MR. CHURCHILL IN THE WHITE HOUSE

ALSO BY ROBERT SCHMUHL

The Glory and the Burden: The American Presidency from the New Deal to the Present

Fifty Years with Father Hesburgh: On and Off the Record

Ireland's Exiled Children: America and the Easter Rising

Making Words Dance: Reflections on Red Smith, Journalism, and Writing (editor)

In So Many More Words: Arguments and Adventures

Indecent Liberties

Wounded Titans: American Presidents and the Perils of Power (editor)

Demanding Democracy

Statecraft and Stagecraft: American Political Life in the Age of Personality

The Responsibilities of Journalism (editor)

MR. CHURCHILL IN THE WHITE HOUSE

THE UNTOLD STORY OF A PRIME MINISTER AND TWO PRESIDENTS

ROBERT SCHMUHL

Liveright Publishing Corporation

A Division of W. W. Norton & Company
Independent Publishers Since 1923

Printed in the United States of America
First Edition

For information about special discounts for bulk purchases, please contact W. W. Norton Special Sales at specialsales@wwnorton.com or 800-233-4830

Manufacturing by Lakeside Book Company
Book Design by Daniel Lagin
Production manager: Julia Druskin

ISBN 978-1-324-09342-8

Liveright Publishing Corporation
500 Fifth Avenue, New York, N.Y. 10110
www.wwnorton.com

W. W. Norton & Company Ltd.
15 Carlisle Street, London W1D 3BS

1 2 3 4 5 6 7 8 9 0

For Gail Bancroft

and Ken Socha—

generous in friendship

and in helping achieve a dream

"No lover ever studied every whim of his mistress
as I did those of President Roosevelt."

—WINSTON CHURCHILL

TO HIS PRIVATE SECRETARY JOHN COLVILLE, MAY 2, 1948

"All goes well & the President [Dwight D. Eisenhower] is a real friend."

—WINSTON CHURCHILL TO CLEMENTINE CHURCHILL, MAY 5, 1959

CONTENTS

PROLOGUE

A devoted fisherman, Winston Churchill never stopped angling, not even at the White House. Though much of his time in Washington, D.C., was spent conferring with presidents—first, Franklin D. Roosevelt, and later, Dwight D. Eisenhower—about grave matters of war and peace, the prime minister's visits were nevertheless spirited, at times entertaining occasions, themselves worthy of a multipart historical docudrama. Whether in residence at 1600 Pennsylvania Avenue itself or the various presidential retreats outside D.C., Churchill was exceptionally adept at making himself at home. When obliged to be attired, this son of an American mother and an English father shuffled about in velvet slippers and a tailored-for-air-raids "siren suit" resembling a romper. With a cigar nearly always in hand, he prowled these corridors of power in the hopes of strengthening his own. Both Roosevelt and Eisenhower eventually adjusted to the unconventional habits—and hours—of their guest, who not only proposed these visits but almost always, by accident or design, stayed longer than initially intended.

Despite a veritable and growing mountain of Churchilliana, no book thus far has been exclusively devoted to the British prime minister's frequent, often furtive visits to Washington, particularly during World War II, and to telling why these sojourns were so historically meaningful. Considered from today's perspective, these trips clearly take on a level of profound diplomatic and military significance, revealing just how influential a foreign leader can become in steering American foreign policy, especially during wartime. In each of his two terms, Churchill trolled the capital with his ideas and viewpoints in hopes of luring presidents to initiate joint activities involving the United Kingdom and the United States. This is one reason his visits lasted as long as they did: gaining acceptance for his endless suggestions and proposals simply took time.

While this book confines itself to Churchill's premierships in the 1940s and 1950s, it's worth contrasting his sway with that of other international leaders and pointing out how unprecedented his access to American leaders proved to be. Imagine the current U.K. prime minister, French president, German chancellor, or anyone else in a position of power abroad settling into a suite in the residential quarters of the White House and having the liberty of talking with the president throughout the day or night. Or imagine Ukraine's president Volodymyr Zelensky, frequently compared to Churchill, spending weeks at America's most famous address, discussing war strategy and access to weaponry with not only President Joe Biden but also with Dr. Jill Biden. Such a scenario sounds ludicrous today, yet that's exactly what happened during the Second World War, the principal focus of this study. Discussing—and debating—high-stakes problems and questions brought Churchill repeatedly to Washington and made 1600 Pennsylvania Avenue a preferred venue for the statecraft he never tired of conducting. To parley one-on-one with the president of the United States amplified the British prime minister's voice on the world stage and elevated his stature on both sides of the Atlantic Ocean.

Churchill's long life—from November 30, 1874, until January 24, 1965—began during the presidency of the eighteenth chief executive, Ulysses S. Grant, and ended with Lyndon B. Johnson, the thirty-sixth president, in office. Twelve Republicans and six Democrats were presidents during those ninety years, and he met, knew, or worked with nine serving or future chief executives. Roosevelt and Eisenhower were, of course, the most significant, because their presidencies took place during the nearly nine years Churchill served as prime minister, from 1940 to 1945, and from 1951 to 1955.

The deliberations between Churchill and FDR about World War II remain unique in history. From 1941 until FDR's death on April 12, 1945, the two world leaders were together well over a hundred days. The majority of this time was spent at the White House; Roosevelt's palatial country residence in Hyde Park, New York; or Shangri-La, the presidential retreat FDR established in the Catoctin Mountains of Maryland, subsequently christened "Camp David" by Eisenhower. Between December 22, 1941, and September 19, 1944, Churchill visited the White House four times, and Hyde Park on four other occasions.

Both Roosevelt and Eisenhower were accustomed to hosting prominent world figures at the White House. King George VI was an overnight guest in 1939, and in 1957, his daughter, the newly crowned Queen Elizabeth II, followed suit, staying overnight on her first state visit as monarch. What makes Churchill's sojourns unusual as well as remarkable are their duration and occurrence at critical moments in the twentieth century. Moreover, his trips to meet with Roosevelt in America took place amid the perils of wartime travel, involving hazardous ocean voyages on battleships. It would not be until the early 1960s that government-owned jets allowed foreign leaders to go from place to place more expeditiously.

In that era before jet travel, Churchill's visits stand out historically for several reasons, not least of which his resolute and relentless encouragement of, in his famous phrase, a "special relationship" between the United Kingdom and the United States. In one major speech delivered at Harvard University in 1943, the prime minister went so far as to advocate common citizenship for the two countries. What better way to establish and deepen this association than by becoming a frequent, front-page visitor at the White House? The initial conferences, with their lively policy sessions and the conviviality of camaraderie, began amid the gloom of war yet for Churchill during a season of revivified hope. Arriving at this point required careful maneuvering: several twists and turns of international politics and diplomacy, featuring two of the twentieth century's foremost defenders of democracy.

When Churchill took up residence in the White House for the first time on December 22, 1941, he no longer felt as though he was alone in defending what he called "our island home." For over a year and a half, the United Kingdom's prime minister repeatedly appealed to Roosevelt to intervene directly in the war that had already claimed, according to Imperial War Museum statistics, no fewer than 43,500 civilians on British soil. In speech after speech, nearly 150 letters or cables, and many overseas telephone calls, Churchill pleaded—as Zelensky, the closest contemporary analogue to a leader acting in wartime, would do eight decades later with Biden—for help and greater American involvement. Then the Japanese assault on Pearl Harbor, a mere fifteen days before Churchill arrived in Washington, brought the United States into the war with the power and potential he longed to have at his side. Years later, in *The Grand Alliance*, Churchill expressed his emotion of "greatest joy": "I knew the United States was in the war, up to the neck and in to the death. So we had won after all!"[1] Victory, so frequently signified by Churchill with an upraised two-finger "V" gesture, took more than three additional years. Yet by the time he reached Washington that extraordinary Christmas season of 1941, and even as the nation mourned the loss of some 2,400 Americans at Pearl Harbor, he understood the difference his new partner could make.

The short, stocky Churchill and the imposing-when-straining-to-stand Roosevelt started taking each other's measure long before the prime minister's trip across the stormy Atlantic. Not even a year into FDR's first term as president, Churchill had invited Roosevelt's eldest son, James, to Chartwell, his country estate in Kent and his refuge for writing, painting, and entertaining since 1922. After their dinner in October 1933, the host and his guests played a game that involved going around the table and telling one another the single wish that he or she most wanted fulfilled. Possibly to impress the twenty-five-year-old Roosevelt, Churchill expressed a bald hope, if not an almost impossible dream. "I wish to be Prime Minister and in close and daily communication by telephone with the President of the United States. There is nothing that we could not do if we were together."[2]

During the rest of the decade—Churchill's out-of-government "wilderness years"—he continued to flatter Roosevelt, noting at one point in *Collier's*, the popular American weekly magazine, "It is certain that Franklin Roosevelt will rank among the greatest of men who have occupied that proud position [of president]."[3] Was Churchill building up a public figure he hoped, at some point, to work with, or was Britain's highest-paid journalist simply rendering an honest analytical judgment? It was probably a combination of both, with blandishment almost second nature to him.

Throughout the 1930s, Churchill became a loud yet lonely voice decrying the dangers of "Nazidom" and "Herr Hitler." His worries and warnings, delivered in print and on the airwaves via American outlets, didn't appreciably decrease the post-World War I appeal of isolationism in the United States, which had been backed by the force of law through the series of Neutrality Acts passed in the 1930s. Yet what Churchill was saying found an audience that included a significant and ardent observer: Franklin Delano Roosevelt. On September 3, 1939, following the Nazi invasion of Poland, Britain declared war on Germany, and Churchill was appointed first lord of the admiralty, a post he previously held during World War I. Eight days later, the president sent a "private" letter to a man he'd met only briefly in 1918: "What I want you and the Prime Minister to know is that I shall at all times welcome it if you will keep me in touch personally with anything you want me to know about."[4]

It was an extraordinary invitation from a head of state to a cabinet-level official, let alone a cabinet-level official of another country: "at all times," "in touch personally," "anything you want me to know about." In the same letter, which had been addressed to "My dear Churchill," the Anglophile president—who wasn't shy in disparaging aspects of Britain's imperial ways that Churchill unfailingly defended—acknowledged that he "much enjoyed reading" Churchill's multi-volume biography of his ancestor John Churchill, the first Duke of Marlborough. How many of the million or so words in *Marlborough: His Life and Times* Roosevelt actually read is unknown, but a copy of the first volume, published in 1933, was inscribed to the president in phrasing intended to ingratiate: "With earnest best wishes for the success of the greatest crusade of modern times."[5] In truth, for both Churchill and Roosevelt, "the greatest crusade of modern times" was still to come, following two future events: Churchill's appointment as prime minister on May 10, 1940, and Roosevelt's request of Congress for a declaration of war on December 8, 1941.

Churchill's visits were almost always extended ones. In a way, it was as though Churchill sought to disprove Benjamin Franklin's adage that guests, like fish, smell after three days. According to the former White House chief usher J. B. West, a self-effacing Iowan who worked from 1941 until 1969 in the executive mansion, adapting to this guest's life-style took time: "The staff did have a little difficulty adjusting to Mr. Churchill's way of living." Deliveries by butlers of alcoholic beverages "wore a path in the carpet."[6] And then there was the matter of how he dressed—or more precisely didn't dress—a subject pursued in the first chapter.

Is it any wonder that Eleanor Roosevelt, who disapproved of certain Churchillian habits and points of view, suggested the purchase of Blair House to accommodate foreign dignitaries? In *The Hidden White House*, journalist and author Robert Klara noted that the First Lady "prodded her husband into acquiring an adjacent guest house after she grew sick of Winston Churchill's smoke-filled, booze-soaked stays."[7] The government bought the nearby real estate in 1942. But Churchill, for all his restless nocturnal perambulations (the near-daily routine of an inveterate night owl), never did move across Lafayette Square to take up residence in the "President's Guest House." The First Lady's attempt at expulsion came to naught.

Instead, stories proliferated about the prime minister's stays. While some are of dubious reliability or impossible verifiability, in many renderings, Churchill becomes amusingly memorable, even strangely mythical. When Biden welcomed U.K. prime minister Rishi Sunak to the White House on June 8, 2023, the two leaders openly joked about Churchill's bathing habits, his roaming the halls at 3 a.m., and the bother he created for Mrs. Roosevelt. "There's an awful lot of stories that are told," Biden remarked. Sunak, who was staying at Blair House, promised the president he wouldn't intrude on the Bidens in their living quarters or repeat his predecessor's risible rituals.

During Churchill's second premiership, from 1951 to 1955, and once afterward, he returned to the White House for meetings and sessions of reminiscence with someone he knew well: Dwight Eisenhower. Preeminent military appointments had sent Eisenhower to London for long periods, beginning in 1942. He and the prime minister met frequently before "General Ike," as Churchill often referred to him, began his career in politics by winning the 1952 presidential election. Churchill viewed the White House as "the summit of the United States," and he wasn't shy in encouraging summits that involved himself.

Churchill biographers have portrayed him as a soldier, politician, statesman, journalist, historian, orator, and painter. He should also be considered an angler among the powerful, and a fearless adventurer, even a daredevil, who insisted on making his personal imprint on world affairs. Before the "Big Three" of Churchill, Roosevelt, and Joseph Stalin met in late 1943, the British prime minister sent a telegram to the Soviet leader that included this sentence: "I have for months past informed you that I will come anywhere, at any time, at any risk, for such a meeting."[8] On the day Churchill composed this "Most Secret and Personal" message, dismissing "any risk" and flattering a mercurial tyrant, he was "home alone" and working at 1600 Pennsylvania Avenue. Roosevelt was away, spending a long weekend at Hyde Park. By then, as one longtime White House maid put it, this particular guest "acted as if he belonged there."

—

MY OWN FASCINATION WITH CHURCHILL BEGAN AT AN EARLY age. I remember reading articles by and about him in *Life* back in the 1950s, when it still circulated in millions of American homes. I watched his highly choreographed funeral in 1965 on a black-and-white Admiral television set and recall being moved by the valedictory Eisenhower delivered during the broadcast. Many of the books published in the months after his death found a home in my already-growing collection of volumes about him. A high-school graduation gift in 1966 was a first edition of Lord Moran's *Churchill*, which had come out earlier that year. Several shelves of Churchilliana now occupy a special section in my library. Two teaching assignments in London—in 2004 and 2012—allowed for visits to Chartwell, the Imperial War Museums, the British Library, and the National Archives to concentrate on Churchill's life and career. Then, in 2017, a research appointment at the University of Oxford provided the opportunity to explore myriad sources that serve as the foundation of this book. Earlier volumes from this pencil considered various aspects of the American presidency, so, you might say, what you're reading here is the literary marriage of two lifelong obsessions—and a wholly novel perspective on one of history's most fascinating and many-faceted figures.

MR. CHURCHILL IN THE WHITE HOUSE

– 1 –

ALONE NO MORE

After battling Atlantic gales and dodging German U-boats for ten days on the HMS *Duke of York*, Winston Churchill was eager to reach the White House. His personal physician likened him to a "a child in his impatience to meet the president."[1] To hasten the journey, the prime minister had requested an aircraft from Hampton Roads, Virginia, where the battleship docked, to fly the last 135 miles to Washington, D.C. Churchill concluded his request with a plea to Franklin Roosevelt to "Please on no account come out to meet me,"[2] but the president disregarded the amiable directive, beginning a custom of etiquette he would continue on subsequent visits. Although mobility could prove arduous for FDR, a paraplegic since 1921, he made the physical effort of personally welcoming Churchill and saying farewell to him almost every time he traveled to America between 1941 and 1944.

On this maiden visit, which began on the evening of December 22, 1941, fifteen days after the Japanese attack on Pearl Harbor, Churchill proposed "to stay a week." As it turned out, he would not depart from the White House until January 14, 1942, some twenty-four days later. There were side trips: first on Roosevelt's private railroad car to Ottawa for a speech to the Canadian Parliament, as well as a photoshoot with Yousuf Karsh (the renowned "Karsh of Ottawa") that produced the often-reproduced bulldog-like portrait of Churchill; and later to Pompano Beach for a few days of relaxation in the Florida sunshine. But most of the time he was away from London, Churchill lived and worked at 1600 Pennsylvania Avenue in Washington.

Churchill had first visited the White House almost exactly forty-one years earlier. In December 1900, the twenty-six-year-old best-selling author of *The Boer War*—a chronicle of the former war correspondent's daring escape from a South African prison—had come to the United States on a lecture tour, a lucrative business practice he continued into the mid-1930s, when writing and speaking still provided the bulk of his income. In addition to his transatlantic authorial prominence, Churchill had been elected for the first time to the House of Commons the previous October. For a budding celebrity and politician, visiting Washington was de rigueur, and he worked with Senator Chauncey Depew of New York, who took him to meet a fellow Republican: the recently reelected president William McKinley. That occasion, though, prompted little notice.

By contrast, Churchill's visit in late 1941 generated massive news coverage across America and the world. Its timing, so soon after the United States entered the war, trained international attention on the two democratic leaders and what they might discuss. Strategy. Tactics. Command. Recruitment. Resources. Supplies. Transportation. Just about every issue, detail, and design would be on the table. "Arcadia," the code name for the bilateral gathering, struck many observers at the time as an ironic appellation because of its suggestion of pastoral placidity and simplicity. Indian secretary of state Leo Amery, a vocal opponent of German appeasement in the Commons, wrote in his diary on December 27, 1941, "I imagine Winston's going [to Washington] has put real life into the Americans who badly need screwing up to an offensive policy. Their whole attitude hitherto has been very timid."[3]

The coincidence of the conference and the holiday season created an incongruous blend of religious ritual and secular stalwartness. Yuletide cheer combined with anxious foreboding. Simultaneous public observance of age-old traditions and the current realities brought the prime minister and the president together, in the full glare of cameras, symbolically conveying their common cause in defense of Western civilization. In the weeks leading up to the conference, the two leaders emphasized that they were fighting together, side by side. Many isolationists, including the celebrated aviator Charles Lindbergh of the America First Committee, quickly abandoned their anti-war position. People across the United States responded to the unprecedented wartime summitry. According to news reports, parents of two sets of twin boys—one in Alabama, and the other in Louisiana—named their newly born sons "Winston" and "Franklin." Some American parents christened their holiday season arrivals "Winston."

By the time Churchill arrived in Washington, the White House had assumed a war footing. Outside and inside, security took precedence as never before. In *Special Agent*, Frank J. Wilson, the head of the Secret Service from 1936 until 1947, described the rapid expansion of protective measures at the White House. The personnel in charge of presidential security—White House and Metropolitan police, Secret Service agents, military guards—more than doubled overnight. Sentries carrying machine guns scanned the sky, and antiaircraft batteries were positioned on the roofs of government buildings, including the White House. Blackout curtains went up on windows. Each room was provided with a pail of sand and a shovel to deal with possible incendiary attacks. Every member of the White House staff was issued a gas mask; FDR even had one attached to his wheelchair. Wilson reveals that a "secluded railroad side track" was put into service for Roosevelt and certain visitors to leave or arrive "in a secret, prompt, and safe manner."[4] In addition, an armored, bulletproof limousine, seized from none other than gangster boss Al "Scarface" Capone, was pressed into service for presidential use. With the public barred from walking on the White House side of Pennsylvania Avenue, work crews were able to quickly dig a tunnel from the basement of the White House to the Treasury building vaults next door, creating a makeshift air-raid shelter. According to Wilson, Churchill's strident displeasure at the racket from the twenty-four-hour a day construction led to a sixteen-hour shift during the remainder of the prime minister's visit.[5] (A more elaborate and permanent protective bunker, with nine-foot concrete walls and ceiling, came into being under the new east wing in early 1942.) The Secret Service established ten safe houses around Washington, where they could spirit the president if the capital came under assault. Yet the White House remained extraordinarily busy. In *The President's House*, William Seale noted, "More than a thousand people were likely to pass in and out of the complex during the day."[6]

With safety a topmost concern, Churchill's arrival wasn't announced in the United States or Britain until he was safely ensconced behind the White House gates. (Interestingly, the official White House press release stated that the purpose of the "conversations" will focus on "the defeat of Hitlerism throughout the world" without ever mentioning Japan or Pearl Harbor.) Official secrecy and voluntary press censorship shielded the prime minister's travel schedule from the public, and similar strictures were imposed by the White House. The exact location of his living quarters remained classified.

Presidential press secretary Stephen Early was factual, if not fully forthright, when he told reporters that Churchill "arrived by air and was met by the President at an air station near Washington." Though not reported, Roosevelt was actually waiting for the plane at Anacostia Naval Air Station, a couple miles from the White House. Early's quotation appeared on the front page of the *Washington* Post on December 23. Another *Post* article on the same page reported: "When he arrived last night, Churchill was attired in the navy pea jacket and the blue yachting cap remembered from photographs of his sea conference [earlier in 1941] with Mr. Roosevelt. This garb was taken by some observers to mean he made the Atlantic crossing by boat, limiting his flying to this continent." Journalists were already watching the visitor closely.

In *Thank You, Mr. President*, A. Merriman Smith, the longtime wire service correspondent at the White House, recalled how the government tried to maintain strict secrecy during the war. The rules that existed for Roosevelt also applied to Churchill when he was in the United States. Early instructed reporters: "Think of him [the president] as a battleship and report his movements just as carefully as you would the position of one of our battlewagons at sea."[7] The most public of public figures, Churchill and Roosevelt, both with healthy predispositions to self-importance, wanted news coverage about themselves—when possible—on their terms. Codes of silence as well journalistic restraint in wartime helped to determine how they would be presented.

Concern for security extended beyond the principals to the mail and packages arriving at the White House. Hundreds of Americans welcomed Churchill to Washington, with many stoking his well-known smoking habit by shipping him box upon box of cigars they hoped he might savor during his stay with the president. Regrettably for the intended recipient, worries about explosives or poisons injected into the tobacco meant the cigars were incinerated rather than smoked. Other less potentially hazardous presents, such as stuffed (or soft) toy animals and painting kits, were distributed to hospitals or benevolent institutions.

At one point during Churchill's visit, a reporter for the North American Newspaper Alliance was granted access to the British embassy to take stock of the letters, cards, and gifts sent to the prime minister upon and after his arrival. "In one corner," the reporter related, "were piled boxes containing 5,000 cigars; in another stood a three-foot tower of letters to Mr. Churchill from strangers." The accounting continued for another eight paragraphs: "a portrait of Franklin D. Roosevelt done on a typewriter," "a bag of lima beans," "crates of eggs," "a bottle of Napoleon brandy 1813," "two bottles of 1848 cognac," and "a Shriner's hat that belonged to a distant relative of Mr. Churchill's mother." Americans who admired Churchill's courage under fire and his rallying oratory expressed themselves in distinctive ways, making personal sacrifices to show their appreciation to someone they knew largely from newspaper accounts, radio broadcasts, or newsreels at the movies. John Martin, who served as the prime minister's private secretary on the trip to Washington, kept among his papers a "SPECIAL DELIVERY" envelope postmarked from Boston that was simply addressed:

Churchill the Magnificent
The White House
Washington, D.C.

ALL THE HOOPLA RELATED TO THE BRITISH LEADER'S VISIT took place after weeks of careful planning. In *The Grand Alliance*, the third volume of his hexalogy *The Second World War*, Churchill admitted that he made the decision to confer with Roosevelt on the morning after the assault on Pearl Harbor. King George VI quickly assented, and Churchill proposed the visit to FDR, who immediately began worrying, on Churchill's behalf, about the danger involved in transatlantic crossings, particularly on his return trip, once the world knew he was nearly four thousand miles from Britain.

But Churchill didn't blink, contending in a December 10 cable to Roosevelt: "We do not think there is any serious danger about return journey."[8] Later that day, FDR fired back: "Delighted to have you here at White House," concluding in true Rooseveltian, glass-always-half-full fashion, "The news is bad but it will be better."[9]

Eager to meet and to solidify the alliance he so desired, Churchill dismissed the risks involved (courage, for him, came naturally) and began preparing for the trip. Prior to departure, he even posed for a War Office photographer's "camouflage trick," the resulting photo showing him purchasing a flag from his wife, Clementine, who was leading a Red Cross drive to support an "Aid for Russia Fund." The picture—intended to give the impression that Churchill was hard at work in London rather than battling storms aboard the *Duke of York*—was released to British newspapers on December 16, a full three days after the British party left for America.

The nautical advisory of "heavy weather" doesn't do justice to what the United Kingdom's war leaders and their aides endured during their transatlantic crossing. Flight Sergeant Geoffrey Green, a clerk and stenographer for the prime minister, kept a detailed diary of the voyage (and the time in Washington) that described the recently commissioned battleship as "rolling and lurching every conceivable way." Rough seas forced the ship to reduce her speed from twenty-four knots to six or seven, resulting in a much longer trip. Green recorded that the times he was summoned to Churchill's cabin the prime minister was usually in bed—and "raising Cain" about how the foul conditions meant a loss of time in the United States.[10] In a letter to Clementine, Churchill remarked, "Being in a ship in such weather as this is like being in a prison, with the extra chance of being drowned."[11]

The only American traveling as part of the prime minister's retinue was W. Averell Harriman, Roosevelt's London-based special envoy and (in FDR's description) "Defense Expediter" for the Lend-Lease program that was designed to provide Britain and other allies with supplies for the war effort. Harriman, too, kept a diary, a practice he continued on subsequent trips. His journals concentrate on Churchill—what he did, what he said, what he expected. An early entry stated that the prime minister spoke "incessantly at meals," and then presented direct quotations from his conversations with Churchill. At one point on December 20 Churchill offered this judgment, "It is in the hands of the U.S. to make this a long or short war," adding: "We must not underestimate the effect of America's entry in the war on all the peoples of the world. They will know there can be only one end. We must use this."[12]

Churchill could have been trying to impress an influential American with White House clout to help his own position, but the statement echoed many of his pre-Pearl Harbor pronouncements and appeals about the dynamism of "the great Republic"—a phrase he repeated—to make the decisive difference in fighting the Axis forces. He also understood the patrician, wealthy, connected Harriman could "expedite" everything from war *matériel* to personal items not readily available back in London. On this trip, the prime minister, according to a January 6, 1942, note from Harriman's secretary, was sent "three dozen silk stockings . . . to give away on his return." Besides the silk stockings, Harriman arranged for eight "Smithfield Virginia Hams" to accompany the British contingent home, with one earmarked for the prime minister's wife. Requests for domestic articles from the States increased on subsequent visits, even among the prime minister's office staff in London.

Clementine Churchill, vastly different from Eleanor Roosevelt in many respects, was well aware what her husband would be doing during that Christmas season. Illustrative of their openness with each other, he dictated during the voyage a nine-page letter to her, cited earlier, that began: "Yesterday, Saturday, finished the longest week I have lived since the war began." Writing the day before arriving—he started composing it on Sunday, December 21—Churchill is unguardedly candid, even reporting at one point, "We made a fine kill of U-boats round Gibraltar, about seven altogether in a week. This is a record." He finished the letter on December 24 by adding in script from the White House: "I have not had a minute since I got here to tell you about it. All is very good indeed; and my plans are all going through. The Americans are magnificent in their breadth of view."[13] As a sign of how engrossed he'd been the first days in Washington, it took him three days to complete his personal letter that began with the salutation "My darling."

Eleanor Roosevelt, by contrast, was not informed about the high-level White House visit until the last moment. In fact, she sounded miffed at learning so late what was happening in her popular syndicated newspaper column, "My Day." Writing the day after Churchill and his entourage came to Washington, Mrs. Roosevelt took note of the situation in the first paragraph of her report published on Christmas Eve, "I was late arriving at the Office of Civilian Defense yesterday morning because the President, who has been very mysterious as to what was going to happen over these holidays, finally decided to tell me that the British Prime Minister, Mr. Winston Churchill, and his party were arriving sometime in the late afternoon or evening. It had not occurred to him that this might require certain moving of furniture to adapt rooms to the purposes for which the Prime Minister wished to use them."[14]

Though FDR's wife of thirty-six years was kept unawares of the arriving company, Wilson in *Special Agent* reported that the president advised him during "the middle of December" that Churchill would be coming to Washington. In addition, Roosevelt's housekeeper and head cook of questionable culinary skill, Henrietta Nesbitt, claimed in her *White House Diary* that she learned of the visit before the First Lady while she was "at the hairdresser's on December 20." A phone call from her secretary conveyed the news and a somewhat bizarre order: "The President had missed his lion-skin rug that Haile Selassie [emperor of Ethiopia] had given him and I had stored at Garfinckel's [a Washington department store]. He wanted that rug on the floor, to show Mr. Churchill when he came, and he wanted it there right away." Nesbitt, who knew the Roosevelts from her Hyde Park days, went on to recount the recovery of "Leo the lion, smelling of mothproofing," and she put the treasured rug "back in place on the President's floor."[15]

At the end of Mrs. Roosevelt's column, she returned to discussing the unknown-until-the-last-minute visitor, whom the president brought to the White House at 6:50 p.m. for a dinner beginning at 8:45. Though the White House usher's diary lists "17 guests" for dinner, the First Lady named just six, concluding: "The gentlemen all gathered together in the President's study after dinner. The ladies were left to talk a little while, and then to go home. They sent their cars back to wait for their husbands."[16] The separation of men and women was the standard (yes, sexist) routine at the time. Serious discussions, it was thought then, took place among those with deeper voices.

Headstrong and honest, Mrs. Roosevelt was willing to criticize publicly both the president and the male-female divide. The previous August, when FDR was planning to confer clandestinely with Churchill off Newfoundland in Placentia Bay, she faced a similar situation. As she reported in her memoir, *This I Remember*, "My husband, after many mysterious consultations, told me that he was going to take a little trip up through the Cape Cod Canal and that he wished to do some fishing. Then he smiled and I knew he was not telling me all that he was going to do."[17] For both the White House visit and the Atlantic Conference four months earlier, Mrs. Roosevelt used the word "mysterious." Over time, especially in her reminiscences after her husband's death, there would be little mystery what she thought of Winston Churchill. Indeed, both Eleanor and Clementine harbored deep reservations about each other's spouses, as we'll see, and their views add complexity to any evaluation of the leaders themselves and how they might have candidly thought about each other.

Roosevelt retired a little before 1 a.m. on December 23, according to the usher's diary. Eight hours later, the prime minister, the president, and hand-picked advisors began the first of five different meetings that Tuesday, not counting their meals together. Churchill came prepared. During the Atlantic crossing, he dictated and revised a multi-section "memorandum" about the war's future, as he saw it, and his agenda of the strategy to guide it. From the start, he sought to assert his experience in combat leadership—gained in World War I and since 1939—to impress the new ally in the fight. He also wanted to make sure the president and those around him (particularly from the military and State Department) understood the plan of action he hoped would be adopted.

The first part of the detailed memorandum focused on "The Atlantic Front," which Churchill argued deserved primacy, even though Japan—not Germany nor Italy—had launched the first assault on American forces. In Part I, he raises the importance of North Africa, noting in italics: *"We ought therefore to try hard to win over French North Africa, and now is the moment to use every inducement and form of pressure at our disposal upon the Government of Vichy and the French authorities in North Africa."*[18] In *The Grand Alliance*, Churchill reported that at their first meeting on December 22 and prior to delivering his memorandum, "I immediately broached with the President and those he had invited to join us the scheme of Anglo-American intervention in French North Africa."[19] Exactly how to approach North Africa occupied several meetings during the Arcadia Conference. As it turned out, the Anglo-America invasion of Morocco and Algeria, which took place nearly a year later (in November 1942) and was called "Operation Torch," became the first major engagement of U.S. forces—land, sea, and air—in the European-North African hostilities against the Nazi troops and their supporters. Throughout this portion of Churchill's assessment, he looked ahead to the next year, to the battles to come. With America at his side, he knew how radically the situation would change.

In *The Grand Alliance*, Churchill doesn't mention that the printed Part II of his memorandum in his account is, in fact, a fourth paper that he substituted for his first analysis of "The Pacific Front."* Again, as with his consideration of the Atlantic situation, what can be expected in 1942 was paramount. The two-time first lord of the admiralty as well as recognized historian underscored his thinking by presenting his words in italic type:

> *We cannot get more battleships than those now in sight for the year 1942, but we can and must get more aircraft-carriers. It takes five years to build a battleship, but it is possible to improvise a carrier in six months. Here then is a field for invention and ingenuity similar to that which called forth the extraordinary fleets and flotillas which fought on the Mississippi in the Civil War.*[20]

He frequently used his detailed knowledge of America's Civil War to drive home points with U.S. audiences.

The final section of Churchill's analytical forecast pushed the war

* All four documents appear in the U.S. government document *Foreign Relations of the United States: The Conferences at Washington, 1941–1942, and Casablanca, 1943*, published in 1968, a quarter century after the conferences took place.

effort into 1943. He was concerned with "bringing the war to a victorious end in a reasonable period,"[21] and he was specific in sketching out definite projects, including "our intention of sending armies of liberation into Europe in 1943."[22] Of course, the liberation of France, Operation Overlord, didn't begin until D-Day, June 6, 1944, and Churchill in his memoir of the war admitted that "the attempt to cross the Channel in 1943 would have led to a bloody defeat of the first magnitude, with measureless reactions upon the result of the war."[23] What's remarkable about the memorandum as a whole—sixteen full pages in *Foreign Relations of the United States*—is its mastery of detail, geography, forces, and planning. Some judgments—such as the possibility of an invasion of western France in 1943—proved unreasonable given the circumstances and conditions at the time. The papers, though never condescending, boldly introduced a resolute and determined military mind to an ally just beginning to embark on a global war. In 1940, the United States had fewer than a half million military personnel. By the end of 1943, the number had grown to over nine million, and in 1945 there were over twelve million in the services.[24]

On the day Churchill presented his far-reaching assessment to Roosevelt, he was also becoming familiar with his surroundings at the White House. Upon arrival and after inspecting several options on the second floor by trying out the beds in each room, he vetoed Mrs. Roosevelt's choice of the Lincoln Bedroom and decided "the Rose Bedroom" was most comfortable for him.*

Flight Sergeant Green used that first full day in Washington to set up his office at the White House, and his diary reflected wide-eyed excitement at his new surroundings: "Most beautiful place I've ever seen—magnificent—all white outside & covers hundreds & hundreds of miles (or so it seemed to me!)"[25] In addition, right as the visit began, the chief White House butler, Alonzo Fields, the first African Ameri-

* The quarters were also referred to as the "Rose Room," "Rose Suite," and "Rose Guest Room" before being renamed the "Queens' Bedroom."

can to serve in that position, learned the Churchillian routine: "On his breakfast tray I was instructed to have something hot, something cold, two kinds of fresh fruit, a tumbler of orange juice and a pot of frightfully weak tea. For 'something hot' he had eggs, bacon or ham, and toast. For 'something cold' he had two kinds of cold meats with English mustard and two kinds of fruit plus a tumbler of sherry. This was breakfast. At lunch he had Scotch and soda. For dinner always champagne, and after dinner, brandy. Then during the evening more Scotch and soda."[26] When the two men got to know each other better, Churchill asked the butler, who assisted four presidents over nearly a quarter-century, to come to his defense should he ever be accused of being a teetotaler. Before long, too, Fields understood, in no uncertain terms, that the prime minister would not tolerate whistling or even talking outside his suite. The regimen kept in London was also to be observed in Washington.

On that December 23 American and British newspapers started devoting their front pages and acres of space inside to the visitor's trip, its importance, and what it could mean to the nascent war effort in the United States. Like Roosevelt, Churchill keenly understood the value of public diplomacy and the stagecraft of statecraft. The day before the prime minister and his contingent of some eighty-five advisors and assistants embarked on their Atlantic crossing, Lord Halifax, the United Kingdom's ambassador to the United States, proposed keeping the journey secret until the prime minister and his party had returned to London. At the time, German U-boats lurked in the Atlantic and sinking the *Duke of York*, Halifax thought, would be the ultimate target. The most critical decision-makers in Britain's war leadership would be lost in one act of aggression. Churchill rejected his ambassador's suggestion of a stealth summit, saying he thought there would be benefits to having wide coverage of his Washington surprise.

Throughout the war, both Churchill and Roosevelt became virtuosos at recognizing when to perform in public for a definite purpose and when to conceal their activities from scrutiny. With America just joining the Allied cause in combat, the prime minister wanted the Axis powers and the world to see the main leaders working together in unity. What was happening now was vastly different from the past. In message after message to Roosevelt and repeatedly in his speeches, Churchill had sought support and involvement from the United States, and he could get perturbed at not receiving the assistance he wanted. Nine days after being appointed—not elected—the "King's First Minister," he handed his private secretary a cable to dispatch. "Here's a telegram for those bloody Yankees," he said. "Send it off tonight."[27]

With what he called "the great Republic in our common cause" now completely engaged, his frustration from unreciprocated wooing ended. Indeed, three years after FDR's death and V-E Day in 1945, Churchill—unlike his father or son who embraced romantic dalliances—admitted to an aide, "No lover ever studied every whim of his mistress as I did those of President Roosevelt."[28] That sustained scrutiny led the prime minister to the White House and to a personal relationship of complexity and intrigue close observers could never satisfactorily explain. The public saw them together as shoulder-to-shoulder allies engaged in a single, all-encompassing cause, yet the two also had their own agendas and definite reasons to pursue them.

For instance, though prescient about the Nazi threat in the 1930s and the Communist menace after 1945, Churchill often viewed current affairs through the lens of history—past events illuminating contemporary affairs. By contrast, one of Roosevelt's most valuable traits was an uncanny ability to look well beyond the present to see the importance of future action in meeting a specific or sought goal. Over time, the two leaders learned how each operated and approached situations.

At the first conference of the "Allied War Council"—the sixteen major U.S. and U.K. leaders—on December 23 at the White House, FDR spoke first. In a memorandum about the meeting, Lieutenant General Henry "Hap" Arnold recorded this statement: "*Objective—1944.* The President then stated that it looked now as if we should project everything into 1944. This was based upon the fact that if we started an idea for production now it will be 1944 before we can get the planes, tanks and ammunition in quantity, so that should be our objective insofar as all new facilities are concerned."[29] Given that this was said in late 1941 and that the Allies didn't land in western France to begin their concerted push across the continent until mid-1944, FDR's early projection seemed almost prophetic, particularly since just two weeks earlier the United States had declared war.

Churchill's first lengthy stay in the White House afforded each man the opportunity to take the other's measure in ways not possible during their earlier meetings off the coast of Newfoundland. The two shared certain characteristics: aristocratic upbringing, naval experience, undeniable ambition, political success, rare resilience, incomparable confidence, oratorical ability, and dramatic flair. As a teenager, according to Andrew Roberts, Churchill "told a friend that he would save Britain from a foreign invasion."[30] Roosevelt, in Robert Dallek's assessment, had dreams "more grandiose than what most teenage boys manifest in their formative years,"[31] even bragging shortly after law school that he aspired to follow in fifth cousin Theodore's White House shoes.

To be sure, there were also stark differences, notably Churchill's belief in the beneficence of the British Empire and its far-flung colonies, with their archaic and dubious practices, a commitment and way of thinking Roosevelt's antipathy to imperialism considered abhorrent. Churchill also tended to be straightforward in dealing with others, while Roosevelt was smilingly circumspect. On a personal level, the monogamous Churchill was devoted to Clementine and regularly confided in her, whereas FDR had a more distant, working relationship with Eleanor and took considerable pleasure in the company of other women. However, right after Pearl Harbor, creating an alliance, secure in a common cause and coordinated approach, took precedence over any individual strengths or drawbacks.

For much of his time in Washington, Churchill seesawed between private meetings about strategy and public events with the purpose of conveying his deliberate, image-conscious message. Indeed, less than a day after arrival, Churchill and Roosevelt conducted a joint news conference for some two hundred reporters, ostensibly about the "Transport of Supplies and Equipment." According to the White House transcript, the president explained "the rules" that "nothing is to be quoted," the use of information on background "may not be attributed" to either figure, and "off-the-record" statements are "not to be disclosed under any circumstances." He introduced the prime minister—"we are very, very happy to have him here"—and from that point Washington's fourth estate peppered Churchill for twelve minutes with questions, not directing a single one to his host.

During press conference "#794" (out of a total of 998 during the Roosevelt presidency), the crowd of correspondents in the back of the Oval Office couldn't clearly see the seated guest, so the sixty-seven-year-old stood up and climbed on his chair. The transcript records that "loud and spontaneous cheers and applause rang through the room."[32] To the question, "Mr. Minister, can you tell us when you think we may lick these boys?" Churchill responded: "If we manage it well, it will only take half as long as if we manage it badly."[33] Laughter, again, filled the room, with accounts of the press conference spread across front pages the next day, Christmas Eve.

In the January 5 issue of *Time* that circulated in late December, the first days of Churchill's "historic" visit received detailed consideration before coverage of its "Man of the Year": Franklin D. Roosevelt. (Churchill was the magazine's choice the year before.) The description of the visitor, who "dropped out of the sky with breathtaking suddenness," came from close perusal at the press session: "Those who crowded up front saw a pudgy man with cheeks like apple dumplings, blue eyes beneath crooked restless eyebrows, the merest foam-flecking of sandy gray hair on his bald pink pate, a long black cigar clenched at a belligerent angle above his bulldog jaw."

At the news conference, FDR wore a black armband, a symbol of mourning to honor his mother, Sara, who had died a little more than three months earlier on September 7 at the age of eighty-six. The year of 1941 proved to be one of the most consequential and calamitous in Roosevelt's life, with the "Man of the Year" designation (his third by *Time*) almost an afterthought. He had been inaugurated for an unprecedented third term on January 20; he signed the Lend-Lease Act, intended "to promote the defense of the United States" and bolster the British war effort on March 11; Marguerite (Missy) LeHand, his personal secretary, de facto chief of staff, and close companion for many years, suffered a debilitating stroke on June 4; his presidential library on the grounds of his birthplace (Springwood) at Hyde Park, New York, was dedicated on June 30; the "Atlantic Conference" with Churchill took place in August, and Pearl Harbor was attacked on December 7. Momentous personal and public milestones were packed into a relatively brief period, and yet—like the prime minister, who at one point in *The Grand Alliance* admitted "I do not know how I got through it all"[34]—the president still joked with reporters, saying wryly in his introduction that his guest "is quite willing to take on a conference, because we have one characteristic in common. We like new experiences in life."[35]

Churchill's public playfulness amid the sobering circumstances that brought him to Washington meant reporters were always on the lookout for nuggets of human interest to color their copy and complete their portrait of the new visitor. The day after the news conference, the Associated Press reported that Mrs. Roosevelt "confided" to the wire service the nearly "boyish glee" Churchill displayed when two poached eggs appeared on his breakfast tray the morning after he reached the White House. Back in London, rationing allowed Britons just one egg per week. Talk of the "he-man breakfast" led the First Lady to tell how she sympathized that the prime minister couldn't be with his family during this Yuletide. "Holidays and work days are just the same," she quoted him saying. "Until this war is over, there is nothing else but work that can be in our minds." One short article took readers closer to Churchill as both "he-man" and warlord.

Amid the portrayals of human interest—photographers had a field day snapping pictures on the White House grounds of Churchill showing off his "siren suit," the one-piece, overall-resembling outfit he donned during the London blitz and continued to wear for comfort in subsequent years—usually sober and restrained commentary often sounded like sycophancy. For many Americans, Churchill was a human symbol of defiance and resistance in battle against enemies of freedom and democracy, someone—given the new circumstances—worth applauding. Bravely overcoming danger to travel to the United States, he personified character traits the U.S. populace could admire. The morning after he arrived, the lead editorial of the *New York Times* offered a journalistic salute akin to the firing of twenty-one guns. The so-called "Gray Lady" almost turned purple in its phrasing: "From the depths of its heart this country will bid Winston Churchill welcome. . . . He comes to us now in a moment of great crisis, when his democracy and our democracy are fighting for their very lives. We clasp his hand and say: Here is not only a great man and a good man. Here is a son returning to his mother's land. Here is a soldier marching under our own flag."

The transcript of the December 23 news conference is one of the few occasions featuring Churchill and Roosevelt together that documents in an official way what they said. In *The Grand Alliance*, immediately after Churchill relates details of his arrival in Washington, he boasts in a revealing and significant passage about all the time they spent together at meetings, events, cocktail hours, meals, and spur-of-the-moment chats in the residential quarters of the White House. The recitation of their various activities leads to a feeling of personal closeness enhanced by domestic proximity: "As we both, by need or habit, were forced to do much of our work in bed, he visited me in my room whenever he felt inclined, and encouraged me to do the same to him."[36] In the Harry Hopkins Papers at the Roosevelt Presidential Library, Hopkins lists eleven lunches and ten dinners (between December 23 and January 14) when he "lunched and dined with President and Prime Minister."

Churchill's memoir-cum-history is invaluable for providing an insider's view of this conference as well as the later ones. Every word, though, comes filtered through his perspective and how he wants a reader—and history—to view him. As he later told the House of Commons in 1948, while working on the six volumes of *The Second World War*, he was willing "to leave the past to history, especially as I propose to write that history myself." One-sided and at times factually incorrect, it is typically the only detailed account that exists. In *Foreign Relations of the United States: The Conferences at Washington, 1941–1942 and Casablanca, 1943*, these statements appear with maddening frequency: "No official record of the discussion at this meeting has been found" or "No official record of this meeting has been found."

A small irony of American history is that Franklin Roosevelt was the only occupant of the White House to establish a presidential library while still in office. He also signed legislation in 1934 creating the National Archives. The president recognized the value of preserving the past and acquiring with a purpose, and in his own life he collected stamps, books, model ships, and other items. Yet he was not someone inclined to produce a paper trail of documents about his meetings and discussions. Spoken words during conversations were the principal currency of his communication, making Warren F. Kimball's three-volume *Churchill & Roosevelt: The Complete Correspondence*—with 1,161 sent by Churchill and 788 by FDR—a trove to keep mining for a better understanding of their relationship, their thinking, and their activities. That Churchill sent 373 more than Roosevelt is telling in itself. He continued making suggestions and fighting his corner often without receiving responses. Intrepid in advancing his ideas and schemes, the prime minister never stopped angling to lure the president to his way of thinking.

Churchill and Roosevelt were almost complete opposites in the way they worked. As Martin Gilbert points out in *Continue to Pester, Nag and Bite: Churchill's War Leadership*, "There can hardly have been a single day of the war when Churchill did not dictate to one or other of his devoted secretarial staff. At the outset of his premiership, he decided that every instruction, suggestion, proposal or criticism emanating from him—and all the answers he received—should be in writing."[37] Churchill's dictation that was subsequently typed and circulated served two purposes: the immediate one—communicating with someone or preparing a speech for delivery—and a more long-term objective—producing documents for use later in his articles or books.

The sheer output of words that Churchill dictated and later edited in typescript would rival the five thousand Charles Dickens set down daily. In the White House, the prime minister needed to participate in meetings about war strategy, planning, and production while keeping up with the day-to-day responsibilities as head of government—and composing his public speeches, with the still memorable phrases, that demand a much different type of prose from mundane memorandums about egg distribution and the like.

Churchill kept his secretarial staff immersed in assignments throughout his waking hours, as he occupied the commodious Rose Bedroom, with its large sitting area for meetings, when he wasn't—as he often tended to be—propped up in bed to receive individual callers. He also used neighboring areas for sessions he scheduled either with people he'd brought with him or with American officials.

The morning of December 24, Secretary of War Henry Stimson went to the White House to talk to Churchill about the situation in the Philippines, where Stimson, a Republican, served as governor-general under Calvin Coolidge before becoming Herbert Hoover's secretary of state. Japan had begun its invasion of the Philippines less than a day after the attack on Pearl Harbor, and by Christmas Eve, U.S. and Philippine forces were engaged in fierce fighting. In a diary entry striking for the details recorded and the involvement of another participant, Stimson reported that he "went over to the White House with General [Dwight D.] Eisenhower of the War Plans Division to back me up in case I was asked questions that I couldn't answer." The talk took place in the map room near the Rose Bedroom, and Stimson looked askance at the prime minister's ensemble: "He was still in deshabille [*sic*], wearing a sort of zipper pajama suit and slippers."[38] This meeting, which isn't mentioned by Churchill in his memoirs, is notable (as we'll point out in the next chapter) because it differs—and dramatically so—from what the prime minister remembered about his first meeting with someone who would play a much larger role in his life later in the war and subsequently.

On both December 22 and December 23, Churchill and Roosevelt had talked past midnight. However, on December 24, when Stimson visited Churchill, the president didn't conduct any meetings until after 11 a.m., with the prime minister not appearing on his schedule until the late afternoon. At a little after 5 o'clock that Christmas Eve, the two leaders stood on the South Portico of the White House for the lighting of the "National Community Christmas Tree."

In his memoir *Washington Goes to War*, veteran journalist David Brinkley, a close observer of Washington, captured the excitement leading up to Churchill's Christmas Eve address. According to the Secret Service, as many as twenty thousand people cleared inspections set up by the military to catch a glimpse—in Brinkley's description—of this "figure almost none in Washington had ever seen, but who had enchanted Americans with his leadership, his oratory, his appetite for food, cigars and whiskey, his wit. He was there, and he would speak beside the Christmas tree."[39]

Since direct quotation wasn't allowed at the previous day's news conference, what Churchill said to the assembled throng and to a radio audience involving every U.S. broadcast network became the first words Americans heard from him since his arrival. He began with a salutation of solidarity: "Fellow workers in the cause of freedom," a minor variation of FDR's greeting a few moments earlier: "Fellow workers for freedom." Purposely, he established a definite connection at the start: "I spend this anniversary and festival far from my country, far from my family, yet I cannot truthfully say that I feel far from home.

Whether it be the ties of blood on my mother's side, or the friendships I have developed here over many years of active life, or the commanding sentiment of comradeship in the common cause of great peoples . . . I cannot feel myself a stranger here in the centre and at the summit of the United States." These sentences created rapport, leading to sobering sentiments about "a strange Christmas Eve," the world "locked in deadly struggle," "terrible weapons" multiplying carnage, with "vulgar ambition" and "morbid lust" the goal of the enemy. Near the end, however, Churchill's words redeem the occasion's principal meaning: "Let the children have their night of fun and laughter. Let the gifts of Father Christmas delight their play. Let us grown-ups share to the full in their unstinted pleasures before we turn again to the stern task and the formidable years that lie before us, resolved that, by our sacrifice and daring, the same children shall not be robbed of their inheritance or denied their right to live in a free and decent world."[40] As in many of his other speeches since becoming prime minister, Churchill combined confidence in victory with the recognition of war's reality. He spoke not about a vague future but of "the formidable years that lie before us," the years he and Roosevelt were discussing and planning.

Indeed, after the tree-lighting, which included participation by the Marine Band, the singing of carols, a prayer from a Catholic bishop, and words from a Girl Scout and a Boy Scout, Churchill and FDR were together almost constantly, from 6 p.m. until 11:45. Not counting cocktails and dinner, just one session of the four that appeared on Roosevelt's schedule that Christmas Eve is even mentioned in the official report. Colonel Leslie Hollis, secretary of the British Chiefs of Staff, recorded a short, four-point memorandum about a meeting on the Pacific front with naval commanders. That report became a cause célèbre within the higher echelons of the U.S. military that detonated on Christmas Day with a force, which almost prompted the resignation of Stimson as secretary of war. When they were together in the White House, Churchill and Roosevelt could consider ideas and operations that their military advisors might question or reject entirely. In this case, the offending and incendiary paragraph reported FDR's "wishes" about military personnel being dispatched to the Philippines, and his view "that there was little likelihood that the land and air reinforcements now on their way from the U.S.A. via Australia could arrive at their destination. His view was that these reinforcements should be utilized in whatever manner might best serve the joint cause in the Far East."[41]

Stimson's diary entry for December 25 is bereft of Christmas cheer. In fact, while Churchill and Roosevelt were attending "the National Christmas Service" at the Foundry Methodist Church in Washington—complete with the singing of "O Little Town of Bethlehem," a carol Churchill had never heard—Stimson steamed about Roosevelt considering the possibility of "the turning over to the British of our proposed reenforcements [*sic*] for [General Douglas] MacArthur." Stimson's anger over the "astonishing paper" grew during the day, and he called Harry Hopkins, at the time Roosevelt's closest advisor on war matters, with his threat of quitting. The nimble "Harry the Hop" quickly "called me back telling me that he had recited what I had said to the President in the presence of Churchill and they had denied that any such propositions had actually been made. I then read to him extracts from the paper . . . and he said that they certainly bore out my view."[42]

Stimson's presidential-directed pique continued to build, and later in his Christmas Day diary entry he made a broader administrative conclusion. "This incident shows the danger of talking too freely in international matters of such keen importance without the President carefully having his military and naval advisers present." The sharp-elbowed cabinet veteran worried that disclosure of the memorandum "would have raised any amount of trouble for the President if it had gotten into the hands of an unfriendly press."[43] From Churchill's first visit through the rest of the war, the secretary of war was often at odds with the British prime minister, and he used his diary as the principal vent for registering his criticism.

The contrasting styles of Churchill and Roosevelt could rankle someone like Stimson, though he wasn't closed-minded. In an entry the next day, he said that Churchill at the Capitol "made a magnificent speech and I think it will do a great deal of good in the country." Still, some members of the British contingent shared Stimson's reservations about Roosevelt. Ian Jacob, a lieutenant colonel who traveled with Churchill on several foreign trips (and later became director general of the BBC), kept a revealing diary during the Washington visit in late 1941 and early 1942. Remarking that unlike the prime minister "the President never had note-takers in his meetings," Jacob, himself an official notetaker, commented, "The President is a most impressive man, and seems to be on the best of terms with all his advisers." However, the next sentences set forth unsparing criticism of FDR: "By the side of the Prime Minister he [FDR] is a child in Military affairs, and evidently has little realization of what can and what cannot be done. He doesn't seem to grasp how backward his country is in its war preparations, and how ill-prepared his army is to get involved in large scale operations."

With that stinging observation as a first volley, Jacob, a member of what Churchill referred to as "my secret circle," complained that "the American machine of Government seems hopelessly disorganized," especially in military affairs.[44] The quotient of condescension is striking; however, in their own ways Jacob and Stimson saw administrative matters similarly. Of course, Churchill had been leading Britain's war effort nearly twenty months, while Roosevelt was still adjusting to the post-Pearl Harbor buildup of personnel and production that the United States would need to wage a war across two oceans. In a sense, Jacob's commentary is unfair, with a strong bias in favor of British procedures. Interestingly, though, his perceptions provide a definite contrast, in tone and substance, to the way Churchill portrayed his time in the White House, whether in reports back to London or later in his memoirs. After Jacob recorded his initial impressions describing the White House, including sketches of room locations and the seating chart for meetings, he focused directly—and sharply—on FDR, stating the president "leads a most simple life" and works in "one of the most untidy rooms I have ever seen. It is full of junk." Jacob's cataloging of the array of items strewn around on book shelves, tables, chairs, and even the floor resulted in a haughty judgment that the disorder "would drive an orderly-minded man, or a woman, mad."[45]

Having set the scene—"typical of the general lack of organization in the American Government"—Jacob later described a formal meeting among the president, prime minister, and their staffs. Even in the conduct of war strategy, he maintained his drumbeat of we-know-better superiority that included an objection to FDR's Scottish terrier, Fala, scampering around the study. At one point, with Churchill "in the middle of an oration," Fala started barking. The frisky first pet and faithful presidential sidekick "had to be ejected" so the meeting could continue.[46]

Jacob was not alone in being bewildered by the distinct approaches of the two allies. The United Kingdom's ambassador to the United States, Lord Halifax, born Edward Wood, had watched Washington's curious ways since his arrival in January of 1941 and noted his activities and rendered his opinions in a near-daily diary. At six feet, five inches tall, the rail-resembling former foreign secretary and appeasement supporter had declined becoming prime minister when Neville Chamberlain resigned on May 10, 1940. In a long political and diplomatic career, he was frequently at odds with Churchill and strongly opposed his posting four thousand miles from London. As Andrew Roberts aptly notes in his biography of Halifax, *The Holy Fox*: "The Rogue Elephant [Churchill] was finally savaging the weakened old elephant [Halifax] to establish himself as undisputed master of the herd."[47] Far from Britain, Halifax could cause less trouble for the prime minister yet still play an important role in dealing with the country Churchill desperately wanted as an ally and partner. Halifax would continue as ambassador until May of 1946.

The wily Halifax exacted some revenge for being exiled to the New World in his diary, with numerous entries about the prime minister, his White House visits, and the governmental activities by both countries that occurred outside of public view. On October 20, 1941, he remarked about Churchill, "With all his faults there is so much that is childishly simple about him." When the prime minister was at the White House on December 27, Halifax echoed Jacob's reservations in describing the drafting of the document that would become known as "The Declaration by United Nations." Grumbling about the Americans' "most disorderly and unbusinesslike methods of working," Halifax is bemused that the result turned out satisfactorily. Yet the process, he admitted, "would drive me to drink." Besides shaking his head at the Rooseveltian manner of conducting business, Halifax never appreciated the mixing of work with day-to-day life at the White House. When the draft of the declaration required retyping elsewhere, Hopkins ushered Halifax to "his bedroom while he dressed, his bedroom serving as bedroom and office. It is the oddest ménage I have ever seen."

Churchill, of course, added considerably to the eccentric nature of the ménage, as he roamed around the White House living quarters in his nightclothes trying to resolve a point or seeking to learn the contents of a newly arrived cable. On that Saturday, December 27, the prime minister scheduled a meeting in his suite with his ambassador for 10 p.m. Two hours later and exhausted, Halifax described Churchill's train of talk as "jumping like a water bird from stone to stone where the current takes you." The undiplomatic diarist attributed the British leader's discursive manner to a self-centeredness acute enough to "make him quite impervious to other people's feelings."[48] Halifax tempers his view by noting that "I forgive him everything for his other great gifts," yet what he recorded in his diary, particularly the "secret" portion only available at the Borthwick Institute for Archives at the University of York, isn't sparing of the qualities and idiosyncrasies he noted. Looking back to Churchill's first visit in a diary note for March 25, 1942, he didn't hold back, remarking that the prime minister had "become much more dictatorial."[49] Often disgruntled and far from home, Halifax provided firsthand observations that help to flesh out the story of a critical period and the central players involved.

In the estimation of many people from different vantage points, neither the prime minister nor the president served as model executives. Roosevelt's close-to-the-vest way of conducting business emphasized small group or one-on-one discussions frequently among officials and advisors with conflicting opinions. To outsiders the process could appear as disorderly as his surroundings, but it was his way of seeing different sides of an issue and keeping those with competing interests on their toes and guessing about the outcome. By contrast, the garrulous Churchill, as noted before, committed his thoughts, proposals, and orders to page after page of dictated memorandums or the individual "minute" addressed to someone in the British government. Decisive rather than digressive in putting words on paper, his ability to concentrate was, indeed, impressive, given demands coming from different directions and departments. In addition, his compositional range was astonishing: a matter-of-fact directive would be tossed off right before tackling a speech for which he often devoted an hour of compositional preparation to each minute for spoken delivery. In *The Grand Alliance*, Churchill recalled that he devoted much of Christmas Day to writing the speech he was scheduled to deliver the next day to a joint meeting of Congress, even excusing himself from an evening White House screening of the 1933 film version of Charles Dickens's *Oliver Twist* to spend more time—he called it his "homework"—to preparing and revising his talk.

Christmas in 1941 is remembered for its somber solemnity. The United States was still grieving over Pearl Harbor, but forced to adapt to the new realities of taking security precautions, preparing for possible military service abroad, shifting to a war-demand economy, devising rationing programs, and everything else. "We are the same people we were yesterday and yet we are different," a newspaper editorial poignantly noted. In some cities religious services on Christmas night were canceled to make sure worshippers stayed at home after dark. In Britain, still recovering from months of German bombing, the scarcity of particular groceries, clothes, soap, petrol, and other items meant a second Yule that combined holiday customs and stoic fortitude.

Despite the cataclysm of global war, radio programming on both sides of the Atlantic tried to provide some solace. The BBC's "Programmes for Christmas Week" included Handel's "Messiah," a spoken version of the Walt Disney film "Snow White," and even a concert of Russian music—titled "Greetings to Joseph Stalin"—celebrating the Soviet leader's birthday. In America on that Christmas night, Bing Crosby sang Irving Berlin's "White Christmas" for the first time during the "Kraft Music Hall" on NBC. With lyrics reminiscing about snowy merriment in bygone days, the song struck a chord, and over time Crosby's rendition became the best-selling single record in history, according to Guinness World Records.

At about the time Crosby was crooning "White Christmas," Halifax stopped by the White House to see Churchill, whom he found attired "in his coloured dressing gown in bed, preparing his speech for the Senate tomorrow, surrounded by cigars, whiskies and sodas and secretaries!"[50] Michael F. Reilly, the head of the White House Secret Service detail and FDR's main bodyguard, provided elaboration on Halifax's description and what life was like in the Rose Bedroom that December. "Never had the staid butlers, ushers, maids and other Executive Mansion workers seen anything like Winston before," Reilly recalled. He explained that the guest ate with the gusto of two or three individuals "consumed brandy and scotch with a grace and enthusiasm that left us all openmouthed in awe." What impressed Reilly and others was "the complete sobriety" that Churchill displayed after his daily sustenance.[51]

According to Roosevelt's calendar for Christmas, he went to the religious service with Churchill, but didn't talk with him one-on-one until 11:40 that night, a session lasting until 1:10 a.m. Meals that day included a luncheon for twenty and dinner for sixty. In his book, *A Rendezvous with Destiny*, Elliott Roosevelt noted that Roosevelt children—he was the fourth of six—or grandchildren weren't able to visit the White House that holiday season. "I suspect," he suggested, "that both my parents were glad to have a household of hungry, demanding Englishmen bustling about on the second floor that Christmas."[52] His mother might not have agreed.

The morning of December 26, Boxing Day in Britain, Churchill polished his speech in his quarters before leaving for the Capitol. Though British prime minister Ramsay MacDonald spoke at a House of Representatives reception in 1929, Churchill was the first foreign leader in the twentieth century to appear before a Congressional meeting of both the Senate and the House. Since so many federal legislators were at their homes and away from Washington for the holidays, Churchill spoke in the Senate chamber rather than in the much larger House of Representatives. (The full text of his speech can be found in the appendix.) Though it was the prime minister's first address to—in his phrase—"a foreign parliament," several senators told reporters afterward it was the greatest speech they ever heard. Churchill poked fun at himself and his mixed heritage before turning to his principal business, the war. "I cannot help reflecting that if my father had been American and my mother British, instead of the other way round, I might have got here on my own," he cracked in his fourth sentence. "In that case, this would not have been the first time you would have heard my voice."[53] Right away, Churchill created an association with his audience in the Capitol and the millions huddled by their radios across America, remarking: "Here in Washington, in these memorable days, I have found an Olympian fortitude which, far from being based upon complacency, is only the mark of an inflexible purpose and the proof of a sure and well-grounded confidence in the final outcome."[54]

Sentence after sentence, each word chosen by the speaker, made his case for joint cooperation, achieving it by combining the immediate concerns with the more enduring principles animating the Allies. He spoke of "deliverance" coming but didn't predict when: "in 1942, or 1943, or 1944."[55] The rhetoric never sugarcoated reality. At one point he admitted, "Many disappointments and unpleasant surprises await us."[56] Viewed *in toto*, the lead article in the next day's *New York Times* remarked that it was "full of bubbling humor, biting denunciation of totalitarian enemies, stern courage and hard facts."

Though Churchill balanced his verbal shelling of Germany, Italy, and Japan, the questions he posed about the Japanese in the wake of the attack at Pearl Harbor attracted much of the attention: "What kind of a people do they think we are? Is it possible they do not realize that we shall never cease to persevere against them until they have been taught a lesson which they and the world will never forget?"[57] Though the development of the atomic bomb and its usage at Hiroshima and Nagasaki was over three years off, the teachers of that unforgettable lesson the prime minister promised would be the men and women working together in Churchill's imperiled empire and Roosevelt's no-longer isolationist republic. At the end, he explicitly drew the United Kingdom and the United States together in what would stand out as his abiding theme and hope, saying "in the days to come the British and American peoples will for their own safety and for the good of all walk together side by side in majesty, in justice, and in peace."[58]

Churchill's oration was an impassioned battle cry—3,228 words (and just over a half hour in length) compared to the more concise 520 words Roosevelt took seven minutes to deliver on December 8, asking the House and Senate for a declaration of war against Japan. Congress formally declared war on Japan shortly after FDR spoke. Three days later, war declarations were also approved against both Germany and Italy, members of the Tripartite Pact with Japan. Germany and Italy had declared war against America earlier on December 11. Besides establishing the transatlantic bond the time demanded, the prime minister's speech also began to plant the first seeds for what he would call "the special relationship" between the United Kingdom and the United States.

Churchill's remarks roused those in the Senate chamber, packed to overflowing. The next morning's *Washington Post* published six photos of Churchill on its front page, and a feature inside (headlined "Big Crowd Thrills as 'Winnie' Appears"), noting that in less than a week he had become a bona fide political personality with popular appeal. The excitement the foreign visitor generated occurred at a time of unprecedented security and anxiety, with the Capitol, it was reported, more heavily guarded than at any prior time.

At a Congressional luncheon following the speech, Churchill commented, "This has been the biggest day of my life," adding, "I was a bit nervous at the prelude, I must say." The news report, published in the *Indianapolis Times* the next day, went on to say that despite his butterflies, the prime minister felt at home among the legislators. That came naturally. By then, he'd served nearly four decades in the House of Commons. When speaking in Parliament, he said he tried to level with the public, adding "Americans want the truth also. . . . I am sure they can stand up to it."

The prime minister also took an additional step to endear himself to Congress and to his mother's people. After the luncheon, he learned that the wife of Senator Ernest (Mac) McFarland of Arizona was ailing and confined to a Washington hospital. Without missing a political beat, Churchill asked to speak to her on the phone to wish her a quick recovery. As he left the Capitol, hundreds gathered at a distance to catch a glimpse of him, and he not only flashed his "V for victory" salute but also hoisted his hat on his cane with a showman's flourish to acknowledge those standing in the back of the huge crowd. On his return to 1600 Pennsylvania Avenue, according to one wire service dispatch, he "paused on the White House lawn and fed peanuts to the gray squirrels." This small, endearing gesture received notice.

Churchill's speech triggered widespread interest in the United States and abroad, with the prime minister reporting back to London on December 27: "Welcome was extraordinary. Work here is most strenuous. . . . My talks with President increasingly intimate and friendly."[59] Interestingly and possibly out of fear of being upstaged, Roosevelt on December 27 released what the press referred to as "the first official report" about the meetings at the White House. Saying at the beginning that a great deal "has been accomplished," the statement went on to say "the position of the United States and of all Nations aligned with us has been strengthened immeasurably. We have advanced far along the road toward achievement of the ultimate objective—the crushing defeat of those forces that have attacked and made war upon us." Surprisingly, at no point in the text did Churchill's name appear. The four-paragraph communiqué—with references to "I" and "my" at key places—was distributed in time to make the Sunday newspapers on December 28, and it helped put an unmistakable presidential seal on the proceedings during the past six days. FDR's perspective was featured on the front pages of the *New York Times*, *Washington Post*, *Chicago Tribune*, *Los Angeles Times*, and other papers.

With the initial conferences on war planning, the Christmas observances, and the oration to Congress behind him, Churchill could establish a routine for working in the White House, and he understood where he ranked there. Roosevelt was both head of state *and* head of the government, while the prime minister, solely in charge of his government's activities, recognized more than others what America could ultimately mean to the Allied cause with its military forces, resources, and *matériel*. That knowledge, however, didn't mean that Churchill, who was eight years older than FDR, would shy away from offering his tutelage or counsel from what he'd learned during the nearly twenty-eight months Britain had been at war. He was particularly well-versed in the need to prepare.

Even before arriving, the prime minister had what might be construed as the effrontery to request that a room in the White House be reserved for him to hang maps and charts on the walls, showing current battles, naval fleet positions, and troop movements. In his underground command center near 10 Downing Street, Churchill had created a similar setup where he could view the sweep of the world at war with the most up-to-date information visually portrayed in terms of geographical positioning, military strength, status of combat, and other aspects.

Among the British staff traveling to Washington was Vivian A. Cox, a lieutenant commander in the Royal Navy. His principal responsibility involved the organization and arrangement of the prime minister's map room, which he set up shortly after arrival and later wrote about in a memoir, *Seven Christmases*, which his nephew, Nick Thorne, edited years later and published in 2010.

Cox reported that the Monroe Room on the second floor of the White House, not far from the bedrooms of both Churchill and Roosevelt, was commandeered to become the map room, and it was frequently visited by the two leaders and their top advisors, as the diary entry by Stimson cited earlier pointed out. What Cox saw and heard—and subsequently described—provides a firsthand view of White House life at this time. It's a human portrayal beyond politics and a preoccupation with war. At one point, he noted: "It was a most fascinating experience, and one that I shall never forget, to see and hear those two leaders openly and fully speaking their thoughts to each other. They were obviously on the most cordial terms. They may have started as 'Mr. President' and 'Mr. Prime Minister' but it was no time before they were 'Franklin' and 'Winston.' "[60] A few paragraphs later, Cox recalled that Churchill came to the map room alone and inquired, "What do you think of the President?" Before the lowly "sub-lieutenant" could muster a response, he heard the prime minister remark: "It is a great blessing for mankind that he was called to his high office at this moment in history."[61]

The map room that Cox and his coworker, Harry McMullan, established became so useful for FDR and his chief advisors that the president requested that a permanent one be created in the White House. Space was found on the ground floor next to the Diplomatic Reception Room, and Cox stayed behind in Washington after Churchill departed not only to make sure maps and charts were effectively displayed but also that military personnel were properly trained to keep all the information as up-to-date as possible. The exact locations of the Allies' Big Three leaders were noted each day and represented in an ingenious, true-to-life way: Churchill with a cigar, FDR with a cigarette holder, and Stalin with a pipe.

Helping Cox to organize and then continue what became a top-secret headquarters of war intelligence for the Roosevelt administration was a reserve officer in the U.S. Navy, Robert Montgomery. Well-known as a Hollywood movie star, Montgomery received his second Oscar nomination for best actor in February of 1942 for his role in the 1941 film *Here Comes Mr. Jordan*. Itching for combat duty rather than map-centric service, Montgomery, the father of Elizabeth Montgomery, who starred in the long-running television series *Bewitched*, was reassigned and subsequently took part in the D-Day invasion but returned to the White House in 1954 to help coach President Dwight Eisenhower in the use of the rapidly expanding new medium of television.

Once long-term staffing was arranged, the cartography center became a daily stop for Roosevelt and military brass who came to the White House. When Churchill returned to Washington later in 1942 as well as twice in 1943, he haunted the map room at all hours, often shuffling around America's premier residence either in bare feet or slippers and clad in his familiar siren suit. Upon entering, he invariably inquired, "How's Hitler?" and—before receiving an answer—offered his own judgment, "the bastard." One time on a 2:30 a.m. visit, the prime minister found the officer on duty slumbering in the darkened room. "Taut watch you keep here, son," he said—but kept that discovery to himself.[62]

Churchill's public activities during his only winter visit to Washington kept him front-page news in the United States and abroad. He, along with Roosevelt, keenly understood the power of leadership by performance—strong words and symbolic actions exhibiting their sense of command. Away from events involving crowds of people and reporters, the prime minister followed his long-established routine of constant communication with government officials among the Allies and back in London. On January 3, 1942, for instance, he cabled "Premier Stalin," who was leading the Soviet Union against Germany's all-out assault, called "Operation Barbarossa," after Hitler broke the pact between the two countries in June of 1941. Churchill complained that an editorial in *Pravda*, reported about in American papers, was unjustifiably critical of the United States for its war tactics in the Pacific, particularly in the Philippines. Noting "the very great danger which might be caused here by continuation of such criticism," the prime minister boasted: "From the very first day of the Nazi attack on you I have laboured to get all possible support for Soviet Russia in the United States."[63] At that point the two comrades with common enemies hadn't met, but that didn't stop the British leader from lodging his objection.

On the same day Churchill chided Stalin and after nearly two weeks in the United States, he wired Clement Attlee, the Lord Privy Seal and leader of the Labour Party in the United Kingdom's Government of National Unity, who became deputy prime minister in February of 1942. The dispatch to Attlee, like the one to Stalin, is stamped on each page of the copy in the United Kingdom's National Archives with a bold warning in bright red ink: "HUSH—MOST SECRET." In it Churchill described residing in the White House and his reaction to it. "We live here as a big family in the greatest intimacy and informality," he observed, "and I have formed the very highest regard and admiration for the President."[64] Churchill's cheery assessment of familial togetherness wasn't shared by everyone. Halifax noted in his diary that he stopped by the White House to meet with the prime minister but discovered that the president was "talking to him in his bedroom!" Note the exclamation point. While the ambassador cooled his heels in the hall, he noticed "Harry Hopkins floating past in pyjamas and dressing gown. Certainly the oddest ménage anybody has ever seen."[65] Halifax never got over—or approved—the unusual scenes on the second floor of the White House.

Two days before Churchill wrote to Attlee praising the convivial domesticity at 1600 Pennsylvania Avenue, the prime minister was the principal character in a moment of "greatest intimacy and informality" that endures in White House history and folklore. Churchill recalled in *The Grand Alliance* that on New Year's Day FDR proposed to him a new collective name for the Allies fighting the Axis countries. Pondering throughout the night, the president had arrived at what he considered a more resonant locution than the "Associated Powers," which had been used thus far during the conference. Roosevelt recommended two other words, "United Nations," and his White House guest, more celebrated as a wordsmith, judged the suggestion "a great improvement." Churchill went on to tell how the nocturnal phrasemaking was reported to him: "The President was wheeled-in to me on the morning of January 1. I got out of my bath, and agreed to the draft."[66]

What Churchill and others who have written about this episode usually fail to note is that the prime minister had arrived back in Washington at Union Station at 8:56 that morning after a nearly nineteen-hour journey from Ottawa. He must have been rushing around in his White House suite, because at 10:45 a.m. he and Roosevelt, accompanied by ten other people in their party, left for religious services at Christ Church in Alexandria, Virginia, George Washington's place of worship. In a proclamation, the president had designated January 1 as a National Day of Prayer to ask, in particular, for "God's help in days to come."

Churchill's unadorned, matter-of-fact recollection of stepping out of his bath to approve the new title assumes greater meaning when explained more fully by Roosevelt and others with knowledge of the whole story. Grace Tully, who had become FDR's personal secretary earlier in 1941 after Missy LeHand's stroke, recalled the president's excitement at coming up with what became a lasting locution. In her memoir—and just about everyone who worked closely with Roosevelt published a book about him—wrote that "the President was so pleased at his choice that he merely barged right in" to the Rose Bedroom to announce his brainstorm. With puckish, juvenile delight, FDR told his Irish Catholic secretary, "You know, Grace, I just happened to think of it now. He's pink and white all over."[67]

Roosevelt relished telling this anecdote, especially the way it related to his coming up with the phrase "United Nations." His sixth cousin, confidante, and presidential library archivist Margaret (Daisy) Suckley noted in her diary that the president "called to W.S.C. & in the door leading to the bathroom appeared W.S.C.: a "pink cherub" [FDR said] drying himself with a towel, & without a stitch on!" Roosevelt announced the phrase and received Churchill's immediate approval. Suckley expanded on the incident to report: "W.S.C. told F.D.R. at their next meeting, that when W.S.C. returned to England & was telling the King about it, he said, 'Sir, I believe I am the only man in the world who has received the head of a nation without any clothes on!' "[68]

Besides making fun of Churchill's awkward circumstance to entertain two women he knew well, Roosevelt either told others or the tale was repeated so often it evolved into an open secret around Washington. In his memoirs, Cordell Hull, who served as secretary of state from 1933 until after the 1944 election, recalled: "On the morning of December 31, while Prime Minister Churchill was having a bath in the White House, the President came to him and suggested that the Joint Declaration carry the title, 'Declaration by United Nations.' The distinguished bather agreed, and thus the term 'United Nations' came into being."[69] The 1945 Nobel Peace Prize recipient for the pivotal role he played in establishing the subsequent world body called the "United Nations" is off by a day in remembering what happened, and he doesn't provide any color, pink or otherwise, but the "distinguished bather" and the presidential phraseology are duly noted by the longest serving U.S. secretary of state.

For both Roosevelt and Churchill, storytelling came naturally, no matter the size of the audience: a single listener or a multitude. To entertain or amuse others made them more human and appealing. And it could even be the same tale. In his diary entry for January 4, 1942, Halifax wrote that he inquired whether noon would be a suitable time for the ambassador to meet the prime minister the following day. Churchill sidestepped that possibility for the reason that FDR might be talking with him in his suite, as he'd done a few days before. Halifax went on to say Churchill told him the president "found Winston with nothing on at all, and he had quickly to drape himself with a towel. 'He is the only head of a State I have ever received in the nude!' "[70]

For both of the principal characters involved, the more repeatable the story, the better. When Canadian Prime Minister Mackenzie King visited the White House in December of 1942, a year after Churchill's first sojourn, Roosevelt explained to him the origin of the phrase United Nations, how "he could hardly wait till the morning to tell Winston," and, above all, the distinctive way the prime minister received word about it. King's diary for December 5 included this detail from FDR: "Winston called out to come in but that he was taking a bath. He [FDR] said he [WSC] walked out of the bath in a few minutes and had not a stripe on him. The President said Winston—pointing at him—I have it: the United Nations."[71]

As frequently as FDR repeated his phrasemaking, it's unclear whether the incident he recounted was the occasion when the pink-hued protagonist uttered the statement most often associated in popular accounts with his initial wartime visit to the White House. Reminiscences of those around Churchill on this trip recount several other memorable moments featuring the fastidious enthusiast of two baths a day and his head-of-state host.

Walter Henry Thompson, Churchill's bodyguard throughout the 1920s and later brought out of retirement in 1939 to serve six more years in that role, recalled that their "first night in the White House" he was checking out the prime minister's suite when he heard a knock at the door. Told to answer it, Thompson was met by Roosevelt in his wheelchair, who seemed hesitant to enter. The veteran Scotland Yard inspector turned to discover that "Winston Churchill was stark naked, a drink in one hand, a cigar in the other." Though FDR offered to leave, Churchill demurred and encouraged what turned into an hour-long chat by declaring: "You see, Mr. President, I have nothing to hide."[72]

The likelihood this reminiscence occurred on December 22 is

highly doubtful. The White House usher's diary notes that dinner was served at 8:45 p.m., and there was a meeting with several people in the president's study that lasted from 10 p.m. until 12:35 a.m. FDR, according to the diary, retired at 12:50 a.m. There wasn't an hour during the first night when the colorful yarn could have taken place. Interestingly, Thompson, who published four memoirs about guarding Churchill, only described the "stark naked" anecdote once, but Erik Larson repeated it nearly word-for-word in his acclaimed narrative about Churchill's first year as prime minister, *The Splendid and the Vile.*

Another Thompson, though, got involved in reciting a similar story, one more faithful to Roosevelt's seemingly unforgettable recollection. In *The War and Colonel Warden,** Gerald Pawle relies on C. R. (Tommy) Thompson's extensive notes and memories to construct a narrative about the longtime naval officer's experiences as Churchill's aide-de-camp and personal assistant throughout World War II. In the chapter "Christmas at the White House," there's a generic description of the prime minister's morning ablution, "often quite a spectacular event," with the bather going underwater and rising to the surface "blowing like a whale." Standing at the ready, a valet would provide a sizable towel and thus swaddled Churchill would often "pace to and fro" dictating to an assistant. Thompson recalled for Pawle one occasion when stenographer Patrick Kinna, bearing "notebook and pencil," was taking down something Churchill was composing, and Roosevelt "entered the bathroom" to discuss the catchphrase and the draft document. In this version, with Kinna as the source, "Naked and unashamed, Churchill declared: "I have nothing to conceal from the President of the United States!"[73]

Martin Gilbert, Churchill's official biographer, confirmed part of Kinna's story by publishing a letter from the stenographer. Dated October 10, 1984, the letter described an incident that Kinna alleged hap-

* Colonel Warden was the prime minister's most frequently used code name when traveling, though he was also known by the aliases of "Colonel Kent" and "Air Commodore Frankland."

pened on December 24, 1941—eight days *before* Churchill pinpointed the naming of the United Nations: "Suddenly President Roosevelt entered the bedroom and saw the British Prime Minister completely naked walking around the room dictating to me. WSC never being lost for words said 'You see, Mr President, I have nothing to conceal from you.' "[74]

Ian Jacob, the British aide with serious doubts about Roosevelt's work habits and surroundings, wrote about yet another sighting of the unclad prime minister by the president. On this particular morning, FDR rolled up to the Rose Bedroom in his wheelchair and inquired if Churchill was awake. Informed that the guest was bathing, Roosevelt didn't bat an eye and entered. " 'Don't mind me,' " said the President, as the Prime Minister grabbed a towel and the door closed."[75]

One other similar episode occurred during Churchill's inaugural White House stay, and, in its way, there's greater drama, if not historical relevance, to it. In his memoir, Cox told of standing outside the map room when he spotted the president and Wendell Willkie coming down the hall. Willkie, a business executive and former Democrat, was the dark horse Republican presidential candidate FDR defeated in 1940. Though the date isn't mentioned, the White House usher's diary establishes it as Tuesday, January 13, 1942, between 10:30 and 11:15 in the morning. As usual, Roosevelt asked if Churchill had arisen, and Cox replied that he didn't think so. Still, the naval officer took the two men to the prime minister's suite and found him "standing in the middle of the floor, naked and unashamed, and looking for all the world like a Botticelli cherub." The British leader is anything but speechless: " 'How very good to see you,' " he beamed with outstretched arms. " 'Pray excuse my state of nature.' "[76]

Churchill's "state of nature" in receiving the incumbent president and his most recent Republican rival was, we now know, a somewhat common occurrence during the prime minister's visits in Washington, with instances of Roosevelt stopping by to talk with Churchill at somewhat awkward moments continuing with regularity after the first visit.

Captain Richard Pim, Cox's superior and supervisor of the prime minister's map room in London who traveled with Churchill on some of his trips abroad, recalled that on May 12, 1943, as the Trident Conference was beginning, FDR was curious if his White House guest "had everything he required." As the president opened the door of the Rose Bedroom, there was Churchill emerging from the bathroom in search of a towel. Though the president apologized, the prime minister put his visitor at ease: "Please do not concern yourself—England has nothing to hide from the President of the United States."[77]

J. B. West, who served as White House chief usher for twelve years during an almost three-decade career assisting six presidents, revealed in his memoir, *Upstairs at the White House*, that his staff of "servants never quite got over seeing him [Churchill] naked in his room when they'd go up to serve brandy. It was the jumpsuit or nothing. In his room, Mr. Churchill wore no clothes at all most of the time during the day."[78] There's a certain locker room hilarity to the different stories, but amid the humor is the humanizing effect of a public figure being caught off guard in his private quarters without considering it unduly consequential. Roosevelt made his New Year's encounter part of his repertoire of White House tales. Interestingly, the president never mentions a riposte or bon mot from Churchill to the naming of the United Nations. Did he really say that he had "nothing to conceal from the President of the United States"? Perhaps that remark is yet another invented expression attributed to the witty Englishman.

Someone brave enough to try to get to the bottom of whatever might—or might not—have occurred was Robert Sherwood. The recipient of three Pulitzer Prizes for Drama, Sherwood was recruited as a speechwriter for Roosevelt during the war, an experience that he used as context for his Pulitzer Prize– and Bancroft Prize–winning book, *Roosevelt and Hopkins: An Intimate History*. At one point, Sherwood brought up a particular story that Hopkins "told many times." In this rendition, the prime minister "protested it was quite all right [for FDR to be in the room]." Then, as Sherwood continued, Hopkins directly quoted Churchill as saying to Roosevelt: " 'The Prime Minister of Great Britain,' he said, 'has nothing to conceal from the President of the United States.' "

The noted playwright turned presidential ghostwriter pivoted to become inquisitive White House reporter-historian. "I asked Churchill if this story was factual," he wrote. "He replied firmly that it was nonsense—that he never received the President without at least a bath towel wrapped around him. And he said, 'I could not possibly have made such a statement as that. The President himself would have been well aware that it was not strictly true.' "[79]

Was Churchill embarrassed by the risible circumstances behind the question? Or did he think an affirmative response might violate the privacy between the two world leaders? Whatever the case—and, as noted, there is evidence the prime minister told both Halifax and King George VI—stories about FDR walking in on Churchill appear with such frequency in books and articles they assume the status of a lasting, laugh-worthy legend.

It's striking and to a degree perplexing that in the telling and retelling of the prime minister having no clothes, the precise wording of his putative retort isn't consistent. In *The President's House*, presidential daughter and author Margaret Truman claimed that Churchill "could easily qualify as the houseguest from hell," going on to report Roosevelt one time found "the prime minister in the all-together. Churchill gave him a cheerful grin and said: 'You see, Mr. President, I have nothing to hide!' "[80]

Nothing to conceal. Nothing to hide. Either way it might have been said rings true as possible, given the circumstances and the speaker's ability for a rapid riposte. In Cox's memoir he devoted a lengthy footnote to the "I-have-nothing-to-hide" episode, revealing that Churchill withheld significant military information from Roosevelt during the Arcadia Conference. The prime minister advised the president that two British battleships were guarding the Suez Canal, when, in fact, they had been mined by Italian frogmen and sunk three days before Churchill arrived in the United States. FDR learned that Churchill misled him a few days after the conference and asked Cox, still at the White House setting up the map room, "How could your man do this to me?"[81] Were the two Allied leaders as close as they purported to be and wanted the public to believe?

Churchill kept other secrets. At their next Washington conference in late June 1942, Roosevelt wanted to know if the British were involved in the assassination of Nazi leader Reinhard Heydrich, director of the Gestapo and architect of the Holocaust. Serving as the principal enforcer of German rule in Bohemia and Moravia, Heydrich became known as "the Butcher of Prague." On his way to Berlin for a meeting with Hitler in May 1942, his car was attacked. He was seriously wounded and died a week later. According to Giles Milton's historical account *The Ministry of Ungentlemanly Warfare*, the prime minister "winked but said nothing" when FDR inquired. Milton adds: "There were some secrets too sensitive to be revealed, even to the American President."[82]

When Roosevelt and Willkie were alone together in the White House the morning of January 13, it's quite possible they were chuckling at Churchill's expense before seeing him. Some days earlier, while the prime minister was relaxing in Florida, he had tried to phone Willkie, whom he had met in London during the previous January. On January 20, 1941, the day FDR was inaugurated for an unprecedented third term, he wrote by hand a letter with the direct salutation "Dear Churchill," asking his former political opponent to deliver it personally. "Wendell Willkie will give you this—He is truly helping to keep politics out over here." Though they had numerous policy differences during FDR's first two terms, Roosevelt and Willkie agreed on the need to prepare for war and to provide assistance to the United Kingdom. In his letter, FDR quoted (not quite faithfully from memory) the Longfellow poem "The Building of the Ship" with the words:

Sail on, Oh Ship of State!
Sail on, Oh Union strong and great.[83]

As an informal envoy of the president, Willkie epitomized bipartisan support for the British as they endured the relentless German bombings during the blitz. Unfortunately, almost a year later, Churchill's telephonic attempt to reach the businessman-politician awkwardly misfired. He related the anecdote in *The Grand Alliance*. Instead of the call going through to Willkie, proposing a possible meeting, it ended up ringing Roosevelt's phone. After some confusion, Churchill admitted to FDR, "I did not mean to trouble you at this moment. I was trying to speak to Wendell Willkie, but your telephone exchange seems to have made a mistake."[84] Upset by the mistake that occurred early in the alliance, Churchill wrote Hopkins to inquire whether trying to contact Willkie had offended the president. Hopkins replied that he didn't think there was any change in their relationship, which came as a relief to the prime minister.

Unraveling amusing events involving a well-known public figure in a private setting can present certain problems. However, the historical stakes increase severalfold if an occurrence involves a potentially serious medical situation. Sir Charles Wilson, who was elevated to become Lord Moran in 1943, was Churchill's private physician from 1940 until Churchill's death in 1965. In 1966, Moran published *Churchill: The Struggle for Survival, 1940–1965*, which became an international bestseller for its revealing, at times compelling, portrait of its subject. It was also, however, a work that received severe condemnation from the Churchill family and close associates for violating patient-doctor confidentiality. Besides troubling ethical concerns, the family and others disputed the rendering of specific occasions, the assertion of psychological judgments, and the use of direct quotations. Longtime private secretary John Colville complained that the doctor-author "was never himself on the stage [at notable events], and only spasmodically an interested, inquisitive spectator in the wings of the theatre."[85] Oliver

Lyttelton, who served as the U.K. minister of production and in other significant positions during Churchill's two premierships, told the *New York Times* in its edition of June 15, 1966, that he considered all of the published dialogue to be "suspect."

Though the book is presented with the verisimilitude of a diary, doubts abound whether the accounts were contemporaneous or pieced together afterward from notes and other published works. Despite such criticism, one particular incident during Churchill's first wartime visit to Washington deserves some probing. The doctor's entry for December 27, 1941, raises several warning flags for a well-known smoker under enormous and constant pressure. The evening following the speech to Congress, we're told, Churchill had difficulty opening a window in his stuffy White House suite to cool it down. (The Washington temperature that night was in the high thirties.) Churchill is quoted as explaining and inquiring: "I had to use considerable force and I noticed all at once that I was short of breath. I had a dull pain over my heart. It went down my left arm. It didn't last very long, but it has never happened before. What is it? Is my heart all right?"[86]

After examining Churchill with a stethoscope, Moran admitted: "There was not much to be found when I examined his heart," but he went on to note the prime minister's "symptoms were those of coronary insufficiency. The textbook treatment for this is at least six weeks in bed." A few sentences about the risks of revealing to the world that Churchill could be viewed as "an invalid with a crippled heart and a doubtful future" led the doctor to evaluate the repercussions of informing his subject: "I felt that the effect of announcing that the P.M. had had a heart attack could only be disastrous. I knew, too, the consequences to one of his imaginative temperament of the feeling that his heart was affected. His work would suffer. On the other hand, if I did nothing and he had another and severer attack—perhaps a fatal seizure—the world would undoubtedly say that I had killed him through not insisting on rest." Moran used the word "attack" twice within four sentences, but downplayed his diagnosis with Churchill, telling him: "There is nothing serious" and "Your circulation was a bit sluggish." The doctor vowed "to tell no one."[87]

In the next two entries, dated December 28 and 29, Moran referred to either "the heart attack" or to Churchill becoming "heart-minded." Interestingly, what he set down for December 31 doesn't address any health issue but rather a change in human attitude he finds striking. The doctor observed that the prime minister of the United Kingdom displayed "indifference" to Canadian prime minister Mackenzie King after his considerably different Washington approach that included "the wooing of the President at the White House. There the P.M. and the President seemed to talk for most of the day, and for the first time I have seen Winston content to listen."[88]

Amid the wooing and the listening, what actually happened to Churchill remains a mystery. Moran deliberately used the phrase "heart attack," and in his thousand-page biography *Churchill: A Life*, Martin Gilbert stated, "Churchill had suffered a mild heart attack."[89] Mary Churchill Soames, the youngest Churchill child, added in her biography, *Clementine Churchill*, "On the night of 26 December Winston suffered a very slight heart attack: so slight was it that his programme remained unaltered, and not a word was said; but it was an indicative sign."[90] More recently, Andrew Roberts in *Churchill: Walking with Destiny* challenged the earlier diagnoses. Relying on studies conducted since the late 1990s, Roberts reports: "Modern medical analysis suggests that he [Churchill] may have had a muscle strain or a strain of the bony and cartilaginous chest wall. Nonetheless, it was a concern for someone who still believed he would not see old age."[91]

What's more puzzling than arriving at an authoritative diagnosis is Churchill's recollection of his own health incident. In *The Grand Alliance*, which appeared sixteen years before Moran's revelation of the event, we read that the prime minister flew down to Florida in early January of 1942 for five days of rest and sunshine. The White House conference meetings and other obligations, in his words, "made this period in Washington not only intense and laborious but even exhausting."

Churchill said he left Washington on January 4, going on to explain: "The night before I started the air-conditioning of my room in the White House failed temporarily, the heat became oppressive, and in trying to open the window I strained my heart slightly, causing unpleasant sensations which continued for some days. Sir Charles Wilson, my medical advisor, however decided that the journey south should not be put off."[92] For the next several pages, Churchill recounts what he did in Florida "in complete privacy" and without further mention of what he contends happened on the evening of January 3*.

So, who was accurate with the date: the doctor or the patient? Was it after the stress of the speech to Congress on December 26 or later on January 3, following the whirlwind trip to Canada, which included another major address? According to Roosevelt's calendar, he and Churchill met at least twice on January 3—and three separate times on January 4, the date Churchill gave for his flight to Florida. On January 4, FDR, Churchill, and Hopkins dined in the president's study. Dinner began at 8 o'clock, and the next notation is that Roosevelt "retired" at midnight. Churchill could not have left the White House until January 5. Churchill was certainly in error about his departure. Then, if you consult Roosevelt's calendar for December 26, he met with Churchill for several hours into the late evening after the prime minister returned to the White House from the Capitol. The next day, Churchill took part in six meetings as well as lunch and dinner, beginning at noon and continuing through the evening. As with the story about the prime minister walking around his White House suite with nothing to conceal, precise details are elusive and impossible to explain with certainty. It's fair to conclude that the six volumes of *The Second World War* are history that, from time to time, provide unhistorical recollections.

* The passage about the heart concern doesn't appear in the 1959 single-book abridgement of his multivolume history. Titled *Memoirs of the Second World War*, this volume includes an epilogue about "the postwar years."

It makes the most sense that the heart-related incident, whatever it might have been, occurred on December 26. During his brief Washington visit in late December of 1941, Canadian prime minister King noted in his diary on December 27 that from his perspective Roosevelt appeared "pretty tired." He went on to observe: "C [Churchill] is beginning to look rather flabby and tired. I could not help thinking of what a terrible thing it is that the fate of the world should rest so largely in the hands of two men to either of whom anything might happen at any moment."[93] As with Roosevelt's inability to walk that was hidden from the public as much as possible by using elaborate stratagems, Churchill kept health matters secretive during both of his terms as prime minister. In this case, wartime censorship helped both leaders project themselves as they might want. Up close, however, as King points out, they looked different.

In his book, Moran included an entry for January 1, 1942. The next one carried the date of January 5, designating "Florida" as the place of its origin. The possibility of illness and exhaustion that Churchill stated as his reasons for the trip aren't even mentioned by the prime minister's medical advisor as justifications for leaving the White House. Instead, he offered more convincing grounds for someone seeking to strengthen a vital relationship to the Allied cause. Moran wrote: "The P.M. decided to come here because he did not want to tax the hospitality of the President, who likes to get away over the weekend to Hyde Park. It was a thoughtful move to give the White House a respite, and we are seeing Winston in a new role." And, pray tell, how did Churchill look in this "new role"? His doctor provided this image: "The blue ocean is so warm that Winston basks half-submerged in the water like a hippopotamus in a swamp."[94] Inspector Thompson, informed by the prime minister that he had no need of a swimsuit, vividly described his protectee: "He'd sun himself in the nude. He looked like a huge, well-adjusted and slightly over-bottled baby boy, all grins and natural surrender."[95] When the bodyguard warned that people using binoculars might glimpse the visitor in the altogether, he was informed: "If they are that much interested, it is their own fault what they see."[96] Whether in the Rose Bedroom or on a secluded Florida beach, Churchill considered himself off stage and able to act naturally and as he wished.

Though Moran and others traveling with Churchill for the Arcadia Conference cited a respite for Roosevelt as the principal motivation for the five-day interlude in the Florida sunshine, the press of governing responsibilities for FDR intersected with war planning and crowded his schedule. The president needed time to concentrate on his State of the Union address, scheduled for delivery January 6, and afterward he wanted to take his first trip back home to Hyde Park since he spent four days there at the beginning of November, over a month before the attack on Pearl Harbor. The prime minister's visit even played a role in his State of the Union. Near the end of the address—after seven references to the "United Nations"—Roosevelt devoted two paragraphs to Churchill, saying at one point: "Mr. Churchill and I understand each other, our motives and our purposes. Together, during the past two weeks, we have faced squarely the major military and economic problems of this greatest world war." Without being specific about his guest's return, he opened the door to future visits "in days to come."[97]

At the same time the president was delivering his State of the Union address, his live-in nonpareil aide Harry Hopkins was being entertained for lunch at the Soviet Union's embassy in Washington by the ambassador, Maxim Litvinov. With shrewd insight and a possible lack of discretion on the part of a Stalin appointee, the ambassador "expressed the belief that Churchill was a great war Prime Minister but would not be very useful after the war was over." The Russian predicted that FDR was "going to be the dominating person at the peace table," adding that the president "had the best grasp of world economic and political conditions of any living man."[98]

Shortly after the State of the Union, Roosevelt headed for Hyde Park. After all of the meetings, meals together, and late-night conversations, the president and the prime minister probably wanted vacations from each other. In a phone call to Mackenzie King on January 8,

1942, FDR reported that Churchill had remained in the United States, though the Canadian prime minister thought the British leader had secretly departed to return to London. Roosevelt confided that he was delighted to be back home and away from Washington to get "a real rest," adding he had "slept for about 2 days."[99]

Both Roosevelt and Churchill returned to the White House on January 11, lunching together before plunging back into their formal and informal meetings. Those sessions continued through dinner on January 14. The prime minister had been a White House guest for sixteen of the twenty-four days he had spent in the United States and Canada. The ever-present Hopkins joined the prime minister and the president at dinner before accompanying them to a "special train" that departed at 9:55 for the trip to Norfolk, Virginia. FDR bid farewell to Churchill in the president's limousine, while Hopkins went to the railroad car with Churchill. In a memorandum about the final hours the prime minister spent in Washington, Hopkins reported that Churchill believed "that great steps had been taken towards unification of the prosecution of the war." The final words of the special assistant's assessment focused on Roosevelt, with the president making "it perfectly clear that he too was very pleased with the meetings. There was no question but that he grew genuinely to like Churchill and I am sure Churchill equally liked the President."[100] For both men, developing a personal relationship that their time together fostered was important, but it was also critical to the public's perception of Allied unity, as America sought to establish its war footing. Still, the depth and affinity of their human relationship would remain ambiguous.

The prime minister and the president, in concert with their advisors, resolved numerous bilateral concerns by establishing U.K. and U.S. committees, including the Combined Chiefs of Staff, the Combined Raw Materials Board, and the Anglo-American Shipping Adjustment Board. Though the Japanese assault at Pearl Harbor forced America into the war, the Arcadia Conference reaffirmed the primacy of the "Germany First" strategy. Devising and working out the details of a large, joint military operation in North Africa began. Possibly most significantly in terms of international affairs and future global cooperation among different societies, the "Joint Declaration" of the Roosevelt-coined "United Nations" received the endorsement of twenty-six countries. Churchill called the declaration "this majestic document," noting that "it set forth who we were and what we were fighting for."[101]

Curiously but impressively for both the Atlantic Charter and the joint declaration, Roosevelt advocated much more than Churchill on behalf of producing formal statements of principles, with precise language the foundation for multinational conduct. Not known as a wordsmith to the degree that Churchill was, FDR saw the value of a "Charter" and a "Declaration" as public proclamations with definite intentions to endure beyond their moment of composition. (It became a practice Eisenhower also adopted in his presidency a decade later.) Moreover, Roosevelt was preoccupied with what was to come, the world's future after the carnage of war. Psychologically, as mentioned earlier, the two men had different orientations to time. The journalist and author Basil Woon noted in his 1942 study *Roosevelt, World Statesman* that during the British contingent's first Washington sojourn that "although the United States had been at war less than a month, President Roosevelt was already occupied with the problems which would have to be solved after victory."[102]

By contrast, Churchill was so absorbed in fighting the war that he wrote Halifax on January 10: "All this fussing about what is to happen after the war is premature at the present time, when we are probably a long way from any satisfactory conclusion. It is only the State Department which is pressing."[103] Immediate circumstances concentrated his thinking, which he explained at length in a ten-page memorandum six days earlier: "We must continue to regard the invasion of the British Isles in 1942 as the only supreme means of escape and victory open to Hitler. He has had the time to prepare, perhaps in very great numbers, tank transporting vehicles capable of landing on any beach. He has no doubt developed air-borne attack by parachutes, and still more by gliders, to an extent which cannot be easily measured."[104] The United States had to guard their Atlantic and Pacific coasts, but the prime minister had to keep in mind that the enemy was just across the English Channel, some twenty or so miles away.

Though Churchill and Roosevelt managed to establish a working rapport during the post-Pearl Harbor conference, the U.K. foreign secretary Anthony Eden worried about the prime minister's prolonged absence from Britain. Eden's private secretary, Oliver Harvey, wrote in his diary on January 8, "A.E. thinks P.M. staying away too long and getting out of touch with opinion here which thinks much more of Russia than of America at present."[105] Such criticism rarely fazed the figure at whom it was directed. He always decided his return.

For Churchill, the lengthy visit wasn't always driven by demands of work. He took advantage of his time abroad to bring back some American-made cinematic diversions. Harriman, expediter extraordinaire, arranged for a dozen current motion pictures (three each from four studios) to be packed in the prime minister's baggage to take home. Hollywood's generosity provided a combination of dramas, comedies, and musicals. One had a conspicuous connection to the person requesting the films. The musical and romantic comedy *Sun Valley Serenade*, starring Glenn Miller and his orchestra, Milton Berle, and Sonja Henie, was set in Sun Valley, Idaho. As chairman of the board of the Union Pacific Railroad, Harriman had the rail company bankroll the construction of the Sun Valley Resort in 1936. What better way to promote train travel to the ski slopes near the new lodge than a big-screen Hollywood production? Another movie was pertinent to the war effort. Released in September of 1941, *A Yank in the R.A.F.*, with Tyrone Power and Betty Grable, sought to be a celluloid commendation for an American flier's courage to serve in the Royal Air Force before the United States joined the fight. Other wartime movies—including *That Night in Rio* (1941), *They Died with Their Boots On* (1941), *Dr. Jekyll and Mr. Hyde* (1941), *Babes on Broadway* (1941), and *The Man Who Came to Dinner* (1942)—starred such A-list actors as Spencer Tracy,

Ingrid Bergman, Errol Flynn, Shirley Temple, Mickey Rooney, and Bette Davis. A Churchill assistant acknowledged the studios' "courtesy," noting: "The Prime Minister gets great relaxation and enjoyment out of pictures and I know that these will give him real pleasure."[106]

The special train from Washington to Norfolk took Churchill to an awaiting Boeing 314 clipper, a long-range flying boat, for a flight first to Bermuda and then back to Britain three days later. The evening he returned, the prime minister briefed the War Cabinet on his extended visit to the United States, stressing the personal dimension to begin before explaining policy decisions. In the minutes and conclusions—written by a notetaker and marked "SECRET" and "TO BE KEPT UNDER LOCK AND KEY" on the pages of the document at the U.K.'s National Archives—it is reported that Churchill "had lived on the closest personal terms with the President. The United States Administration were tackling war problems with the greatest vigour, and were clearly resolved not to be diverted from using all the resources of their country to the utmost to crush Hitler, our major enemy." Nine sentences of matter-of-fact, institutional prose about "the general course of the discussions" followed the short introduction. More revealing, however, are two typed pages that are inserted and available along with the printed version in the National Archives. The wording of the prose seemed more typical of Churchill—for instance, the word "Olympian" that he used in his speech to Congress reappeared—and the statements provided a clear-eyed assessment of the Washington conference. Early paragraphs—of the ten *in toto*—established the tone and subtly suggested rarely heard, we-know-better criticism echoing some of Jacob's observations quoted earlier: "An Olympian calm had obtained at the White House. It was perhaps rather isolated. The President had no adequate link between his will and executive action. There was no such organisation as the Secretariat of the Cabinet or of the Chiefs of Staff Committee." Near the end there was a straightforward warning of the need to be careful and not overly pushy with the powerful new ally: "The Prime Minister thought there was little risk of the Americans abandoning the conventional principles of war. They were not above learning from us, provided that we did not set out to teach them."[107]

Churchill's post-Arcadia reservations weren't the only ones among high-level officials. On the American side, Secretary of War Stimson noted in his diary shortly before the final conference sessions that he had "received word of some propositions for the creation of a future strategic joint organization, between America and Britain for war strategy, which seems to me completely wrong. The British are evidently taking advantage of the President's well-known shortcomings in ordinary administrative methods and are striving to take advantage of his readiness to accept shortcuts and back door information, which has not passed through his regular constitutional advisers."[108] Although Stimson frequently found fault with Churchill, their judgments of White House administration were similar, and problems originated with the president. A less than structured organizational system produced consequences affecting the day-to-day operations of cabinet members and their departments. Especially as America's participation in the war was taking shape, such "shortcomings" were evident on the inside. Stimson's diary is a trove of behind-the-scenes intrigue that's peppered with often acerbic appraisals.

His memoir, *On Active Service in Peace and War*, was more reticent, and he praised the new alliance: "The most important single accomplishment of this meeting was that it laid the groundwork for the establishment of an effectively unified Allied high command. The Combined Chiefs of Staff, set up in Washington in early 1942, rapidly became a fully developed instrument for the coordination of land, sea, and air warfare."[109] Still, the veteran cabinet official who served in three different administrations noted executive deficiencies in the two principal leaders he viewed close-up in World War II: "Both Mr. Roosevelt and Mr. Churchill were men whose great talents required the balancing restraint of carefully organized staff advice."[110]

Ten days after reporting to the War Cabinet, Churchill stood in the House of Commons on January 27 and delivered a prepared speech of over eleven thousand words about the "War Situation." The remarks roamed widely about different phases of the conflict and allowed the prime minister, who also served as minister of defence, to make his case that recent setbacks in battle, though lamentable, didn't forecast the future. Churchill devoted several sections of his *tour d'horizon* to his transatlantic trip: the creation of the Combined Chiefs of Staff Committee, the naming of what turned out to be a short-lived position of supreme commander for the Pacific, the coordination of massive amounts of combat supplies to be manufactured in U.S. factories, and all the rest. As he emphasized with the War Cabinet, the personal, one-to-one association and collaboration proved significant to Churchill, who of the Big Three—Churchill, Roosevelt, and Stalin—logged far more miles than either his American or Soviet counterpart. During the war, he made some twenty-five journeys outside Britain, displaying his energy, bravery, and ambition. He knew his personality was essential to his power, and he was willing to go where he thought he could have the most impact for his cause—and for himself.

Churchill told the Commons that after Pearl Harbor was attacked he "was sure it was my duty to cross the Atlantic and establish the closest possible relationship with the President and Government of the United States." A few sentences later, he described the evolution of that "relationship": "During those three weeks which I spent in Mr. Roosevelt's home and family, I established with him relations not only of comradeship, but, I think I may say, of friendship. We can say anything to each other, however painful. When we parted he wrung my hand, saying, 'We will fight this through to the bitter end, whatever the cost may be.' "[111] Churchill's judgment or perception of the "friendship" between the two leaders became an abiding refrain, often expressed in florid phrasing, though FDR was more restrained in precisely classifying or describing the relationship. Did Churchill still view himself as something of a suitor, the loyal lieutenant of the principal figure in "the grand alliance"? Or was this rhetorical wishful musing?

Before he sat down, Churchill admitted "to feeling the weight of the war upon me even more than in the tremendous summer days of 1940"—with the Dunkirk evacuation, the fall of France, the beginning of the Battle of Britain, and the persistent threat of a German invasion across the English Channel. The battlefield had greatly expanded the past year and a half, but the prime minister could now count on direct participation "to the bitter end" from an ally he'd courted since war clouds first formed. The daredevil prime minister would continue to take the initiative to remain close to his "friend," coming back to Washington with regularity.

Over a month after Churchill and his entourage decamped from the White House in January, his time in residence at 1600 Pennsylvania Avenue continued as a topic of discussion. In Halifax's diary for February 18, 1942, he reported on a conversation with Dean Acheson, then-assistant secretary of state, about the taxing nature of playing host to Churchill. According to Halifax, Hopkins "confessed" to Acheson "that to have Winston here more than twice a year would be very exhausting." Hopkins went on to admit he "never got to bed before two or three, as Winston had always gone into his room after finishing with the President for one more drink, and at 6:45 in the morning the door had opened and Winston, slipperless, had come in, saying, 'Have you done anything about what we were discussing last night?'—after four hours!"[112]

Eleanor Roosevelt, who was irritated for not being informed that the holiday season would be so different from any previous one, was also aware of the post-visit fatigue Churchill caused and Hopkins identified. In *This I Remember*, she reported that her husband "worked long hours every day" when the prime minister was living in the White House. She makes sure to point out the "long nap every afternoon" that Churchill took, adding: "While he was sleeping, Franklin had to catch up on all his regular work. . . . It always took him several days to catch up on sleep after Mr. Churchill left."[113] As we'll see, Mrs. Roosevelt was usually diplomatic and complimentary in writing about Churchill, but she harbored serious reservations, substantive and social, about the recurring

White House guest. This first, extended visit allowed her to view him in several settings and to see him in relation to the president. From the outset she worried that the war's principal decision-makers acted on occasion like youngsters, amusing themselves by playing games. Curtis Roosevelt, the eldest grandson of the president and First Lady, remembered his grandmother telling him about Roosevelt and Churchill sitting in the White House map room observing the locations of naval activities and battles. In her vivid metaphor, slapping both men, the pair seemed like "two little boys enjoying themselves in the bathtub with their toy boats."[114]

Joseph P. Lash, her close friend who years later wrote the Pulitzer Prize-winning biography *Eleanor and Franklin*, spent the New Year's Day of 1942 at the White House. In his journal at the Roosevelt Library, he recalled that following lunch he joined the First Lady and her secretary-cum-assistant Malvina Thompson in "E.R.'s sitting room" to discuss the two leaders. They asked Lash for his opinion: "I said PM was richer temperament, but Pres. a more dependable person, a steadier man in a crisis. Tommy clapped her ahnds [*sic*] and said she and Mrs. R felt the same. Pres. more hardheaded, less brilliant but more likely to do the right thing. I said Pres. gave impression of being more under control—never let himself go."

Once Thompson departed, Lash reported that Mrs. Roosevelt told him she needed contact with people "to get refreshment & strength for her duties & work." According to his handwritten, difficult-to-decipher notes, she went on: "Pres. seemed to have no bond to people. Not even his children. A completely political person!"[115] Nearly thirty-seven years of marriage provoked chilly conclusions about this "completely political person," who had already won three presidential campaigns and was contemplating a fourth.

The First Lady's opinion was shared by another woman important to the president. Missy LeHand, the subject of speculation about how close she was to Roosevelt, admitted to the journalist and author Fulton Oursler that FDR spent a considerable amount of his time alone.

In his autobiography, *Behold This Dreamer!*, Oursler described what White House life was like for LeHand before her illness: "Here she sat with her knitting, keeping company with a very lonely man, who, so she told me once, was really incapable of a personal friendship with anyone."[116] Someone with "no bond to people" and "incapable of a personal friendship" projected the persona that others with less knowledge of him viewed differently. Roosevelt had earned his nickname of "the Sphinx" for a reason. He often flashed an inscrutable smile that concealed his thinking. Would he and Churchill have a different—and special—relationship?

Certain people, it's often said, can change the chemistry of a room when they walk through the door. During Churchill's first extended stay in Washington, he altered established routines of the White House and everyone who lived there, including its principal occupant. As the war continued to grind on, with serious setbacks the first several months of 1942, the prime minister kept returning to not only change the chemistry at 1600 Pennsylvania Avenue but also to fight for his own battle plans. The "summit of the United States" would be for him a prime place to exercise leadership en route to becoming a world statesman.

– 2 –

DEFEAT AND DISGRACE

Almost everything seemed to be going wrong. Arriving in Washington after a nonstop flight from Scotland, a jet-lagged and impatient Churchill hoped to go directly to the White House. But the president, he soon learned, wasn't there: Roosevelt had decided to spend a few days at his ancestral home in Hyde Park, New York, more than three hundred miles away. To see him, Churchill would need to follow him there. Was this some kind of power play? Why? Were other unexpected clouds on the horizon?

Churchill's second wartime visit to America bore almost no resemblance to his first six months earlier. This time—a week in June of 1942—Roosevelt initiated the meetings, and the two leaders kept out of public view. There would be no religious or secular ceremonies. No press conferences. No speeches. No broadcasts. Where they were and what they were doing were cloaked in secrecy and mystery.

The uneasiness of war's hard truth replaced the uncommon excitement that surrounded Churchill's previous sojourn. Prior to departure and aware of the potential danger, King George VI requested a letter that, in the event of the prime minister's death, would tell the sovereign Churchill's choice of a successor. The dapper, forty-five-year-old Anthony Eden, the secretary of state for foreign affairs, was Churchill's pick to form a new government.

The early months of 1942 cast a pall over the war's progress and put the Allies on their collective back foot. Japanese forces engineered the fall of Malaya and the surrender of Singapore, involving the capture of some eighty-five thousand British troops. Escalating the sense of gloom were the loss of the Dutch East Indies, the conquest of Burma, and the occupation of the Philippines, leading to the Bataan Death March for approximately seventy-five thousand American and Filipino troops. In addition, slaughterous battles between the Allies and the German army's Afrika Korps continued in Libya and Egypt, while on the Eastern front the Wehrmacht's assault on the Soviet Union brought millions of combatants into the fight with considerable impact on what Churchill and Roosevelt would discuss. It was time to take stock and to scrutinize the whole war effort.

A veteran of battlefield combat before and during the Great War, Churchill maintained that it took a minimum of two years' training from experienced military professionals to mold first-class fighting troops. With just a half year of mobilization, the United States would need time to develop the necessary forces across the branches of the military. Moreover, FDR was also having to make a formidable personal transition—from "Dr. New Deal" to "Dr. Win the War." The older, more defense-seasoned Churchill hoped to put the president back on "the rails"—in the phrase of General Alan Brooke, the crusty, opinionated chief of the Imperial General Staff—while increasing their camaraderie.[1]

When the prime minister and his seven-person entourage set down on the Potomac River the evening of Thursday, June 18, Churchill recorded that the Boeing Clipper flying boat took twenty-eight hours to cross the Atlantic. After more than a day in the air, the group spent the night at the British embassy on Massachusetts Avenue in Washington. Lord Halifax, Britain's ambassador, noted that the prime minister was irked the president wasn't in Washington but in the Hudson Valley. Had the prime minister known, he would have directed his specially outfitted aircraft to New York City, "where he could have flown on more easily."[2] FDR had arrived at Hyde Park on Thursday morning before the prime minister landed.

From the perspective of Halifax, Churchill began to display "a better temper" after the champagne began to flow and the traveler had a chance to hold court with the ambassador, his wife Dorothy, and three members of Churchill's party. What's amusing, and revealing, about the observations Halifax recorded is that he never missed an opportunity to needle his longtime Conservative Party colleague. Churchill yakked until 1:30 a.m., and the ambassador's wife noticed the prime minister's traveling companions dozing off on the darkened porch, where everyone sat. This unusual scene prompted Halifax to render a judgment that Churchill "certainly is a most extraordinary man; immensely great qualities, with some of the defects that sometimes attract to them. I couldn't live that life for long."[3]

Early the next morning, a U.S. Navy plane carried Churchill and a few aides from the Anacostia Air Station to the New Hackensack Field in Dutchess County, New York. Built by the federal government a decade earlier, the facility—later renamed the Hudson Valley Regional Airport—was about a dozen miles south of FDR's estate at Hyde Park and then operating as a training base for pilots heading off to war duty. When Churchill arrived, he began the first of four excursions to the Roosevelt homestead. As he had done the past December, the president was waiting near the runway to greet his guest—who at the time was recovering from the jolt of his arrival.

In *The Hinge of Fate*, the fourth volume of *The Second World War*, Churchill recalled that the president witnessed "the roughest bump landing I have experienced."[4] That part of the prime minister's introduction to Roosevelt's tranquil neighborhood proved much less compelling than their drive to the palatial home of Springwood and the property surrounding it. The host, FDR, despite his paralytic legs, served as driver and guide in ferrying the guests to his favorite refuge from the rigors of Washington. Churchill's recollection of the ride revealed a veteran journalist's eye for detail. He explained how the president's car was modified to allow him to use his hands and arms to operate the vehicle. FDR even flexed his muscles and "invited me to feel his biceps, saying that a famous prize-fighter had envied them. This was reassuring; but I confess that when on several occasions the car poised and backed on the grass verges of the precipices over the Hudson I hoped the mechanical devices and brakes would show no defects."[5]

The prime minister's personal assistant, C. R. Thompson, recalled this particular presidential tour somewhat differently. The bucolic Hudson Valley setting was anything but sedate, as FDR in Thompson's phrase, "took a boyish delight" in trying to elude the Secret Service detail responsible for guarding the president and the prime minister. Roosevelt's automobile antics on narrow, jungly paths that the much larger security car couldn't navigate made the Secret Service look like the Keystone Cops from the silent film era. Thompson remarked that "when we last caught a glimpse of our escorts they were charging backwards and forwards" at a sharp turn "without making any headway at all. The President kept to the woods and we never saw another Secret Service car till we broke cover close to the house."[6]

Why was Churchill, who knew from his youthful days as a war correspondent the arresting value of on-the-scene action in his accounts, reluctant to depict for readers this vehicular cat-and-mouse game? Did it portray a head of state in a juvenile and frivolous manner at a time requiring no-nonsense, mature resolution? Was it a statement by a physically disabled person that it was possible to escape and enjoy freedom on his terms, if only for a few exhilarating moments? Whatever the case, the prime minister's new view of the president diverged considerably from the one he'd observed at the Atlantic Conference off Newfoundland or in Washington at the Arcadia Conference. FDR became a different person when he was at home and off the political stage. Not long after arriving, Churchill learned that the squire of Hyde Park could act and entertain there without any of the decorum dictated by White House protocol. Some three hundred or so miles removed from Washington, this setting enhanced their rapport, and Churchill kept returning.

Hyde Park served as Roosevelt's hideout from the constant demands of the presidency, a position he'd occupied for nearly a full decade by then. He enjoyed sharing and showing off the domain that his father, James, had purchased in 1866, sixteen years before FDR's birth there. The large home, outbuildings, and grounds, according to the National Park Service, are "the only place in the United States where a President was born, maintained a lifelong connection, and lies buried." Particularly after he contracted polio in 1921 at the age of thirty-nine and lost the ability to walk without assistance, Hyde Park allowed Roosevelt to move around with greater freedom. Indeed, life there seemed light years removed from the capital's often fishbowl existence. That the president welcomed the prime minister to his familial surroundings signified their relationship had become a more personal one in a relatively short time.

At Hyde Park, FDR was able to spend time with people rooted, as he was, in the Hudson Valley. One of them, Margaret "Daisy" Suckley, FDR's sixth cousin and never-married confidante, was usually involved in the president's activities there. In a symbol of their closeness, she gave him the Scottish terrier Fala that went nearly everywhere with its besotted owner. Suckley, who worked at the Roosevelt Library, was invited to the first lunch with Churchill after his arrival. In her diary, she described the interaction between the president and the prime minister after watching them during the meal. "There seemed to be real friendship & understanding between F.D.R. & Churchill," she recalled. "F.D.R.'s manner was easy and intimate—His face humorous, or very serious, according to the subject of conversation, and entirely *natural.* Not a trace of having to guard his words or expressions, just the opposite of his manner at a press conference, when he is an actor on a stage—and a player on an instrument, at the same time."[7]

On this first visit to Hyde Park Churchill brought with him a gift for a devoted book collector, who could boast that he'd already established his presidential library. In a May 27 message to Roosevelt, Churchill reported: "I am venturing to send you a collection of the books I have written, which I have had bound up, hoping you will find a place for them in your shelves." He concluded, "Kindest good wishes. Former Naval Person," the phrase he often used in referring to himself in their correspondence.[8] True to his word, the London bookbinders Sangorski & Sutcliffe prepared a complete set of Churchill's published volumes in red leather, with gold lettering on the spine and the Roosevelt crest decorating the front cover. Some two dozen titles (the oldest, *The Story of the Malakand Field Force*, was first published in 1898) made up the collection, and they currently occupy special shelf space in FDR's study at the Roosevelt Presidential Library and Museum. As time passed, Churchill continued to add to the uniquely bound collection as new volumes appeared after the initial gift in 1942. For instance, his 1943 war speeches were brought together in *Onwards to Victory*, a copy of which he presented to Roosevelt at the second Quebec conference in September of 1944 right before what would be his last visit to Hyde Park. The inscription was brief but characteristically original:

> To F.D.R.
> From WSC
> A fresh egg from the
> faithful hen!
> Quebec 1944

The president's appointment calendar for June 19 makes no mention of touring, lunch, policy discussions, or any other activities. The phrasing is informational and without elaboration: "Winston S. Churchill arrived in Hyde Park for the Second Washington Conference June 19–25, 1942 and then accompanied FDR back to Washington." James Roosevelt, then a major in the Marine Corps who would later be awarded a Navy Cross and Silver Star, joined his father in welcoming Churchill at the airport. In his memoir *My Parents: A Different View*, the eldest son of Eleanor and Franklin described the British leader in less than reverential terms. Bothered by what Churchill considered "the intense heat," he—as James told it—"agreed to a swim," but, unfortunately, there was a small problem about a sizable shape. Locating swimming trunks wide enough in the waist presented a challenge, but a suitable bathing costume, as the British say, was eventually discovered. The thirty-four-year-old Roosevelt, who at six feet four was a little taller than his father, remembered that Churchill provided "a remarkable sight when he emerged in his suit with cotton in his ears, a wide-brimmed sun hat on his head and a long cigar in his mouth. Setting the hat and cigar aside for a few moments, he jumped into the pool and bounced about like a rubber ball for a few moments." After cooling off in the pool, the guest enjoyed some brandy as he sat in the shade with his cigar. Roosevelt wryly noted, "He could do justice to a bottle of brandy."[9]

As the prime minister became more acquainted with his surroundings in the Hudson Valley, he probably came to understand why Roosevelt traveled home so often. On this trip, FDR spent all of June 18 there without any scheduled activities, according to his appointments calendar. Three months earlier, the president had written a "Dear Winston" letter that began by mentioning some military setbacks, including the surrenders of Singapore (in February) and the Dutch East Indies (in March), before complaining about news commentators in the press "who cannot get politics out of their heads in the worst crisis."[10] The self-described "amateur strategist" continued to discuss specifics of the war effort for five paragraphs, but he then took a dramatic, personal turn with advice about the restorative power of spending time where it was possible to be your unguarded self. Roosevelt recommended his own elixir: "Once a month I go to Hyde Park for four days, crawl into a hole and pull the hole in after me. I am called on the telephone only if something of really great importance occurs."[11] Despite the concern and sincerity of the suggestion, Churchill never found time during the war years to adopt the Rooseveltian regimen of regular respite. As previously described, he made more than two dozen trips abroad during the war, and each of his four White House visits in 1941, 1942, and

1943 also involved excursions elsewhere while staying most of the time in Washington.

When he was returning to the White House after one side trip, Churchill remarked without elaborating, "Business kept me company."[12] For his chapter in *The Hinge of Fate* about his second wartime visit to the United States, he continued to stick to business, telling next to nothing about his nonworking hours. Others who were there reported about his dips in the pool or his requests for a butterfly net, which, alas, wasn't on hand at Hyde Park for any of his desired lepidopterological quests.

The day following Churchill's arrival at Hyde Park, William D. Hassett, the president's assistant secretary since 1935, noted how the British visitor made himself at home during his stay at Springwood. Saying FDR was "enjoying as he always does, his conferences with the Prime Minister," Hassett continued that, in Roosevelt's opinion, "Churchill is a delightful companion." The former newspaper reporter then offered a thumbnail sketch of "Winnie," who is the epitome of informality. The morning after arriving, the prime minister was "out on the lawn barefoot and later was seen crossing the passage to Harry Hopkins' room still barefoot."[13]

Two afternoon meetings appear on the president's calendar for that Saturday, June 20. The first one, listed at 2 p.m., pertained to the "Atomic Bomb Project," which Churchill always referred to by its codename "Tube Alloys" and involved the work by American, British, and Canadian scientists to develop what became war-changing weaponry. The second meeting, an hour later, involved Churchill, Roosevelt, Hopkins, and W. Averell Harriman, the president's special envoy in London, about an unspecified subject. In a page of "Personal Notes" about his time at Hyde Park, Harriman recounted how Roosevelt served as chauffeur to show off his property on the way to his private cottage over six miles from the main home. FDR had built what he called "Top Cottage" as a bungalow, where he could relax and entertain. Three miles from it was Eleanor Roosevelt's larger home of Val-Kill. Similar to their separate bedrooms at the White House, both retreats demonstrated the fierce independence of each figure, hideaways of their own from the public—and, indeed, from each other. The president and First Lady were at liberty to welcome whomever they wanted to surroundings they called their own.

What Harriman jotted down revealed that, among his many wartime roles, he played the prime minister's Boswell, capturing his bon mots during conversations. After Roosevelt commented about the chilly nature of Edwina Mountbatten, the wife of Louis Mountbatten, then a member of the U.K.'s Chiefs of Staff Committee, Churchill replied: "There's spark in the flint." Later, when Harry Hopkins mentioned he was considering his third marriage, the prime minister put romantic notions in their proper perspective, as far as he was concerned: "You are married to the war. That should satisfy you." It didn't. Louise Gill Macy became Mrs. Harry Hopkins six weeks later during a White House ceremony.

Though he set down direct quotations attributed to Churchill, Harriman paraphrased Roosevelt. At one point, the future New York governor noted FDR's dilemma of pinpointing the most appropriate location for the first major American offensive. "When I was alone with the President," Harriman reported, "he told me he was having difficulty in finding a place where the soldiers thought they could fight, but he was going to insist on some action ________."[14] The blank space at the end of the sentence prompts questions, even today. Was it an attempt to withhold the naming of a potential target out of fear the personal document could somehow fall into enemy hands? The phrase "where the soldiers thought they could fight" is somewhat curious, too. Which soldiers? Roosevelt's uniformed military advisors or possibly his own sons then seeing action? As often was the case, there does not exist an "official record" of either Hyde Park session in the official U.S. government document published years later.

While FDR pondered where to send troops to fight, a major concern facing Churchill on his third transatlantic crossing in less than a year involved the continuing debate between Britain and America over launching military operations to create a "second front." At the time, the Germans were fighting the Soviet army in Russia, and Stalin was pleading with Churchill and Roosevelt to land troops in western Europe to reduce the Wehrmacht's onslaught. In August of 1939, the Soviet Union and Germany had signed a nonaggression treaty, known as the Molotov-Ribbentrop Pact, which was negotiated by the Soviet minister of foreign affairs Vyacheslav Molotov and his German counterpart, Joachim von Ribbentrop, a former wine and champagne merchant who catered to Hitler and had few friends in German government circles. The Nazis broke the agreement on June 22, 1941, by invading the Soviet Union in Operation Barbarossa, the largest land offensive in history, and by establishing the Eastern front of what the Soviets came to call "the Great Patriotic War." Pulling some German divisions from the east and forcing them to fight elsewhere on the continent, Stalin argued, would make it easier to defend Mother Russia while bringing more Allied forces into combat nearer the U.S.S.R.

A strategic dispute between Britain and the United States focused primarily on timing—determining the opportune moment to mount an invasion from the West. Exactly *where* to strike was critical, too, but the *when* for a decisive landing became an issue that was constantly debated from every possible perspective. Should it take place sooner or later? When was the optimal time for an assault?

From meetings conducted in London during April of 1942, Churchill knew from General George Marshall, the U.S. Army chief of staff, and Hopkins that the Americans favored a cross-Channel assault as expeditiously as possible. In fact, Roosevelt had written another "Dear Winston" letter on April 3 that the two emissaries personally delivered. "Your people and mine demand the establishment of a front to draw off pressure on the Russians," FDR wrote, "and these peoples are wise enough to see that the Russians are today killing more Germans and destroying more equipment than you and I put together." The message included a flourish of command: "Go to it!"[15]

Roosevelt's ardent desire to assist the Soviets became even more apparent in late May of 1942 with a visit to Washington by Molotov, the Soviet minister and the namesake of the "Molotov cocktail," a sarcastic reference to what he alleged were humanitarian aid packages instead of incendiary bombs during the Winter War between Finland and the Soviet Union in 1939 and 1940. Shortly after arriving, Molotov, described on the president's calendar as "Commissar for Foreign Affairs" and assigned the same White House suite as Churchill, began his personal offensive to have FDR agree to launch a second front. During their meeting on May 30, Molotov reported that he had conferred with Churchill en route to the United States and that the prime minister did not provide a direct response to British participation in the proposed invasion. In no uncertain terms and echoing Stalin's stern appeals, the Soviet official wanted to find out whether the United States was ready to open a second front. "If you postpone your decision," he said in language that sounded threatening, "you will have eventually to bear the brunt of the war, and if Hitler becomes the undisputed master of the continent, next year will unquestionably be tougher than this one."

Responding to this stark statement, Roosevelt turned to General Marshall and asked if the U.S. military was getting ready to mount a second front. Marshall affirmed that his forces were training for such an assault. The president then told Molotov he could inform Stalin that he anticipated "the formation of a second front this year."[16]

Marshall judged that Roosevelt was inappropriately specific by adding "this year" to the statement, and when Churchill heard about it, he seriously doubted that Britain and America could mount a successful invasion in a matter of a few months. The prime minister needed to find out for himself exactly what the president had in mind. During this trip back to Washington, he hoped to gain some guidance on U.S. planning while also making the case that he considered it imperative to delay such a critical and complicated action. When would there be action? Now or later?

Secretary of War Henry Stimson was adamant about the need to prepare for a cross-Channel operation as soon as possible. Indeed, on the day Churchill arrived in the United States, Stimson argued for a concentrated buildup on British soil—code-named Operation Bolero—prior to the invasion. He did so in a detailed, ten-point letter to Roosevelt that maintained, "Geographically and historically Bolero was the easiest road to the center of our chief enemy's heart."[17] As became clearer each day that June week, Stimson proved to be one of the strongest American proponents of a cross-Channel assault, and his four-square position put him on the opposite side of Churchill. Moreover, while pointing out advantages of Bolero, Stimson criticized any operation in North Africa as a distraction from the main concern of attacking "our chief enemy's heart."

Stimson wasn't the only high-level figure to develop a strategy for the future prior to the conference. As he had the previous December, Churchill arrived prepared. He had set down an eleven-point memorandum on June 15 that he widely circulated as well as a detailed letter to Roosevelt that he composed at Hyde Park. In the memo drafted to focus the conference's initial discussions, he tactfully yet explicitly looked ahead to 1943—and *not* 1942—for the major undertaking needed to create the much-anticipated second front. Saying the British government doesn't "favour an operation that was certain to lead to disaster," he hammered home his thinking: "We hold strongly to the view that there should be no substantial landing in France this year unless we are going to stay."[18]

If an extensive European assault and campaign wouldn't be possible over the next months, the prime minister proposed "to take some of the weight off Russia" by conducting a "French Northwest Africa operation,"[19] a possibility first raised at White House meetings six months earlier. The memorandum established what Churchill considered realistic. The Allies, in his opinion, would definitely not be ready in 1942 to produce what would be needed for a second front in western Europe, but the combined British and America forces would be well served if they could see action and gain battlefield experience later in 1942. Despite the convivial setting of the conversations in the Hudson Valley, Churchill's first visit to Hyde Park became, in effect, spring training for the major-league battles that would take place in Washington over the coming days.

Collegiality wasn't on Stimson's mind as he considered "the crisis which has arisen owing to Churchill's visit." He and Marshall fretted that Roosevelt would undercut or radically alter the War Department's planning. The cagey cabinet veteran viewed Churchill and Roosevelt as being "too much alike in their strong points and in their weak points. They are both brilliant. They are both penetrating in their thoughts but they lack the steadiness of balance that has got to go along with warfare."[20] Stimson didn't include this observation in his memoir. His war primarily took place in the corridors of power, and he kept battling despite decisions that went against his and Marshall's strategy.

The prime minister and the president took an overnight train to the capital Saturday evening in advance of the conference that was code-named "Argonaut"—the same one later used for the conference in Yalta during February of 1945—with their military advisors set to begin Sunday. Routing FDR to and from Hyde Park varied for the sake of security precautions, and the private cars usually moved along the tracks well after sunset in what were referred to as "blackout trips."

Grace Tully, FDR's personal secretary, was on duty at Hyde Park that weekend and traveled back to the White House with the two leaders. She noticed that Churchill didn't seem as exuberant as usual on the trip. Roosevelt confided to her that British forces were under assault in Libya, adding, "I think Winston is terribly worried, Grace."[21]

While uneasiness about what was happening in the Mediterranean region occupied Churchill's thoughts, a more personal one received Tully's attention during the train journey. En route to Washington, the prime minister's valet appeared in the main cabin, carrying slippers with his chief's initials on them. Bending down to remove Churchill's shoes, the valet heard, "God, no, not here," and the man for whom this was a nightly routine got up to go to his compartment to change his footwear.[22] Even though he'd become well aware of the assistance Roosevelt required to get around, Churchill saw the slipper ritual as an occasion for embarrassment. His self-image, even in relative privacy, dictated avoidance of any scene reflecting high-horse superiority.

As soon as it became publicly known that Churchill had returned to America—front pages on June 19 announced his arrival—talk of opening a second front began to drive the press coverage of the meetings. The most prominent banner headline in the *New York Times* declared "Churchill Here For Talks on Second Front." American proponents of a European invasion were undoubtedly responsible for whispering carefully selected points to reporters and columnists to help shape public opinion. For example, Washington's most influential newspaper of the time, the *Evening Star*, published a page-one report on June 19—under the headline "Roosevelt and Churchill Discuss War Tasks at Secret Rendezvous"—emphasizing U.S. thinking and preparation, with the president's press secretary Stephen Early admitting that all the conjecture about mounting a second front was "perfectly justified."

The surreptitious nature of the "parleys," a favorite word then, and the centrality of a second front to the conference agenda dominated what the public learned during the next few days. As mentioned previously, both Churchill and Roosevelt understood the value of news coverage to frame how people viewed a subject, but for this visit they maintained strategic secrecy. They didn't make themselves available to reporters. The only widely reported item of human interest that appeared during this visit was provided by a New York genealogist, who revealed that Churchill and Roosevelt were "eighth cousins once removed," a relationship discovered by tracing the families of their mothers. There was just one occasion necessitating photographers (a group picture of the Pacific War Council) and it occurred on the prime minister's last day at the White House. Unlike the three weeks the previous December and January, planning and policy deliberations trumped publicity, as the pair confronted their problems and prospects.

The Anglo-American entourage traveling from Hyde Park arrived in Washington at 9:25 on the morning of June 21. That Sunday German forces were continuing their drive toward the Libyan city of Tobruk near the border with Egypt, and a Japanese submarine surfaced in the Pacific Ocean off the coast of Oregon to fire on Fort Stevens. Though there were no casualties and only minor property damage, fear spread in the United States of a possible attack elsewhere from the sea. The two leaders faced difficult circumstances both far and near.

John Martin, Churchill's private secretary, reported that he and his British colleagues were taken to the quarters in the White House where they had worked before. Eleanor Roosevelt offered her welcome, and the secretary commented that "we felt as if we were coming home."[23] Martin, however, didn't mention how sultry Washington was at the time. The temperature reached 96.3 degrees later in the day.

Churchill took up residence in the Rose Bedroom, where he had stayed previously and which he described in his memoirs on this occasion as a "very large air-conditioned room, in which I dwelt in comfort at about thirty degrees below the temperature of most of the rest of the building."[24] According to the White House Historical Association, the private and residential apartments on the second floor received cooling units during FDR's first term, but the president preferred to work in the Oval Office in his shirt sleeves with the windows open.

Shortly after getting settled and while sitting in the president's study, Roosevelt handed Churchill a telegram that had just arrived. It announced the surrender of the British and Dominion forces at Tobruk on the Mediterranean Sea. The cable said twenty-five thousand troops were taken prisoner, but the actual number was closer to thirty-three thousand. With a deep-water harbor and a port for delivery of supplies, Tobruk changed hands four different times during the war, underscoring its strategic importance for both the Allies and the Axis. British and Australian forces battled Italian troops in January of 1941 to win control of Tobruk. Then, for more than a year, Italian and German commanders plotted how to recapture the seaside garrison that occupied such a pivotal location on the way to Alexandria and the Suez Canal. In April of 1941, Nazi general Erwin Rommel, who earned the nickname of the Desert Fox, launched an offensive with the objective of seizing Tobruk from the Allies. It failed then, but the Axis forces fought battle after battle in the desert around Tobruk until the fortified base fell—with both military and political consequences. The dramatic saga of the ingenious tactics used to guard the port and its surroundings later became the subject of several popular movies, including *The Rats of Tobruk* (1944), *The Desert Rats* (1953), and *Tobruk* (1967).

Shock at the news made Churchill demand verification from London. The situation, the prime minister learned, was more calamitous than the initial bulletin. In his memoirs, Churchill didn't try to cushion the reality of the collapse. "This was one of the heaviest blows I can recall during the war," he wrote. "Not only were its military effects grievous, but it had affected the reputation of the British armies." The bombshell of what happened left the prime minister despondent, and he later wrote a judgment no one in leadership would want to compose: "Defeat is one thing; disgrace is another."[25] Tobruk was the second largest capitulation of U.K. forces after the surrender of Singapore four months earlier. In addition, myriad weapons and vehicles were seized.

Rommel's reaction to the seizure of the garrison and all of its captured military booty became widely quoted, with the words wounding the commanders responsible for losing such a strategic stronghold. The head of the Afrika Korps told some of the captured officers: "Gentlemen, you have fought like lions and been led by donkeys."[26] Military historians consider the taking of Tobruk as Rommel's greatest military triumph, and it resulted in his being named field marshal.

According to Churchill, Roosevelt responded to the setback with both sympathy and a question. The president didn't seek amplification or inquire about blame. He was already focusing on the future in a spirit of compassion and partnership. Churchill recalled that Roosevelt simply asked: "What can we do to help?" In his account, the prime minister rapidly answered: "Give us as many Sherman tanks as you can spare, and ship them to the Middle East as quickly as possible."[27]

Almost every retelling of the two leaders reacting to the news about Tobruk that has appeared since 1950, when *The Hinge of Fate* was published, cite Roosevelt's empathetic concern and his sincerity in reaching out to offer assistance.[28] Conveying compassion came naturally to FDR, who had fought back from the infirmity of infantile paralysis with greater solicitude for those experiencing misfortune. That the president offered consoling words is undeniable. Yet what he might have said—his exact words—is another matter. Did the literary-minded Churchill embellish a scene to make it more dramatic? If so, for what reason?

What makes someone wonder how Roosevelt spoke at the time is the remembrance of Eleanor Roosevelt and her account of meeting Churchill shortly after he learned Tobruk had fallen. Noting that the prime minister seemed "stricken," she recalled that "his immediate reaction was to say: 'Now what do we do?' "[29] In this revealing recollection, "his immediate reaction" is *not* to tell the First Lady about her husband's expression of sympathy or his offer of assistance. Rather, it is to pose his own plaintive question about the unknown future. By then, of course, he knew his troops would be receiving help from America that he desperately wanted.

In a way, Churchill's recollection elevates FDR, while Mrs. Roosevelt's makes someone think twice. Is Churchill expressing exasperation or frustration with the question Mrs. Roosevelt attributed to him, or is he sincerely seeking advice and assistance? More important for the sake of history, which question—Roosevelt's or Churchill's—was asked in the immediate aftermath of the bulletin's arrival? Both? Neither? It's not really known, but Mrs. Roosevelt kept repeating her version of the story in subsequent books, including her autobiography, without Churchill offering a dissent.[30]

Roosevelt's immediate decision to strengthen the British military spoke more loudly than either of the reputed questions now quoted in historical accounts, and his White House visitor became the beneficiary of what FDR called "the arsenal of democracy." That phrase, with power of its own, came into popular usage during a radio broadcast the president delivered on December 29, 1940, eight weeks after he won his third term and nearly a year before Pearl Harbor. That same night, across the Atlantic, the Luftwaffe dropped one hundred thousand incendiary bombs on London, causing widespread destruction throughout the city.

Still, since 1950, when *Hinge of Fate* appeared, historians and biographers have noted the heroic-sounding commiseration behind Roosevelt's six words, elevating the scene and making it as humanly dramatic as any other occasion involving the two leaders during the war. The prime minister felt the humiliation of "disgrace," and FDR didn't hesitate to reach out. Yet why did Churchill wait so long to provide such a memorable account of this critical moment? That intrigue persists by scrutinizing the historical record closer to the time of the episode.

On May 19, 1943, Churchill delivered his second address to Congress, and the circumstances nearly a year later couldn't have been more different from the dark days of June 1942. By then, North Africa was securely in Allied control, thanks at least in part to Roosevelt's commitment to Churchill after Tobruk's fall. The speech provided an ideal opportunity to help a fellow politician looking ahead to a reelection campaign the following year. By invoking FDR's putative question, the prime minister had a chance to reinforce the strong, personal relationship of the two comrades in arms as well as boost the electoral position of the leader he'd wooed for so long. Two months before, Churchill had told Eden that FDR planned to seek reelection for a fourth term in 1944.[31] Whether informed by Roosevelt, Hopkins, Harriman, or someone else, Churchill knew another White House campaign would surely affect the president's decision-making right up to Election Day, nearly twenty months in the future. Well ahead of any partisan political brawl, it was a perfect time to recall FDR's reaction.

The prime minister, however, took a different tack on Capitol Hill, focusing more on himself and unnamed "American friends." He related the fact that the president handed him the bulletin about Tobruk, adding, "That indeed was a dark and bitter hour for me, and I shall never forget the kindness and the wealth of comradeship which our American friends showed me and those with me in such adversity." His partners in war found "the means" to help "restore the situation."[32] The explanation is thankful yet vague, particularly concerning FDR's role.

Six days after what was hailed in the press as an oratorical tour de force, Churchill on May 25 brought up Tobruk again during a joint press conference with Roosevelt in the White House. The prime minister recalled receiving the cable from the president and then admitted: "I don't think there was anybody—any Englishman in the United States so unhappy, as I was that day, since [General John] Burgoyne surrendered at Saratoga [during the American Revolution]."[33] As before, Churchill placed emphasis on himself by speaking in the first-person, and this time he didn't mention the offer of American assistance. Close analysis of multiple sources before *The Hinge of Fate* was published makes one seriously wonder whether FDR's compassionate question was, indeed, asked.

Whatever might have been said in the president's study on June 21, 1942, General George Marshall, a by-the-book military officer and staunch defender of the army he led throughout World War II, became involved in the details of the conversation between Roosevelt and Churchill. He argued that his own troops were counting on receiving and using the three hundred Sherman tanks now being offered to other combatants. Churchill acknowledged, "It is a terrible thing to take the weapons out of a soldier's hands." But Marshall followed the commander in chief's orders, even when his experience made him think differently about a decision or a strategic trial balloon. He saluted civilian control of the armed forces but firmly put a stop to Roosevelt's attempt for greater familiarity, with its suggested intimacy, when the president once called him "George." He preferred "general." The future secretary of state and secretary of defense was known for somewhat frosty formality—as well as being the namesake of the Marshall Plan, which helped to rebuild Europe after the war. In his memoirs, besides including the quotation of FDR, Churchill summed up the reaction to the fall of Tobruk and the gift of needed equipment by invoking the trite yet appropriate adage: "A friend in need is a friend indeed."[34]

The repercussions of the Libyan debacle affected how the two leaders and their advisors began their formal meetings at the White House that Sunday. Marshall informed Stimson that a "good deal of a pow-wow and a rumpus" took place among the Allied leaders. The Libyan setback scrambled strategy and put a more intense focus on northern Africa in the thinking of some conference participants. Stimson learned that Churchill made "a terrific attack on Bolero," the full-scale operation intended to build up U.S. forces and supplies in Britain as the necessary prelude to the future cross-Channel invasion. However, it was decided, according to Marshall's report that he conveyed to Stimson, "that we should go ahead full blast on Bolero until the first of September."[35]

Meanwhile, across the Atlantic, members of Parliament and political commentators in Britain demanded to know who was responsible for the Tobruk disaster—and why the prime minister was over in Washington on another of his trips at such a critical time. The fires of controversy and blame began to burn with uncommon ferocity, and Churchill started to make plans to take the initiative in his own political self-defense at the same time as he participated in the ongoing conference.

American newspapers bannered their front pages with the Tobruk story the day after it fell. James B. Reston, a thirty-two-year-old *New York Times* reporter who would go on to win two Pulitzer Prizes and become a leading columnist and editor at the paper, contributed the main dispatch from Washington: "News Puts Damper on Churchill Visit." His opening paragraph put the situation at home and abroad in stark terms, "Washington was in a sober and realistic mood tonight," noting that the fall of Tobruk "put a damper on the unrestrained second-front speculation that has surrounded the Roosevelt-Churchill talks." Reston acknowledged that it was difficult to be specific in describing the talks because everything was taking place behind closed doors in complete secrecy. All the news fit to print was, at best, sparse.

For over five hours on June 21, the prime minister and the president talked with their major military planners about Operation Bolero, the methodical movement of U.S. troops and equipment to Britain for the invasion of western Europe. Besides Churchill and Roosevelt, the other participants in the deliberations included General Alan Brooke, chief of the Imperial General Staff, General Hastings (Pug) Ismay, Churchill's chief staff officer, Marshall, and Hopkins.

Uninvited but eagerly awaiting a call from FDR was Secretary of War Stimson. The diary he kept reflected the seething disappointment of an insider relegated to playing the part of an outsider, something of a political voyeur, forced to rely on reports from others to find out what was happening. During all the conference sessions between June 21 and June 25—Churchill's time in residence at the White House—Stimson was involved in just one formal discussion: on Monday, June 22, from 11:10 a.m. until 12:35 p.m. Recounting that meeting, Stimson said Churchill was "evidently staggered by the blow of Tobruk" but clear-eyed in assessing what transpired: "He said it was just plain bad leadership; that Rommel had out-generaled them and out-fought them and had supplied his troops with better weapons." When the topic turned to Bolero, which Stimson favored, the secretary of war could readily tell others didn't agree with him, and he also sensed his strong opposition to a military campaign in North Africa wasn't shared by the two leaders.[36]

Though the secretary of war kept stressing the importance of the Bolero buildup in Britain, he can tell that FDR was considering some kind "of a diversion from Bolero."[37] Stimson worried that Roosevelt, under Churchill's influence, would support an action sidetracking preparation for an assault on the European continent. Stimson didn't hold back in recording his differences, making what he wrote in his diary direct evidence of the internal tension and disagreement that animated the upper ranks of the government. Troubled "that the whole war effort might be endangered," the seventy-five-year-old Stimson ventured a scathing assessment of the sixty-year-old Roosevelt following the one session he attended: "Altogether it was a very unhappy meeting for me. The President was in his most irresponsible mood. He was talking of a most critical situation and in the presence of the head of another government with the frivolity and lack of responsibility of a child."[38]

After Stimson returned to the War Department, he continued to boil and to do what he could to defend his ground. And he wasn't alone. Marshall and other officers fought as best they could for a concentrated, deliberate expansion of an invasion force to confront the German military directly in western Europe. As far as they were concerned, embarking on another operation would be a costly, undesirable digression that could jeopardize the overall strategy. The elected president and his appointed war commanders were of two minds. Churchill's second visit to the White House did, indeed, pose a "crisis."

What was most intriguing about the Monday meeting with Stimson—the president's first of the day, although his last one on Sunday, about "Submarines and Pacific," went until 1 a.m.—concerned the roster of figures involved. Roosevelt and Churchill took part, as did Navy Secretary Frank Knox and Hopkins. That was all. No Brooke, no Ismay, no Marshall, no active, uniformed military figure on either side. Stimson, who in 1910 was defeated as the Republican Party's candidate for governor of New York, had served as secretary of war during William Howard Taft's administration from 1911 to 1913 and as secretary of state throughout Herbert Hoover's one term. Knox, a Rough Rider in Theodore Roosevelt's regiment in Cuba for the Spanish-American War, had sought the vice presidency in 1936 as Republican candidate Alf Landon's running mate. Stimson and Knox were the two most prominent Republicans serving in FDR's executive branch, and it was almost as though the meeting was arranged to showcase the avowed bipartisanship Roosevelt sought to promote for the American war effort. Unlike the scabrous partisanship that exists in the twenty-first century, Roosevelt wanted prominent Republicans out front to project a united, national cause.

Interestingly, Churchill made no mention of this session in his memoir. Instead, the prime minister adopted the opposite viewpoint that Stimson presented by arguing in favor of an analysis of possibilities for operations in North Africa, Norway, and even the Iberian peninsula in 1942. An invasion of western Europe, as envisaged by the American military planners, was something for the future, possibly in 1943. Churchill's hesitance on the European option and his enthusiasm for other action created constant friction in U.S. officialdom that took a long time to resolve.

Debating strategy occupied much of Churchill's attention during his June visit, but there were other obligations to fulfill. Hopkins told him the president wanted him to meet and speak with two up-and-coming major generals: Dwight D. Eisenhower and Mark Clark. The two were "brought to my air-cooled room" in the White House, where he remarked: "I was immediately impressed by these remarkable but hitherto unknown men. . . . We talked almost entirely about the major cross-Channel invasion in 1943, 'Round-up' as it was then called, on which their thoughts had evidently been concentrated."[39] At that time, Churchill kept dangling an unspecified date a year off for the invasion. It sounded definite without being so. A principal reason for Eisenhower to talk with Churchill about the possible invasion was that he was departing for London to become commanding general of the European theater shortly after he left this White House meeting, arriving there even before the prime minister returned home.

In *The Hinge of Fate*, Churchill wrote that Eisenhower and Clark came to see him on June 21, the Sunday when Tobruk fell. According to the president's calendar, their talk occurred the following day, June 22, which is correct. Getting a date wrong certainly isn't an egregious offense. However, Eisenhower should not have been "hitherto unknown" to Churchill. As noted in chapter one, Eisenhower had been involved in a meeting with the prime minister previously—on December 24, 1941, when he and Stimson went to the White House to discuss the situation in the Philippines.

Well-known public figures meet multitudes of people in their work. But Churchill, somewhat amazingly, failed to remember the first time he was introduced to *both* Roosevelt and Eisenhower, current and future occupants of the White House. To call it a strange coincidence borders on understatement. Both, in their way, reminded the British leader when they first shook hands. When a chipper Churchill announced how happy he was to meet FDR at the Atlantic Conference in 1941, a somewhat miffed Roosevelt corrected the prime minister that the two had met earlier—at a July 1918 London dinner during the Great War, when FDR was a thirty-six-year-old assistant secretary of the Navy on a fact-finding trip, and Churchill, then forty-three, was serving as minister of munitions. (Roosevelt didn't impart that he wasn't impressed nearly a quarter-century earlier.) In Eisenhower's case, one of the last letters he wrote to Churchill near the end of his second premiership harkened back to "the moment we first met in Washington, December, 1941." A few sentences later, he also reminded "Winston" of his White House visit in June of 1942 "when we had to face the bitter reality of the Tobruk disaster."[40]

During Churchill's second stay in the White House, he received an urgent appeal from Eden to return to London to deal with the fallout from the disastrous surrender and other problems. Churchill didn't listen, and Eden thought the prime minister "appeared peevish and reluctant and implied he was doing most important things over there."[41] Churchill kept to his agenda, continually conferring with American officials or with the British military leaders traveling with him. After the session with Eisenhower and Clark, he and Roosevelt conferred about aircraft allocation, submarines and shipping, and sending U.S. troops to the Middle East. Unlike their first conference six months before, this one probed the war's progress with greater attention to the details of combat within the broader Allied strategy.

Throughout Churchill's visit, secrecy concerning his whereabouts and activities largely prevailed. For instance, in "The Day in Washington" column of the *New York Times* for June 24, the opening sentence read, "President Roosevelt and Prime Minister Churchill continued their conferences and invited the Pacific War Council and a bipartisan Congressional delegation to meet with them separately tomorrow." The first part of this matter-of-fact advisory was intentionally inaccurate, an example of fog-of-war disinformation. Roosevelt and Churchill had no plans for conference sessions because the prime minister was scheduled to make a clandestine side trip nearly five hundred miles from Washington.

Churchill, accompanied by Stimson, Marshall, Brooke, Ismay, and others took the president's train for a night journey to Fort Jackson in Columbia, South Carolina. At the massive army training facility midway between New York City and Miami, nearly ten thousand fledgling soldiers engaged in drills of various kinds, including a thousand parachutists performing a mock airborne assault. Ismay, who had been in the British military since 1905, wasn't impressed with what he saw during the exercises and war games. Churchill didn't agree and said so, as he recalled in his memoir: "'You're wrong. They are wonderful material and will learn very quickly.' To my American hosts however I consistently pressed my view that it takes two years or more to make a soldier. Certainly two years later [in June 1944, with D-Day June 6] the troops we saw in Carolina bore themselves like veterans."[42] Given the degree to which Churchill influenced Roosevelt during America's initial months of combat, it's legitimate to wonder whether a certain period of time might also have been necessary for a commander in chief to acquire the experience and expertise for making sound, life-or-death decisions involving military strategy. The prime minister's purposeful angling to assert his thinking on Allied decision-making continued.

Regardless of what he said—or didn't say—about Tobruk's fall, Roosevelt's human compassion in dealing with Churchill on this visit extended to his guest's personal well-being. Sir Charles Wilson, Churchill's doctor who later became Lord Moran, reported a remark

Roosevelt made to him the evening before the party left for Fort Jackson: "You, Sir Charles, do not know the South Carolina sun in June. Be careful of the Prime Minister tomorrow." The president's concern for potential solar effects on the fair complexion of the prime minister involved more than a remark to the physician traveling with the prime minister. The president prepared a telegram, labeled "SECRET," that he dispatched to Marshall: "To be delivered to General Marshall immediately upon his arrival at Camp Jackson stop You and Sir Charles Wilson are in command stop enough said stop Roosevelt."[43] Why Marshall rather than his superior, Stimson, would have been the recipient of the presidential directive is curious; however, the secretary of war took note of Wilson's dutiful supervision, noting the "doctor watched over him the whole day like a hen over a chicken but the little man came along in good shape."[44] The phrase "little man" is much more than a two-word physical description of the five foot six Churchill by the nearly six foot Stimson.

Roosevelt's spoken and written warnings about the blazing Southern sun and blistering heat aptly depicted conditions at Fort Jackson June 24. Churchill wore a sun hat throughout the maneuvers, while Stimson stood out in his distinctive pith helmet. The group was probably glad to fly back to Washington, where temperatures fluctuated between the high 50s and low 80s that Wednesday. Besides keeping a close eye on his most important patient, Wilson offered a candid assessment of Churchill's reaction to reviewing the Yankee recruits and their prospects: "He does not believe that these troops are, as yet, sufficiently hardened to be war-worthy on the battlefields of Europe."[45] Churchill's two-year rule for soldier development, undoubtedly, shaped his thinking during the remainder of his visit and into the summer.

The British prime minister wasn't the only foreign dignitary staying at the White House during the fourth week of June in 1942. King Peter of Yugoslavia arrived while Churchill was away for a full round of military meetings, formal ceremonies, and social occasions. The king, then just twenty, led his country's government-in-exile after Yugoslavia was invaded by German forces in 1941, and he traveled from his headquarters in England for his talks in the United States. During the German occupation of Europe, London became the center for royalty and deposed government officials to live and conduct their resistance efforts against Nazi rule.

Churchill, Roosevelt, and King Peter met from shortly after midnight on June 25 until 1:25 a.m., with the focus of discussion on "North Africa," according to the president's calendar. A military operation thousands of miles removed from the English Channel and western Europe now seemed to concentrate the thinking of the two Allied leaders. Was the concept of a second front being redefined? Were Roosevelt's military commanders going to be challenged to consider a theatre of combat not related to Bolero? What had happened to FDR's pledge to "Commissar Molotov" and to his "Go to it!" enthusiasm that he expressed to Churchill in his letter of April 3? With justification Stimson kept worrying that the emphasis on Bolero was weakening as the prime minister and president talked, and that realization provoked even greater conflict between the White House and the War Department.

After the late-night session with FDR and King Peter, Churchill continued to work, ending shortly before 4 a.m. He had one more day to emphasize what he considered the most effective plans for Allied forces in the coming months. Thursday, June 25, brought two groups to the White House to hear directly from Churchill and Roosevelt. The bipartisan congressional leadership gathered at 11 a.m. for a thirty-five minute, basically pro forma briefing, followed by a much longer, and larger, meeting of the Pacific War Council. Representatives of eight countries, including Canada, Australia, New Zealand, and China, focused on fighting the Japanese and the overall state of the war. Bringing the War Council together provided the only occasion during Churchill's visit when he appeared in public and in front of photographers for next-day coverage. (News and pictures of the tour of Fort Jackson weren't released until days later.) For once, the British leader, still shaken by Tobruk, was unsure how to act for the picture-taking. Canadian prime minister Mackenzie King heard him explain his dilemma: "If one were smiling, the public would think they were taking things too lightly. On the other hand, if we looked serious, they thought there was a crisis."[46]

Worrying how to appear was just one complication of Churchill's final day in Washington. He also had to navigate the second front debate and whether the Allies should launch an invasion of Europe. Meeting with representatives of British Dominions, many of whom were serving on the Pacific War Council, he argued—as he'd done frequently before—that overwhelming force would be necessary to avoid another Dunkirk, the evacuation from France in late May and early June of 1940 to rescue 338,000 British and French soldiers after the Nazis had overrun western Europe. According to meeting notes that Mackenzie King kept, Churchill spoke of the potential massacre of large numbers of French people by German troops if an invasion lacked the necessary fighting personnel and ordnance. At the same time, the prime minister saw no problem in talking openly about the Allies planning such an offensive "to keep the Huns believing that an attack was going to be made" as a deliberate deflection to pull German divisions from the Eastern front to relieve some of the strain on the Soviet forces.[47] Churchill talked about a second front being imminent, but his mind was made up that a premature action would be suicidal and not be able to defeat the enemy. He repeatedly invoked the spring of 1943, but that wasn't firm, just something off in the distance for supporters of a second front in Europe.

To the War Council, both Roosevelt and Churchill emphasized recent Allied accomplishments in the Pacific, notably the Battle of the Coral Sea in early May, the first time a major Japanese advance was repelled by the Allies, and the Battle of Midway a month later, which proved to be one of the most consequential clashes of World War II and provided a decisive victory for the American Navy six months after Pearl Harbor. More than anything, as Canada's prime minister observed, the highly publicized session was little more than a photo opportunity "to give the gathering a significance in the eyes of the public."[48] With Churchill and Roosevelt together, the posed pictures, with or without smiles, conveyed the true meaning the council wanted to project: the Allies were united—and the Axis powers as well as the world could see the wartime comradeship shared by several countries.

Despite disagreements among the British and Americans over Bolero or other operations, the president and prime minister wanted to project optimism, with some of the council members telling reporters about the encouragement the two leaders provided the United Nations. Despite the surrender and setback of Tobruk, the Allies argued they were formulating strategy and making decisions that, ultimately, would lead to victory.

As Churchill was nearing the end of his time in Washington, the United States announced a major military personnel appointment. Front-page stories—in some cases more prominent than the dispatches about Churchill and Roosevelt meeting together—bannered the arrival in London of Major General Eisenhower for his new leadership post there. The largest headline on page one of Washington's *Evening Star* for June 25 proclaimed:

GEN. EISENHOWER TO COMMAND AMERICAN SECOND FRONT EFFORT; WHITE HOUSE REPORT CHEERING

Churchill's visit had begun with the second front as the principal focus of attention, and a week later there was a figure by name and rank directly associated with it. This, of course, took place despite Churchill's lingering reluctance to support a European invasion except as a ruse to convince the Germans of impending action.

The *New York Times* in its front-page account on June 26 emphasized Eisenhower's role in preparing an assault of Europe and even used the caption "May Lead Invasion" along with a file photo of the major general. Nine months earlier Eisenhower held the two-rank lower classification of colonel. The Washington-datelined story in the *Times* made a direct connection between the naming of Eisenhower to his "new command" and the Churchill-Roosevelt talks, noting that "Churchill had reached an agreement with President Roosevelt on the feasibility of planning for a second front, despite current setbacks in Libya and Egypt." All the journalistic attention to the fifty-one-year-old Eisenhower made this son of Abilene, Kansas, a 1915 West Point graduate, widely known for the first time. His rapid ascent in the Army mirrored his equally swift emergence as a prominent figure in the public eye.

Although the prime minister's second wartime visit to the White House was almost completely different from his first one, it ended exactly the same way as six months earlier—with a three-person dinner: Churchill, Roosevelt, and Hopkins. The president's special assistant presented the two leaders with the draft of a joint statement they edited and approved for release after Churchill returned to Britain. The phrase "second front" never appeared in the ten-paragraph, three hundred-fifty-seven-word statement. Secrecy exceeded specificity, with vague reference to "coming operations" intended to "divert German strength from the attack on Russia."[49] Finding a way to help the Soviets and weaken the Germans in eastern Europe remained unresolved, and that dilemma would intensify, only contributing to Stalin's anger. According to Imperial War Museum statistics, nearly three million Soviet prisoners of war perished between June of 1941 and early 1942. Millions of others—precise numbers are unknown—were killed in battle. Stalin persisted in demanding relief from his two major allies, as Molotov's clandestine May trip to London and Washington dramatized.

Unlike his first wartime visit that lasted over three weeks, the prime minister felt greater urgency to return to Britain to deal with the aftereffects of Tobruk and other war-related concerns, including the alarming number of shipping losses. In 1942, the Royal Navy saw its fleet seriously reduced, with the enemy sinking aircraft carriers, cruisers, destroyers, submarines, and other vessels.

Churchill and his entourage left the White House at 8:50 p.m., an hour before Roosevelt departed by train to go back to Hyde Park—and eight days of recuperation from the meetings and social occasions involving an energetic houseguest and war comrade. Several full days of animated talk—with meetings running until 1 a.m. or later on two different occasions—tested his stamina, as each of Churchill's visits tended to do.

The secrecy that prevailed throughout Churchill's time in the United States extended to his departure from the White House and how he was spirited from 1600 Pennsylvania Avenue to reach the four-propeller flying boat that was designed for him and his retinue. Of his six transatlantic trips during the Second World War, this was the only one when he flew both ways, an indication of the gravity of the moment. Ever hospitable, Roosevelt accompanied Churchill through the tunnel connecting the White House to the next-door Treasury building at 1500 Pennsylvania Avenue for the clandestine getaway. The tunnel had been constructed shortly after the war began as an escape route for the president if the White House came under attack. Vaults deep below the Treasury offices were converted into a bomb shelter with living quarters for Roosevelt, his family, and others. En route on the stealth departure, the president jocularly told the prime minister, "I am going along with you, Winston, only to make sure that you don't steal any of [Treasury Secretary] Henry Morgenthau's gold."[50] The grim realities of war didn't keep FDR from a final needle directed at his departing guest.

Churchill's relatively brief visit wasn't universally cheered by the public as his first one was. Indeed, an airmail letter sent to the prime minister at the White House and preserved in the papers of his secretary, John Martin, conveyed a two-word, typed message in capital letters: "GO HOME."[51] That note was sent shortly after Churchill's arrival was announced. An anonymous missive of displeasure is one thing, but what about a potential assassination attempt?

Though the incident wasn't disclosed until years later, the Secret Service thwarted a would-be gunman from firing at Churchill on his way to the flying boat at the Baltimore airport's terminal for British

Overseas Airways Corporation (BOAC). A Secret Service agent, Howard Chandler, overheard a BOAC guard muttering to himself, "I'm going to kill that bastard Churchill. I'm going to kill him." Chandler apprehended the guard, an American hired by the British carrier, near the plane's door. Had the man, later judged to be insane, not been talking to himself, it's possible he could have gotten off a shot at point-blank range. Roosevelt's chief bodyguard, Michael Reilly, who was on the scene and later revealed what happened, commented that Churchill was "within one minute of assassination."[52] After the foiled assailant was led off, Reilly personally escorted Churchill to the plane without informing him of the episode.

Even though this trip to the White House didn't receive ubiquitous approval or nearly as much press attention as the previous one, Churchill continued to intrigue Americans and to exert a strong hold on them. He fascinated people in different walks of life across the country. An editorial, headlined "Wings," which appeared in the Asheville, North Carolina *Citizen-Times* June 28, 1942, a day after the prime minister's return to London, captured Churchill's appeal. The prose, complete with a quotation from Shakespeare's *Midsummer Night's Dream*, matches the warmth of feeling about the subject, who's referred to twice as a "chubby little man with the fat, black cigar" but never identified by name. This wartime wizard has removed the customary distance between a foreign leader and the citizens of another country:

> The peripatetic Premier is home. He has annihilated time and space. He has spanned a broad ocean between two mighty lands,
>
> Swift as a shadow, short as any dream
> Brief as the lightning in the collied night.

The editorial ends with a rhetorical yet ringing question for American readers: "Where are the isolationists of yesteryear?"

The Britain to which Churchill returned was still psychologically rebounding from the trauma of Tobruk. His first major business when he arrived back at 10 Downing Street the evening of June 27 was a meeting of the War Cabinet, where he talked about the "defeat" in the Middle East and the Roosevelt administration's offer of assistance. General Brooke followed Churchill with a summary of his meetings in Washington. His just-the-facts presentation stood in stark contrast to the way he described his time in Washington for the diary he kept. On the flight back to Britain, he observed that Roosevelt had "a wonderful charm about him. But I do not think that his military sense is on a par with his political sense."[53] This jab at FDR prompted Brooke to compare Roosevelt to Churchill in a reflection he added later to his immediate observations. Like Stimson, Brooke harbored doubts about the two war leaders' combat acumen. He acknowledged FDR's lack of "military knowledge" and Marshall's importance in advising the commander in chief. Churchill, however, was different, and he watched him at close range. "Winston never had the slightest doubt that he had inherited all the military genius from his great ancestor Marlborough!" Brooke fumed. "His military plans and ideas varied from the most brilliant conceptions at one end to the wildest and most dangerous ideas at the other. To wean him away from these wilder plans required superhuman efforts and was never entirely successful in so far as he tended to return to these ideas again and again."[54]

The surrender at Tobruk, with its military, political, and public relations reverberations, haunted Churchill's second sojourn in the White House, and the "disgrace" of it stalked his days in Westminster after his return to London. Loud voices in Parliament forcefully questioned the direction of the war, with the setbacks thus far in 1942 uppermost for scrutiny. The prime minister, who was also "defence minister," needed to defend himself against a motion of censure put forward following Tobruk. In a sweeping, ten-thousand-word speech on July 2, 1942, Churchill made the case for the national government, the war cabinet, and himself. One of the most stinging charges leveled at him was that he was absent from the home front at a critical time. Did the prime minister need to be abroad when British forces were under such perilous assault? Saying he was "on an important mission in the country of one of our great Allies," Churchill argued that "our American friends are not fair-weather friends" and "in this particular case the bonds of comradeship between all the men at the top were actually strengthened."[55]

Churchill expanded on his defense by contending that his time at Hyde Park and in Washington solidified the alliance between the United Kingdom and the United States. At no point, however, did he refer to Roosevelt by name nor did he describe how FDR responded at seeing the prime minister's reaction to the bulletin about Tobruk's fall. Curiously, despite the breadth of his oration, he kept details about the weeklong visit to himself. What prompted him to avoid discussing Roosevelt? Was it purposeful, possibly out of fear of being upstaged in the minds of Parliament members and the broader public because he sensed his own vulnerability? The main point he wanted to announce from the American sojourn was "that the two great English-speaking nations were never closer together."[56]

When the time arrived to vote, 475 supported Churchill, while 25 favored the motion to censure. The prime minister had weathered the storm and could look ahead to the future, one of continuous challenge and constant travel. The next month, in fact, he flew to Moscow for his first meetings with Stalin, and he persisted in advocating for military operations somewhere other than western Europe. The prime minister's advocacy ultimately prevailed in late July, when Roosevelt—in a rare move during World War II—overruled Stimson, Marshall, and his other military advisors by ordering U.S. involvement in an invasion of North Africa.

Always sensitive to political winds, the president realized that Americans were becoming impatient for action of some type against Germany, and the midterm elections were approaching on November 3. Though Marshall kept arguing strongly against any British-advocated diversion, the four-star general and army chief of staff saluted and years later expressed a realization about the shaping of war strategy when there is civilian control of the armed forces. Speaking in 1956, he frankly admitted, "We failed to see that the leader in a democracy has to keep the people entertained. That may sound like the wrong word, but it conveys the thought. The people demand action. We couldn't wait to be completely ready."[57]

For a popularly elected commander in chief, quotidian politics is an ever-present consideration, if not a deciding factor. FDR had not won the White House three times and the New York governorship twice without having acute political antennae that operated nearly every waking hour. In talking with Marshall about the operation, which was renamed "Torch" after being called "Gymnast," Roosevelt put his hands together in a prayerful pose and made a mock-solemn appeal: "Please make it before Election Day."[58] Possibly more than anyone else, he understood the impact a major military operation would have across the country among the voting-age populace. In the Pacific, the Battle of Midway signaled a possible turning point against the Japanese. Now it was time to confront Germany as boldly as possible.

Five days *after* Americans went to the polls on the third day of November, over one hundred thousand Americans and British under the command of Eisenhower, landed on the beaches of Algeria and Morocco in the first successful joint undertaking by U.S. and U.K. forces across the Atlantic. The military victory over the Axis combatants—including troops of Vichy France and naval contingents of Germany and Italy—gave the Allies control of the western Mediterranean region and a beachhead for future operations to the east in northern Africa to the Suez Canal as well as across the Mediterranean to the European continent. However, as FDR feared, delay in launching the invasion proved costly to the Democratic Party's strength in Congress and Roosevelt's support on Capitol Hill. In the Senate, Democrats lost 9 seats (creating a 57 to 38 majority), while in the House of Representatives the Democratic advantage dropped from 105-seat dominance to a narrow 13-seat margin, 222 to 209. The midterm results provided a warning sign to Democrats that FDR might be losing some of his political clout at a key moment in the war and two years before he planned to face the voters again.

Operation Torch wasn't the second front in Europe that so many people in and out of the U.S. government wanted to see mobilized as soon as forces were battle-ready and the necessary ordnance and machinery positioned for use. Yet, after Churchill's June visit and the repercussions of Tobruk, the prime minister and the president had reason to share a newfound confidence. On November 13, Churchill wrote Roosevelt: "Our enterprises have prospered beyond our hopes and we must not neglect the good gifts of fortune."[59]

For Americans, December marked a full year of war. Nearly four million service members were now engaged in the military on land or sea and in the air. December also marked Churchill's thirty-first month at 10 Downing Street. As the new year approached, neither leader could have predicted that they would be together during six different months in 1943—January, May, August, September, November, and December—nor that they would confer in five separate countries: Morocco, the United States, Canada, Egypt, and Iran. Roosevelt would become the first president to fly to an international conference, while Churchill would log thousands more miles than FDR to make sure his proposals—and personality—helped shape the war's progress. Many of the days he spent away from London in 1943, he was living and working in the White House, even at one point when Roosevelt wasn't there.

– 3 –

"WINSTON'S TRAVELLING CIRCUS"

During the eleven months between June 1942 and May 1943, the tide of war dramatically turned to the Allies' advantage, so much so that Churchill's third summit at the White House almost took on the trappings of an early victory celebration. Instead of the weeklong, close-to-stealth sojourn involving a handful of aides that occurred the year before, Churchill arrived on May 11 for a front-page-worthy stay of sixteen days, accompanied by a retinue of 150 military advisors and staff members, including 6 joining him in residence at the White House. In a secret diary, Lord Halifax, the U.K.'s ambassador to the United States, mocked the scores of British subjects descending on Washington as "Winston's travelling circus," displaying (from his somewhat jaundiced perspective) an "amusing form of megalomania on Winston's part."[1]

What caused the prime minister to be decidedly more public? Why the projection of grandiosity? After defeats and setbacks during much of 1942, including the fall of Tobruk in June and the fiasco of the Dieppe raid in France that August—with over half the Canadian, British, and American landing force of 6,100 killed, injured, or captured—the Allies won significant victories in the second battle of El Alamein in Egypt during late October and early November as well as Operation Torch in North Africa that November. Looking back at that time,

Churchill boasted, "It may almost be said, 'Before Alamein we never had a victory. After Alamein we never had a defeat.'"[2] On November 10, the prime minister famously told a dinner audience at the Mansion House in London, "Now, this is not the end. It is not even the beginning to the end. But it is, perhaps, the end of the beginning."[3] The next day he declared in the Commons, "Historians may explain Tobruk. The Eighth Army has done better; it has avenged it."[4]

Besides applauding the success in the desert—in no small measure because three hundred Sherman tanks shipped from America after Tobruk joined the fight—Churchill called "this Battle of Egypt" one aspect of a coordinated Allied plan in the western Mediterranean region. He was referring to Operation Torch, the invasion by Anglo-American troops of North Africa under the command of General Dwight Eisenhower, the first major U.S. assault in the European-North African Theatre. In his speech of November 10, the prime minister made a point of sharing credit for the turn of fortune, noting: "The President of the United States, who is Commander-in-Chief of the armed forces of America, is the author of this mighty undertaking, and in all of it I have been his active and ardent lieutenant."[5] The self-appointed junior officer might wryly depreciate Churchill's combat status—he'd actually served as a lieutenant colonel in the Great War a quarter-century earlier—but, even with whatever measure of megalomania within him, he understood his place in the hierarchy of United Nations' leadership.

Nine days before Roosevelt met the train from New York carrying Churchill and his entourage to Washington following their transatlantic crossing on the *Queen Mary*, the prime minister had written Harry Hopkins a "most especially secret" telegram offering to stay at the British embassy because of several domestic issues FDR was juggling, including strikes by coal miners, as well as the war effort. Churchill then went beyond matters of lodging to raise a more compelling reason for a full-scale conference—and to hoist a warning flag. "I am conscious of serious divergences beneath the surface which, if not adjusted, will lead to grave difficulties and feeble action in the summer and autumn. These difficulties we must forestall."[6] The prime minister seemed to sense a weakening of Allied unity and of his influence on the overall war strategy.

Though Churchill wrote Hopkins, the president personally responded a few hours later and said he was "delighted" about the prime minister's upcoming visit. "I agree most heartily that we have some important business to settle at once; the sooner the better," Roosevelt remarked, signing off by saying: "I want you of course to stay here with me."[7] Despite the availability of the Eleanor Roosevelt-inspired Blair House across the street, the British leader would return to the White House following a voyage, which, for part of the way, included protection from ten U.S. warships. Peril, from sea and air, still lurked.

Throughout what Churchill dubbed the Trident Conference and while he and the president at public occasions kept advancing their common cause, the Combined Chiefs of Staff fiercely argued behind the scenes over war strategy, tactics to use, and where combat resources deserved to go. Was the United States tacking to the Pacific to take on the Japanese rather than concentrating on first defeating Germany? Would a cross-Channel operation be feasible within the next year? Do other points of attack exist in Europe for establishing the long-debated and delayed second front against the Axis in Europe? Answering these questions and many others would occupy the principals and their staffs for two weeks, as the Allies squabbled and fought among themselves to reach agreement about their next steps and ultimate objectives.

W. Averell Harriman accompanied Churchill to Washington, as he'd done during the prime minister's first visit. Similar to that time, he kept a record of his conversations with Churchill. During dinner on May 6, the discussion turned to the ship's security, despite the fact that the *Queen Mary* at that point was being protected by an aircraft carrier, two cruisers, four destroyers, and a flying boat overhead. On the ship as a decoy measure, posters in Dutch suggested Queen Wilhelmina of the Netherlands was a passenger rather than the British prime minister, a believer in the principle: "The more tales, the more safety." As they talked, Churchill revealed what he planned to do if a German submarine attacked. He had already ordered mounting a machine gun to his lifeboat, bragging: "I won't be captured. The finest way to die is in the excitement of fighting the enemy." When Harriman conceded that talk of a possible attack alarmed him, the prime minister responded with an invitation: "You must come with me in the boat and see the fun."[8]

On the voyage over, Churchill prepared another of his detailed papers: in this case about "the Indian and Far Eastern spheres." One section was both strategic and personal, acknowledging the need "to make a long-term plan for the defeat of Japan" but within the context "of the prime struggle against Hitler."[9] Though the United States entered the war after a Japanese attack, the prime minister didn't want anyone to lose sight of "the prime struggle" that he and FDR kept affirming since meeting at Placentia Bay in August of 1941.

After Roosevelt met Churchill at the train on the evening of May 11, they returned to the White House. The Rose Bedroom on the second floor was ready for his third occupation of it, and the two leaders began to repeat their established routine in Washington. They spent most lunches and dinners together with meetings usually scheduled for late morning (because the prime minister arose most days well after the sun) and late afternoon (to accommodate Churchill's daily nap). Of course, after-dinner discussions occurred with regularity: until 1:25 a.m. on May 14, 12:45 a.m. on May 18, 1:25 a.m. on May 19, 1:20 a.m. on May 20, 2:00 a.m. on May 24, 1:55 a.m. on May 25, and 1:50 a.m. on May 26, according to Roosevelt's calendar. The day after Churchill departed (on May 26), FDR set off for Hyde Park to recuperate from his night-owl guest. That, too, had become presidential practice.

The first afternoon that the prime minister and his delegation were in Washington (May 12), the Combined Chiefs of Staff met with Roosevelt and Churchill at the White House for over an hour-and-a-half. The first of six dozen-person sessions during Trident, the prime minister and president spoke almost exclusively and followed a parallel approach in remarks to the highest-ranking military advisors—plus Hopkins on the U.S. side. While Churchill kept posing questions—

thirteen separate ones in the notes he dictated before the meeting—Roosevelt matter-of-factly assessed battle conditions involving the United Nations. Even though Churchill told the group they had "the authority and prestige of victory,"[10] he, along with FDR, recognized how much further the Allies needed to go for the ultimate one.

In notes he took about the May 12 meeting, Roosevelt's chief of staff Admiral William D. Leahy reported that Churchill "made a convincing argument for a strong effort during 1943 to force Italy out of the war," but maintained that a cross-Channel invasion could *not* occur in the spring of 1944. Roosevelt didn't agree and advocated that the Allies launch the operation earlier and not later than 1944. Since his first post-Pearl Harbor meetings with Churchill, 1944 was the year FDR had targeted for major operations. The president, according to Leahy, "expressed determination to concentrate our military effort first on destruction of Nazi military power before engaging in any collateral campaigns and before exercising our full effort against Japan."[11] The tension between the two leaders' viewpoints on war strategy animated discussions by the two sides during the next several days—with the prime minister and the president sticking to their guns on the policies they backed from their own, sometimes differing, perspectives.

The opening volleys helped set the agenda for the conferences of the Combined Chiefs of Staff while offering guidance about the priorities of various operations and locations of future engagements. With marching orders delivered, the brass retreated to their meeting tables for prolonged debate. The prime minister and president received briefings about the discussions but mostly kept their own dispute-free, hail-fellow schedules. Both politicians to their core, they viewed the world, even one embroiled in global war, from that vantage point.

As seen during earlier visits, how the two men conducted business was often subject to criticism by those with whom they worked. The day before Churchill arrived, Secretary of War Henry Stimson reported that he spoke with General George Marshall, the army chief of staff, about a preparatory meeting to Trident involving Roosevelt and the

Joint Chiefs of Staff. Marshall recounted that the commander in chief "agreed" with his military commanders on the "American policy" to be advanced during Trident. Stimson, however, wasn't certain the president would remain steadfast in supporting the policy. "I fear it will be the same story over again," Stimson fretted. "The man from London will arrive with a program of further expansion in the eastern Mediterranean and will have his way with our Chief, and the careful and deliberate plans of our Staff will be overridden."[12] The charms of a certain "man from London" were well-known to the people around the president, and at various points during 1943 the emotional connection between Roosevelt and Churchill seemed as strong, if not stronger, than at any time in their working relationship. They weren't hesitant in expressing their opinions to others.

For instance, at the Casablanca conference, which took place over ten days in January of that year and was the last time the prime minister and president were together before Trident in May, Churchill refused to watch FDR's plane become airborne as it began its return to America from Morocco. According to Kenneth Pendar, the U.S. vice consul in Marrakech, Churchill told him, "Don't tell me when they take off. It makes me far too nervous. If anything happened to that man, I couldn't stand it. He is the truest friend; he has the farthest vision; he is the greatest man I've ever known."[13] For someone intrepid in traveling to Washington, Moscow, and elsewhere throughout the war, Churchill was anxious, even fearful, on behalf of another person he had gotten to know since 1941.

For Roosevelt, a moment of candor and regard also occurred in North Africa. During a battlefield visit in Tunisia preceding the Tehran "Big Three" summit of FDR, Churchill, and Stalin in late November 1943, he spoke one-on-one with General Eisenhower. Telling the commanding officer of his "disappointment" that Torch began after the midterm elections, the president then brought up "instances of disagreement with Mr. Churchill, but earnestly and almost emotionally said: 'No one could have a better or sturdier ally than that old Tory!' "[14]

The liberal FDR needles Churchill as an "old Tory," but you also hear affectionate admiration in what was said.

Over time and especially from late 1943 onward, disagreements between Roosevelt and Churchill increased, and their relationship changed. But what the public saw through the news coverage of Churchill's third White House visit was the president's incandescent smile and the prime minister's upraised fingers in a "V for victory" sign. Friction that existed between the two leaders was kept behind closed doors among themselves. Robert Sherwood's classic description of Roosevelt's "heavily forested interior" often created an outer mask for his genuine opinions and emotions.[15]

King Peter of Yugoslavia was a White House guest during Churchill's previous visit. During Trident, while Churchill made himself at home in the Rose Bedroom, other White House quarters were occupied, though more briefly, by the president of Czechoslovakia Eduard Benes and the prime minister of Canada Mackenzie King. Earlier that May, Madame Chiang Kai-shek, wife of the Chinese generalissimo and president, and the president of Bolivia General Enrique Peñaranda, stayed at 1600 Pennsylvania Avenue. Crown Princess Martha of Norway, a flirtatious favorite of FDR, was also a frequent guest at the time, and she accompanied the president to Hyde Park after Churchill's departure.

Churchill, Roosevelt, and Benes discussed the future of Germany and the fate of war criminals at an 11 a.m. meeting on May 13 in the White House Study. Later, the prime minister and president ate lunch and dinner together before an 11 p.m. meeting with Hopkins and Harriman back in the study. However, in a common refrain when Churchill was in the White House, the U.S. government document about the proceedings reported "no official record . . . has been found" of this meeting.[16] That phrasing or similar terminology appeared twenty-four times in the 197 pages about the "Proceedings of the Conference." This particular late-evening session lasted until 1:25 a.m., according to the president's calendar, with no mention of what was discussed.

Both Churchill and Roosevelt carried out their public commitments while the military chiefs and advisors argued over strategy and plans. On the morning of Friday, May 14, as FDR conducted the first of four news conferences during Trident, Churchill began to prepare remarks recognizing the heroism of the British Home Guard on its third anniversary. Slated for broadcast throughout Britain, the United States, and elsewhere, the talk was scheduled for delivery at 12:30 p.m. direct from the White House.

There was just one problem. At 10:45 a.m., the speaker had no script for his remarks, and he hadn't begun to organize his thoughts. Elizabeth Layton Nel, one of Churchill's devoted secretaries and the only woman among the prime minister's staff at the conference, later described the somewhat frantic scene of her boss lounging in bed, shuffling his papers, awaiting the arrival of his muse. "Suddenly he began to dictate, and we [Nel and another stenographer] took it in turns," she recalled. Finishing shortly after noon and with five minutes to spare, Churchill rushed from the Rose Bedroom to the assembled microphones.[17]

The fifteen-minute speech, published in its entirety by several newspapers in the United Kingdom and the United States, provided the first comments on Trident by a principal participant. At his news conference that morning, Roosevelt had dodged a direct question about the summit, saying: "There isn't any—any news yet, because we are still conferring. And I don't believe there will be anything until the visit is practically over."[18] Churchill, by contrast, avoided details but delivered reassurance and inspiration: "These are great days; they are like the days in Lord Chatham's time [the British leader during the Seven Years' War], of which it was said you had to get up early in the morning not to miss some news of victory." The prime minister continued to speak in general though strategic terms, rhetorically conveying a sense that preparation was essential and that it was "no good having only one march ahead laid out; march after march must be planned as far as human eye can see."[19] Despite the hasty composition, the broadcast served its purpose in stirring fashion, and near the end there was promise of a "deadly grapple on the Continent." At what point? Following which "march"? Nobody dared say.

Secrecy also surrounded a cryptic message Churchill received that day: "Mincemeat swallowed rod, line and sinker by right people and from best information they look like acting on it."[20] Operation Mincemeat, one of the most daring and elaborate ruses during the war, involved the planting of bogus documents on a dead body made to look like a Royal Marine. The papers, which were found on the corpse along the coast of Spain, described an Allied invasion of Greece, Sardinia, and the Balkans with the purpose of diverting Axis forces from the intended target: Sicily. The Nazi high command, informed by sympathetic Spaniards, believed the disinformation "Major Martin" was carrying and directed multiple divisions away from where the Allied troops were actually heading. As a result, the invasion of Sicily that began in July of 1943 came as a surprise to German defenders. Churchill always encouraged out-of-the-box, "corkscrew" thinking, and this intelligence stratagem worked to perfection. It took a decade before the hoax and its consequences became widely known.[21]

After Churchill and Roosevelt made their vague public statements that Friday, the two leaders presided at another meeting of the Combined Chiefs of Staff about the theatre that included India, Burma, and China. FDR strongly supported assisting China against the Japanese, a viewpoint the prime minister didn't as heartily espouse. Churchill was less inclined to devote forces and resources there, leading Lieutenant General Joseph Stilwell, the commander of U.S. forces in China, Burma, and India, to claim that the Chinese were suspicious of the British. Churchill didn't appreciate the airing of such an opinion nor did he think the charge was accurate. Stilwell, called "Vinegar Joe" for his abrasive personality and aversion to collegiality, didn't back down, pushing for more supplies shipped into China on a monthly basis.

A perturbed Churchill held his ground and pushed back against "the unfounded suspicions of the Chinese."[22] The two-hour meeting ended with disputes between the Americans and the British out in the open and with the request that the military advisors work on plans to assist the Chinese. To blunt Stilwell's accusation, Churchill made clear that British forces "were perfectly prepared to fight in true brotherhood with their Allies."[23] In a diary entry, General Alan Brooke took on Stilwell directly, calling him "a small man with no conception of strategy."[24] The chief of the Imperial General Staff subsequently amplified his opinion by lambasting Stilwell as "a Chinese linguist [with] little military knowledge and no strategic ability of any kind. His worst failing, however, was his deep rooted hatred of anybody or anything British!"[25] The illusion of "true brotherhood" among the English-speaking Allies was repeatedly tested during the Trident Conference.

Churchill and Roosevelt kept their distance from another joint session of their strong-willed advisors for the next five days, as they considered less controversial subjects and talked among themselves. The two leaders, in fact, took a completely different tack, escaping from the councils of war at the White House shortly after the stormy Friday meeting adjourned.

Instead of a weekend at Hyde Park, where Churchill had begun his previous trip to America, the president decided to take the prime minister to what had become since the previous summer his secret retreat in Maryland's Catoctin Mountains. Called by FDR "Shangri-La"—the mythical Himalayan paradise described in James Hilton's popular 1933 novel *Lost Horizon*—the presidential getaway was later renamed Camp David by President Eisenhower to honor his father and his grandson. Churchill became the first foreign dignitary Roosevelt brought to Shangri-La, where, according to the National Park Service, FDR spent sixty-four days during nineteen separate visits in 1942 and 1943.

In that pre-helicopter era, the party was driven the sixty-five miles northwest of the capital in an armored limousine. Recalling the trip, Churchill engaged in a contretemps with Eleanor Roosevelt over—of all things—the seating arrangement in the presidential vehicle. Mrs. Roosevelt chose for herself a small front seat to allow Churchill to sit next to FDR. "I would not have this," Churchill ventured, "and the

British Empire went into action."[26] The prime minister put his foot down and got his way with the First Lady shifting to her husband's side. The self-identified personification of "the British Empire"—an unusual characterization in itself—and America's First Lady frequently didn't see eye to eye. Their clashes tended to intrude on matters both substantive and insignificant, with words over etiquette or protocol sometimes disguising deeper differences, including how each viewed Britain's imperial and colonial ways.

En route to Shangri-La, Churchill's grasp of U.S. Civil War lore—knowledge he loved to flaunt—commandeered the conversation when the travelers passed through Frederick, Maryland. The setting of John Greenleaf Whittier's poem "Barbara Frietchie," Frederick served as an important crossroads for Union and Confederate troops. Once, according to the legend Whittier made popular in verse, a "rebel horde" marched through town and saw the American stars and stripes flying at the ninety-year-old woman's house. After a shot was fired by one of Stonewall Jackson's men:

> It shivered the window, pane and sash;
> It rent the banner with seam and gash.
>
> Quick, as it fell, from the broken staff
> Dame Barbara snatched the silken scarf;
>
> She leaned far out on the window-sill.
> And shook it forth with a royal will.
>
> "Shoot, if you must, this old gray head,
> But spare your country's flag," she said.

Churchill inquired about the house and proceeded to recite the poem from memory. In his memoir, he said nobody in the car corrected his imperfectly remembered lines or remarked that he made the poem's namesake twenty years younger than Whittier. Incredibly, indeed curiously, the misremembered lines appear in *The Hinge of Fate*, even though Churchill would have had easy access to Whittier's work when drafting his memoirs.[27]

C. R. Thompson, the prime minister's personal assistant traveling with him, noted that Churchill said "he hadn't read the ballad for at least forty years." Calling the rendition, even with the mistakes, "an extraordinary feat," Thompson remarked, ". . . Harry Hopkins talked about it for days. But Mr. Churchill's memory was phenomenal."[28] Prodigious recall notwithstanding, imprecision in remembering a once-famous poem pales in comparison to failing to remember his initial personal meetings with Roosevelt and Eisenhower, as previously discussed.

Following the interlude of patriotic verse, Churchill talked more generally about the Civil War by focusing on two prominent Confederate generals, Stonewall Jackson and Robert E. Lee—"two of the noblest men ever born on the American continent."[29] Lee, in particular, fascinated Churchill to the point that in 1930 he composed a counterfactual narrative for the American magazine *Scribner's* with the eyebrow-arching title "If Lee Had Not Won the Battle of Gettysburg." This fabulistic composition described how Lee's hypothetical victory resulted in the "Confederate States" achieving independence and troubled coexistence with the "Union." The bizarre scenario went on to outline how the "two Americas" joined with Britain to avert the Great War. Though fanciful throughout, Churchill's genuine admiration for Lee was clear, saying the Virginian was "an almost unique example of a regular and professional soldier who achieved the highest excellence both as a general and as a statesman."[30] Years after this fable appeared, Churchill returned to writing about Lee—heaping more praise on him—in the fourth volume of his *History of the English-Speaking Peoples* that was titled *The Great Democracies*.[31]

The sojourn at Shangri-La was primarily a holiday for the two leaders. FDR devoted some of the time to his prized stamp collection, his vicarious way of traveling the world and learning more about it.

The pair even tried their hands at fishing as they sat by a stream at the 125-acre retreat.

While the two leaders clandestinely enjoyed crisp spring air in the Maryland mountains—the fishing pictures show a less than sportively clad Churchill swaddled in a long overcoat and wearing a fedora—newspapers devoted acres of weekend space to the summit and its purported consequences. The press, though, confronted a substantial obstacle. Reporters remained completely in the dark about the substance of the discussions, especially the policy and planning differences.

"The News of the Week in Review" section of the *New York Times* on Sunday, May 16, displayed five pictures of Churchill and Roosevelt together: one for each of their meetings since 1941, with a photo from a few days earlier the dominant one. Writing the main dispatch about the conference, Arthur Krock, already a two-time winner of the Pulitzer Prize and the newspaper's principal Washington correspondent, noted in the opening paragraph that the prime minister's "pressing business is war, and war is what the President and he have been talking about." If that sounds imprecise, seven paragraphs into the article—and after references to Churchill's speech honoring the Home Guard—Krock confessed: "Outside the high confidential circle in which the talks between the President and Mr. Churchill are proceeding, no one knows anything in detail of what goes on." Though lacking insider intelligence, Krock composed seven additional paragraphs of suppositions and speculations. At one point he acknowledged that "the Pacific will remain in the secondary category of the whole war problem for the present," a welcome statement for the British to read, given their fervor for a Germany first policy.

On the editorial page of the *Times* the same day, Churchill was treated in a jocular fashion. In comparison to his last visit, night had brightened and sunnier prospects contributed to a more buoyant mood. The "Topics of the Times" column began with a lighthearted question: "Could it be that Winston Churchill came to Washington chiefly for the trip?" Worries of combat fade as the nearly four thousand-mile journey is described as something of a lark for "a portly, not to say stout

Prime Minister." From this perspective, Churchill's energy and courage place him at the center of strategic action: "He flies to Cairo to plan the finish for Rommel. He flies to Moscow to do his bit in planning the finish at Stalingrad. He braves the Atlantic to plan heaven knows what." The phrase "heaven knows what" telegraphed that genuine news about the conference eluded journalists who seem forced to interject wisecracks about Churchill's physique to enliven their commentary.

Interestingly, that Sunday's edition of the *Times* included a full-page advertisement that obliged readers to do a double take. Presented with headlines, articles, and a detailed map, the two-line, eight-column banner across the top in capital letters announced:

VISIT OF MR. CHURCHILL TO UNITED STATES OCCASIONS PLEA TO OPEN GATES OF PALESTINE TO SAVE EUROPEAN JEWS

A smaller headline beneath the large one above read:

MR. CHURCHILL, CHAMPION OF HUMANITY, ONE WORD FROM YOU NOW CAN SAVE THE LIVES OF UNTOLD THOUSANDS

Sponsored by the "Committee for a Jewish Army of Stateless and Palestinian Jews," the appeal contained statements from Churchill about Palestine becoming a "Hebrew Nation" and praised him "as an indomitable fighter" and an inspiration for "the gallant British people." At the time, Roosevelt was aware of Nazi atrocities in persecuting European Jews, but he was reluctant to act on proposals of assistance. The ad served as implicit criticism of the president—maybe some other world leader can help—and it provided information, in the exact style of a newspaper, about a human catastrophe that expanded and metastasized as the war ground on.[32]

With genuine news elusive while the leaders were away from the capital, reporters scrambled to develop stories bearing any relationship to the summit. Washington's *Sunday Star* published a human-interest feature about Phyllis Moir, Churchill's secretary during his 1932 U.S. lecture tour, who nearly a decade later wrote a highly publicized memoir about that experience. What she told the reporter left no doubt about her admiration—"Hours do not exist for him"; "His mind brims over with ideas"; "He is the hardest worker I ever saw"; "He listens to his own words like a composer to music." The stocky U.S. visitor, in her view, was a singular figure.

In different yet related ways, the ad in the *New York Times* and the interview with Moir reflected both the regard and curiosity Americans had for Churchill three years into the war. In newspaper lingo, he was good copy, and what the public saw often included the human element that Churchill liked to stress in projecting his persona. Being "at the summit of the United States" put him in the world's spotlight, and he knew it.

Despite all the attention Churchill received in the press, the weekend whereabouts of the two leaders remained secret, but what Eleanor Roosevelt told a New York audience shortly after the side trip must have displeased, if not worried, the Secret Service. Speaking at the College of the City of New York, she reported, according to the *New York Herald Tribune*, that she, FDR, and Churchill were driving "to a little place in the country . . . to pass the night." The prime minister inquired about antiaircraft protection, routine procedure for him in Britain. The president replied there wasn't any, adding, "It's hardly visible from the air. It's really just a camp."

Later in her remarks, Mrs. Roosevelt made a not-so-subtle critique of imperialism and the unnamed defender of the British Empire. "We cannot after the war, look down on any people, or race or religion," she said, "but must treat them all as human beings deserving of our respect. . . . We have imposed civilization upon them in the name of the white man's burden." What became a preoccupation of the First Lady was shared with the president. Notwithstanding Churchill's traditional and firmly rooted views, both Roosevelts were looking beyond "English-speaking peoples" in shaping the postwar world.

The prime minister and the president returned from Shangri-La for a White House lunch on Monday, May 17. Bernard M. Baruch, the well-known New York financier and presidential advisor, joined the prime minister and president—the three men were friends of long standing—for a discussion that also included the ever-present Hopkins. Years later, Baruch recalled a personal moment during the lunch, when Hopkins acted annoyed at Baruch's complaints about the pace of production for the war effort. As the successful investor turned counselor told it, FDR didn't find fault with the Baruch approach and even praised it: "Every time Bernie sticks his nose into anything, production increases." The president regarded Baruch as "the burr I stick under the tails of these boys" to get results.[33] The smiling, jovial politician realized the value of having a tough taskmaster, with a badgering propensity, in the trenches of war production.

Earlier in the war, Churchill had appointed Lord Beaverbrook (the influential newspaper publisher Max Aitken) to a succession of offices—minister of aircraft production, minister of supply, and minister of war production—and the Beaverbrook-style drew similar expressions of vituperation from those on the receiving end of his orders. Leadership often involved appointing less than diplomatic characters to make government work more efficiently. Though without portfolio in May 1943, Lord Beaverbrook traveled with the large British party to Washington and even spent the weekend at Shangri-La courtesy of Roosevelt's personal invitation. As with Hopkins for FDR, Beaverbrook, never a favorite of Clementine Churchill, qualified as both a friend and fixer for the prime minister. Hopkins and Beaverbrook suffered periodic exiles when the president or prime minister deemed distance preferable for either personal or political reasons.

After the lunch with Baruch, Churchill disappeared from FDR's calendar for the next two days, except for a three-person, hour-long conversation on Tuesday, May 18, with the Duke of Windsor, the former King Edward VIII, who abdicated in 1936 to marry the twice-divorced American socialite Wallis Simpson. Since 1940, he had served as royal governor of the Bahama Islands, and on this trip to Washington he planned to attend Churchill's second address in less than eighteen months to a joint session of Congress. The prime minister sequestered himself in the Rose Bedroom from the evening of May 17 through the morning of May 19. He had to prepare.

Working like a journalist with one eye on the clock, the prime minister began composing his speech late that Monday evening after he had dinner and watched the movie *Divide and Conquer*, the third documentary in Frank Capra's seven-part *Why We Fight* series. Churchill returned to his suite and announced to his secretary, Elizabeth Nel, that he needed to start on what he'd say at the Capitol and to a worldwide radio audience at noontime Wednesday. Nel, who was portrayed (in a less than factually accurate manner) in the 2017 film *Darkest Hour*, recalled that Churchill paced back and forth for hours with "his hands gesturing, his voice rising and falling." The process of dictated composition lasted until 2:30 a.m. At one point, while walking behind the secretary's chair, the prime minister abruptly changed from his dinner jacket to "his famous green and gold dressing-gown with the red dragons."[34] He was very much at home in the White House and working as he did back in Britain.

On Tuesday morning, May 18, Churchill invited Lord Halifax to come to the Rose Bedroom, where the ambassador found him working in bed, sharpening his speech for Congress. Halifax listened to what the prime minister planned to say and particularly liked "a good purple passage about the Japanese."[35] Unlike the talk honoring the Home Guard, the address to the joint session at the Capitol took much longer to write, revise, and practice. Churchill felt he had to provide a detailed report about the war, one that was both realistic and reassuring. Crafting the speech, which in its final form encompassed nearly 5,600 words, the prime minister knew he had to take on opponents of the Germany first strategy that he and Roosevelt initially endorsed nearly two years earlier.

Albert (Happy) Chandler, a Democratic senator from Kentucky

(who subsequently became a colorful and controversial commissioner of Major League Baseball), had emerged during Churchill's visit as an outspoken proponent of concentrating on defeating Japan before invading Europe. Previously a defender of the Roosevelt Administration's military policy, Chandler devoted a three-hour Senate speech to elevating the Pacific theatre over Europe just two days before the prime minister arrived at the Capitol. Influential on the Military Affairs Committee, Chandler was striving to change the policy as senators and representatives assembled to hear from the foreign dignitary, who was protected with such stringent security measures that Capitol Hill, according to one newspaper account, "looked like a fortress."

Never inclined to retreat from an argument, Churchill devoted his opening paragraphs to pressing for all-out combat to eclipse the Rising Sun as a belligerent. Bearding Chandler, he said, "Let no one suggest that we British have not at least as great an interest as the United States in the unflinching and relentless waging of war against Japan. And I am here to tell you that we will wage that war, side by side with you, in accordance with the best strategic employment of our forces, while there is breath in our bodies and while blood flows in our veins."[36] Both sentences prompted ovations, a common occurrence in the almost hour-long oration. The *Times* of London kept score and recorded cheering nineteen times, applause on five occasions, and laughter after eight statements.

Besides declaring the Allies' commitment to fighting Japan, Churchill tried to repair any ill will between Britain and China, as he'd heard earlier from Stilwell. "I regard the bringing of effective and immediate aid to China as one of the most urgent of our common tasks," the prime minister asserted. A few paragraphs later he stopped smoothing over disagreements he faced since arriving in Washington to hark back to the Allies' defining strategy: Germany's defeat first and then Japan.[37] The paunchy pugilist walked a tightrope of contending approaches by balancing statements to appeal to competing viewpoints. The warlord was also the savvy politician appearing before fellow vote-seekers who had definite ideas of their own. Decades of debate in the House of Commons provided transferable lessons.

With his critics assuaged, Churchill provided a *tour d'horizon* about the progress of battle—with victories, setbacks, and references to "Corporal Hitler" noted. He trumpeted Operation Chastise, the dam-busting RAF raids of Germany's Ruhr Valley that were carried out the night of May 16 into the early morning of May 17. The daring attacks by Lancaster bombers were front-page news one day before the speech to Congress, providing a boost in Allied morale on both sides of the Atlantic.

Churchill also applauded the success of the campaign in Africa and recalled the pain of Tobruk the last time he visited Washington, noting "the kindness and the wealth of comradeship which our American friends showed" amid such adversity.[38] As noted in the previous chapter, he mentioned that "the President handed me a slip of paper" about the fall but doesn't explain what the president might—or might not—have said at the time. If FDR's six comforting words of help were so meaningful, repeating them in the Capitol would seem strategically and politically prudent. Indeed, Roosevelt's name wasn't mentioned. Did he fear accusations of foreign involvement or interfering in American domestic politics?

Near the end of his address—the entire text appears in the appendix—Churchill assumed the mantle of the historian by discussing a central lesson of the U.S. Civil War and its possible meaning to the global conflict then being waged. Like Eleanor Roosevelt, he talked of a recent trip outside Washington "not far from the field of Gettysburg, which I know well, like most of your battlefields." Churchill explained that the Battle of Gettysburg in 1863 was a decisive battle, a turning point, but savage fighting continued for a long time. Lee didn't surrender to General Ulysses S. Grant until April 9, 1865, almost two years later. In other words, victory wasn't imminent, overconfidence was a danger, and the Allies needed "to search our hearts and brace our sinews and take the most earnest counsel, one with another, in order that the favourable position which has already been reached both against Japan and against Hitler and Mussolini in Europe shall not be let slip."[39] Shrewdly, Japan is placed before Europe in the order of enemies and the country itself is cited rather than the surnames of Axis leaders. Oratory, too, can often be strategic.

Churchill's speech was broadcast on all four national radio networks—CBS, NBC, Mutual, and Blue—with CBS counting its audience at being over fourteen million listeners. In New York City, twelve different stations carried the address. For its coverage, the *Chicago Daily Tribune* displayed little restraint with a boldface page-one headline:

**PULVERIZE JAPS
AFTER HITLER:
CHURCHILL VOW**

Surprisingly, for a newspaper well-known for promoting isolationism, vilifying Roosevelt, and scorning the British, the reporting more closely resembled a confection of public relations from the British Information Service than a usual *Tribune* dispatch. The article-cum-encomium began by describing how "the prime minister came to the joint session as he frequently has confronted a hostile opposition in his own parliament—and carried the day" before stating that the "performance throughout measured up to the most redoubtable exploits of the man who has made himself the dominating figure on the allied side."

Colonel Robert McCormick's crusading *Tribune* wasn't alone in recognizing the merits of Churchill's address. Members of Congress told reporters that the disquisition gave them confidence in the strategy of the United Nations, with one senator—Burnet Maybank of South Carolina—judging that he'd just heard "the greatest speech ever delivered before Congress," according to the *Times* of London. The next day, Roosevelt told the Pacific War Council he considered the address "the clearest and best exposition of global war that has ever been given."[40]

After his speech, Churchill continued his one-on-one campaign to shore up Congressional support for the war cause by attending a luncheon in the Capitol for legislative leaders as well as key members of the Senate Foreign Relations Committee and the House Foreign Affairs Committee. The prime minister answered questions for nearly an hour, though none was posed by Chandler. He, deliberately, hadn't been invited. The next time Churchill came to Capitol Hill to deliver his third address to Congress (on January 17, 1952), Vice President Alben Barkley told the prime minister that as Senate majority leader in 1943 he had called Roosevelt to see about arranging the lunch. According to Barkley, FDR "let out a whoop that practically shattered my eardrums, and said: 'For heaven's sakes, do! Give him a glass of scotch and a good lunch, and, while you're entertaining him, I will get rid of some desk work.' "[41]

Whether Churchill actually ate or drank at the Congressional lunch is unknown, but the president's secretary, Grace Tully, recalled what happened at the White House as soon as Churchill returned to 1600 Pennsylvania Avenue. Tully and Roosevelt had listened together to the speech on the radio, and the president was enthusiastic in welcoming the prime minister for the second lunch he was given that afternoon. As he settled down with the president, she noticed Churchill seemed fidgety and immediately guessed he was wondering when FDR "would get around to offering him a much needed stimulant." After a few awkward moments, the British leader took the initiative of asking for an adult beverage, and Roosevelt, who avoided alcohol at lunch, apologized for his inattentive faux pas.[42]

Churchill was sixty-eight-years-old in May 1943, but keeping a full day's schedule—as long as he could quench his thirst along the way—didn't overtax his constitution. That Wednesday morning he revised his speech in the morning, delivered it early in the afternoon, and returned to talk with FDR. Late in the afternoon, no doubt after his quotidian nap, he and the president participated in a meeting with Canadian prime minister Mackenzie King, who had arrived at the White House the morning of the speech and stayed the night. Churchill told King that enroute to the Capitol Hill he felt like the Dickens character Sydney Carton in *A Tale of Two Cities* prior to his execution, an odd analogy for someone with no shortage of self-confidence.[43] The last afternoon activity on Churchill's agenda for May 19 was almost as important as his address to Congress. The prime minister and the president convened another (and critical) meeting involving the Combined Chiefs of Staff before they had dinner. They then took part in another discussion with King that started at 11:40 p.m. and continued past 1 a.m. A long day, to be sure.

At the parley of the Combined Chiefs, the military leaders on both sides wrangled over war strategy and the next moves to initiate after the North Africa campaign, which had ended six days earlier with the surrender of Axis forces in Tunisia. While the Americans, led by Marshall, pushed to prepare for a cross-Channel invasion, the British favored more of a cross-Mediterranean campaign—transporting troops and equipment from North Africa for an invasion of Italy. Several hours of going back-and-forth yielded a victory for each side: twenty-nine divisions were to be earmarked—in Brooke's phrase—"for entry into France early in 1944" and there would also be "a continuance of pressure against Italy."[44] Both Allies had fought on behalf of their positions and came away with a strategic trophy they wanted.

At the meeting, Churchill told the group he was pleased with the approval of the cross-Channel operation, adding that he had always favored this action to create a second front in Europe but delays kept occurring.[45] This assertion, recorded in the official minutes, contorted candor. Churchill's support of what came to be known as Operation Overlord, including D-Day on June 6, 1944, evolved over time, though he kept making statements indicating his approval whenever Americans raised the subject. Words came easily to the prime minister, but deciding exactly what to do—as opposed to talking about it—proved difficult for him. Doubts whether a cross-Channel invasion would be successful haunted him and his thinking.

Canadian prime minister King became privy to Churchill's apprehension during conversations the two had in the White House both before and after the address to Congress. According to King's recollection, Churchill foresaw catastrophic problems with the proposed operation in western France. He worried that the Allies would suffer a similar fate they experienced at Dieppe in northern France on August 19, 1942, when over half the landing force of six thousand became casualties or prisoners in the first hours of battle.[46] Even at the White House dinner after the cross-Channel decision was made on May 19, Roosevelt brought up the U.S. troops assembling in Britain and what they'd face during an invasion of western France. King noted Churchill's qualms in his diary, stating the prime minister "used a very significant expression when reference was made to crossing from Britain—that sooner or later, we all have to die."[47]

Besides Dieppe, Churchill was tormented by the disastrous Gallipoli campaign during the Great War, when, as first lord of the admiralty, he pushed for a second front to eliminate the Ottoman Empire from battle. He hoped this action would secure a naval route for the British to join their ally, Russia. However, as deaths and casualties mounted—nearly sixty thousand Allied forces died—Churchill became the failure's scapegoat and left the Admiralty. For decades afterward he couldn't escape the dark cloud of Gallipoli, and its shadow followed him to every government office he occupied. Avoiding the recurrence of such a debacle concentrated his mind.

Until the military commanders and their political superiors ultimately approved the specific dimensions of Overlord, Churchill found ways to drag his feet and to dodge a final decision. In postwar years, however, he fought to erase criticism that he stood in the way of the operation Americans thought necessary. Preparing for his first White House conference after Pearl Harbor, he recalled that he "always considered that a decisive assault upon the German-occupied countries on the largest possible scale was the only way in which the war could be won, and that the summer of 1943 should be chosen as the target date." The thin-skinned Churchill attacked insider accounts promoting the "false assumption" of his opposition.[48] After the war was won and he had endured repeated accusations of his reluctance, Churchill fought back using his most potent personal weapon: the English language.

During this May visit, Churchill participated in another gathering of the Pacific War Council. Similar to the one the year before, the proceedings on May 20 focused on reports about the war's progress for representatives from eight of the United Nations engaged in Pacific operations. But, unlike the June 1942 gathering with Tobruk's fall dampening spirits of those assembled, the mood in 1943 was realistic yet confident.

At one point, T. V. Soong, China's bespectacled foreign minister and brother of Madame Chiang Kai-shek, tangled directly with Churchill about the combat ability of British forces in the different theatres of war. He inquired with his elbows out: "How can the Englishmen, who were so feeble in their conduct of the war in Malaya, fight such magnificent battles as they have fought in Africa?"[49] The prime minister vigorously pushed back, complaining that he didn't think someone from an Allied country should meddle in day-to-day staffing selections and related matters. While FDR repeatedly sided with China during the war, Churchill was developing a different reputation vis-à-vis the Chinese, and it was being openly challenged.

With high-level officials from the British Commonwealth on hand for the Pacific War Council, Churchill convened a session of the Dominion countries. King had pushed for explicitly identifying the Dominions—Canada, Australia, New Zealand, South Africa, and India—by name in the speech to Congress; however, Churchill was firm that when he said "we" he meant the United Kingdom and the United States. Although the prime minister spoke for nearly an hour, only about five minutes were unfamiliar to the participants, prompting Lord Halifax to aver: "I never saw anybody who loves the sound of words, and his own words, more."[50]

Halifax rarely missed a chance to take a dig at someone he often viewed in uncomplimentary ways. In fact, after listening to the prime minister's reports to the War Council and the Dominions, the ambassador found himself playing host to a social gathering Churchill orchestrated to please Hopkins. The *soirée* included dinner at the British embassy and—believe it or not—a fashion show choreographed by Hopkins's wife, Louise, a former editor at *Harper's Bazaar*. Churchill wanted to return home, where clothes had been subject to rationing since 1941, with contemporary American fashions for his wife and daughters, a chivalrous act he initiated during an earlier visit to Washington. Modeling Yankee couture continued well into the evening, allowing Halifax to take another swipe at his favorite target: "I saw no reason why it should ever end, and it did not in fact end until 1.30. a.m."[51] For FDR, not having to entertain his White House guest gave him a night off. According to his calendar, he ate dinner alone in his study and retired at 9:10 p.m.

Except for a quick lunch on May 21, Churchill and Roosevelt kept to themselves on Friday. Late in the day, they formally met with their chiefs of staff to review a draft outlining the decisions the military advisors made. The prime minister and the president interrogated the officers on the use of the Azores Islands, the bomber offensive from the United Kingdom, defeating the Axis powers in France, the Burma-China theatre, and future Pacific operations. Near the end of the discussion about European combat, Churchill made clear there needed to be "a new code word to cover post-Husky operations."[52]

"Husky" was the codename of the Allies to refer to the planned invasion of Sicily. That operation began seven weeks later on July 9, again with Eisenhower in command. Both war leader and wordsmith, Churchill was looking ahead to future battles and to giving them appropriate names. In his opinion, codenames needed to be vivid and strong, and in one instance he took grave exception to what was proposed to be "Operation Soapsuds" for a bombing mission. His purview encompassed the big picture as well as individual brushstrokes.

Throughout this session, the fourth of six that brought together the two leaders and their military brass, the uniformed commanders kept their focus on specific plans for battles and operations. Resolving the thorny issues of those plans almost brought the Allies to blows, as the two sides argued their cases for doing—or not doing—certain operations. Brooke worried that Churchill or Roosevelt would disagree with the joint planning "and reopen some of the differences which we had reconciled with such difficulty!"[53] That didn't happen, and the war-within-the-war reached a temporary, hard-fought truce.

After returning from Shangri-La, Churchill told King he planned to spend the next weekend resting in his comfortably air-conditioned surroundings of the Rose Bedroom. By the end of the week, however, he'd changed his mind and decided to move to the British embassy to cultivate closer relationships with influential Americans. Given that he wanted to bring together U.S. government officials and those prominent in other Washington circles, he undoubtedly thought it more fitting to conduct such sessions away from the White House.

On that Friday night, Lord Halifax, as nominal host, brought together such figures as Supreme Court Chief Justice Harlan Stone, who had been on the high court since 1925 and became Roosevelt's choice to lead it in 1941; Director of Economic Stabilization James Byrnes, who spent a quarter-century in the House and Senate before receiving three major, rapid-fire appointments from FDR, and Eugene Meyer, a financier and also the publisher of the *Washington Post*. As could be predicted, Halifax complained that the discussion among a dozen or so lasted until 1:30 a.m.—"These habits are paralyzing to me"—but noted the value of the occasion. Churchill made clear "the impossibility of isolationism" as well as the importance of the president involving representatives of both parties at any postwar peace conference. Domestic politics also entered the discussion, as the assembled Americans "seemed completely confident that the President would stand and win for the Fourth Term."[54]

Once FDR successfully challenged the two-term precedent George Washington established in the eighteenth century, the door opened to extending executive service even longer. What Churchill had been told in March of 1943 was now common knowledge in the capital.[55]

The next day, the parade of Americans to the British embassy continued, with Churchill making his case to cabinet officials, senators, and House members. If he had wanted a quiet weekend at leisure, this wasn't it, as he dedicated hour after hour to talking about the war and how he saw the postwar world taking shape. At one point, when meeting with legislators, he compared how he felt a year ago to his sunnier outlook in 1943. Churchill told the group that when Tobruk fell "he had been the most miserable Englishman in America since [General John] Burgoyne surrendered at Saratoga" during the Revolutionary War.[56] The prime minister understood his reference would resonate with his audience and dramatize the considerable difference in the war's progress from one spring to the next.

On Sunday, while still at the embassy, he again spent time with prominent Americans—including his friend Bernard Baruch and William (Wild Bill) Donovan, the director of the Office of Strategic Services, which later became the Central Intelligence Agency. At lunch, Churchill returned to an idea he raised at the lunch the day before and that would, as time passed, animate his thinking about the relationship between the United Kingdom and the United States. The two-word phrase he kept using then to describe what he was proposing was "fraternal association." Churchill discussed several aspects of a postwar world before sketching out his vision for a new confederacy between the British Commonwealth and the United States. It was almost as though he was using his own heritage—the son of a British father and an American mother—to propose a working relationship beyond two-nation camaraderie. Halifax summarized Churchill's recommendation by noting, "He could see small hope for the world unless the United States and the British Commonwealth worked together in what he would call fraternal association."[57]

As Churchill talked, he went so far as to bring up specific ways of formalizing the association, including a common passport or some form of common citizenship. Voting privileges? Possibly after a period of residency. Even being "eligible for public office in the territories of the other" wouldn't be out of the question.[58] In future months and years, Churchill repeatedly returned to this idea of fostering greater interconnection between "English-speaking peoples," especially between British subjects and American citizens. This recommendation, in fact, became the thematic thrust of a lecture he delivered at Harvard University a few months later in 1943 and is discussed in the next chapter. Eleanor Roosevelt took umbrage at such a limited, single-language association; however, the prime minister saw the world after combat as one led by a fraternity made up of the United States, the United Kingdom, and the British Commonwealth. The British Empire might be in decline, but working together with America he imagined a new form of global leadership that still recognized Britain's role and influence.

At the same time Churchill was visiting Washington in May of 1943 and occasionally recalling the calamity of Tobruk, Hollywood was distributing a feature film that used the British capitulation in the desert as the springboard to a war story of recovery—and triumph. After the battlefield successes in North Africa, Billy Wilder cowrote and directed *Five Graves to Cairo* that put Erwin Rommel, the once-acclaimed Desert Fox, in the bull's eye of the German military's reversals in Africa. Wilder, who began his film career in Berlin before emigrating to the United States to escape Nazism, based his action on a fictional British survivor of Tobruk, who took on Rommel and his compatriots through a convoluted set of circumstances.

At one point in what's now considered a classic World War II drama, Rommel—played by legendary cineaste Erich von Stroheim—brags, "We should take that big fat cigar out of Churchill's mouth and make him say heil five times." In the context of the war's momentum, the line is less a belligerent threat than a laugh-producing pronouncement. By the time of the movie's release, Rommel had escaped from Africa, and a May 23 headline in the *New York Herald Tribune* reported "Rommel Myth Collapse Is Major Allied Victory." To moviegoers in America and Britain, Rommel was no longer invincible, and Tobruk, regardless of what actually happened, could be viewed differently.

At the same time that Churchill was meeting with a succession of Americans at the embassy, Roosevelt deserted Washington, his guest, and the conference to spend much of Saturday and Sunday relaxing at his retreat in the Maryland mountains, which was much closer than going all the way to Hyde Park. He arrived back at the White House a little after 10 p.m. on Sunday, May 23, and Churchill must have had someone, possibly Hopkins, inform him of FDR's return. Halifax recorded that the prime minister left the embassy at 11—"and no doubt kept the President instead of me up till 1.30."[59]

The ambassador's cheeky remark was inaccurate, and the next day's *Evening Star* published this front-page headline with the honest truth:

PRESIDENT AND CHURCHILL CONFER UNTIL 2:30 A.M.

FDR's press secretary Stephen Early provided the report's specific information, noting that the prime minister spent the weekend at the embassy without revealing where Roosevelt had been. The *Evening Star* article disclosed that plans for the war's future were finalized by the military advisors and presented to the two leaders "for study." How much actual "study" occurred during the late-night conversation is unknown.

Churchill and Roosevelt were constantly together during the next two days, as they worked to conclude the Trident Conference and set policy for the war's next operations. A luncheon meeting on May 24 focused on atomic energy and the development of the atomic bomb. That discussion included Vice President Henry Wallace, the highest-ranking American official, besides the president, monitoring work on atomic energy, and Frederick Lindeman (Lord Cherwell), an Oxford don and Churchill's chief science advisor On his trips to meet with Roosevelt, Churchill kept asking about the status of the research and testing taking place in the United States. This particular meeting—on FDR's calendar the stated subject is "Post-War Topics"—lasted over two hours.

Wallace was the second of three vice presidents elected with Roosevelt as the Democratic standard-bearer. A two-term secretary of agriculture, Wallace succeeded John Nance Garner for the 1940 campaign and then was himself replaced on FDR's ticket in 1944 by Harry Truman, a senator from Missouri since 1935. During his three months as vice president, Truman was never briefed about the military implications of the secret experiments involved in the Manhattan Project. Remarkably, when he became president April 12, 1945, the British prime minister and his longtime friend from Oxford, referred to as "the Prof," knew more than Roosevelt's successor about the capability of this devastating weaponry.

The fifth meeting of the political leaders and their military chiefs began after the session devoted to atomic energy. Churchill and Roosevelt worked methodically through the report submitted by the generals and admirals, stopping at individual sections for clarification or comment. The status of the Azores, specifics of the cross-Channel assault, elimination of Italy from the war, bombing Axis oil refineries near Ploiesti, Romania, and proposed actions in the Burma-China theatre, all received detailed scrutiny. Churchill spoke twenty-one times and Roosevelt thirteen times during the meeting.

As the group discussed the invasion of Europe through western France, FDR interjected a political dimension: What about having a French division as part of the Allied landing in France? Churchill responded that General Charles de Gaulle, then the leader of the London-based Free French Forces, and General Henri Giraud, the civilian and military commander in chief in North Africa, were competing for primacy as opponents of the Nazi-collaborating Vichy government in France. Though Roosevelt never liked de Gaulle—and de Gaulle knew it—the president was sensitive to the symbolism of the French participating in the planned invasion from the start. Since de Gaulle lived in London from 1940 until the liberation of Paris in late August of 1944, Churchill had regular encounters with him and learned how difficult his self-absorption, along with his devotion to his native land, could be. Still, despite their personal feelings, political considerations deserved attention in planning an operation on French soil.

Near the end of the meeting, after the prime minister and the president said they agreed with the various conclusions of the document, Churchill balked at giving his approval. He wanted to learn more about the plans for Mediterranean operations after the invasion of Sicily, slated to begin six weeks later, and also how the information about Burma would be transmitted to the Chinese. The prime minister pushed to take up these subjects when the two sides gathered again the next morning. He'd never be mistaken for a rubber stamp.

Even though the joint, multi-person meeting didn't adjourn until shortly before 7 o'clock, the summitry didn't end with the arrival of dusk. At midnight, according to the president's schedule, FDR began a two-hour discussion with Churchill, Ismay, Hopkins, and Harriman before retiring at 2:10 a.m. Were the Allies at odds? Perhaps America's growing military capacity was making Roosevelt more confident in his power as commander in chief and less willing, as in the past, to follow Churchill's lead.

A key area of difference between the prime minister and the president concerned where their forces would fight after Sicily. In his memoir, Churchill claimed that Roosevelt hadn't directed the War Department "to become more precise on the invasion of Italy, but as this was the main purpose for which I had crossed the Atlantic I could not let the matter rest."[60] The wording reflected a certain restrained tension, but the reality was different. In bulldog fashion, Churchill kept pushing for invading the European continent from the South, while the Americans, most notably Marshall, thought the cross-Channel operation deserved primacy in the planning.

Secretary of War Stimson learned of the "debate between the President and the Prime Minister," commenting that Churchill "was as obstinate as a little Dutchman and fought to the end and finally said, 'Well, I will give up my part of this if you will let me have George Marshall to go for a trip to Africa.'" As he had in June of 1942, Stimson became incensed at Churchill. He figured out what was afoot: the British leader was campaigning to get his way and wanted to persuade Marshall to his approach. Stimson's anger and frustration boiled over to include Roosevelt: "nobody has any say and Marshall is going to pack up his bag tonight and start on his hard trip tomorrow morning."[61]

Both strong-willed and tough-minded, Churchill and Roosevelt fought their corners and at times couldn't resolve disputes. Churchill's "grand alliance" wasn't always a harmonious one, despite the bonhomie on display whenever the pair appeared in public and in front of cameras. Years later, when Churchill composed his multivolume remembrance of World War II, most conflict among the victorious Allies received subordinate, even *sotto voce*, treatment when compared to what he said about the Axis enemies.

Recalling his May visit of 1943, Churchill commented: "The fact that the President and I had been living side by side seeing each other at all hours, that we were known to be in close agreement, and that the President intended to decide himself on the ultimate issues . . . exercised throughout a mollifying and also a dominating influence on the course of Staff discussions."[62] With that sentence, Churchill gave preeminence to Roosevelt, which he had consistently done. The phrases—"living side by side" and "known to be in close agreement"—sought to convey a cozy camaraderie for war decision-making and avoidance of most clashes over policy and strategy. Of course, Churchill's retrospective narrative didn't appear until well after Roosevelt's death, when resurrecting past quarrels would do nothing to advance his notion of a "fraternal association."

The final full day of the Trident Conference, which followed the long midnight session, combined group meetings and a much-requested appearance by Churchill to answer questions from the White House press corps. Brooke complained that the prime minister wanted a change in the agreement between the United Kingdom and the United States that he thought "would have crashed the whole discussion" and wrecked Trident's outcome. Luckily, as often happened, Hopkins played the out-of-public-view *deus ex machina*, intervening to resolve the matter and calm the waters through "wording which only altered details and none of the principles."[63] Brooke, however, wasn't the only British critic of the prime minister's Washington sojourn. Near the end of the long conference, Oliver Harvey of the Foreign Office tartly said about Churchill, "It is high time the old man came home. The American atmosphere, the dictatorial powers of the President and the adulation which surrounds him there, have gone to his head."[64] The comment is telling. Is it any wonder why Churchill kept wanting to cross the Atlantic to take up residence in the Rose Bedroom?

Once the leaders and their military aides agreed on the final report, Roosevelt hosted a White House luncheon for the British and American teams. Lord Halifax sat next to the president, learning that "the big American circus people" informed FDR that "if they could get Mussolini to take on show with their circus, they would pay $500,000 a month for it" and make money with the act.[65] Why the president of the United States would have been talking to circus people during the war seems bizarre, but the anecdote is amusing in evoking the strutting, jaw-out "Il Duce" and his potential big-tent appeal across the United States.

At their news conference late that Tuesday afternoon, the president played ringmaster, with the prime minister the featured act. In the transcript of the exchanges between the reporters and the prime minister, the words "laughter," "loud laughter," "much laughter," or "more laughter" appeared almost two dozen times. Though rare in Britain at the time, Churchill knew the significance of news conferences in America, especially to Roosevelt, so he played to the fourth estate with American references and gag lines. Early on, he repeated his quip that during his last White House visit he felt like General Burgoyne at Saratoga. Later, he quoted a Confederate general of the Civil War as saying, "We got there firstest with the mostest." At the end of the session, the prime minister thanked the journalists before climbing onto his chair and flashing his trademark "V for victory" sign.[66] Each time Churchill had met the Washington press (in 1941 and now in 1943), the somewhat less than acrobatic sexagenarian mounted a chair for comic effect, ingratiating himself to a group he wanted to cultivate. Like FDR, Churchill—who devoured newspapers wherever he went—understood it meant more to appear in news columns and on the front page than inside, where the editorials and commentary amplified opinions often at odds with the president or the prime minister.

Although the conference, had, in effect, concluded, the two leaders didn't want to telegraph to the world that Churchill would soon be leaving the White House on yet another dangerous transatlantic trip. Maintaining secrecy and exercising deception came naturally to both men. Roosevelt's last words to the press were intended to keep everyone guessing: "Don't get the idea that the conferences are concluded. They are not. They are continuing." Churchill immediately chimed in: "We have a lot of ground to cover."[67]

A few hours later, Churchill, Roosevelt, and Hopkins met over dinner, as they had twice before at the end of earlier visits, to discuss a joint message to be sent to Stalin and how to handle the exchange of information on the research about "Tube Alloys" or the atomic bomb. For the second time in two days, the top-secret Manhattan Project, which had begun the summer before, received attention at the highest level, with Churchill working aggressively to keep Britain a partner and player in designing nuclear armaments. Sophisticated weaponry had fascinated him since before the Great War.

Three evenings in a row Churchill and Roosevelt talked long into the night—until 2 a.m. or so on May 24, May 25, and May 26. Yet, still, before 8 o'clock the morning of May 26, the president accompanied Churchill to his Boeing flying boat for its takeoff from the Potomac River. The prime minister's party, including Marshall, headed first to Newfoundland, then Gibraltar, and finally Algiers for meetings with Eisenhower and others about the invasion of Sicily and what Churchill hoped would be the location of the next major assault: Italy. He'd kept up his own fight for an assault on Europe from the south.

When the prime minister was nearly four thousand miles away from U.S. shores, the White House released a one-sentence statement about Trident: "The recent conference of the Combined Staffs in Washington has ended in complete agreement on future operations in all theatres of the war."[68] Three different drafts of detailed "communiqués" had been prepared, but at their last meeting Churchill and Roosevelt decided that a succinct explanation, trumpeting "complete agreement" throughout "all theatres," would be better than going into specifics, and they, of course, wanted to avoid any mention of discord. Roosevelt sent Eisenhower a copy of the statement to deliver to Churchill and appended a personal note to it that, in part, said, "I miss you much. It was a highly successful meeting in every way and proved that it was well timed and necessary."[69]

Roosevelt's personal sentiment—"I miss you much"—was intriguing when compared to what Stimson wrote on May 27, the day the message was sent. That afternoon the secretary of war went to the White House for a meeting with the president. Discussing the just-ended conference, Roosevelt commented "that Churchill had acted like a spoiled boy the last morning," as he argued one point. Stimson said the prime minister "persisted and persisted until Roosevelt told him . . . that he had better shut up."[70] Stimson applauded FDR for being persistent himself. Was Roosevelt being sincere in his recorded exasperation, or was he making an important cabinet member, often at odds with the prime minister, think differently (and better) about the president's toughness? Was the "spoiled boy" routine becoming tiresome to FDR? Five hours after this meeting, the president left for Hyde Park and a five-day respite without a single appointment or meeting on his schedule.

In his journal focusing on that day and Roosevelt's escape from Washington, William Hassett, the assistant secretary to the president, observed that the visitor, who arrived on May 11 and didn't depart until May 26, was "a trying guest—drinks like a fish and smokes like a chimney, irregular routine, works nights, sleeps days, turns the clock upside down." This assessment is much different and more negative than how Hassett saw the visitor previously. While at Hyde Park, he recorded that Roosevelt slept ten hours each evening four straight nights.[71]

On his flight across the Atlantic, Churchill composed a wide-ranging, six-page letter to his wife, Clementine, that demonstrated spousal frankness. He reported that Roosevelt refused to tell his wife anything he considered secret "because she is always making speeches and writing articles and he is afraid she might forget what was secret and what was not." He judged that his "friendship with the President was vastly stimulated" during the stay, and he even advised FDR to deliver speeches like the one he had to the joint session of Congress—"but I was very careful not to presume outside my proper sphere."[72]

Missing from Churchill's chatty letter, with its modestly critical treatment of the president, is any hint of a judgment about Roosevelt that the prime minister's doctor, Sir Charles Wilson, who became Lord Moran in early March of 1943, recorded. On May 25, the last day of Trident, Moran wrote that he went to the Rose Bedroom and—according to this account—found his patient pacing the floor until he stopped "and said abruptly, 'Have you noticed that the President is a very tired man? His mind seems closed; he seems to have lost his wonderful elasticity.'"[73] Is the quotation accurate? Was Churchill beginning to sense—or even see—Roosevelt's physical decline, which became much more noticeable as months passed? Or could it have been that the president was becoming weary of Churchill's behavior after their fifth extended war conference? For whatever reason, Churchill discerned a difference that might alter their relationship.

Churchill spent a week in the Mediterranean region before returning to London on Saturday, June 5—a full month after he departed for America. Almost immediately upon arrival, he assembled the War Cabinet at 10 Downing Street to report about the Washington conference and the tour of North Africa. While the letter to his wife emphasized personal dimensions of his White House stay, including the happy benefit of his "specially cooled room" during a late-spring hot spell, what he said to his government colleagues focused on combat strategy and broader policy objectives. He emphasized the value of joint-country conferences in nurturing "the harmony of Anglo-American co-operation."[74] Churchill acknowledged disagreements between the staffs before reporting that "personal contact" helped to resolve the differing, often strongly held viewpoints.

In addition, Churchill stressed that he considered it necessary to take on Italy and to secure a foothold in Europe there. He wouldn't surrender on his southern strategy. At every turn, Americans registered their criticism, but the prime minister explained how he conducted his campaign for approval by going directly to North Africa and taking Marshall with him for meetings with Eisenhower. Another long, dangerous trip had paid off, arguing that the U.S. Army chief of staff "seemed likely [to] return to the United States a convinced supporter of the projected operations in this theatre."[75]

With face-to-face jawboning, the force of his personality, and clever scheming, Churchill made his case repeatedly to those who questioned and, in some cases, opposed his thinking. A little over a month after Churchill arrived safely back in London, Operation Husky began, with Sicily falling to the Allies six weeks later on August 17. By then, however, the prime minister had made yet another transatlantic trip, taking him back not only to the Rose Bedroom at 1600 Pennsylvania Avenue but also to the Roosevelt estate at Hyde Park not once but twice. And, for the first time, this journey would be a family adventure—with Churchill treating the White House even more like his own home.

– 4 –

FORWARD TOWARD VICTORY

Winston Churchill's second visit to America in less than three months—1943 was the only year during the war when he made two transatlantic round trips—enhanced his stature, especially in the United States, as the most conspicuous Allied leader. Lionhearted and adventurous, traits in abundance since youth, he dramatized himself to the world as both war strategist and man of action. When he judged his involvement could bolster battlefield objectives or the larger cause of freedom, he—unlike Franklin Roosevelt or Joseph Stalin—didn't hesitate to strike out on secret missions by ship, plane, or train. Remarkably, between January 12, 1943, and January 18, 1944, Churchill traveled outside Great Britain 171 days, including a full month at the White House and Hyde Park.

A principal reason for Churchill's return to North America was the first Quebec conference, assigned the codename "Quadrant," that August. A second Quebec conference took place almost exactly a year later. On this trip, similar to earlier ones, Churchill came prepared—with detailed memorandums and an entourage even larger than the one in May: an official party of 238 persons.[1] Unlike previous wartime journeys and a sign that security for travelers was less of a worry, this trip involved other members of the Churchill family: his wife, Clementine, and his youngest daughter, Mary, who as a subaltern (or junior officer) of the British Auxiliary Territorial Service was serving as the prime minister's aide-de-camp. Still, as in May, a small flotilla of military ships, including an aircraft carrier, guarded the passenger liner *Queen Mary* across the Atlantic.

The Churchills, along with their retinue, sailed clandestinely from the River Clyde in Scotland on August 5, arriving at Halifax in Nova Scotia on August 9. The next day—and after about twenty-four hours on a private train—Britain's war leadership reached Quebec City for deliberations at the Citadel, the oldest military building in Canada, and the Chateau Frontenac Hotel. Though the main focus of the trip, the conference—the third of six that brought Churchill and Roosevelt together that year—competed with other meetings and events south of the Canadian border.

Right from the start, the two leaders and their advisors faced several daunting questions. When should the assault of Nazi-occupied Europe begin, and where was the most advantageous place for such an invasion? Who would command such an attack? How many forces and resources did the Pacific-Asian Theater need to defeat the expansion-obsessed Empire of Japan? The complexities behind each question (and a multitude of other ones) meant teams of officers and aides were assigned to come up with preparatory studies and plans.

As he'd done twice before, Averell Harriman, the London-based U.S. emissary, accompanied Churchill on the Atlantic voyage. He continued his practice of jotting down detailed notes after their conversations during meals or playing the card game bezique. Early in the voyage, Harriman observed that the prime minister's "mind is always on the war. Out of a clear sky Friday night [August 6] he said the single sentence 'We are going to win this war.'"[2]

The next day, according to Harriman, Churchill complained that relations with Stalin were becoming more frustrating, stating that the Soviet leader wasn't responding to cables. That irritation persisted and grew during the trip, with the president's chief European expediter monitoring the changes in mood. On August 24 at Quebec, when

Stalin informed Churchill and Roosevelt that he wanted more participation in decision-making, the two Allied leaders expressed joint annoyance, particularly since "Uncle Jo" (Harriman's spelling) hadn't bothered replying to earlier messages. Roosevelt admitted he was "mad," but Churchill went further with a reaction he confided to Harriman that he "foresaw 'bloody consequences in the future' (using 'bloody' in the literal sense). 'Stalin is an unnatural man. There will be grave troubles.'"[3] Almost a year earlier, Churchill had traveled to Moscow to meet with Stalin. A fervent critic of Bolshevism and communism for decades, the British leader understood that an ally in war against a mutual enemy could, given different circumstances, reverse course and become an adversary when hostilities ended.

Shortly after Churchill arrived at the Citadel, the main site of Quadrant, he telegraphed FDR and used the name "Warden" that he often assumed for security reasons on overseas missions: "The Warden family are looking forward keenly to their visit to Hyde Park where we propose to arrive the afternoon of the 12th. Are we right in thinking we should all bring our thinnest clothes?"[4] At six on the evening of August 11, Churchill and daughter Mary—Clementine stayed behind in Quebec to rest after the ocean crossing—climbed back on the train for another full day of rail travel to Roosevelt's estate in the Hudson Valley. Exact times for each trip during his thirty-seven-day stay in North America aren't recorded, but a tally using available sources in the National Archives of the United Kingdom and press reports show that the prime minister spent about 160 hours, nearly an entire week, going from place to place on a schedule that would have tested the stamina of a fifty-year-old, let alone someone approaching seventy. Eight lengthy rail journeys added up to traveling thousands of miles, and most of that time he kept secretaries busy taking down his dictation.

En route to Hyde Park in a six-car private train arranged by the president of the Canadian National Railways, the Churchill party took a ninety-minute detour to Niagara Falls to show Mary the three waterfalls that help form the border between Ontario and New York. Alerted to the morning pause of the prime minister's rail trip, anxious reporters crowded around for comment on the natural grandeur. "I saw them before you were born," Churchill remarked to one questioner. "I came here first in 1900." The response quickly prompted a follow-up query. Do they appear as they did four decades ago? "Well, the principle seems the same," Churchill admitted. "The water still keeps falling over."

Numerous newspapers printed the prime minister's quip in articles about his sightseeing, though specific details were sparse because of wartime security. The Associated Press dispatch that the *Evening Star* in Washington published on August 12 was vague as to why the British leader left the site of the Quadrant conference so soon after arriving to travel to "an unannounced destination." The *Times* of London duly reported Churchill's reaction to his second examination of the falls while also maintaining secrecy: "the prospective route has not been divulged." Anyone, Axis spy or average citizen, could have guessed the prime minister planned to rendezvous with the president. But where exactly? Roosevelt had returned to the White House on August 9 from a weeklong fishing trip in Canada, so they might meet in Washington. In fact, on August 11, FDR left for Hyde Park, arriving there the morning of August 12, a Thursday, to await Churchill's arrival at 6:30 that evening.

What's the prime minister's first recollection of his second visit to the president's country estate? In his memoirs he recalled, "It was indeed so hot that I got up one night [of the two-night stopover] because I was unable to sleep and hardly able to breathe." Churchill sought refuge from the heat by going outside and sitting by the Hudson River to await the sunrise.[5] With the temperature reaching 90 degrees one day and never dropping below 70, the Hudson Valley was considerably warmer than London's average of the low 60s at that time and even cooler at night.

Churchill's discomfort didn't go unnoticed. One account, provided by an aide, noted that the prime minister's "sudden appearance in the garden in his night attire greatly surprised the Secret Servicemen patrolling the grounds."[6] It wasn't just the president's security detail that had to cope with the visitor's impromptu response to an inability to sleep. There were more general worries. Churchill's bodyguard, Walter Henry Thompson, found Roosevelt's estate anything but a holiday, and his chapter-and-verse disapproval struck at the heart of the pleasures FDR relished when he returned to his homestead. Thompson admitted that he "hated Hyde Park," in part because it posed so many difficulties in providing security. He also loathed the Roosevelts' outdoor lifestyle. "Day and night I was on the alert," he later wrote, "chasing over the damn acreage with a creel on my hip . . . or a whole hamper of sandwiches on my head, and mustard on my trousers . . . not infrequently challenged by unfamiliar American police (this was the worst!), and a bad bed at night right under a revolving floodlight."[7]

The Scotland Yard veteran, Churchill's shadow throughout the war, never appreciated the quaint, bucolic charm of Hyde Park. But for Roosevelt, an overnight train trip from the White House and he was home, back to being a "country squire" (in one popular description of him), and far removed from the exigencies of the capital. FDR welcomed the company he invited there—and this time, as before, he met Churchill's private train at the "Roosevelt siding" and worked to keep his guests entertained. Margaret (Daisy) Suckley, the president's distant cousin, noted in her diary that Roosevelt told her to arrange pictures of and by Churchill in a prominent place to be admired by the visitors, a political as well as endearing gesture.

Suckley's on-the-scene observations of the weekend provided details unavailable elsewhere. During a luncheon picnic, with Eleanor Roosevelt cooking up hot dogs on "a broiler on wheels," Churchill snuck treats to Fala, the Scottish terrier Suckley had given the president. She described the prime minister, who's unembarrassed about diving into the pool after the meal, as "a strange looking little man. Fat & round, his clothes bunched up on him. Practically no hair on his head, he wore a huge 10-gallon hat. . . . His humorous twinkle is infectious."[8]

More substantively, what Suckley saw that weekend, as the two leaders talked and engaged in planned activities, resulted in her drawing conclusions about each and the dynamics of their relationship. "I took away the impression that Churchill *adores* the P., loves him, as a man, looks up to him, defers to him, leans on him," she wrote. "He is older than the P., but the P. is the bigger person, and Churchill recognizes it. I saw in Churchill, too, an amount of real greatness I did not suspect before." Suckley's judgments competed with her clear-eyed reporting, noting that Churchill at the picnic had a "special little ice-pail for his scotch" and his appearance at the pool made him look "exactly like a kewpie" doll in his shorts.[9]

Out in the sunshine among others, Churchill enjoyed some relaxation after another ocean crossing and two day-long train journeys. However, according to one of her biographers, Eleanor Roosevelt wasn't enjoying herself. The First Lady expected serious examinations of current issues and controversies, but, in this account, she only heard pleasant prattle during meals and elsewhere.[10]

Other sources, though, told a different story. Joseph P. Lash, then serving in the U.S. Army Air Force, received a letter from Mrs. Roosevelt, a close friend, that she sent to him at the time. In it, she wrote, "A well-known and frequent guest [Churchill] tonight read us letters from Germans taken from airmen who have been brought down in the last few weeks." The pilots "said they could stand no more," which was "sad and encouraging from our point of view."[11] Morale in the Luftwaffe was dwindling and a telling fact about the enemy. In addition, Harriman, who was sitting on Mrs. Roosevelt's left while Churchill was on her right, described an evening's dinner exchange right before the Churchills departed for their return to Quebec. As the prime minister had done during his May trip and as he would explain in greater detail a few weeks later at Harvard University, Britain and the United States should—in his opinion—enter into a "fraternal relationship" following the war. Mrs. Roosevelt, according to Harriman, took exception to the proposal—and said so. The diplomat noted: "Mrs. Roosevelt seemed fearful this might be misunderstood by other nations and weaken the United Nations concept." Churchill, according to Harriman, didn't agree and kept riding his hobbyhorse of a postwar U.K.-U.S. fraternity.[12] Mrs. Roosevelt might have preferred longer, more wide-ranging talks, but substantive matters received consideration amid the social talk. When Churchill and Mrs. Roosevelt butted heads, a somewhat regular occurrence in Washington or at Hyde Park, both stood their ground, often leaving the president a bemused spectator of their exchanges.

Despite their differing viewpoints, Mrs. Roosevelt devoted one of her "My Day" newspaper columns to the visit by the prime minister and his retinue. Following security protocol, the First Lady refrained from mentioning Churchill's time at Hyde Park until he was safely back at Quebec. Wire service reports that weekend talked of "a preliminary meeting somewhere" taking place at "an undisclosed point in the United States." By the time news of what headline writers referred to as the "Secret Parley" had circulated widely, Churchill was back in Canada, and Roosevelt had traveled to the White House for a full day of meetings before departing for Quebec City the evening of August 16.

Mrs. Roosevelt's column, written to appear on August 17—United Features Syndicate distributed "My Day" to nearly a hundred newspapers at the time—revealed that the visit to Hyde Park was no longer a "secret."[13] She focused less on the prime minister and more on Mary, "a friendly soul," who "enjoyed doing the things that are part of our country life here and would normally be part of the country life at home." Eating slices of watermelon at a picnic became an entirely new experience for the foreign guests, with the president (according to Samuel I. Rosenman, FDR's sometime speechwriter and a justice of the New York State Supreme Court) warning the young woman "not to swallow any of the pits lest they grow into watermelons in her stomach."[14]

Though Mary received attention in several paragraphs, her father is described as enjoying "leisurely talking at meals and sitting out under the trees." Despite what she referred to as the "serious work" conducted by the two leaders, they were also able to unwind, with Churchill quoted as saying, "You know one works better when one has a chance to enjoy a little leisure now and then." Amid the pressures and vicissitudes of war, moments at ease were important to the prime minister and the president, just as occasional leaves were invaluable for battlefield combatants. The First Lady, who cultivated the persona of having a deep bond with people of every class and race, wanted her readers to see two public figures as regular people in a near-holiday environment.

Along with the outdoor picnics and dips in the pool, Churchill and Roosevelt began to set forth their positions for the upcoming conference—with the cross-Channel invasion and who would command the operation uppermost in their deliberations. They also discussed anti-submarine warfare, the French Committee of National Liberation, and relations with neutral Ireland, according to the U.S. Government's official history.[15]

Surprisingly, Churchill devoted just one paragraph and a portion of another to the three days at Hyde Park in his war memoirs. Besides grumbling about the heat, Churchill portrayed Harry Hopkins as being out of favor with Roosevelt to the point that FDR didn't speak to his aide when he arrived at a lunch. However, the president's mood seemed to change with the prime minister on the scene. "In two days it seemed to be like old times," Churchill observed. Hopkins is quoted as remarking, "You must know I am not what I was." The statement, revealing about both Roosevelt and Hopkins, led to Churchill's comment: "He had tried too much at once. Even his greatness of spirit broke under his variegated activities."[16]

Churchill's ten sentences about Hopkins—the incident is worth keeping in mind for this book's next chapter—offered a portrait in miniature of a three-person relationship that was critical, if not indispensable, to the alliance between the United States and Britain as well as the conduct of the war. There's a certain heartless fickleness to Roosevelt, which Churchill forthrightly recorded. Suffering from stomach cancer since the late 1930s, Hopkins had served the president as a tireless, all-purpose adviser while living in the White House. Churchill took credit for helping to restore Hopkins to some semblance of his old self for a brief time—but the memoirist judged that his friend's spirit was diminished, if not destroyed.

At the time, Hopkins had just celebrated the first anniversary of his marriage to Louise Gill Macy, a fashion writer. They'd wed in a White House ceremony on July 30, 1942. Not long afterward, the new Mrs. Hopkins wanted to find a place to call home rather than continuing to live in a suite at 1600 Pennsylvania Avenue. Moreover, Hopkins' personal relationship with Roosevelt was affected when he married for a third time. (Divorced in 1930, his second wife died in 1937.) Someone else had come between the president and his right-hand aide. Lash received an August 1943 letter from Eleanor Roosevelt that said, "Harry & Louise are going to move to their own house but no one seems to have hard feelings though P[resident] doesn't like their going."[17] The breach was significant and subsequently treated as such in historical accounts. David L. Roll observed, "A narrow but unmistakable fissure was opened. In love with Louise, Hopkins seemed to be no longer 'the half man' whose company FDR could completely dominate."[18] Doris Kearns Goodwin went further, "On the surface, Harry's relationship with the president remained as before, but underneath, the cord of communion was cut," adding ominously that "a frost descended on their relationship."[19] For FDR, loyalty didn't exist in half or three-quarter measures. The Hopkins family eventually moved to their own residence in Georgetown later in 1943.

It's curious that Churchill decided to make Hopkins the focus of how he remembered his second visit to Hyde Park. Was the prime minister finding it more difficult to shape Allied war strategy without the clout of the once-close confidant of the president? Was Roosevelt being less amenable to Churchill's ideas and suggestions? While at Hyde Park—and on 10 Downing Street stationery—the prime minister dashed off a handwritten note to "My dear Franklin" that proposed going immediately to Quebec. "The eyes of the world are on the

Conference & I doubt if much progress will be made till we are on the spot," he asserted, advancing Sunday (August 15) or Monday (August 16) to start the proceedings.[20] FDR balked, returned to Washington on August 16, and didn't arrive in Quebec until the next evening. For whatever reason, the president kept to his original plans. Churchill's emphasis on global interest, "eyes of the world," as a principal impetus to change the agenda showed his desire to project his persona on the world stage, always a consideration in his personal and political calculus. As part of the same note, the prime minister also brought up the possibility of spending time at *both* Hyde Park and the White House following the conference.

No response from Roosevelt to the recommendations has ever been found. In contrast to Churchill, the president's paper trail of documents is a village street as opposed to a coast-to-coast highway. That, however, doesn't mean that there was a paucity of papers related to the Quebec conference crossing FDR's desk before he boarded the *Ferdinand Magellan*—the specially armored and heaviest rail car ever built in the United States—for the sixteen-hour trip to Canada. The U.S. government report about Quadrant included over four hundred pages of "Substantive Preparatory Papers." In several of the documents, the necessity of launching a cross-Channel invasion assumes paramount importance. One memorandum, prepared by the War Department, concluded in eye-grabbing italics: *"It is clear that the soundest course of action is to mass air, sea, and land power in the U.K. for a cross-channel assault. But even more vital to the achievement of victory than the particular course of action chosen, is the pressing necessity of deciding what that course of action shall be and then sticking vigorously and wholeheartedly to that decision."*[21] American strategists and policymakers knew what they wanted to have happen, and Quebec would be the place, once again, to make their case, which was first proposed by the United States early in 1942 and strongly advocated since then.

Churchill, however, continued to ponder the potential human cost of a massive assault across the English Channel. Maybe a maneuver through the Balkans or landing from the Mediterranean would provide a secure toehold for the long-desired second front and result in less hazardous access to the continent for its eventual occupation. The prime minister harbored persistent doubts but kept pushing his military staff to prepare plans for a possible invasion of northwestern France.

Just before departing for Canada, Churchill met with Lieutenant General Frederick Morgan to review the state of the program. The prime minister took high-decibel exception to the codename assigned to the operation by the British Inter Service Security Board. The board had given the action-to-be the flaccid label "Mothball." Churchill was beside himself at the prospect of "Operation Mothball" and its resonance for posterity. "Do you mean to tell me that those bloody fools want our grandchildren 50 years from now to be calling the operation that liberated Europe Operation Mothball?" the prime minister gruffly inquired. "If they can't come up with a better code name for our landing than that, I damn well will pick the code name myself." After a few moments, he erupted, "Overlord. We shall call it Overlord."[22]

The impact of code names to describe planned actions in wartime assumed its own importance in Churchill's preparation for the Quebec conference and his meetings with Roosevelt. He insisted on having the final say on proposed etymological ruses, and one of the last directives (addressed to General Hastings Ismay, Churchill's chief military assistant) that he dictated before the *Queen Mary* docked in Halifax set forth explicit instructions for composing and assigning code names. Words always mattered to Churchill—in 1938 he memorably said, "Words are the only things that last for ever"—and he was inventive in his examples of terms that work and those that don't. Terms of overconfidence or suggesting "an air of despondence" should never be codewords for actions involving combat. Also to be avoided were "names of a frivolous character, such as 'Bunnyhug,' 'Billingsgate,' 'Aperitif,' and 'Ballyhoo.' " The memo continued to suggest that figures of mythology, war heroes, and well-known race horses offer worthwhile possibilities for consideration.[23] To a writer and war leader, linguistic precision was consequential in its own way, too. Operation Overlord trumped Operation Mothball permanently and powerfully.

Though Churchill doesn't disclose the substance of any conversations he had with Roosevelt at Hyde Park, Overlord and the planning for it received serious attention. In a diary entry for August 15, General Alan Brooke, chief of the Imperial General Staff, recorded that the prime minister noted that in meetings involving Churchill, Roosevelt, and Hopkins, the presidential advisor "pressed hard for the appointment of [General George] Marshall as Supreme Commander for the cross Channel operations and as far as I can gather Winston gave in, in spite of having previously promised me the job!!"[24] Britain's foremost uniformed military commander was furious, particularly since the prime minister had assured him not once but three times of the prestigious assignment. Churchill's demeanor conveying the decision incensed Brooke, too: "He offered no sympathy, no regrets at having had to change his mind, and dealt with the matter as if it were one of minor importance!"[25]

Brooke's reaction was worlds removed from Churchill's, who recalled in his memoirs that the general "bore the great disappointment with soldierly dignity."[26] Four days after Brooke learned his fate, he described an argument he had with the prime minister over possible combat in southeast Asia by seething that he "behaved like a spoilt child that wants a toy in a shop irrespective of the fact that its parents tell it that it is no good!"[27] He subsequently repeated his "spoilt child" assessment in his diary without backing down from his high-pitched criticism. A few months earlier, Roosevelt had compared Churchill to "a spoiled boy." The label wasn't flattering or collegial.

Brooke's account identified Hopkins as the person pushing for an American to command Overlord. Churchill's recollection differed. In *Closing the Ring*, he admitted that he had offered Brooke the post "*early in* 1943" and received Roosevelt's agreement. However, as preparations for the invasion increased, the balance of military power shifted with Churchill taking note of the larger number of American forces that would see action in the operation. Given what Churchill referred to as "the very great preponderance of American troops," he "took the initiative of proposing" an American to serve as commander.[28]

Whatever the actual circumstances as to the person making the proposal and where it occurred—there's little doubt it was Hyde Park—an American would lead Overlord and Brooke wouldn't. On September 6, the *Evening Star* in Washington published an exclusive on its front page, saying that General Marshall "will direct any invasion from England, it was reported here today on the highest authority." The Associated Press distributed a dispatch based on the reporting in the *Evening Star* for next-day use and many newspapers repeated the scoop's main points, including the *New York Times*, *Chicago Tribune*, and *Los Angeles Times*. Nine months before Overlord, the world was learning what was afoot, even if important details would later change.

In the 118 pages published in the "Proceedings of the First Quebec Conference," over two dozen meetings involving Churchill and Roosevelt are noted between August 17 and 24. The description of the initial session continues a pattern established during the first Washington conference in late December 1941, with government historians acknowledging their inability to document the leaders' conversations: "No record of the discussion has been found, as it was not Roosevelt's practice to record his private conversations with Churchill."[29]

Detailed minutes do exist for the two plenary sessions conducted by the prime minister and the president with the Combined Chiefs of Staff. During the one on August 19, the eight participants on the British side and the six for the Americans immediately considered "the Report of Progress" in the war, and Churchill's first statement raised his lingering unease about Overlord should the German army have more than a dozen mobile divisions in northern France at the time of the invasion. This concern was dismissed by Hopkins, the only participant at the meeting without a defined military role. (Churchill was the U.K.'s "minister of defence," and FDR was commander in chief.)

The prime minister rebounded (in the phrasing of the minutes) "to emphasize that he strongly favored Overlord for 1944. He was not in favor of Sledgehammer in 1942 or Roundup in 1943"—earlier code names for the invasion of France.[30] Interestingly, the paragraph Churchill devoted to his acceptance of Overlord in *Closing the Ring* was an almost word-for-word appropriation from the minutes in the Joint Chiefs of Staff files. Verbs in the present tense shifted to the past, and third-person constructions became first-person for the sake of his history-memoir.[31]

After hesitating and dragging his feet on mounting a second front, Churchill accepted (at least for now) May 1, 1944, as the target date for the sea, air, and land campaign in western Europe. Another central decision that was made in Quebec established the Southeast Asia Command (for the China-Burma-India Theater), and the Anglo-American leadership also resolved to defeat Japan within a year after Germany surrendered.

Though there were just two plenary sessions—on August 19 and August 23—with the Combined Chiefs of Staff, Churchill and Roosevelt continued their routine of conferring at meals and during the late evening hours. On the president's calendar for August 20, this notation appears: "FDR and Prime Min Mr. Winston S. Churchill held their usual lengthly [*sic*] discussions after dinner and both retired very late." Omitted in the official history of Quadrant is an incident Britain's foreign secretary Anthony Eden recorded in his diary. Cordell Hull, then seventy-two and in his tenth year as U.S. secretary of state, wanted to head to bed about midnight, but Churchill, just a couple years younger, objected with a grouchy outburst: "Why, man, we are at war!"[32]

After the conference, which concluded on August 24, and a few days at a Canadian fishing camp, the prime minister headed south, embarking on another long rail journey. This time the destination was Washington. On the way, according to Churchill secretary Elizabeth Nel, the prime minister asked his Canadian-born assistant about her mother, who had flown to Quebec from Vancouver to visit her daughter. Realizing the expense involved for the mother, Churchill said "he wished to make her a present of half her fare across the continent," noting her boss "never forgot those who worked for him."[33] The prime minister also didn't overlook what other public figures—then and now—might try to sidestep. When Churchill returned to London, he personally paid for two first-class tickets on the *Queen Mary* to Halifax: one for his wife and the other for her assistant, Grace Hamblin.

When Churchill's train pulled into the secret siding at the Bureau of Engraving and Printing near the White House at 4 p.m. on Wednesday, September 1, Roosevelt was there, waiting to greet the prime minister. This time Clementine was with him. More late nights would lie ahead for the prime minister and the president, as they mulled at greater length some of the subjects they'd begun discussing at Hyde Park and Quebec. During the next ten days, Churchill became not only completely at home in the White House but also more revered than before among American thought leaders and opinion shapers. It was as though he grew in public stature with each Washington sojourn, reason enough for him to want to keep returning to the Rose Bedroom.

For newspaper reporters, the frequent White House guest continued to be page-one copy, both for war-policy pronouncements and personality profiles. In a lengthy *New York Herald Tribune* account announcing Churchill's arrival and the "indefinite time" for his visit at 1600 Pennsylvania Avenue, a detail that was reported seemed both astonishing and amusing: "A separate truck, piled high with much-traveled and somewhat battered luggage, transported the Churchill party baggage to the White House."

On September 1, Washington's temperature reached 95 degrees at 4:50 p.m., weather considered objectionably oppressive by the British visitors. John Martin, the prime minister's private secretary, noted in a letter from the White House that Washington in late summer "has a most foul climate. . . . My tuxedo for dinner is a cruel penance. The PM has a beautifully cool air-conditioned room, but we work next to him (and sleep) in the atmosphere of a hot-house."[34]

Martin wasn't alone in making the White House his residence or work place—or both—until late on September 11. He was part of the seven-person entourage that included three Churchills, C. R. Thompson (the prime minister's personal assistant), Walter H. Thompson (the bodyguard), and Frank Sawyers (valet). As visitor quarters at the White House became crowded, so, too, did places for Churchill and those with him to carry out their duties. Seventeen more people in the prime minister's party, with access for work at 1600 Pennsylvania Avenue, were also staying at the Hotel Statler. In her memoir, Nel recalled that the usual office space wasn't large enough, and Churchill's staff moved into a sitting room "which in a very short time changed its appearance into that of a paper junk-shop." The cluttered, near-chaotic surroundings presented challenges for Nel and her coworkers to the point where she had to "set my typewriter (our own noiseless machines travelled with us) on the rear portion of a grand piano, in front of which I sat on the back of an armchair."[35]

Much of Churchill's dictation concentrated on the situation in Italy—after weeks to establish specific terms the Italian government surrendered on September 8, which brought several German divisions into the fight against the Allies in Italy—and communicating with Stalin about Quadrant as well as the possibility of a Big Three meeting in the future. (In messages about dealing with Stalin, Churchill frequently referred to the Soviet leader as "UJ" shorthand for Uncle Joe, or the Great Bear, or simply Bruin.) The unresolved conditions in Italy preoccupied the prime minister and the president during much of their time together in the White House, even affecting Churchill's schedule. As a result he decided to stay longer in the United States while the situation in Italy remained unresolved.

Churchill and Roosevelt conducted meetings at all hours between September 1 and September 9, a total of fourteen sessions not counting meals, according to the official history of the visit and FDR's calendar. On two days—September 2 and 3—the president wheeled himself into Churchill's room in the late morning to confer in the Rose Bedroom.

As happened during the three previous stays of the prime minister, the two talked well past midnight or 1 a.m. all six nights that Churchill slept at the White House. On September 6, when the prime minister was returning to Washington after a day-long trip outside the capital, Roosevelt took advantage of Churchill's absence by retiring at 8:10 p.m.

Although some in Churchill's retinue found life in the capital sweltering, the prime minister acclimated to his now-familiar surroundings without difficulty. He felt no need to repeat what he'd done at Hyde Park in August to escape the heat. In fact, Alexander Cadogan, Britain's permanent under-secretary for foreign affairs since 1938 who had participated in the Quebec conference and then traveled to Washington, recorded wry impressions of his nation's war leader while abroad. In his diary, he complained that he didn't "know what Winston's doing" and that plans of the visit constantly changed. Frustrated at the situation, the mustachioed diplomat explained, "Winston will, I think, settle down in U.S.!" The next day, Cadogan composed a letter to his wife of thirty years, Lady Theodosia, with a close-up description of a public figure at home overseas: "The P.M.'s sleeping arrangements have now become quite promiscuous. He talks with the President till 2 a.m. and consequently spends a large part of the day hurling himself violently in and out of bed, bathing at unsuitable moments and rushing up and down corridors in his dressing-gown."[36]

These Churchillian escapades in the White House remained private until long after they occurred. Cadogan's diaries weren't published until 1971, three years after his death and six after Churchill's. However, throughout this stay in 1943, the prime minister juggled his schedule to combine time for White House meetings or work sessions in his room (often propped up in bed) along with widely covered public appearances that showed off his performative personality.

On his second full day in Washington, September 3, he purchased a $100 war bond from Treasury Secretary Henry Morgenthau Jr. in a White House ceremony staged in front of a throng of reporters, photographers, and crews for what were characterized as "sound movies." The lighting to record the event was so intense that Churchill—according to newspaper reports—quipped, "I'll be so much roasted that you will have to turn me around and cook the other side." Even in his formal remarks, noting the day of the event marked the fourth anniversary of Britain's entry in the war, the prime minister engaged in levity, directed at Morgenthau, the guardian of the Treasury Department since 1934. "I have often thought of you, Mr. Secretary, as one of the bravest men in the world," Churchill said. "You ought to have the Congressional Medal of Honor, the Victoria Cross and all of the other decorations of the Allies for being able to lie down at night and sleep quietly among all of those astronomical figures in modern finance."

While Churchill entertained White House journalists—one dispatch pointed out he was wearing a white cotton suit "and clutching his inseparable cigar"—the president was engaged elsewhere, leading Clementine and Mary Churchill on a sightseeing excursion around the Washington area. His limousine picked them up after lunch at the Pentagon, which had been completed earlier in 1943 in the record time of a little more than sixteen months and was the largest office building in the world until 2023, when the Surat Diamond Bourse in India claimed that distinction. On their tour agenda was a visit to George Washington's home at Mount Vernon. Daisy Suckley had traveled from Hyde Park to the capital and joined the group on the outing. When they returned, she found the White House usher Wilson Searles "having a fit" over the lack of planning for the Churchill family visit. In her diary, Suckley brashly set down her opinion: "Mrs. R. should be here to attend to all this sort of thing—The P. shouldn't have to—and it *has* to be *done*."[37] At the time the First Lady was on a five-week tour to buck up the troops in the South Pacific, a journey that started shortly after the Churchills stopped by Hyde Park in August.

In launching the $15 billion loan drive—which reached nearly $19 billion of sales in less than a month—Churchill surprisingly preceded the president. Roosevelt waited until Wednesday, September 8, to make his pitch in a Fireside Chat, his twenty-sixth of the thirty he delivered over a dozen years. He connected progress in the war, including the armistice with Italy, to raising funds to achieve "overpowering superiority" in the fight. Midway through his twelve-minute talk, FDR made a point of focusing on his current White House guest, remarking that "Mr. Churchill and I are here together in Washington at this crucial moment." Stressing that planning propelled their numerous conferences, the president cautioned, clearly with sales in mind, that "we have never lost sight of the fact that this war will become bigger and tougher, rather than easier, during the long months that are to come."[38] The president, who didn't get to bed until 2:15 a.m. on September 8 and started his meetings right before 8:30 later that morning, retired at 12:20 a.m. after his broadcast, a reception, and additional conversations. The next evening, though, he left for a break at Hyde Park, with Churchill following later to the president's retreat.

Beforehand, though, Churchill had to wrestle with an itinerary packed with strategy meetings, public events, and speeches. On September 4, the day after he performed to sell war bonds, he spoke at a quickly arranged Saturday luncheon sponsored by the White House Correspondents Association, the Overseas Press Club, the National Press Club, and other organizations. Some 250 Washington journalists crowded into a ballroom at the Hotel Statler, located four blocks from the White House, to listen to a speech and question-and-answer session they were unable to cover as they usually did. This time ground rules forbade any quoting of what the prime minister said. Follow-up stories focused on how Churchill handled himself rather than the substance of his remarks. In addition, the White House was silent on the war in the Mediterranean region, making reporters hungrier than usual for actual news.

Washington Post columnist Barnet Nover, the president of the Overseas Press Club, introduced Churchill "as one of the ablest practitioners of our craft," going on to say "that Mr. Churchill, the great statesman, the great leader, has best revealed himself as the great journalist." Connecting language and leadership served as a prelude to

Nover's compliment that during the eight-month bombing of London and other British cities in 1940 and 1941, the phrase-making premier "spoke words that marched like an army with banners, and were responsible for victories of the spirit without which our present victories on land and sea and in the air would not have been possible."

At this time, as fall approached in 1943, Churchill's reputation in the United States reached its apex since he'd become prime minister. His first visit after Pearl Harbor captured the country's attention, with its dramatic element of surprise inspiring widespread fascination as well as acclamation. Yet what seemed arresting nearly two years later was that his bulldog determination united with his oratorical gifts to produce a noticeable difference in the war's progress. To Americans and people elsewhere, he demonstrated an eagerness to go anywhere to defeat the Axis powers and to defend democracy. A man in perpetual motion, he became the face and voice of the fight for Western civilization, someone to admire for that era's influencers.

While Churchill and Roosevelt conferred at Hyde Park before Quebec, the *New York Times* foreign affairs columnist Anne O'Hare McCormick, the first woman to win a Pulitzer Prize in a journalism category, offered a striking word sketch: "Behind his look of a mischievous cherub Mr. Churchill is John Bull in person, a John Bull spiced with wit and malice and with a prophet's tongue, but a hard fighter and a debater who sticks to his point with furious persistence." Shortly after the Washington luncheon with journalists, Walter Lippmann devoted his widely syndicated newspaper column to an encomium about the visiting prime minister. Quoting Chaucer, Alfred North Whitehead, and John Henry Newman, he revised the title of a W. B. Yeats poem, "The Fascination of What's Difficult," to call his disquisition on Churchill "The Fascination of Greatness." Though widely recognized for his Olympian restraint, Lippmann didn't hold back in evaluating his subject: "Mr. Churchill is not only the Prime Minister of Great Britain. He is also the one certainly authentic example of greatness in a public man who moves among us."

Respected at the time as the most significant commentator in American journalism, Lippmann had published his sixteenth book, *U.S. Foreign Policy: Shield of the Republic*, three months earlier. No aspect of the war escaped his purview, with some sentences in his column about Churchill as warlord reading like an erudite fan letter. However, his points, in retrospect, seem reasonable in the context of the moment and the prime minister's standing in the United States: "The fascination of Churchill is not merely in his wit, or even in his humor, which keeps him so near to his fellow men, or in his genius for war." Arguing that the secret of Churchill's greatness and fascination came from "his magnanimity," Lippmann suggested ". . . when men age, they may grow vain, irascible and self-centered. Or they may grow wise, benign, compassionate and universal. Churchill has aged well." The maturity that produced respect for others encompassed friend and foe alike, so that "even in his wrath against the enemy, which is awe-inspiring, there is not the malice of the small man but the chivalry of the good warrior."

Lippmann's enthrallment with Churchill epitomized the far-reaching American attitude then. Beyond Washington, Churchill had achieved a level of respect rarely, if ever, enjoyed by a foreign figure. Indeed, during this late-summer visit, the *Chicago Tribune* reported that a Republican politician in Illinois told a picnic gathering that he had a suggestion—albeit an unconstitutional one—that would keep Roosevelt from running for a fourth term in 1944. He recommended that both the Democratic and Republican parties nominate Churchill to be their presidential nominee. With Churchill in the White House—in this case as president—"America would have no future worries," Richard J. Lyons, the losing Illinois GOP Senate candidate in 1944 exclaimed. Facetious though the proposal was, it reflected genuine, even bipartisan, regard. In his memoir, *Washington Goes to War*, David Brinkley, who began his career in journalism writing for United Press International in the 1940s before making his name in broadcast news at NBC by coanchoring the nightly *Huntley-Brinkley Report* throughout the late 1950s and 1960s, observed that it had become "routine now in the letters to the newspapers for people to say the British so loved Roosevelt and the Americans so loved Churchill the two allies could exchange national leaders and both would be happy—possibly even happier."[39]

For this sojourn in the Rose Bedroom, Churchill devoted more of his attention to the fourth estate than during his previous visits. On September 4, he lunched with several well-known Washington news figures, including Lippmann, Eugene Meyer, the editor and publisher of the *Washington Post*, and Sir Wilmot Lewis of the *Times* (of London). The next day at a White House luncheon, he met with another leader in American journalism: Helen Ogden Mills Reid, the vice president of the *New York Herald Tribune*, Lippmann's flagship newspaper.

Roosevelt and Reid shared the opinion that Britain's policy on India was anachronistic colonialism that deserved change. Churchill, however, defended the existence of British rule. After the meal and while talking outside on the South Portico of the White House, the subject of Indian independence arose. Before Reid launched into her criticism, Churchill preempted her by posing two questions, according to one witness: "Are we talking about the brown Indians in India who have multiplied alarmingly under the benevolent British rule? Or are we speaking of the red Indians in America who, I understand, are almost extinct?"[40] Another version of this story quoted Churchill articulating more colorful words but landing the same rhetorical punch: "Madam, to which Indians do you refer? Do you by any chance refer to the second greatest nation on earth which under benign and beneficent British rule has multiplied and prospered exceedingly, or do you mean the unfortunate Indians of the North American continent which under your administration are practically extinct?"[41]

The first rendering was based on C. R. Thompson's "recollections," which were subsequently repeated by Mary (Churchill) Soames in her memoir, *A Daughter's Tale*. Both Thompson and Mary Churchill participated in the lunch and adjourned to the South Portico with the other guests. They heard the actual exchange. The other direct quotation is an example (among many) of the way a Churchill statement received embellishment to be more pointed and entertaining when restated on later occasions.

Wherever Churchill went as prime minister, he kept up a constant flow—torrent would be more accurate—of memorandums and messages to U.K. government officials, Commonwealth leaders, public figures among the Allies, and others. The White House was no different from Downing Street, Chequers, or anywhere else. The sheer volume of words he composed and sent out is staggering, and on occasion he used dispatches to individuals to help work out ideas he subsequently developed for more formal or public settings.

On September 5, he sent his longtime friend, Jan Smuts, a field marshal of the British Army as well as prime minister of South Africa, a detailed telegram—"For you alone"—that provided Churchill's perspective on several dimensions of the war. The sixth point would assume greater significance over time: "I think it inevitable that Russia will be the greatest land power in the world after this war which will have rid her of the two military powers, Japan and Germany, who in our lifetime have inflicted upon her such heavy defeats. I hope, however, that the 'fraternal association' of the British Commonwealth and the United States together with sea and air power, may put us on good terms and in a friendly balance with Russia at least for the period of re-building."[42] The prospect of postwar Russian power—behind the "iron curtain"—became an abiding worry in later years, but his focus on a "fraternal association" of the United Kingdom and United States as a bulwark of freedom served as a central principle in addressing an audience the day after he wrote Smuts.

During two of his previous three visits to the White House, Churchill delivered major speeches—in both cases to joint sessions of Congress. On September 6, Labor Day in 1943, he had a much different oratorical challenge. Roosevelt had worked behind the scenes to encourage his alma mater, Harvard University, to confer an honorary doctorate on the British leader. His address of acceptance at Cambridge, just outside Boston, would be the centerpiece public occasion of his two weeks in America after Quadrant, and it would be nationally broadcast. A major Churchill speech was announced in newspapers the day before, though details were withheld and sketchy for security reasons. A boxed item on the front page of Sunday's *Washington Post* merely said the address "will not be of political significance and will be made from a city which will be identified later." A sense of mystery was injected into the prime minister's American visit.

As tended to be his routine during the war for composing addresses, Churchill waited until the deadline stared him in the face before finishing his text, which he'd begun in the White House. His doctor, Lord Moran, remarked on Churchill's "irritability" during the train journey from Washington, adding: "For some reason, which I have not yet fathomed, he is taking the speech he is to make at Harvard very seriously."[43] Elizabeth Nel recalled that she and a colleague "worked until 4.30, getting his speech ready" that Monday morning by typing the words he dictated for delivery.[44] If Churchill approached his speech with puzzling earnestness, his doctor also wondered why the honored guest wore what he did to the formal ceremony. "He was attired in a black coat and bow tie," Moran observed. "But Winston would not be Winston if he was strictly conventional. Beneath the gorgeous scarlet robe appeared a pair of rather inadequate grey flannel trousers."[45] In fairness, the trousers represented something of a graduation from his usual White House attire: his comfortable, bespoke—often tailored in velvet—siren suits.

Similar to the introduction at Saturday's lunch with the Washington news people, the honorary degree citation emphasized Churchill's literary abilities before noting others. The twenty-nine words that James Bryant Conant—then finishing his first of two decades as Harvard's president—spoke in awarding the Doctor of Laws echoed Lippmann's panegyric: "An historian who has written a glorious page of British history; a statesman and warrior whose tenacity and courage turned back the tide of tyranny in freedom's darkest hour."

In his memoir, Churchill reprinted several paragraphs from the address—the entire text is in the appendix—and proclaimed that it was "a public declaration to the world of Anglo-American unity and amity."[46] Since his visit in May, he'd continued to develop his theory of a "fraternal association" between Britain and America, and this academic audience allowed him to deliver to a broad audience a detailed argument in the context of the two Allies waging war shoulder to shoulder. Identifying "ties of blood and history," Churchill placed himself at the center of this fraternal fellowship: "Naturally, I, a child of both worlds, am conscious of these [ties]." In a portion of the address not quoted in his memoir, he publicly opened a door that revealed not only his thinking but also his own confidence in making such a bold suggestion: "The gift of a common tongue is a priceless inheritance and it may well some day become the foundation of a common citizenship. I like to think of British and Americans moving about freely over each other's wide estates with hardly a sense of being foreigners to one another."[47]

Before Pearl Harbor, fear of international entanglements influenced, to one degree or another, American public opinion and governmental policies. The isolationist impulse served as a defining characteristic for millions, especially in the Midwest. Now, not even two years later, a foreign leader speaking on U.S. soil had the temerity to float the idea of "a common citizenship." The audacity of the proposal raised eyebrows—but not for everyone.

Robert Sherwood, the acclaimed dramatist who was drafted to be one of Roosevelt's speechwriters, substantiated that FDR and Churchill discussed the idea, with the likelihood that the subject arose at the White House as the prime minister mulled what he'd say to an academic assembly that would also be broadcast on the radio. Sherwood said Churchill "certainly talked to Roosevelt before suggesting even the remote possibility of 'common citizenship' and was assured by the President that the United States had advanced so far from its isolationist position that this would not outrage public opinion or provoke another Boston Tea Party."[48] After Churchill's death, his long-serving private secretary and dedicated diarist, John (or, as he was called, Jock) Colville, reported Churchill's judgment, expressed in 1952, "that if Roosevelt had lived and Churchill had been returned to office in 1945 the United States and the United Kingdom would have progressed far along the road to common citizenship."[49] In the twenty-first century and post-Brexit, it is inconceivable such a consolidated community could be a serious consideration, but Churchill and Roosevelt actively entertained the proposition.

Besides the remarks about a new kind of citizenship, Churchill also championed the adoption of a program of "Basic English"—"about 650 nouns and 200 verbs or other parts of speech." Applauding Harvard academics for contributing to this effort that, he thought, would enhance freedom of movement in the world and possibly help preserve peace, he concluded his linguistic sales pitch by declaring: "Let us go into this together. Let us have another Boston Tea Party about it."[50]

Churchill, of course, was well aware that any reference to the Boston Tea Party would gobsmack a gathering meeting a few miles from where angry colonists rebelled against the British for demanding, in the slogan of that time, "taxation without representation." He also recognized that there were a substantial number of critics of the British Empire in the United States—most notably Franklin D. Roosevelt. Churchill circumvented any contemporary imperial concerns by musing aloud about a future very different from the past. As with his other declarations that day, what he said was intended to resonate with an academic audience: "The empires of the future are the empires of the mind."[51] The line is certainly poetic, but an exact meaning probably eluded many in the audience packed into Harvard's Sanders Theatre for the ceremony.

At the end of his address, Churchill provided inspiration that "in this tremendous, thrilling, formative epoch in the human story" the trials of war were met head-on by "a generation that terror could not conquer and brutal violence could not enslave." He continued his high-minded oratory with its deliberate appeal to his American listeners, inviting them to join him "on the stage of history."[52]

No second-guessing introvert, Churchill was well aware of his own place on that stage, right at the front, but he would occasionally seek verification or validation of where he stood. For the Harvard address, which several newspapers (including the *New York Times*, *Washington Post*, *New York Herald Tribune*, and *Boston Globe*) reprinted in full, he requested "a tabular report of the reactions of all important American newspapers to my Harvard statement, showing which are for and which against."[53] This elaborate survey of press coverage was ultimately set into type and published for distribution within the U.K. government.

Just how involved was Churchill in making sure London colleagues learned about his Harvard speech and its reception? A memorandum, dictated on September 17 during his return from North America, provided explicit directions for the report's presentation, including his eagerness to circulate it as soon as possible after his return. The lengthy synopsis, titled "War Cabinet Paper No. 398," was delivered widely on September 20. Churchill always cared about what he wrote and said, how it was received, and who was informed about it. But the speedy transmission also indicated a certain amount of vanity as well as ardor to underscore a particular public activity. Given all that happened while he was away from Downing Street since early August, it was revealing that this detailed report occupied so much of his attention.

Moreover, in retrospect, the person who was responsible for assembling and interpreting all the news coverage was more than a low-level, paper-pushing embassy employee. During the war, Isaiah Berlin left academic life at the University of Oxford, where he was emerging as a respected figure in philosophy and the history of ideas, first to work for the British Information Services in New York before moving to Washington as first secretary of the British embassy. In both U.S. postings—from 1940 until 1945—Berlin, a pipe-smoking polymath fluent in five languages, analyzed journalism and engaged in countless conversations with well-known Americans as grist for weekly reports that told London officialdom about American public opinion. At the embassy, where he began working in 1942, the self-described "Russian Jew"—he had been born in Latvia and lived in Russia before his family moved to England—took charge of the report about the Harvard speech. Berlin's summary took note of the positive coverage, saying the reportage included "a very large amount of praise of the Prime Minister's person and achievements and an exceptional volume of homage to his eloquence."[54]

Berlin's complimentary statements about the Harvard address echoed earlier ones he drafted for Whitehall consumption. During the May 1943 visit of the prime minister, he wrote that "Churchill's visits and speeches create a volume of goodwill towards Britain which nothing else can parallel."[55] Berlin detected even greater admiration for the prime minister a few months later. His dispatch on September 12 stated that the White House visit, the Harvard talk, and "the flood of excellent war news, induced uncommon exhilaration in Washington." The report described the "altogether exceptional position which Mr Churchill occupies in American national life and politics."

Berlin, who was thirty-four in 1943, captured the high-water mark of Churchill's U.S. reputation during his first premiership by focusing on his "magnificent gusto," "electrifying utterances," the "life-giving properties of his visit," and "the thrilling effect of his all-embracing and infectious imagination."[56] During the September visit, Berlin even had a fleeting encounter with Churchill at the White House, when a cable arrived at the embassy that required immediate delivery to the prime minister. In a letter to his parents back in Britain that he composed later in the month, he boasted that he'd shaken hands with his hero, who "was wearing his 'siren suit', looked like a sweet old man out of Dickens—& I was v. pleased even with this momentary contact with a genius (he quite clearly is that the moment you meet him)."[57]

Berlin's esteem for Churchill remained a constant of his thought, and his experience at the British embassy during his paladin's Washington stays fortified that viewpoint. However, his opinion of Roosevelt was anything but consistent, and the time when the prime minister traveled to North America for the Quadrant conference revealed significant reservations of the American president Berlin closely watched from his perch a couple of miles from the White House. In a seven-page typed letter to his parents that's dated August 16—immediately following Churchill's visit to Hyde Park—Berlin wrote of his interest in American politics, with its emphasis on individuals instead of institutions. Calling himself "a gossip-loving character," he offered a stunning analysis of Washington's first citizen: "The President really is very queer—not at all what you think he is. I have reached the conclusion that despite the gay and generous nature and all the manners and sweep of an old-established landowning squire, he is (a) absolutely cold, (b) completely ruthless, (c) has no friends, (d) becoming a megalomaniac and is pulling our Mr Churchill along rather than vice versa." Berlin's unambiguous disapproval continued, and he delivered a broadside that FDR couldn't be trusted, in part, because the president "does not like the rich, it is true, but neither does he like the poor or really anyone." By contrast, in this observer's opinion, Mrs. Roosevelt "is the opposite in every respect, a sentimental, gushing, heavy liberal, with a great deal of native shrewdness which the very ugly often develop."[58]

Though just a letter home, this stinging—and penetrating—assessment was based on Berlin's extensive reading and capital-city chatter with government officials, politicians, and journalists. Then in an unprecedented third presidential term and with talk of a fourth circulating, FDR received unrelenting scrutiny, and the repurposed Oxford don, who would become a visiting professor at Harvard first in 1949 as well as later, followed White House intrigue to prepare his weekly reports for London. At the end of this epistle home, he jotted in his difficult-to-decipher script, "This is a terribly boring letter!" In retrospect, it seemed anything but boring, especially compared to what Berlin later said in public about Roosevelt, which was laudatory yet not as effusive as his admiration for Churchill.[59]

As Berlin began his project to compile and assess all the coverage of the Harvard address, Churchill returned to the White House on his private train. Cadogan, who had gone along on the trip, portrayed the prime minister as an animated performer for people he encountered along the rail route. He flashed his "V for victory" sign from his window and even rushed "to the rear platform of the car, in a flowered silk dressing-gown, to attract and chat with anyone he can find on the platform at stopping-places. Makes Clemmie and Mary do the same—only they are conventionally dressed!"[60] Applause animated him.

When Churchill arrived back at the White House the morning of September 7, mail had already begun to pile up about his address. One take-a-bow message came in a note from Harriman that concluded "your words will live in English literature." Churchill's thank-you reply the next day was typed on White House stationery with the word "At" added at the top of the letterhead.[61] On his fourth wartime visit to Washington, Churchill (and those working with him) either felt very much at home—or they had depleted their stock of Downing Street stationery during their many weeks away from London. The first page of the address itself was also prepared on White House stationery. Across the top these words appeared and were underlined: "Prime Minister's Broadcast Speech." There was no reference to Harvard or the occasion for delivery.

While Churchill was basking in the acclaim of Americans, the Foreign Office back in London took a decidedly different view of the prime minister's time in the United States after the Quebec conference. Oliver Harvey, Eden's private secretary and frequent naysayer of the king's first minister, was particularly caustic in a diary entry for September 6, the day of Churchill's Harvard visit. He noted the prime minister planned to stay more than a week longer. "Whilst his influence on the President in military matters may be excellent," Harvey claimed, "the President's influence on him in political matters is disastrous. The P.M.'s American half comes up more and more."[62]

Four days later, Eden weighed in, expressing double-barreled annoyance in his own diary that took aim at both Churchill and Roosevelt. The secretary of state for foreign affairs griped about the "exasperating difficulty" in conducting business with the prime minister while he was abroad. He also objected to Roosevelt's refusal to approve any high-level meetings of the Allies in London, which Eden viewed as "almost insulting considering the number of times we have been to Washington." He elaborated on his criticism and sharpened his point: "We are giving the impression, which they are only too ready by nature to endorse, that militarily all the achievements are theirs and W, by prolonging his stay in Washington, strengthens that impression."[63] Despite whatever signals of disapproval he might have been receiving from Britain, Churchill didn't deviate from the schedule he had set and wanted to complete. Were all the compliments and cheers he was receiving in the United States deafening him to opinion back home?

How the prime minister was acting stateside also annoyed those lower on the ladder of governmental service. Flight Sergeant Geoffrey Green, the clerk and stenographer who accompanied Churchill on several trips abroad, jotted in his notebook for September 7 that the P.M. was "just a spoiled child at times and *must* have his own way, even where Yanks are involved."[64] The repeated comparisons of the prime minister's behavior to that of a "spoiled" youngster couldn't be dismissed as fleeting occurrences. At the time, of course, such displays were well out of public or press view.

During Churchill's remaining days in America on this White House visit, he concentrated on the war situation, deliberately avoiding high-profile public events. (Clementine and Mary received newspaper coverage after the Harvard trip by appearing at Washington activities, which served to keep the prime minister on peoples' minds.) The Allied invasion of Italy, which began on September 3 with an amphibious landing, and the complications arising from the Italian government signing an armistice resulted in British and American military brass shuffling in and out of the White House for meetings the rest of the week. The armistice was announced on Wednesday, September 8, the day before the U.S. Fifth Army and the British Tenth Corps landed at Salerno and Taranto. As it turned out, fighting in Italy continued until Germans surrendered there on May 2, 1945—two days after Hitler committed suicide and four days after Mussolini was executed by antifascist partisans—but the Allies had begun a critical phase of combat on the European continent while Churchill and Roosevelt huddled together in Washington.

Amid all the field reports flowing into the White House and the British embassy, Churchill was forced to handle an immediate, intensely personal crisis. First Sea Lord Dudley Pound, admiral of the British fleet and nicknamed "Churchill's Anchor," came to see the prime minister in the Rose Bedroom. The sixty-six-year-old Pound didn't shroud what he wanted to say. He thought he had suffered a stroke and knew he was no longer capable of performing his duties. He asked to resign. The night before, both Roosevelt and Churchill suspected Pound was seriously ill. A rapidly growing brain tumor took Pound's life six weeks later.

After Churchill met with Pound on September 9, he turned to wrapping up his conversations with Roosevelt and mapping strategy for the coming months, which included looking ahead to the first Big Three summit. The president, who delivered his Fireside Chat about the new bond drive the night before, planned to leave for Hyde Park later that Thursday for a four-day weekend out of the swirl of Washington.

Besides lunch and dinner with Roosevelt, Churchill prepared an eight-point memorandum that reviewed the war's status after "the Italian Surrender." What he wrote was specific, detailing how the captured Italian fleet could be used "to intensify the war against Japan," the possibility of "the conversion of Italy into an active agent against Germany," "the requirements of 'Overlord,'" and other matters. The statement—"to take stock of the new world situation"—served as the point of departure for the final meetings of the two leaders and the Combined Chiefs of Staff in the late afternoon of September 9. At one point in their deliberations, Churchill remarked "that we must be worthy of good luck as we have been of bad in the past."[65] The future looked bright, but darkness could return with the campaign in Italy just beginning and Overlord some nine months away.

When Roosevelt left the White House the evening of September 9 for another "blackout trip" to Hyde Park, Churchill—along with his wife and daughter—remained in Washington at 1600 Pennsylvania Avenue. In his memoir, Churchill recalled that FDR "asked me to use the White House not only as a residence but for any conference I might wish to hold. . . . I availed myself fully of these generous facilities."[66] Having a world leader other than the president living and working in the White House is unprecedented—but, by Churchill's fourth prolonged stay, he felt comfortably at home in America's "Executive Mansion." Without delay, he scheduled a full-dress conference session for Saturday, September 11.

At this meeting in the State Dining Room of the White House, Churchill directed the discussion to consider the complexities of invading Italy and the necessity to strengthen battle operations there. Surrounded by all the top uniformed U.S. and U.K. military leadership, the head of the British government showed no hesitancy to bring up the use of Balkan forces in Italy, the possibility of another bombing attack on the oil refineries at Ploesti, the conditions in the South Pacific, and even the subdued nature of a speech Hitler delivered in Berlin the day before. Churchill knew this meeting was his last chance on this visit to deliver his war strategy to Marshall, Leahy, and others, so he took advantage of the occasion—as well as the presidential surroundings.

In his memoirs, the prime minister said he considered it "an honour to me to preside over this conference," which "seemed to be an event in Anglo-American history."[67] General Hastings Ismay, the prime minister's top military aide, described the meeting in more personal terms. "It was like a family gathering, and every sort of problem was discussed with complete frankness," he recalled. "I wonder if, in all history, there has ever existed between the war leaders of two allied nations, a relationship so intimate as that revealed by this episode."[68] The forty-eight hours Churchill served as the highest-ranking executive in the White House demonstrated not only the state of the relationship between the prime minister and the president in September of 1943. The unusual situation also revealed the extent to which Churchill was willing to take charge and assume command regardless of the circumstances, however out of the ordinary they might be.

Just before the Churchills departed from Washington late Saturday to travel overnight to Hyde Park, the prime minister hosted a dinner and another meeting—this time, though, at the British embassy, where he had met with Dominion representatives based in Washington on September 10. The guest list included three of the longest serving cabinet members in the Roosevelt presidency. Secretary of State Cordell Hull and Interior Secretary Harold Ickes had been in office since FDR's first inauguration in 1933, while Henry Morgenthau became secretary of the treasury a year later. Sam Rayburn in his first (of three) stints as Speaker of the House and Admiral Leahy were there as well, with Leahy subsequently jotting in his diary, "The general conversation at dinner was about the war and post-war prospects."[69] Churchill had temporarily shifted to a different location, yet what obsessed him continued to be the paramount reason he'd been selected prime minister in 1940. Every occasion existed to be seized.

When Churchill's private train arrived near Hyde Park the morning of September 12, Roosevelt was waiting, as usual, to welcome his visitor. The only problem this time was that for some reason—overslept? not dressed? still dictating?—Churchill didn't disembark. According to William Hassett's journal that day, FDR "drove Mrs. Churchill up to the house and returned for the Prime Minister, who, after further delay, finally emerged from his train."[70]

In his memoir, Churchill devoted just one sentence to the day-long visit and never divulged why he was tardy in exiting from his special car—which Hassett judged to be more commodious and elegant than the *Ferdinand Magellan*. All Churchill recorded was that he "broke the train journey to say good-bye to President Roosevelt, and was thus with him at Hyde Park when the Battle of Salerno began."[71] He didn't acknowledge a significant personal event related to the day. It was his and Clementine's thirty-fifth wedding anniversary, which FDR made a point of toasting before taking his visitors back to the train later that evening. Churchill also didn't mention items of entertainment packed in his battered luggage. Courtesy of another Harriman request made to Hollywood executives, five escapist movies were going back to London with the Churchill party: *Claudia*, *Heaven Can Wait*, *Holy Matrimony*, *Stormy Weather*, and *Winter Time*. The first three were comedies and the last two musicals. It shows Harriman's clout that *Claudia* and *Winter Time* weren't released to the public until later in 1943.[72]

Daisy Suckley, who earlier in her diary reported that Churchill brought two more of his signed books in the special red leather binding for FDR's collection, found an occasion on this stopover to reciprocate in her way. She gave Mary Churchill a book she had coauthored in 1942, titled *The True Story of Fala*. Targeted for a youthful readership, the copy was distinctive because it featured the signature of the president as well as Suckley.

Like her brother Randolph, Mary followed her father into the writing trade. Married in 1947 to Christopher Soames, a prominent Conservative politician and government official for decades, Mary Soames became a successful author, who specialized in books documenting the lives of her parents. On her trip to Canada and America, the youngest Churchill child kept a diary, a habit she started years before. Her entries in 1943 included sharp-eyed observations about her two visits to Hyde Park as well as Washington.

Just before she and her father arrived at Hyde Park on August 12, she noted that Secret Service agents took over from "our beautiful Mounties." To her, the president's guards "look so criminal & tough they scare me to death." Her first impression of FDR was that he's "an enthralling personality," while Mrs. Roosevelt is "a great and noble character."[73] However, after Mary spent more time with the president in Quebec and at the White House in early September, she became more discerning, commenting he's "magnetic & full of charm—his sweetness to me is something I shall always remember. But he is a 'raconteur'—& it can be tedious. But at other times, it is interesting & fun."[74]

During the day-long stop over at Hyde Park on September 12, three days before her twenty-first birthday, she continued to watch her host, a figure conspicuously different from her father. Individual adjectives provided an ambiguous portrait: "He seems at once idealistic, cynical, warm-hearted & generous, worldly-wise, naïve, courageous, tough, thoughtful, charming, tedious, vain, sophisticated, civilized." Her conclusion: "I must confess he makes me laugh & he rather bores me."[75]

While the subaltern-diarist sized up America's commander in chief, she saw her father through the eyes of a devoted and loving child, experiencing "the golden peaks of my life." After lunch the two are lying on the lawn—the sixty-eight-year-old "warming his tummy"—and Churchill, a highly accomplished artist, described to his daughter "the colours he would use were he painting—& commented on the wisdom of God in having made the sky *blue* & the trees *green*—& 'it wouldn't have been *nearly* so good the other way round.'"[76]

Decades later in her first book, she recalled the September visit to Hyde—"the day passed very happily"—but appended Clementine's comments about Roosevelt. She said her mother "never really fell under 'FDR's' powerful spell, spotting very quickly that his personal vanity was inordinate." The granddaughter of an earl and wise to the customs of nobility, Churchill's wife disapproved of the president calling her "Clemmie" shortly after they met. "It was surely meant as a compliment," Mary wrote, "but my mother always regarded the use of her own, or other people's, Christian names as a privilege marking close friendship or long association."[77]

Clementine wasn't alone in resenting the familiarity that the president sought by fostering personal rapport. The day before the attack on Pearl Harbor, Lord Halifax—born Edward Wood—was summoned to the White House, and he reported that Roosevelt inquired "whether my friends called me Edward or by some nickname, and then said that he

Churchill makes a donation to his wife, Clementine, for the Red Cross Aid to Russia Fund she chaired. The picture—a "camouflage trick" (in Churchill's phrase)—was taken by a government photographer on December 9, 1941, but not released to the press until December 16, when Churchill was clandestinely sailing to the United States. (IMPERIAL WAR MUSEUM)

Churchill's arrival in Washington on December 22, 1941, became public only after he was safely behind the gates of the White House, with these photos documenting the first moments between the prime minister and President Franklin Roosevelt. On this trip Churchill stayed until January 14, 1942. (AP IMAGES)

Roosevelt and Churchill deliver remarks during the lighting of the National Community Christmas Tree from the South Portico of the White House on December 24, 1941. (FRANKLIN D. ROOSEVELT PRESIDENTIAL LIBRARY)

The two leaders conduct a press conference at the White House less than a day after Churchill began his first visit to Washington, enabling them to emphasize their comradeship not long after Pearl Harbor and America's entry into the war. (FRANKLIN D. ROOSEVELT PRESIDENTIAL LIBRARY)

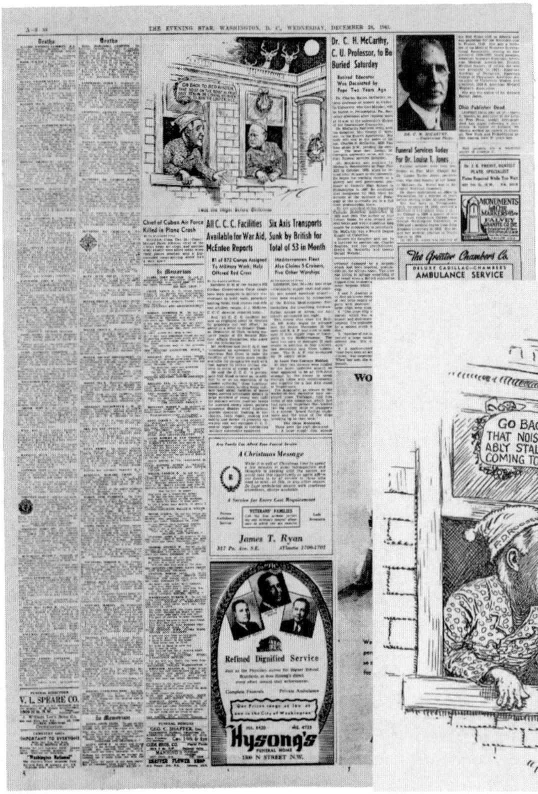
THE EVENING STAR, WASHINGTON, D. C., WEDNESDAY, DECEMBER 24, 1941.

Dr. C. H. McCarthy, C. U. Professor, to Be Buried Saturday

Chief of Cuban Air Force Killed in Plane Crash

All C. C. C. Facilities Available for War Aid, McEntee Reports

Six Axis Transports Sunk by British for Total of 53 in Month

Funeral Services Today For Dr. Louise T. Jones

Ohio Publisher Dead

The Greater Chambers Co.
AMBULANCE SERVICE

A Christmas Message

James T. Ryan

Refined Dignified Service

Hysong's
1300 N STREET N.W.

V. L. SPEARE CO.

The president and prime minister are portrayed as living side-by-side in the White House in this illustration, *'Twas the night before Christmas*, which was published in Washington's *Evening Star*. (CARTOON BY CLIFFORD KENNEDY BERRYMAN)

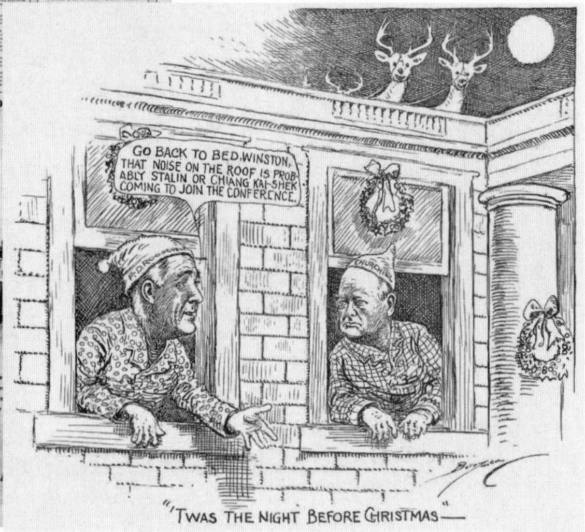

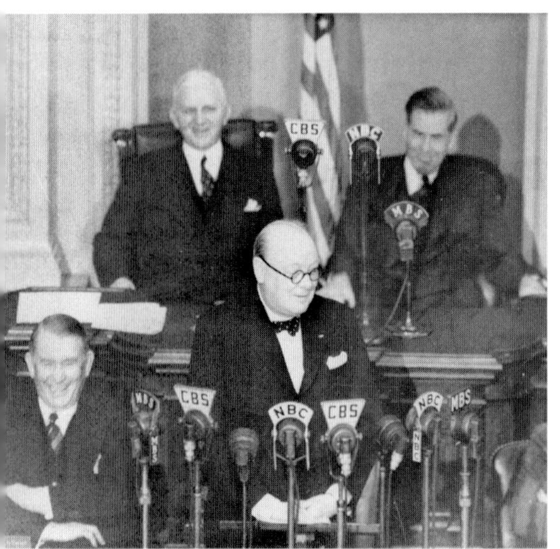

Despite the grave time, Churchill prompts an outburst of laughter during his first address to Congress on December 26, 1941. He subsequently delivered two more speeches as prime minister on Capitol Hill: in 1943 and 1952. (IMPERIAL WAR MUSEUM)

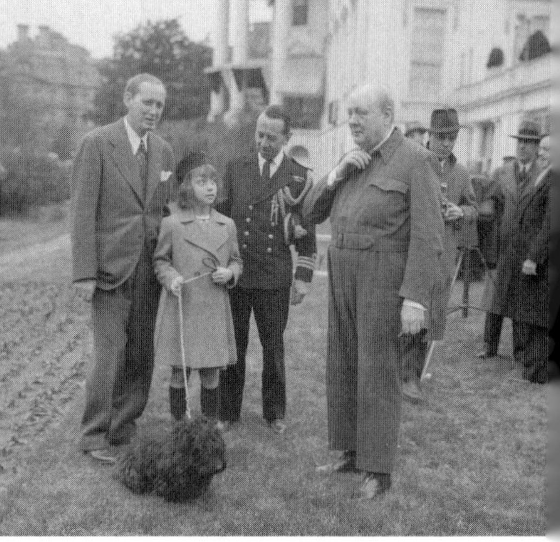

Churchill shows off his "siren suit" for photographers outside the White House on January 3, 1942. With him (left to right) are presidential assistant Harry Hopkins; his daughter Diana Hopkins, who's walking FDR's dog, Fala; and Commander C. R. Thompson, the prime minister's aide-de-camp throughou the war. (IMPERIAL WAR MUSEUM)

SPECIAL DELIVERY

Churchill the Magnificent
The White House
Washington, D.C.

Sacks full of letters and gifts arrived at the White House during Churchill's first wartime visit. This envelope, among the holdings of the Churchill Archives Centre in Cambridge, was kept by John Martin, the prime minister's private secretary. (AUTHOR'S PHOTOGRAPH)

Mail Churchill received at the White House wasn't always complimentary. This two-word epistle—"GO HOME"—arrived in June of 1942 at a difficult time for the Allies. (AUTHOR'S PHOTOGRAPH)

The Pacific War Council met at the White House on June 25, 1942. Canadian prime minister Mackenzie King is standing between Churchill and Roosevelt. Behind King is British ambassador to the United States, Lord Halifax. (FRANKLIN D. ROOSEVELT PRESIDENTIAL LIBRARY)

Not long after Churchill began a June 1942 visit to Roosevelt's estate at Hyde Park, New York, the president took him to his private retreat, Top Cottage, located several miles from the main home. (FRANKLIN D. ROOSEVELT PRESIDENTIAL LIBRARY)

Churchill never minded being photographed indulging in a favorite habit. Here he lights up before a May 14, 1943, broadcast from the White House, recognizing thc valor of the British Home Guard on its third anniversary. (AP IMAGES)

A David Low cartoon, which originally appeared in the popular Evening Standard in London on May 14, 1943, captures the Allies' mood with the tide turning in their favor. A seemingly amused Harry Hopkins glances over at the upbeat leaders. (EVENING STANDARD LTD)

THE LONDONER'S DIARY

PORTENT

Roosevelt took Churchill to his secret camp, Shangri-La, outside Washington in Maryland's Catoctin Mountains for a weekend in May 1943. The two fished part of one day at what is now known as Camp David. (FRANKLIN D. ROOSEVELT PRESIDENTIAL LIBRARY)

Churchill examines a $100 war bond presented to him by U.S. Treasury Secretary Henry Morgenthau Jr. in a White House ceremony on September 3, 1943. The prime minister had come to Washington after the first Quebec conference and stayed nearly two weeks before returning to London. (AP IMAGES)

Churchill acknowledges cheers at Harvard University on September 6, 1943. He received an honorary degree and during his address proposed "common citizenship" for peoples of the United States and Great Britain. (HARVARD UNIVERSITY ARCHIVES, HUP CHURCHILL, WINSTON [25], OLVWORK614662)

With Roosevelt in the driver's seat, the president greets siren-suited Churchill upon arrival at Hyde Park on September 12, 1943. Churchill decided to stay at the White House for meetings, even though Roosevelt had departed earlier for his Hudson Valley home. (IMPERIAL WAR MUSEUM)

Churchill made the Rose Bedroom his White House residence and office during all of his overnight visits in the 1940s and 1950s. This photo was taken before extensive remodeling of the White House during the Truman presidency. (HARRY S. TRUMAN PRESIDENTIAL LIBRARY)

President Dwight D. Eisenhower and Churchill take time for photographers shortly after the prime minister's arrival at the White House on June 25, 1954. (DWIGHT D. EISENHOWER PRESIDENTIAL LIBRARY)

Churchill bows to First Lady Mamie Eisenhower as she welcomes him to the White House in 1954 during his second term as prime minister. (DWIGHT D. EISENHOWER PRESIDENTIAL LIBRARY)

The prime minister and president are flanked by their principal advisors on international affairs. U.S. Secretary of State John Foster Dulles is next to Churchill, and U.K. Foreign Secretary Anthony Eden is beside Eisenhower. (DWIGHT D. EISENHOWER PRESIDENTIAL LIBRARY)

Eisenhower bids Churchill farewell at the end of their meetings in 1954, the prime minister's last White House stay while in office. (DWIGHT D. EISENHOWER PRESIDENTIAL LIBRARY)

Keen to sustain the "special relationship" between the United Kingdom and the United States, Churchill came to Washington in 1959 to spend time with the president and other prominent Americans. While in the capital, the two visited John Foster Dulles at Walter Reed Army Medical Center, where the former secretary of state passed away from cancer nineteen days later. (DWIGHT D. EISENHOWER PRESIDENTIAL LIBRARY)

Churchill and Eisenhower helicoptered to the president's farm in Gettysburg during the 1959 visit. With the president serving as golf-cart chauffeur, the two toured the grounds of the farm and also inspected Civil War battlefields from the air. (DWIGHT D. EISENHOWER PRESIDENTIAL LIBRARY)

On April 9, 1963, President John F. Kennedy conferred honorary American citizenship on Churchill in a White House ceremony. Churchill's son Randolph (on Kennedy's left) read a statement written by the new citizen, a hero to Kennedy. (ABBIE ROWE, NATIONAL PARK SERVICE / JOHN F. KENNEDY PRESIDENTIAL LIBRARY AND MUSEUM)

This cartoon, titled *The Bridge* and drawn by Leslie Illingworth, appeared in Britain's *Daily Mail* the day after the citizenship celebration, symbolizing Churchill's transatlantic connection between the United Kingdom and the United States. (DMG MEDIA LICENSING AND PROVIDED BY THE BRITISH CARTOON ARCHIVE, UNIVERSITY OF KENT)

would like to call me Edward. I said I was greatly flattered, and longed to counter by saying that I would call him Frankie!"[78] American political etiquette, as practiced by a Democrat's democrat, always tried to reduce the distance between and among people—even those from other countries accustomed to different standards of protocol. (As touched on previously, one American refused to allow FDR's familiarity: George Marshall. "General Marshall" was never "George.") Clementine's reservations about Roosevelt tended to be personal, while Eleanor's about Churchill encompassed both personal and policy-related concerns, notably his affection for alcohol and his constant drumbeat about the boon to the world of a U.K.-U.S. alliance.

While the prime minister and president spent time basking in the sunshine, reports continued to arrive about Operation Avalanche, the code name of the Allied landing at Salerno. Axis forces mounted such a ferocious counter-attack that doubts about the strategy and execution started to circulate. "These things always seem to happen when I am with the President," Churchill is quoted as telling his doctor, Lord Moran, obliquely referring to the fall of Tobruk in June of 1942, when the prime minister was also at the White House. Moran remarked, "Poor Winston, he had been so anxious to convince Roosevelt that the invasion of Italy would yield a bountiful harvest at no great cost."[79] Churchill's prolonged hesitancy to support the cross-Channel operation derived in part from his desire to storm the European continent from the south. That thinking and its consequences were now under serious scrutiny in Washington and London as fighting intensified in Italy.

According to Daisy Suckley, Churchill's last words to Roosevelt were "God Bless You," a rather strange farewell for someone Churchill expert Richard M. Langworth once labeled an "optimistic agnostic." FDR replied, "I'll be over with you, next spring."[80] Was the president contemplating a transatlantic journey around the time of Overlord? Would he partially make up for Churchill's multiple ocean crossings by finally traveling to London or somewhere else in the United Kingdom?

What about the political repercussions of such a trip if FDR decided to seek a fourth term in the 1944 election?

For political and personal reasons, Churchill yearned to greet Roosevelt in London and went so far as to provide detailed architectural drawings of a spacious apartment the president would occupy while there. These plans were brought back to FDR by Eleanor after her four-week trip in the fall of 1942 to tour the British home front and meet U.S. troops. As late as May 20, 1944—seventeen days before D-Day—Roosevelt wrote in a "Dear Winston" letter that he couldn't embark on a foreign trip "for over a month. Of course, I am greatly disappointed that I could not be in England just at this moment, but perhaps having missed the boat it will be best not to make the trip until the events of the near future are more clear."[81] Despite all of Roosevelt's travel during World War II, he never made the effort to go to Britain. For meetings between America's chief executive and his British counterpart, Churchill had to cross the Atlantic six times as well as go to locations in North Africa, the Middle East, or the Soviet Union. On this particular trip in 1943, he logged nearly five thousand miles on train tracks in America and Canada for the journey that took him from Halifax and back.

During the more than thirty-seven-hour rail journey from Hyde Park to Halifax to reach the battleship HMS *Renown*, Churchill dictated memorandums and correspondence much of the time. One dated September 13 was addressed to "My dear Franklin" and included the text of a "telegram to U.J." ("Uncle Joe" Stalin) for which he sought the president's approval. The final paragraph of the letter turned familiar, if not intimate, while also conveying a broader message justifying the prime minister's commitment to the demanding travel agenda he had begun in 1941. Expressing gratitude for the "charming hospitality" at the White House and Hyde Park, he connected the relations between the Allied leaders and his vaunted objective: "You know how I treasure the friendship with which you have honoured me and how profoundly I feel that we might together do something really fine and lasting for our two countries and, through them, for the future of all."[82]

The next day Churchill sent Deputy Prime Minister Clement Attlee and Foreign Secretary Eden a "Most Secret and Personal" cypher telegram reporting that Roosevelt "thinks we should be prepared to raise with Stalin . . . the post-war world organization." The prime minister concluded his message by saying that whatever is decided it shouldn't affect "the natural Anglo-American special relationship."[83] During each trip to the United States in 1943, Churchill persistently invoked "the doctrine of the fraternal association of our two peoples," as he publicly proposed at Harvard. However, the phrase "special relationship," with its greater emotional resonance, subsequently became indelibly identified with Churchill, when the expression entered popular usage after Churchill's "Sinews of Peace" ("iron curtain") speech, delivered at Westminster College in Fulton, Missouri on March 5, 1946. Midway in that controversial address, the by then former prime minister said: "I come to the crux of what I have travelled here to say. Neither the sure prevention of war, nor the continuous rise of world organisation will be gained without what I have called the fraternal association of the English-speaking peoples. This means a special relationship between the British Commonwealth and Empire and the United States."[84] Over two years earlier, while returning from the Quebec conference and more than two weeks in the States, he was introducing a two-word phrase to his thinking and writing that to this day often features, whether positively or negatively, in discussions about the relationship between the United Kingdom and the United States.

The *Renown* docked back on the River Clyde in Scotland on September 19. Churchill had been gone over six weeks. Shortly after he reached London the next day, he convened the War Cabinet, and this meeting was attended by Lord Halifax, who had been in Britain on home leave since early August and periodically participated in sessions of the War Cabinet. (On August 18, after that day's meeting, he noted in his diary, "Winston is deluging them with telegrams."[85])

Churchill also showered the House of Commons with words on September 21, when he returned there and spoke, according to an Associated Press report, for two hours and seven minutes—with an hour-long intermission for lunch after the initial seventy-five minutes. The first portion of his prepared remarks contained over eight thousand words, and his grasp of details reflected how closely he had monitored dispatches from the battlefield, especially Italy, during his time in North America. Near the end of his speech, Churchill compared the attitude of Americans to the British and praised the U.S. commitment to the war as well as the strengthening linkage between the Allies. The prime minister had basked in Yankee adulation during his trip and that undoubtedly shaped aspects of his viewpoint. "I was made conscious of the resolve and desire of all parties to drive forward the war on all fronts and against all foes with the utmost determination," he stated. "I was also conscious of a feeling of friendliness towards Great Britain and the British Commonwealth and Empire such as I have never known before."[86]

Besides describing the war picture from his vantage point after his extended stay in North America, Churchill also looked ahead to future battles in an original way. "I call this front we have opened, first in Africa, next in Sicily, and now in Italy, the Third Front," the prime minister said responding to a question from a House member. "The Second Front, which already exists potentially and which is rapidly gathering weight, has not yet been engaged.... At what we and our American Allies judge to be the right time, this front will be thrown open, and the mass invasion from the West, in combination with the invasion from the South, will begin."[87]

Churchill said as much as he could in public to provide a prelude to Overlord. In covering the speech, Washington's *Evening Star* published "a condensed text" on September 21 and used a seven-column front page headline: "Churchill Promises Mass Invasion of Europe's Coast From West." The eight-column banner above it leads to a copyrighted story from the Associated Press: "Marshall Slated as Global Commander." The first sentence made a reader think the issue of who would be in charge of the second front was settled: "The blunt fact about Gen.

George C. Marshall is that he is tentatively slated to become virtual commander-in-chief of all Anglo-American forces in the field, ground, sea and air, and put into execution the pattern of victory East and West shaped at the Quebec Conference." That, of course, didn't happen, with Eisenhower receiving the appointment three months later.

As the first Big Three conference in Tehran—involving Churchill, Roosevelt, Stalin—approached in late November, concern about the planned invasion that was scheduled for the spring of 1944 circulated among Washington officialdom. Secretary of War Henry Stimson considered any efforts to delay or abandon Overlord attempted sabotage—with Churchill, in his opinion, the principal culprit. In a diary entry for October 28—exactly a month before the Tehran talks began—Stimson thundered that his British nemesis was determined "with all his lip service [of support] to stick a knife in the back of Overlord and I feel more bitterly about it than I ever have before."[88] Three days later, he remained infuriated and pointed at the "dirty baseball on the part of Churchill." What worried Stimson most was the fear that the prime minister would influence Roosevelt's commitment to carry through with Overlord. Smoldering suspicions among the Allies continued for months.

The meetings in Tehran, however, proved decisive in reinforcing the resolve to launch a full-scale second front in the spring of 1944. Though Churchill kept in regular communication with the president, the prime minister didn't meet with Roosevelt or return to America until three months after D-Day. By then, Roosevelt was embarking on his fourth campaign for the White House, a quest that on November 7, 1944, won for him yet another term as president. The two leaders continued to work together and FDR maintained he would make his promised trip to London, but their relationship after Churchill left Hyde Park in September of 1943 and Tehran on December 1 became increasingly more complicated. Their own "special relationship," cultivated by Churchill during his four extended White House visits, took a definite turn into new, uncharted territory.

– 5 –

A SECRET RENDEZVOUS

If 1943 was Winston Churchill's American *annus mirabilis*, a remarkable year when fascination with him reached its apex, 1944 turned into an enigmatic study in contrasts. One year after two lengthy sojourns in the White House and a multitude of extensively covered public occasions, the British prime minister never traveled to Washington and, uncharacteristically, avoided the limelight when he did come to the States that year. Though Operation Overlord opened the Western European front with D-Day on June 6 and Paris was liberated on August 25, there were salient reasons a foreign figure, even an admired one, sidestepped the hoopla and hubbub of visiting Franklin Roosevelt in 1944.

Churchill's final American trip to confer with Roosevelt took place in complete secrecy and lasted just thirty-two hours. This excursion to FDR's Hudson Valley White House at Hyde Park—instead of Washington—followed the second Quebec conference in September of 1944. The Anglo-American wartime alliance was in a state of change, and so, too, was the relationship between the prime minister and the president.

Churchill and Roosevelt met to discuss what they hoped would be the concluding stages of World War II in Quebec and at Hyde Park over eight days that September. It was the prime minister's sole transatlantic journey that year and the two leaders' only time together in 1944. By contrast, during 1943 and in five different countries, Churchill and Roosevelt spent some sixty days participating in conferences or engaged in one-on-one consultations. Those, in effect, two months together, which involved Joseph Stalin for four days at Tehran, helped map out policy proposals to defeat the Wehrmacht and Japan—and end the war.

In 1943, uppermost in the minds of Roosevelt and Stalin, if not the uncertain and fence-straddling Churchill, was the cross-Channel invasion. Overlord began six months after the last meeting between Churchill and FDR in 1943 and a little more than three months before their time together the following year. By then, the Allies were advancing across France, Belgium, and Luxembourg toward the Siegfried Line in western Germany. Victory seemed tantalizingly close, and press reports from Quebec mentioned wagering taking place on the precise date the German military would capitulate. Still, strategizing about conquering Hitler and his forces as well as defining the role Britain and the Soviet Union would play in the Pacific theatre defined the discussions of the two leaders and their advisors.

The road to Quebec City and Hyde Park was circuitous and cluttered with frustrated hopes. On March 18, 1944, Churchill proposed to Roosevelt an early April conference in Bermuda, adding a last item to the telegram that he was "hardening for OVERLORD as the time gets nearer."[1] FDR declined this meeting, saying he needed rest to overcome a lingering "attack of grippe."[2] Two days later, the president followed up with a telegram, keeping the door slightly ajar: "I join you in hoping that we may arrange to have a meeting before the great event [D-Day] is launched."[3]

Churchill persisted with his desire for talks, even writing on May 25 that "a very good place in London which would give you perfect safety and comfort" would be at his disposal.[4] FDR kept refusing Churchill's overtures from March into August. In a June 1 telegram, the prime minister admitted that a rendezvous in America seemed politically problematic: "It would probably be better for me not to come in to the United States as you approach the election crisis or our enemies might try to make mischief."[5] The phrases "election crisis" and "our enemies" reveal Churchill, someone careful in composition, taking sides in the eyes of his "top secret" reader. Six weeks later (on July 16), he was still pushing and sounding agitated that nothing had been arranged: "When are we going to meet and where? That we must meet soon is certain. . . . I would brave the reporters at Washington or the mosquitos of Alaska!"[6] In reply, Roosevelt floated the idea of a conference to be conducted on battleships off the coast of Scotland in mid-September, saying: "This would get me back in plenty of time for the election, although that is in the lap of the Gods."[7] Nearly a month later, on August 11, Roosevelt wrote that he was unable to sail to Scotland but that he can "arrive in Quebec on the 10th or 11th of September."[8] The president was finally on board.

Thirty-one days later, what was code-named the Octagon conference began. However, questions surrounding Churchill's sixth trip to North America since 1941 prompt any observer to wonder why scheduling this meeting took half a year. Questions abound. Did FDR procrastinate to keep Churchill at arm's length to evade his newest ideas and stratagems? The prime minister was insistent about meeting, even broaching a trip to Washington after suggesting it might be hazardous amid "the election crisis." Had he become insecure in dealing with Roosevelt? Perhaps he thought that he (and by extension the British Empire) was now playing second fiddle, as FDR and Stalin commanded vastly larger forces and flexed more military muscle. What was behind the president's numerous hints of trips to the United Kingdom without following through?

Despite the continuity of friendly messages and acts of kindness by both men, two episodes in 1943 reveal Rooseveltian machinations that raise doubts about the authenticity of the relationship between the president and the prime minister. Did bonhomie conceal the exercise of *realpolitik* and a measure of duplicity? Tellingly, in each case, FDR was scheming to establish a stronger connection to Stalin—and Churchill was either completely left out or the object of squirm-producing ridicule.

On May 5, 1943, six days before the Trident Conference began, FDR wrote "My dear Mr. Stalin," proposing "an informal and completely simple visit for a few days between you and me." He suggested the meeting could take place "either on your side or my side of Bering Straits," making the point that Iceland wasn't a real possibility because of the "difficult flights" involved—and holding talks there "would make it, quite frankly, difficult not to invite Prime Minister Churchill at the same time."[9] Nearly eight weeks later, Churchill learned from the London-based U.S. emissary W. Averell Harriman of Roosevelt's idea of a two-person meeting with Stalin. The prime minister fired off a cable to FDR the next day, June 25, and made no effort to hide his displeasure: "You must excuse me expressing myself with all the frankness that our friendship and the gravity of the issue warrant. I do not underrate the use that enemy propaganda would make of a meeting between the heads of Soviet Russia and the United States at this juncture with the British Commonwealth and Empire excluded."[10]

How did FDR react to Churchill's high-pitched concern, with its appeal to their "friendship"? He lied. On June 28, Roosevelt wrote: "I did not suggest to UJ that we meet alone but he told [Joseph] Davies [Roosevelt's envoy and former ambassador to the U.S.S.R.] that he assumed (a) that we would meet alone and (b) that he agreed that we should not bring staffs to what would be a preliminary meeting."[11] Eight paragraphs of soft-pedaling justifications followed the prevarication to help reduce Churchill's bitterness.

As it happened, Roosevelt and Stalin didn't meet until late November of 1943, with Churchill also participating. The Tehran conference was the first time the Allies' Big Three assembled since the Second World War began. While the talks progressed, FDR kept worrying that he wasn't creating personal rapport with Stalin. In this case, it was more than using someone's first name or a nickname to establish greater familiarity. Frances Perkins, the first woman in U.S. history to serve as a cabinet member and the secretary of labor throughout Roosevelt's presidency, recorded in a memoir how FDR made a breakthrough with his Soviet counterpart. Frustrated that he couldn't connect with Stalin, he warned Churchill that he was plotting to defrost Stalin's icy exterior. The president informed the Soviet leader that "Winston is cranky this morning, he got up on the wrong side of the bed."[12] Roosevelt continued to make fun of Churchill, his manner, and his way of doing things until Stalin roared with laughter and came over to shake FDR's hand. According to Perkins, Roosevelt judged that his fun-poking shtick at Churchill's expense had worked, with the result being that "we talked like men and brothers."[13]

In his war memoirs, Churchill mentioned that Stalin "indulged in a great deal of 'teasing' of me"[14] at a dinner on November 29. Stalin raised the prospect of executing fifty thousand members of the German general staff, and Churchill objected that "such infamy" would "sully my own and my country's honour."[15] Churchill walked out of the hall in anger. FDR's performance of strategic ridicule occurred two days later (on December 1). What was Churchill thinking about his relationship to the two other leaders as the conference concluded? The U.S. government publication about the Tehran conference reduced Roosevelt's mockery to a footnote in the proceedings, mentioning "jocular remarks at Churchill's expense" that relied on the Perkins account.[16] Though the president's disparaging conduct was not formally recorded in the minutes, the anecdote—thanks largely to FDR's retelling of it—appeared in John Gunther's *Roosevelt in Retrospect*, Elliott Roosevelt and James Brough's *A Rendezvous With Destiny*, and elsewhere.

Cutting, personal humor for the purpose of ingratiating oneself at the expense of another is always a double-edged sword. In this case, Roosevelt was trying to establish a connection with a cold, standoffish figure by belittling a comrade in arms, who always traveled to meet them. How seriously did FDR and Stalin take Churchill? Were the two figures, meeting for the first time, trying to assert through statements they considered humorous that they were more powerful than the British prime minister? Gunther, one of America's most respected foreign correspondents before becoming a best-selling author, reported that "the baiting [by FDR] went a little far." Wanting to learn more, he "asked someone who was present if this episode actually had taken place as frequently described. 'You bet it did, and it wasn't funny, either!' "[17] Mary Churchill Soames later told an interviewer: "My father was awfully wounded at Teheran. For reasons of state, it seems to me President Roosevelt was out to charm Stalin, and my father was the odd man out." She went on to admit: "My father was very hurt, I think."[18]

At the beginning of 1943, after the conference in Casablanca, Churchill considered FDR "the truest friend" and "the greatest man" he'd known. This judgment, though, was uttered *before* the prime minister knew of the president's mendacity trying to justify his approach to Stalin in May and Roosevelt's attempt at deprecating drollery to benefit himself with a powerful figure he'd met just a few days before. Both activities must have prompted Churchill to question where he stood with someone he wanted to trust and call a friend. Was Roosevelt's conduct in either instance how true friends treated each other?

During the conference in Iran, which lasted from November 28 through December 1, Churchill arrived at a painful perception he would later vividly express. "I realized at Teheran for the first time what a small nation we are," he said. "There I sat with the great Russian bear on one side of me, with paws outstretched, and on the other side the great American buffalo, and between the two sat the poor little English donkey who was the only one, the only one of the three, who knew the right way home."[19] Despite the vast differences involved among the three major Allies, Churchill's self-image combined a realistic assessment of national power along with his own confidence in developing strategy and policy. This latter characteristic kept driving him to arrange summits with other leaders, including the one with Roosevelt in 1944 at Quebec and their subsequent discussions at Hyde Park. He had felt alone for over a year and a half before Pearl Harbor, and now, in a different way, he felt squeezed between two more potent forces that diminished his clout. He had struggled mightily to woo Roosevelt—only to see the president, as time passed, more inclined to pursue Stalin with his superior military capability and territorial dominance.

FDR's willingness to say or do what he thought would benefit him, his standing with others, and his exercise of power undoubtedly created uncertainty for Churchill. How the president acted toward the prime minister could at times even seem puzzling. Roosevelt, for instance, made a point of leaving from Hyde Park for Quebec two-and-a-half hours earlier than the scheduled departure time arranged by the White House. The reason for the change? FDR wanted to arrive at the conference site first so he could welcome Churchill and his party.

When the *Ferdinand Magellan* arrived at Quebec City, the president immediately invited Canadian prime minister Mackenzie King on board for a visit. Roosevelt told King he wanted to arrive before Churchill, prompting this biting comment from the three-time prime minister of America's northern neighbor, who had been in office since 1935: "It seemed to me that the President was rather assuming that he was in his country."[20] Could FDR, who invariably greeted Churchill on transatlantic visits to the United States, have wanted to continue that custom, or could it have been a stunt of one-upmanship with the U.S. president arriving ahead of the United Kingdom's prime minister in one of the most significant Dominions?

Considerations of protocol or pretension aside, King noted Roosevelt's physical changes—"very much thinner" and "distinctly older and worn"—since their last meeting. "I confess I was just a little bit shocked at his appearance," King admitted.[21] At this time, the Canadian was seven years older than Roosevelt. Like Churchill, King had been born near the end of 1874. During their chat, the prospects for FDR in the November election came up. He, according to King, expressed uneasiness, claiming that "we cannot get our people to register; cannot get the vote out."[22] For FDR, electoral apprehension and worry, even about the mechanics of casting ballots, loomed as factors in his political calculus.

During the Quebec conference, at Hyde Park, and subsequently, gauging the president's health and the impact of November's voting on decisions became unavoidable concerns for Churchill and the people around him. The 1943 conference in Canada had looked ahead to a summit with Stalin joining Churchill and Roosevelt as well as to Overlord with its establishment of the second front the Soviets had sought since before Pearl Harbor. A year later, the principal topics on the conference agenda included the role Britain's navy would play in fighting Japan, continuation of Lend-Lease to assist the United Kingdom, and the controversial "Morgenthau Plan," advanced by Treasury Secretary Henry Morgenthau Jr. This proposal advocated removing Germany's war-making ability by eliminating the country's industrial capacity in the Ruhr Valley. Each subject addressed the future, particularly charting a path to victory in the Far East and dealing with the aftermath of defeating the Third Reich.

Though Churchill cabled back to the deputy prime minister and the war cabinet on September 13 that the conference "opened in a blaze of friendship,"[23] that blaze was tamped down during several meetings by friction between the two sides. The U.S. account of the proceedings included the description of a dinner (held on September 13, the day the cable praising the joint friendship was sent), where Morgenthau's ideas received an airing. Churchill pronounced the plan to be "unnatural, unchristian and unnecessary."[24] Later in this account, the displeased prime minister turned to Roosevelt and inquired, "Is this what you asked me to come all the way over here to discuss?"[25] The next day, according to the official proceedings, Churchill and Roosevelt met to create a committee on the Lend-Lease agreement and the prime minister became "nervous and eager" for the president to initial the prepared document, accepting the terms. After some time passed and unable to contain his agitation, Churchill asked the president two more questions even more pointed than the one posed the previous day: "What do you want me to do? Get on my hind legs and beg like Fala?"[26] The prime minister's language assumed a new edge of dissatisfaction and frustration directed squarely at Roosevelt.

During their six days in Canada, Churchill and Roosevelt spent most of their time together at luncheons and dinners, eleven in all. There were seven other meetings involving the two leaders, usually with a small number of other participants. Two plenary sessions (September 13 and 16) brought the prime minister, the president, and their chief military strategists together. Just before the conference concluded, Churchill and Roosevelt received honorary degrees from McGill University in a ceremony at the Citadel that was followed by a joint press conference. The contingent of some 150 reporters received a short, three-sentence "communiqué," summarizing the work of the lone meeting the two men had in 1944. The key sentence reported: "In a very short space of time they reached decisions on all points both with regard to the completion of the war in Europe, now approaching its final stages, and the destruction of the barbarians of the Pacific."[27]

Near the conclusion of his remarks to the assembled journalists, Churchill harked back to a phrase he used earlier in the week. "I have enjoyed this conference very much," he said. "It has been conducted in a blaze of friendship." He went on to declare that "it has been the most agreeable of all the conferences which I have ever attended."[28] Given what we know Churchill said behind closed doors in previous days, were these statements a truthful reflection of what had occurred? What did Churchill actually think after the meetings ended? Four days later, according to an account of Lord Moran, the prime minister delivered a very different assessment. On the *Queen Mary* sailing out of New York City on September 20, Churchill's doctor asked, "Did you find this conference less tiring than the Cairo meeting [in 1943]?" The patient answered with a question and an explanation: "What is this conference? Two talks with the Chiefs of Staff; the rest was waiting for the chance to put in a word with the President. One has to seize the occasion. There was nothing to tire me."[29]

If Moran's account is accurate, the prime minister, away from the earshot of reporters, definitely saw himself in a subordinate position, a donkey (if you will) overshadowed by the much larger, less domesticated buffalo. Looking back nearly four decades later, John Colville, who served as Churchill's assistant private secretary from 1940 to 1941 and again from 1943 to 1945, noted that the power dynamics for the Allies began to change in 1943. As "the arsenal of democracy" expanded in productivity and military forces surged in numbers, Americans—in Colville's opinion—became "less sensitive to British views."[30]

Still, Churchill sought time when he could get it with Roosevelt, always talking publicly about their "friendship," ablaze or otherwise. Even on this brief trip, with the shortest amount of time in the United States, FDR played host to "Winston and Clemmie," as he called the couple. For the fourth time, Churchill and Roosevelt met at the president's Hyde Park estate, his Hudson Valley White House. This visit, however, was different. That it even occurred wasn't revealed to the public until late in the afternoon of September 26, shortly after Churchill arrived back in London and ten days after the Quebec conference concluded.

Withholding any announcement of the prime minister's whereabouts maintained secrecy about his travel, but in this case there was another governing consideration. Roosevelt's presidential campaign was scheduled to have its formal beginning on September 23 with a speech in Washington at a dinner of the International Brotherhood of Teamsters. In remarks that evening, FDR memorably criticized his Republican opponents for slandering his Scottish terrier and devoted companion, Fala: "I don't resent attacks, and my family doesn't resent attacks, but Fala does resent them. . . . I think I have a right to resent, to object to libelous statements about my dog." Though Roosevelt talked extensively that evening about the war, he made no mention of Churchill or meetings with him. The prime reason was that GOP politicians had seized on the Quebec conference as being little more than political theater, starring Roosevelt and Churchill, rather than serious strategy sessions. Representative Everett McKinley Dirksen of Illinois, who became well-known in the 1960s as the Senate minority leader with an unforgettable foghorn voice, was one of the most vociferous Roosevelt critics in Congress, saying as the conference in Canada began that "the fourth-term candidate"—a barbed label Dirksen repeated often—benefited politically from the summit because, as newspapers reported, it was "the first time the British Prime Minister has ever been used in an American election campaign."

People around both leaders filtered much that they said and did with a close eye on what might happen at U.S. polling places on November 7. Near the end of the Quebec sessions, Robert J. (Robin) Cruikshank, a prominent British journalist who during the war worked with Isaiah Berlin in Washington as director of the American division of the Ministry of Information and helped with press relations at Quebec, wrote Churchill's principal private secretary, John Martin. In a memorandum marked "SECRET," he offered a warning. "I think I should advise you that a visit by the Prime Minister to the United States will be turned to mischief by considerable sections of the Press in that country," Cruikshank counseled. He elaborated on his concern by stating that FDR's opponents in politics and in the press would try to show that Churchill favored the president's reelection. The veteran in journalism and government, with many years of experience in America, became even more blunt in cautioning against the prime minister spending any time in one particular state: New York. The governor of New York, Thomas Dewey, was FDR's Republican opponent, and Roosevelt had preceded Dewey as governor a decade earlier. "The fight in that State will be very hot," Cruikshank argued. "If the Prime Minister should visit that State it will be said by many political zealots that he has done so to give the weight of his vast prestige in the U.S. and the magic of his name there to support a hard-pressed candidate."[31]

The strongly worded memorandum had no influence, but the strict wartime secrecy kept Americans and the British from learning about the Churchills' stop at Hyde Park until several days after FDR launched his campaign. A brief Associated Press dispatch from Quebec that circulated on September 18 reported: "Prime Minister Churchill left here by train for an undisclosed destination yesterday." The tight lid of censorship was on—and it stayed firmly in place throughout the next week.

Though FDR's calendar available in his presidential library listed "no appointments" for either September 18 or 19, Churchill's private train arrived near Hyde Park the morning of the eighteenth, a day after Roosevelt had returned from Quebec. Besides the Churchills, the British retinue included several of the prime minister's closest associates, while the president was surrounded by some of his top advisors, including Admiral William D. Leahy, FDR's chief of staff, and advisor Harry Hopkins. For lunch the first day, the Duke of Windsor (formerly King Edward VIII) was an invited guest—King George VI wanted Churchill to make clear to the Duke that his older brother would *not* be welcome to take up residence in England—and on one of the evenings Treasury Secretary Morgenthau came over to Springwood for dinner from his nearby home in the Hudson Valley.

Roosevelt left no formal record of Churchill's visit, and what the prime minister recorded about it tests whether a reader should trust what is written in a memoir, even by someone who in 1953 would win the Nobel Prize in Literature (as the citation stated) "for his mastery of historical and biographical description as well as for brilliant oratory in defending exalted human values." At the end of chapter ten of *Triumph and Tragedy*, Churchill devoted portions of three paragraphs (two of which averaged just thirty-two words each) to his time at Hyde Park. In the first one, he noted: "On Sunday, September 17, I left Quebec by train with my wife and daughter Mary to pay a farewell visit to the President at Hyde Park."[32] In truth, Mary Churchill didn't travel with her parents on this trip, as she had the year before. She was on duty with her battery at another Hyde Park, this one in London, for her assignment with the Auxiliary Territorial Service. In 1944, her involvement in that transatlantic journey was limited to welcoming her mother and father on their return at London's Euston Station, as she later noted in two of her books. Her memoir, *A Daughter's Tale*, even includes a picture with this caption in the photographic section: "Meeting my parents at Euston Station on their return from Quebec, September 1944."

After that inaccuracy by Churchill, the next paragraph in *Triumph and Tragedy* repeats almost word-for-word what he wrote in chapter five of *Closing the Ring* about Harry Hopkins and "his altered position" vis-à-vis Roosevelt in the summer of 1943.[33] Was Hopkins at Hyde Park in both 1943 and 1944? The answer is yes, according to the U.S. government report, John Martin's *Downing Street: The War Years*, and David L. Roll's *The Hopkins Touch*. Churchill's literary assistant, William Deakin, an Oxford historian who assembled and oversaw the text and documents in the preparation of the war memoirs, could not find evidence of Hopkins being at Hyde Park in 1943, so the passage was deleted in the British edition of *Closing the Ring*, published nine months after the American one. U.S. readers learned about the diminished state of Hopkins in two separate volumes of Churchill's war memoirs.[34]

As happened with a number of the president's associates, Hopkins drifted apart from FDR, and the former secretary of commerce turned foreign policy advisor lost much of his influence by 1944. With an upcoming election, Roosevelt wanted to minimize criticism of his administration—and of himself. As the war years progressed, Hopkins had turned into a lightning rod for Republicans and certain journalists to attack. In addition, as noted in the previous chapter, when he moved out of the White House in 1943, "Harry the Hop" could no longer jump to be at the president's beck and call at all hours.

Years later, as Churchill composed his "history," he misremembered that the lunch he originally thought occurred in 1943 really took place a year later. While Churchill described the uncomfortable lunch, his longtime aide-de-camp, Commander C. R. Thompson, noticed more awkwardness at a Hyde Park dinner in 1944. With Hopkins there, the unflappable Roosevelt seemed ill at ease in his own home. The friendship between Churchill and Hopkins continued, but the Roosevelt-Hopkins breach was evident to others. As Thompson recalled, "The

President and Hopkins were worlds apart and the forced cheerfulness was just a façade. It was all most depressing and in sharp contrast to our happy times together in the past."[35]

A more telling description of what happened at Hyde Park after the Quebec conference can be found in a diary Clementine Churchill kept and sent to her children. For September 18, she reports that FDR, Eleanor Roosevelt, and their daughter Anna met the train when it arrived. Married at the time to John Boettiger, Anna impressed Mrs. Churchill: "So far as I have been able to observe she seems the nicest of the large Roosevelt brood."[36] The prime minister's spouse isn't shy in commenting on the visitors to Springwood, including Admiral Leahy and "Windsor," but Hopkins received detailed consideration: "Harry Hopkins also appeared and stayed till the next morning. He seems to have quite dropped out of the picture. I found it sad and rather embarrassing. . . . I cannot but feel that this is a disadvantage to Anglo-American relationship."[37]

The most revealing portion of her journal focused on FDR, and to begin it the diarist switched to the first-person plural "We," making it sound like the wife and her husband might have discussed matters of power between themselves. She wrote that "we" wondered whether Leahy occupied Hopkins' right-hand place. "One must hope that this is so," she observed, "because the President, with all his genius does not—indeed cannot (partly because of his health and partly because of his make-up)—function round the clock, like your Father. I should not think that his mind was pin-pointed on the war for more than four hours a day, which is not really enough when one is a supreme war lord."[38]

Clementine Churchill's up-close appraisal of FDR's restricted regimen was consistent with medical documents at the Roosevelt Library. During a physical examination in May of 1944, the president's blood pressure was alarmingly high (196/112), and he was told—a month before D-Day—to reduce his work load to four hours a day, avoiding as much "irritation" as possible.[39] Daisy Suckley on September 18, the same day Mrs. Churchill was describing, admitted that FDR "worries me. He gets so awfully tired, and has no chance to rest."[40] The state of the president's health was not only noticeable to those around him, as questions of his fitness found their way into political speeches and journalistic commentary. To try to suppress this talk, Eleanor Roosevelt devoted her September 25 "My Day" column to denouncing opponents' "gossip" about FDR's physical condition: "Now that he has been to Quebec and back, I hope everyone realizes that the people who spread these rumors are not really concerned about the President's health."[41]

For her column that appeared September 19, Mrs. Roosevelt began: "Yesterday we had a picnic lunch," remarking, "Here our picnics are pretty simple to arrange, with a built-in grill and everything conveniently at hand."[42] With the wartime and campaign-season secrecy in full effect, there was no mention of any British visitors to Hyde Park. Though the column is mostly happy-go-lucky in tone, the First Lady's mood that day was anything but that. In a letter late that evening (September 18) after she finished her column, she complained to her close friend, Joseph P. Lash, about being "a glorified housekeeper" before exploding: "These are the days when the resentment at the tyranny of people & things grows on me until if I were not a well-disciplined person I would go out & howl like a dog!" A few sentences later, Mrs. Roosevelt got personal: "I do not agree with Mr. Churchill on Spain & he insists on bringing it up at every meal. He talks picturesquely but I'm almost tempted to say stupidly at times."[43]

Mrs. Churchill's account in her diary was similar to the one of her daughter Mary in 1943, descriptive and assertive: "Life at Hyde Park is a succession of picnics."[44] Besides the pleasure of picnics, Mrs. Churchill joined the First Lady "for two terrific walks" and went with FDR to "the President's Museum," where—she noted in her diary—she "managed to hook out of it a horrible caricature of your Father by Paul Maze."[45]

A woman of definite opinions, she spoke her mind, engaging in spousal image-management to the point of ripping up a sketch by a respected artist who had known Churchill since the Great War and had encouraged him to take up, in a phrase Churchill used as the title of one of his books, "painting as a pastime." Her pushing for the disposal of what Maze had drawn was, to a certain extent, a foreshadowing of the more dramatic destruction of the Graham Sutherland portrait of Churchill, which was funded by members of the House of Commons and the House of Lords to honor his eightieth birthday in 1954. Neither Clementine nor her husband approved of the painting's depiction of its subject, with Churchill dismissively pronouncing it as "a remarkable example of modern art." It was subsequently removed from their home at Chartwell and burned. Unflattering art didn't deserve public display, they must have presumed.

In his memoir *I Was There*, Leahy described in detail what occurred each day of the Churchill visit. On September 18, we're told, that Hopkins arrived at Hyde Park at noon, "bringing with him the Duke of Windsor."[46] Hopkins stayed after lunch to help draft a joint statement for Churchill and Roosevelt on dealing with the new government in Italy and relief for the Italian people. The message concluded with a Churchillian flourish of wanting to hurry "the day when free elections can be held throughout Italy, and when Italy can earn her proper place in the great family of free nations."[47] The text of the statement wasn't released to the public until Churchill had returned to London, eight days later.

Even though Hopkins was now being treated differently by FDR, he continued to carry out assignments when asked. While he was off composing the message about Italy, Leahy was watching Hyde Park activity. The chief of staff related that he was "impressed . . . that the Prime Minister, one of the most powerful men of the age, bowed respectfully to the former King upon the latter's departure." Leahy commented that Churchill was "thoroughly British . . . in his manner and social customs."[48]

What Leahy didn't mention was that Churchill had taken the then-king's side in the abdication crisis that roiled the United Kingdom (and British Empire) in 1936. Out of government during what became known as his "wilderness years," Churchill suffered the indignity of being shouted down in the House of Commons for rising to speak in support of the embattled sovereign. Fellow MP Leo Amery jotted in his diary on December 7, 1936—five years to the day before Pearl Harbor—that his longtime friend (and occasional political adversary) appeared "completely staggered by the unanimous hostility of the House, as well as by being called to order by the Speaker." A few sentences later in the entry, Amery noted that Churchill "is personally very fond of the King and the thought of the King's difficulties may also have helped to upset his judgement."[49] Churchill (and the king) lost the battle, but that didn't mean that the figure Leahy called "the most powerful individual that has appeared in England since Henry VIII" wouldn't continue to display his esteem for the monarchy as an institution. During his career in government, Churchill knew and served at the same time while four kings and two queens occupied the throne—with George VI and his daughter, Elizabeth II, reigning throughout his nearly nine years as prime minister.

Leahy's close scrutiny of Hyde Park socializing extended to lunch on September 19 at "Mrs. Roosevelt's farmhouse," meaning Val-Kill, a few miles from Springwood. The admiral's account described verbal jousting between the First Lady and Britain's first minister. The point of contention this time? According to Leahy, it was "an hour of argument . . . on their general attitude toward a reorganization of the world." Mrs. Roosevelt contended that peace could "best be maintained by improving the living conditions of the people in all countries." This global aspiration was met with a somewhat more parochial and bare-knuckle proposal, advanced by the prime minister. Churchill claimed, as he'd done so often in the past, that the "only hope for a durable peace was an agreement between Great Britain and the United States to prevent international war by the use of their combined forces if necessary. He expressed a willingness to take Russia into the agreement if the Russians wished to join."

While the president was contemplating the creation of the

"United Nations" as a new, postwar organization dedicated to peacekeeping, Churchill was thinking in terms of the current war structure rather than more broadly at the shape of the world once the fighting ended. Leahy witnessed the strong-willed back-and-forth—both demonstrating "conviction" in his opinion—and judged what he heard "an extremely interesting and instructive hour."[50]

FDR often dodged debate or argument with a joshing remark of deflection, but his spouse was unafraid to speak her mind, taking stands whether at a lectern or at a lunch. With Churchill, she was willing to spar over numerous subjects, whether it be the Spanish Civil War or how the world might look in future decades. As time passed, she seriously wondered what he thought of her and her views.

Mrs. Roosevelt was poles apart from Mrs. Churchill. Clementine could find fault with the president over his considerable self-regard and his "great cheek" for calling her "Clemmie" straightaway, yet she never challenged him directly. When Clementine died in 1977, at the age of ninety-two, her daughter Mary wrote in the *Sunday Times Weekly Review* on December 18, "Winston told her everything: so she bore also the burden of at times anguishing knowledge. This made her fend off any close companionship outside the immediate circle of her family, and she suffered times of great loneliness, although surrounded by people." While FDR kept Eleanor mostly in the dark, Churchill was something of an open book with Clementine, meaning a dignified smile rather than a remark would be her form of communication in certain situations, whether in London or on a trip abroad.

Besides deciding on what to say in the Anglo-American statement on postwar Italy, the prime minister and president devoted time at Hyde Park to how to handle the top-secret work being carried out on the development of the atomic bomb. According to Leahy, the discussions revolved around whether the British should receive "all of the information . . . about the manufacture and use of atomic energy for *war* purposes." Would the United States try to control the new weaponry, guarding against other countries having the ability to develop the lethal technology?

FDR's approach was for him, characteristically, a combination of open *and* closed, a politician threading the needle to offer something but not the most valued asset. Leahy noted that Roosevelt did not want to divulge military secrets, but, given that the British helped with early experiments, they could share in some of the findings and their applications. The president foresaw atomic energy developing "for successful use in industrial and scientific fields."[51] "Dr. Win-the-War" understood that what was being engineered could change the world militarily and more broadly.

It's possible Churchill avoided any mention of the ongoing research in his remembrance of this visit to Hyde Park because he and FDR were at odds over precisely what the British would receive. However, the formal *aide-mémoire* Roosevelt and Churchill initialed about "tube alloys" includes this striking sentence: "The matter should continue to be regarded as of the utmost secrecy; but when a 'bomb' is finally available, it might perhaps, after mature consideration, be used against the Japanese, who should be warned that this bombardment will be repeated until they surrender."[52] While the United States dropped atomic bombs on two Japanese cities, Hiroshima and Nagasaki, less than a year later, Britain's first nuclear weapon wasn't detonated until 1952, nearly a year into Churchill's second premiership. The Soviets joined the United States in having an atomic bomb in 1949.

When Churchill and Roosevelt were conversing among themselves without advisors, what they were contemplating to do or what they together decided they wanted to achieve could produce angst, even anger, among their staffs and subject specialists. During the brief Hyde Park stopover in 1944, Alexander Cadogan, Britain's permanent under-secretary of state for foreign affairs and the highest-ranking civil servant in the department, represented the United Kingdom, during the first month of the Dumbarton Oaks conference in Washington, which was taking place at the same time as the Quebec conference and the subsequent discussions at Hyde Park. The session at Dumbarton Oaks, located in the Georgetown section of Washington, helped establish a foundation for inaugurating the United Nations as a peacekeeping organization a year later. Cadogan had been summoned to Quebec and following his return to Washington found out that he hadn't seen a telegram from Churchill that required a Foreign Office reply. In his diary for September 20, the day the Churchill party set sail to return to Britain, the diplomat was undiplomatic in expressing his frustration at the way high-stakes international affairs were being conducted. He failed to receive a telegram, and, when provided a copy, he described it trenchantly as "a message from P.M. to A [Anthony Eden], reporting (probably incorrectly) what President had said to him (probably also incorrect) about future procedure. What a way of doing business!"[53]

Cadogan wasn't alone. On the day Churchill arrived in Canada to begin the Quebec conference, Alan Brooke, who was promoted to field marshal early in 1944, set down his assessment of the prime minister he'd served since the war began: "He knows no details, has only got half the picture in his mind, talks absurdities and makes my blood boil to listen to his nonsense." His criticism builds to a paradoxical yet, from his perspective, justified crescendo: "Never have I admired and despised a man simultaneously to the same extent. Never have such opposite extremes been combined in the same human being."[54] No man, they say, is a hero to his valet, but war comrades in the heat of battle can be just as censorious, too.

Brooke wasn't alone. General Hastings Ismay, the prime minister's principal military aide throughout the war years, became so exasperated by his leader's behavior during the Quebec meetings that he submitted his resignation.[55] It wasn't accepted, and he accompanied Churchill on the *Queen Mary* for the voyage from New York, with Brooke flying back to Britain on his own after a fishing holiday in Canada. With nerves of key participants frayed, the September sojourn would be the last trip for the British to North America during the war.

Identical to 1944, Churchill and Roosevelt were together for just one conference in 1945. This one, the weeklong Big Three summit at Yalta, February 4 to 11, couldn't have been more different from the second Quebec conference or any of the previous ones during the war. Stalin refused to leave the U.S.S.R. and proposed the Black Sea resort city in Crimea. "We could not have found a worse place for a meeting if we had spent ten years on research," Churchill quipped acidly.[56] Declining in health, Roosevelt still made the journey and presided at plenary sessions. The public—in the United States and elsewhere—was largely in the dark, with the whereabouts of the president a mystery for three weeks after his fourth inauguration. In his memoirs, Churchill describes FDR as looking "frail and ill" before the summit.[57] Afterward at Alexandria, Egypt, Churchill's reaction is more funereal: "The President seemed placid and frail. I felt that he had a slender contact with life."[58] That would be the last time the two men were together. They first met as the leaders of their countries on a battleship in August of 1941, and their final talk took place on another war ship about three-and-a-half years later, a fitting parting perhaps for a pair of sea dogs. A poignant fact of history is that as the United States became more powerful militarily and internationally Roosevelt's personal capacity to govern was noticeably declining along with his own constitution.

Roosevelt died on April 12, forty-four days after arriving back at the White House, at the conclusion of his grueling fourteen-thousand-mile, thirty-six-day journey. Churchill's security guard, Walter Henry Thompson, provided an unforgettable scene of the prime minister's immediate reaction to the news. An urgent summons at 3 a.m. (Friday, the 13th, in London) brought Thompson to Churchill's bedroom, where the figure he'd protected so long was alone, pacing the floor. Thompson recalled the prime minister continuously "talking of Roosevelt—weeping, reminiscing, smiling, going over the days, the years; recalling conversations, wishing he had done this, wondering what had been meant when Roosevelt said this or that; agreeing, disagreeing, reliving."[59] At one point, Churchill mentioned the possibility of flying to Washington for the funeral, inquiring if Thompson would accompany him.

Churchill's impulse to attend the funeral resulted in him contacting Lord Halifax, the ambassador in Washington. Halifax noted that the prime minister "was wondering about coming over himself and two reflections were immediately obvious: (1) That the effect here would be tremendous, but—(2) Was it perhaps out of proportion, having regard to the risks and the strains involved."[60] In "the middle of the night" (Washington time), the ambassador received word that Churchill had decided against making the trip. The next day, however, Halifax informed London that the newly inaugurated Harry Truman "would immensely value the opportunity of a talk with Winston, if he was coming over."[61] That overture reopened Churchill's consideration of going to Washington, and, according to Cadogan, after debating the pros and cons the prime minister "said he would decide at aerodrome. Party due to get off ground at 8.30!"[62]

In the end, following a full day of weighing options and ordering his plane to be ready to depart at the airfield, Churchill chose to remain in Britain. Condolence messages sent that Friday to Mrs. Roosevelt—"I have lost a dear and cherished friendship which was forged in the fire"—and to Hopkins—"I had a true affection for Franklin"—became his primary means of conveying sympathy. In his memoirs, Churchill contends that "pressure" was "put on me not to leave the country at this most critical and difficult moment, and I yielded to the wishes of my friends."[63] The prime minister cabled regrets to the new president, and Foreign Secretary Anthony Eden represented the United Kingdom at the funeral.

Even today, Churchill's on-again, off-again wavering remains intriguing, bordering on inexplicable. He knew of FDR's physical decline from their interactions at conferences in 1944 and early 1945. After they were together (by Churchill's computation) "one hundred and twenty days of close personal contact" and they had exchanged "over seventeen hundred messages,"[64] Churchill's absence still raises many unresolved issues. Why did he wrestle with making a final decision for an entire day? Perhaps he considered "the risks" Halifax mentioned too great to overcome, since the Luftwaffe would have been on alert to target aircraft heading toward Washington at the time. With the war approaching its denouement, a transatlantic trip may have been considered overly chancy to the effective resolution of the combat and to postwar planning. The personal ties between the comrades in arms could have weakened since earlier days. Did the mushrooming military might of the United States change the dynamics of the relationship between the two Allies, resulting in Churchill having far less of a say?

For whatever reason, Churchill, who had never refused to travel anywhere despite the danger involved, decided against another transatlantic crossing. He called for adjournment of the House of Commons on April 13 and delivered a tribute at Westminster on April 17, two days after Roosevelt was buried. One passage captured the human dimension of their many hours together in the White House and elsewhere. "President Roosevelt's physical affliction lay heavily upon him," Churchill observed. "It was a marvel that he bore up against it through all the many years of tumult and storm. Not one man in ten millions, stricken and crippled as he was, would have attempted to plunge into a life of physical and mental exertion and of hard, ceaseless political controversy. Not one in ten millions would have tried, not one in a generation would have succeeded . . . in becoming indisputable master of the scene."[65] Calling the United States "the great Republic," he concluded his eulogy, "For us, it remains only to say that in Franklin Roosevelt there died the greatest American friend we have ever known, and the greatest champion of freedom who has ever brought help and comfort from the new world to the old."[66]

Harold Nicolson, the prolific writer and critic who served in Parliament between 1935 and 1945 and knew Churchill well, observed in a letter to his son, Nigel, that "Winston rose and spoke about Roosevelt. I did not think him very good."[67] Others who witnessed the tribute shared Nicolson's opinion that the eulogy, though moving in places, lacked Churchillian grandeur. John Colville jotted in his diary that he saw the prime minister "feverishly composing" his remarks right before delivering them, leading Churchill's aide to comment the result was "adequate but not one of his finest efforts."[68] It remains somewhat puzzling still today why the testimonial seemed merely "adequate." Had the flame of their perceived friendship dimmed and inhibited his elocution?

Ten days before Churchill returned to Downing Street on October 26, 1951—this time by the Conservative Party winning a general election—he was asked after a campaign speech what he considered his "biggest mistake in the war." Lord Moran recorded what he said was Churchill's response: "Not going to meet Truman after Roosevelt's death." A long pause followed before Churchill added: "It wasn't my fault. I wanted to cross the Atlantic. But Anthony [Eden] put me off. He telegraphed from Washington that they did not want me."[69]

Churchill's focus on his "mistake" of not immediately cultivating a working relationship with Roosevelt's successor—the prime minister wouldn't meet Truman until the Potsdam conference outside Berlin began in July of 1945—seems, in its way, strange. Paying personal respects to the leader who had helped Britain in its darkest days and served as his host for so many days between 1941 and 1944 wasn't mentioned, while the foreign secretary received the blame. Never lacking in determination or a strong sense of command, the prime minister certainly could have put his foot down and attended had he really wanted to go.

Churchill revisited his decision not to go to Washington two years later with the publication of *Triumph and Tragedy*. For this recollection, he reiterated his regret of failing to meet the new president, but he also criticized FDR for excluding Truman from learning about the administration's clandestine work to end the war and prepare for peace during the new vice president's initial months in office. "It seemed to me extraordinary," Churchill observed, ". . . that Roosevelt had not made his deputy and potential successor thoroughly acquainted with the whole story and brought him into the decisions which were being taken. This proved of grave disadvantage to our affairs."[70] In his final days, FDR disregarded the inevitable and also continued to operate largely on his own, as he had since becoming president in 1933.

During the same conversation when Churchill discussed his "biggest mistake," Moran also recorded an intriguing judgment from his patient. Churchill, we're told, offered his opinion that he had "great influence over President Roosevelt until about three months before Yalta; then he ceased to answer my letters."[71] If accurate in assigning the date, that would mean personal messages from FDR stopped around the time of the November 1944 election. Churchill continued to receive responses under Roosevelt's name, but the prime minister suspected White House staff members composed them. It bothered Churchill that he had to inquire whether a cable he sent on March 17, 1945—eighteen days after FDR returned from Yalta—was received by the president. The poignant nature of this message suggested that the prime minister realized the Roosevelt to whom he said farewell in Egypt no longer exerted the power he had witnessed since 1941.

With the end undoubtedly drawing near, Churchill set down a personal remembrance of their wartime comradeship. "Our friendship is the rock on which I build for the future of the world so long as I am one of the builders," he wrote. "I always think of those tremendous days when you devised Lend-Lease, when we met at Argentia, when you decided with my heartfelt agreement to launch the invasion of Africa, and when you comforted me for the loss of Tobruk." A few sentences later, Churchill commented in words of hope that also strained truth, "I shall be looking forward to your long-promised visit"—a promise, of course, never kept.[72]

Churchill's affectionate reminiscence was intended for an audience of one, but it took two weeks for him to receive a reply, leading to an unavoidable question: Were the two leaders genuinely close on a person-to-person basis, or did wartime camaraderie join them together in a relationship of allies fighting common enemies? Though Roosevelt never mustered the will nor found the time to go to Britain, there could be no doubt of the president's exhausting hospitality to Churchill on each of his visits to the United States. He arranged to meet the prime minister on arrival and bade farewell on departure. To Eleanor Roosevelt's chagrin, he constantly invited him to stay in the living quarters of the White House, despite the availability of Blair House. He welcomed him to his family home in the Hudson Valley and took him to Shangri-La. He stayed up later than his customary hour to retire, talking with his notoriously late-to-bed guest. He organized means of travel and tight security measures when the prime minister needed them.

From Churchill's first White House sojourn until Roosevelt's death, the pair kept exchanging gifts of one kind or another. Churchill made sure each of his books was bound in red leather, embossed with gold lettering, and autographed for FDR's library collection, while Roosevelt reported in a letter to the prime minister, dispatched on D-Day, that he was sending two electric typewriters to Churchill for the simple reason the president had learned Churchill liked the typeface of a particular American-made machine. They regularly traded pictures, even of themselves. Some gifts seemed touchingly thoughtful. On October 16, 1943—between the prime minister's triumphant September visit to Washington and the Tehran conference in late November—Roosevelt sent a memo to his secretary, Grace Tully, "Take up with General [Henry] Arnold [head of the Army Air Forces during World War II] and find out what is the latest date that I can deliver a Christmas tree for Winston Churchill and send it over by a bomber or otherwise in order to reach him at Chequers, England, before Christmas." The presidential instructions became more specific that the tree "should be packed in burlap and sent to wherever General Arnold says." A subsequent memo from Tully to the superintendent of the Roosevelt estate at Hyde Park, William Plog, explained: "An Army truck will pick this tree up on December 11th."[73]

Two days after his tree inquiry, Christmas and Churchill were still on Roosevelt's mind, and he wrote Tully again, saying that "Mr.

Churchill was perfectly thrilled by the set of maps" hanging in the White House Study. FDR wanted her to inquire whether *National Geographic* would "make a similar set for me to send to the Prime Minister for Christmas."[74] In January 1945, before leaving on the trip to Yalta, Churchill dictated a brief reminder for himself to ask the president the details for a shipment of "golden orfes"—a type of pond fish—the prime minister wanted to send him.

Though public service occupied the majority of his adult years, Roosevelt listed his occupation, even for voting purposes, as "tree farmer." Across the Atlantic, Churchill raised (and enjoyed feeding) different species of fish at Chartwell. Each figure wanted to share with the other presents possessing personal meaning.

Considerate as both leaders could be, neither was shy about commenting on the other out of earshot of reporters or people they didn't know well. According to Frances Perkins, FDR told her that Churchill came up with ideas almost as naturally as breathing. However, the rate of production and the quality of creation were often at variance. Pointing out an example of success—the Mulberry harbors effectively used in the D-Day invasion of Normandy—Roosevelt said it was "one of those brilliant ideas that he has. He has a hundred a day and about four of them are good." During a visit to Hyde Park, the prime minister saw old naval ships stored along the Hudson River and blurted out to the president: "By George, we could take those ships and others like them that are good for nothing and sink them offshore to protect the landings."[75]

When they were together and in written communication, FDR referred to Churchill as "Winston." Behind his back the somewhat patronizing nickname of "Winnie" was often heard, even early on. Elliott Roosevelt, the son of Eleanor and Franklin who rose to the rank of brigadier general in the Army Air Corps during the war, described a discussion with his father during the Atlantic conference in August of 1941. Even then FDR called Churchill, "A real old Tory, of the old school." In addition, if the exchange is accurate, a few sentences later the elder Roosevelt asserted: "Don't forget one thing.

Winnie has one supreme mission in life, but only one. He's a perfect wartime prime minister. His one big job is to see that Britain survives this war."[76]

In private Churchill could be stinging, too. A few weeks after the Tehran conference, Colville recorded that "the P.M. turned and said to Commander [C. R.] Thompson, 'But, Tommy, you will bear witness that I do not repeat my stories so often as my dear friend, the President of the United States.' "[77] The remarks to Perkins and to Thompson reflected a combination of personal annoyance along with a degree of respect.

One of Churchill's most often quoted *bon mots* about Roosevelt, recorded by Colville in a diary entry on May 2, 1948, bears repeating: "No lover ever studied every whim of his mistress as I did those of President Roosevelt."[78] Witty and vivid, the remark reveals strategic calculation to attain something that's greatly desired from someone else. Viewed in this context and spoken well after Roosevelt's death and Churchill's electoral defeat in 1945, is it accurate to see their bond as a "special relationship," or is the association closer to a shotgun liaison, given the extreme circumstances and exigencies of global war? Policy disagreements and America's expanding military capability may have changed the power equation to the point that Churchill sensed he was on different footing with Roosevelt near the end of the war compared to the first years of battle. Could it even be said FDR wooed Stalin in a manner similar to Churchill's earlier pursuit of Roosevelt?

Throughout their joint appearances in public and with the press, the word "friend" can often be found in transcripts of their remarks, as each leader (albeit Churchill more frequently) characterized how one regarded the other. Lifelong politicians, both understood the necessity of presenting a united front and the significance of displaying diplomatic stagecraft to complement their country's statecraft. However, it's no secret that what the public saw at choreographed appearances was far from the complete picture of what happened behind the closed doors and heavy curtains of the White House. Wartime censorship also played into the hands of savvy manipulators of the images they wanted to project.

Neither Churchill nor Roosevelt lifted the veil (or heavy curtains) to provide anything resembling a complete portrait of their relationship. Clues, though, can come from observers and writers who, to varying degrees, had firsthand knowledge, with each person attempting to come to terms with this historic human alliance. These views offer distinct, illuminating vantage points in helping to make an overall assessment possible.

As one of Roosevelt's speechwriters, Robert Sherwood witnessed the prime minister's visits to the White House and later interviewed Churchill while conducting research for his book, *Roosevelt and Hopkins: An Intimate History*. After explaining what happened at the Atlantic conference in 1941, Sherwood offered his opinion and the context for understanding why the two leaders approached subsequent meetings as they did: "It would be an exaggeration to say that Roosevelt and Churchill became chums at this Conference or at any subsequent time. They established an easy intimacy, a joking informality . . . and also a degree of frankness in intercourse which, if not quite complete, was remarkably close to it. But neither of them ever forgot for one instant what he was and represented or what the other was and represented."[79] The principal profession of each was politics—an honorable profession with often ambiguous choices and circumstance—and they both saw much of the world and their time together from that perspective.

Shortly after sizing up how Churchill and Roosevelt operated when they were together, Sherwood offered more encompassing analysis. In this interpretation, the British leader "quickly learned that he confronted in the President a man of infinite subtlety and obscurity—an artful dodger who could not readily be pinned down on specific points." Roosevelt didn't make a decision until he had to do so, often keeping associates of opposite viewpoints guessing. While FDR mulled and seemed flexible, Churchill was different. From Sherwood's reading of the two, the president "learned how pertinacious the Prime

Minister could be in pursuance of a purpose. . . . [I]t was this quality which, at times, made him extremely tiresome to deal with and, at other times—and especially times of most awful adversity—made him great."[80] Cartoonists readily portrayed Roosevelt as a sphinx, who, despite his public joviality, combined mystery with his leonine demeanor. As noted earlier, people closest to him always sensed a certain distance and understood their inability to crack the bedeviling riddle of his complex personality.

For a leader like FDR, who, beginning in 1941, had occupied the presidency longer than any predecessor and had become accustomed to getting his way, anyone who could be "extremely tiresome" might well have been viewed more negatively as time passed. That attitude could have affected one-on-one conversations and complicated decisions. The fact that Roosevelt traveled as much as he did, starting in January of 1943, but never visited Britain, despite his repeated assurances, remains mysterious. From the fall of 1942 onward, King George VI and Churchill were ready to welcome FDR on an unprecedented royal visit. The president kept promising, telling Eden at the end of the second Quebec conference (immediately before he left for Hyde Park and Churchill's last visit there) "win or lose, he would come to us after the election, end of November."[81] The foreign secretary's diary entry for September 16, 1944, wasn't the last word about a possible visit. As late as March 13, 1945, a month before FDR died, King George VI wrote the president to say he looked forward to seeing him in Britain later that year.

Ian Jacob, who was promoted during the war from colonel to lieutenant general and accompanied Churchill on his conferences abroad, intently observed the interactions between the prime minister and president in his role as assistant military secretary to the British War Cabinet. He later reflected on the relationship of the two leaders. Early on, during 1941 and 1942, Jacob watched as "the friendship seemed to be firmly established; both men could communicate with each other without danger of being misunderstood." However, even with that foundation, he underscored the limitations that existed, "Each is bound to think first and foremost of the true interests of his own country."[82] Those "true interests" supersede true friendship, leading Jacob to comment that "friendship can only be a term to be used in a restricted sense."[83]

Especially as America entered the war and began building an all-out effort to win, Churchill sensed he could help Roosevelt—and help himself at the same time. From 1941 into 1943, the prime minister advanced his agenda, and Jacob remarked that "it is fair to say that Churchill felt that he could convince the President of the wisdom of any course he wanted to pursue by written memoranda and by conversation. He liked to be in the White House, and to have informal meals with the President and Harry Hopkins, followed by long talks." Those conversations, usually well past midnight and involving adult beverages, might have been exhilarating at first, but in Jacob's judgment over time they "tended to be a little one-sided, tedious."[84]

For whatever reasons, Roosevelt reduced the time he spent with Churchill after 1943, which marked the last time the prime minister visited FDR in Washington. By then, many of the major decisions about the direction of the war had been made, and the president's big-picture approach was beginning to turn to what would happen once the fighting stopped. As in other matters, Churchill was different and continued to take, according to Jacob, "a deep interest in all the details of military operations." Their relationship, friendship with restrictions, changed, and their times together in 1944 and 1945 became relatively brief.[85]

A close-up appraisal of the Churchill-Roosevelt association was the subject of a 1984 conversation among Averell Harriman, his wife (since 1971) Pamela, who had been married to Randolph Churchill from 1939 until 1946, and the historian Arthur M. Schlesinger Jr. Churchill fascinated Schlesinger and among his papers are multiple files about Churchill and his meetings with Roosevelt. His series, *The Age of Roosevelt*, never advanced beyond its third volume and 1936, but he continued adding to his research for a future study. That never happened, but he devoted a lengthy journal entry to the way the leaders approached each other.

Schlesinger told the Harrimans he had been reading the correspondence between Churchill and Roosevelt and wondered "whether the two men really liked each other, or liked the theory of liking each other in the great historic context." In short, were they friends? Mrs. Harriman said they most definitely were not. "They had nothing in common," Schlesinger quoted her as saying. "They were not each other's type. They were not amused by the same things. They did not like the same sort of people. Churchill liked men. Roosevelt liked women. . . . But they had to get on with each other, and both worked at it."[86]

To "get on" with someone—in other words, to be friendly—and to have to keep working at getting on shouldn't be confused with establishing a friendship that binds two people together beyond a working relationship for a certain reason at a specific time. Withstanding assault in the same foxhole during wartime can foster a cozy, temporary familiarity, but it doesn't necessarily forge an enduring association.

A very different vantage point for assessing Churchill and Roosevelt came from Walter Graebner. He went to London in 1937 as the first foreign correspondent for *Time* magazine, and at the end of the war he shifted from being the London bureau chief for *Time* to assuming the directorship of advertising and promotion for *Time* and *Life* in Europe. After covering Churchill as a journalist, he then worked closely with the former prime minister on the publication in *Life* of excerpts from his war memoirs as well as other articles. Graebner, for example, arranged for *Life* to publish a lavish cover story—on January 7, 1946, a week before Churchill began a sixty-five-day stay in America—featuring eighteen color paintings, which a headline referred to as "a great statesman's avocation."

Graebner collected reminiscences and anecdotes about their association for a book, *My Dear Mr. Churchill*, which appeared shortly after Churchill's death in 1965. Graebner recalled that "Churchill never seemed to wish to be drawn out in any conversation in which Roosevelt was mentioned, and I have never been able to tell whether this was because he grieved so much over the loss of a friend or whether the two had drifted apart toward the end of the President's life." For someone who thrived on animated conversation, this reticence spoke volumes. Was Churchill afraid that any suggestion of criticism would be interpreted that they didn't "get on"? Graebner, a publishing executive important to Churchill's out-of-office livelihood, admitted: "I cannot remember Churchill ever saying more than one sentence in private which could have been a clue to his real opinion of the man: 'I always had the greatest respect and fondness for him,' was all he ever said to me."[87]

Roy Jenkins, who served in the House of Commons with Churchill for sixteen years (from 1948 through 1964) and met him for the first time in 1941, shared certain similarities with Churchill that sharpened his opinion of "the greatest human being ever to occupy 10 Downing Street," as he asserted in the final words of his thousand-page biography, *Churchill*.[88] Both Jenkins and Churchill possessed considerable literary talent, as their many books proved. Both had firsthand knowledge of the workings of the British government. Both had been chancellor of the exchequer and home secretary. Both had switched party affiliations during their political careers. Both took a keen interest in American history, with Jenkins's last book of the eighteen he wrote a biography of Franklin Roosevelt, which appeared after his death in 2003.

Appraising the Churchill-Roosevelt relationship and its human chemistry, Jenkins, who served as the president of the European Commission and as chancellor of the University of Oxford, focused on the prime minister's decision not to attend FDR's funeral and wondered "whether Churchill had cooled on Roosevelt to an extent which had drained away the emotional impact of his death."[89] Noting lingering friction from the Yalta conference, where Roosevelt seemed to side more with Stalin than Churchill, Jenkins amplified an earlier judgment of the prime minister's "close surface friendship with Roosevelt" and argued that "the emotional link between Churchill and Roosevelt was never as close as was commonly thought. It was more a partnership of circumstance and convenience than a friendship of individuals, each of whom . . . was a star of a brightness which needed its own unimpeded orbit."[90] Each figure a bright star? It might be more accurate to view Churchill and Roosevelt in galactic terms, boldly moving on their respective paths amidst planetary chaos and confusion.

Trying to make sense of a complicated human relationship that began over eight decades ago and lasted less than four years becomes even more daunting if aspects of the relationship remain unknown or in dispute. What does a survey of the historical record actually reveal when pieces of a puzzle don't seem to fit? Edith Benham Helm, who was the White House social secretary for twenty-five years, the longest of anyone, and during the administrations of Woodrow Wilson, Roosevelt, and Truman, alleged in a memoir that Churchill "was at the White House oftener and for longer stays than the public realized, I feel sure. Once he and Mrs. Churchill were there a full month while the Roosevelts were at Hyde Park, and the secret was so well guarded that no word ever leaked out."[91]

As previously noted, Churchill did live and work in the White House for a couple of days in 1943 while FDR was enjoying a long weekend in the Hudson Valley. But were there "oftener" and "longer stays," including "a full month" when the Churchills stayed at 1600 Pennsylvania Avenue? Mrs. Roosevelt wrote the foreword to Helm's book, endorsing its merits. Was she aware of what had been reported inside of it? Neither the Churchill Archives Centre at Churchill College in Cambridge nor the White House Historical Association in Washington could substantiate that such an extended "secret" visit ever took place.

Still, what Helm divulged prompts lingering intrigue because almost two decades after her account appeared, J. B. West's *Upstairs at the White House* came out. The former White House usher disclosed somewhat cryptically that "Mr. Churchill was in and out of the White House secretly several times during the war. Each time his departure was as sudden as his arrival. Many times the public had no idea he was in Washington."[92] As with Helm's recollection, can this be accurate, or was Churchill such an outsized figure that tales of mythical stays and sightings turned into fodder for gossip and folklore about the president's work place and residence?

With the tight censorship rules that existed in journalism and other forms of communication until the end of hostilities in 1945, clandestine meetings or stays might have occurred. If they did, however, revelations about them in memoirs or interviews would have provoked widespread attention in postwar America and elsewhere. To be sure, the public ultimately learned that Roosevelt surreptitiously entertained Lucy Mercer Rutherfurd at the White House and at his retreat in Warm Springs, Georgia—where he died while she was visiting there in 1945. The two began an affair in 1916, when Mercer was Eleanor Roosevelt's secretary. Eleanor's discovery of the liaison and her threat of divorce led FDR to promise he would not see the woman again, a pledge he didn't keep. In 1920, she married the wealthy Winthrop Rutherfurd, but still maintained contact with Roosevelt. On September 1, 1944, nine days before Roosevelt departed for the Quebec conference, he diverted the *Ferdinand Magellan* to stop in Allamuchy, New Jersey, to spend several hours with the recently widowed Lucy Mercer Rutherfurd at the Rutherfurd mansion and farm.[93] These formerly hidden "facts" are now well-known, but the allegations of Helm and West are a different matter. What prompted two White House insiders with knowledge of day-to-day activities at 1600 Pennsylvania Avenue to make their claims?

Though questions about the Churchill-Roosevelt relationship persist, it's reasonable to conclude that it significantly changed, particularly after 1943. Whatever their personal feelings for each other, Churchill and Roosevelt began their work together after Pearl Harbor in 1941 to fight a world war and to defend Western democracy. The prime minister kept returning to America and to the White House to confer about these objectives with the president, who was always charming and always calculating. Their work, their politics, their power took precedence over individual concerns and reservations. They might well have had a relationship of chummy convenience, but it was also one of conviction, of cooperation, and of common cause.

– 6 –

THE COLD PEACE

More than a decade of defeat and tumult passed between Winston Churchill's final Washington visit to meet with Franklin Roosevelt and his triumphant return to the Rose Bedroom of the White House during Dwight Eisenhower's first term. For Churchill, the roundabout route to becoming prime minister a second time in the 1950s principally involved looking back to the stormy war years and peering ahead to a world transformed by ideological conflict. Throughout these years of becoming a senior statesman and internationally recognized author, he kept a close eye on America and its leaders. Churchill's path back to power, with several Washington stopovers and recurring journalistic attention, set the stage for his final days "at the summit of the United States."

Though sixteen years younger than Churchill and a newcomer to the hurly-burly of vote-seeking politics, Eisenhower had an advantage that Roosevelt lacked with the British prime minister. Until their initial meetings in 1941, FDR and Churchill had briefly met but never conferred one-on-one. They didn't really know each other. Eisenhower, by contrast, worked closely with Churchill during much of the war, and afterward the two spent time together.

Influential in their wartime collaboration was Eisenhower's remarkable rise in the army and the significant overseas assignments he received. When they first met on Christmas Eve in 1941, Eisenhower was a brigadier (or one star) general and assistant chief of staff for the War Plans Division. Six months later, following promotion to the two-star major general rank, he was named commander of the European Theater of Operations, based in London. As a three-star lieutenant general, he commanded Operation Torch, the Allied invasion of North Africa in November of 1942. The next year, the new four-star general directed the invasion of Sicily and Italy before becoming Supreme Commander of the Allied Expeditionary Forces. This appointment brought with it the responsibility for leading the sea, air, and land assaults on D-Day as well as the subsequent combat in western Europe until Germany's unconditional surrender on May 7, 1945. A few months before that, Eisenhower had become a five-star general. In less than a decade, he had advanced from a lieutenant colonel to the highest possible army rank. And, of course, eight years later in his first attempt at winning elective office, he wrested the White House from the Democratic Party for the first time in two decades.

Throughout the years of combat, Eisenhower and Churchill established a working and personal relationship that over time developed into a genuine friendship. The two figures would argue and vigorously defend their positions; however, by Churchill's later years Eisenhower was unequivocal in his admiration and unafraid to say so. Churchill's White House visits in the 1950s and other circumstances reflected a human bond stronger than the one between Churchill and Roosevelt. To be sure, the presidency of Harry Truman came between the Roosevelt and Eisenhower administrations. However, during those nearly eight years (between 1945 and 1953), Churchill and Eisenhower continued to be involved and to receive widespread attention before the general decided to turn to the preoccupation of Churchill's life: politics. What happened before both Churchill and Eisenhower simultaneously occupied the highest governmental offices for their countries is critical in understanding the context and continuity of their relationship. So, too, is the ebb and flow of Churchill's reputation in the United States.

Churchill, Truman, and Eisenhower were together at the Potsdam conference, which took place between July 17 and August 2, 1945, just outside Berlin. At the time Eisenhower was serving as the military governor of the U.S. Occupation Zone in Germany. The day before the first session of the conference for the Allied leaders—Churchill, Truman, and Stalin—the prime minister and new president met for the first time. In his diary, Truman wrote of Churchill: "He is a most charming and a very clever person—meaning clever in the English not the Kentucky sense." But charm and cleverness didn't disguise the candor of the man from Missouri: "He gave me a lot of hooey about how great my country is and how he loved Roosevelt and how he intended to love me etc. etc."[1] At Potsdam on July 26, results of the British national election, conducted earlier in the month, were announced—and Churchill was no longer the king's first minister. Clement Attlee, the deputy prime minister in the United Kingdom's wartime coalition government and the Labour Party leader, replaced Churchill for the last days of the conference, and retained the office until Churchill's return to power on October 26, 1951.

In *Crusade in Europe*, Eisenhower recounted how he helped cushion Churchill's defeat by providing him with a luxurious place to recover from the rigors of war and electioneering. "Mr. Churchill wanted and needed a short rest," Eisenhower observed. "I was pleased and honored that he asked me to put him up; his suggestion implied that he felt for me some little fraction of the great respect, affection, and admiration I had developed for him." Beginning on September 2, thirty-eight days after leaving 10 Downing Street and the same day Japan formally surrendered, Churchill took up residence at a villa on Lake Como in Italy, which Eisenhower called in military lingo "one of the pleasantest parts of our theater."[2] For nearly three weeks, the seventy-year-old Churchill painted and began to ponder the next phase of his life. At the top of his out-of-office agenda was writing his own history of the war as well as deciding the most effective ways for delivering his ever-darkening outlook of a postwar world defined by the Soviet

Union's ideological and territorial hostility to its former comrades in arms. As became clear early on, America would play a central role in his six-volume memoir, *The Second World War*, and also in advancing his assessment of the benumbing frost of the Cold War between the West and the East.

Churchill never resided at the White House during Truman's presidency. His visits to Washington in 1946 and 1949 occurred while he was leader of the opposition in the Commons. (Attlee did stay at the White House on November 10 and 11, 1945.) After returning as prime minister, Churchill made two January trips, in 1952 and 1953, to see Truman in Washington—but for two principal reasons neither time served as an occasion for occupying the Rose Bedroom as he had during Roosevelt's presidency. The living quarters of the White House were renovated from November 21, 1948, until March 27, 1952, forcing the Trumans across the street to live at Blair House. In 1953, most of Churchill's time in the United States was spent in New York meeting with president-elect Eisenhower, though the prime minister did confer with Truman on January 8 at the White House and later at a dinner held at the British embassy.

During his first American visit after losing the 1945 national election—he arrived on January 14, 1946, fifteen days before the death of Harry Hopkins—one event made history, though it took place almost a thousand miles from the nation's capital. Accepting a Truman-endorsed invitation to speak on March 5, 1946, at Westminster College in Fulton, Missouri, the former prime minister and the president traveled together by train to the small, 212-student liberal arts school in Truman's home state. After the president offered a welcome and introduction, Churchill delivered what he titled his "Sinews of Peace" speech. At one point, he noted that "an iron curtain has descended across the Continent" of Europe. That stark symbol of a divided world pitting democratic nations against countries in the orbit of totalitarian Communism captured global attention and turned the address, in popular parlance, into the "iron curtain" speech.

Churchill's *tour d'horizon* of what he considered the international dilemma after World War II quickly brought brickbats for its perceived warmongering from Stalin as well as strident criticism from influential Americans (including Eleanor Roosevelt and Walter Lippmann). Truman tried to dodge the controversy by telling reporters he hadn't read the text beforehand, a retort somewhat at liberty with the truth.

However, besides his time with Truman, Churchill went with Eisenhower, now army chief of staff, to Richmond, Virginia, for a speech on March 8 to that commonwealth's general assembly, the oldest legislative body in the Western Hemisphere. During his introduction, Eisenhower called Churchill "one of the great men of the world," and Churchill returned the compliment by saying about the general: "I have formed impressions that will last me all my days of . . . his great power of making the soldiers and officers of our two countries work together . . . as if they were the soldiers of one single nation."[3] Later in his speech, Churchill broadened his theme beyond one person to say he had "a very simple message which can be well understood by the people of both our countries. It is that we should stand together."[4] The former prime minister in 1946 sounded very much like the honorary degree recipient at Harvard three years earlier.

Shortly after his time in Virginia and with journalistic commentary about the Fulton speech still reverberating internationally, Churchill stopped by the White House on March 11 to bid farewell to Truman. The next day he went to Hyde Park to pay his respects at FDR's grave. Eleanor Roosevelt accompanied him and devoted her "My Day" column, circulated on March 14, to Churchill's fifth visit to the Hudson Valley since 1942. As she had done the week before after the "iron curtain" speech, she combined deference and disapproval in her assessment of her guest's view of the world situation, remarking: "No matter how much any of us may differ at times with the ideas which Mr. Churchill may hold, none of us will ever cease to be grateful to him for the leadership which he gave during the war."[5] As the years passed, Mrs. Roosevelt's opinion of Churchill continued to mix positive and negative judgments, with her reservations or differences becoming more pointed after he returned to 10 Downing Street in 1951.

Throughout his mid-January to late-March stay in America during 1946—in some respects, with his Fulton address and the spadework he did for his war memoirs, the United States became a staging ground for the next phase of his public life and his dramatic political comeback—Churchill made three separate trips to Washington, proof that he never wanted to be too far removed from the U.S. power center. He also continued to be the subject of far-reaching press attention. In honor of the first anniversary of FDR's death, the April 15, 1946, issue of the *New Republic* was devoted to "Roosevelt: First Appraisal by Those Who Knew Him." Churchill's remembrance appeared first *before* a statement from Truman. After returning to Britain, he concentrated on his war memoirs, an unavoidable genre of the time. In fact, later in 1946, three books written by Americans appeared and leveled blistering criticism at Churchill, sullying his reputation and casting him in a distinctly different light from Eisenhower's assessment of global greatness. These authors recognized that Churchill had performed on the stage of history, but to them what happened behind the curtain deserved exposure, too. The figure portrayed didn't agree—and said so—while Eisenhower, to his embarrassment, played a role in some of the revelations.

Harry Butcher's diary, *My Three Years with Eisenhower*, was published on April 25, 1946, after ten excerpts had come out in the *Saturday Evening Post*. Among other revelations, Butcher paraphrased Eisenhower describing how Churchill consumed soup, including that because of his build he "almost had his nose in the soup" and it "disappeared to the accompaniment of loud gurglings."[6] Besides the close-up reenactment of table manners, readers learned about Eisenhower's "suppressed yawn" at a dinner Churchill hosted as well as other such incidents. Churchill read one of the magazine extracts and wrote Eisenhower that "I think you have been ill-used by your confidential aide. . . . Great events and personalities are all made small when passed through the medium of this small mind."[7] Eisenhower chastised Butcher for disclosing private matters, but the book, with several scenes dramatizing Churchill's attempts to change Eisenhower's battle plans, became a commercial success.

Four months after readers became privy to the interactions of two principal figures in the Allies' high command, Louis Adamic produced an entire book—*Dinner at the White House*—ostensibly about a ninety-minute experience involving Churchill's first visit to meet with FDR after the United States declared war. A naturalized American citizen from Slovenia and prolific writer about the value of ethnic diversity, Adamic and his wife were invited by Eleanor Roosevelt, an admirer of his 1941 book *Two-Way Passage*, to dine at the White House on January 13, 1942, the evening before Churchill left the capital to return to London. Early in this muckraking memoir, we're told the prime minister "waddled into the room" for pre-dinner drinks, and Adamic offered his initial opinion of Churchill: "I had long considered him dangerous. . . . His large, round mug was perfectly smooth, blandly innocent—except for the eyes and mouth which were shrewd, ruthless, unscrupulous."[8] For more than two hundred additional pages, Adamic combined reportage with a drumbeat of caustic commentary, noting at one point that the prime minister was: "A very great leader and—so far as I'm concerned, and because of what he represents—also evil."[9]

Eleanor Roosevelt devoted her syndicated newspaper column on August 24, 1946, to Adamic's dinner-based diatribe. She tempered her reaction with praise of the author before offering words that seem to approximate sympathy: "I am sorry that Mr. Adamic felt that Mr. Churchill was an evil influence."[10] Mr. Churchill, however, felt no sympathy, and had his London lawyers sue the author and his publisher, Harper and Brothers. Adamic had imputed that aspects of British policy related to Greece were, in part, influenced by Churchill's dealings with a bank that had offered him assistance in 1912. According to press coverage, Churchill received "substantial" monetary damages, and the passage in question was removed from unsold and future copies of the book. Documents in the Churchill Archives note that a £5,000 cheque was deposited in Churchill's bank account on January 14, 1947, as settlement of the case, a sum not released to the press. The amount would be worth approximately £250,000 in today's currency. Like Butcher's, this slim volume received considerable attention. In a Sunday *New York Times* review on September 15, the twenty-eight-year-old Harvard history professor Arthur M. Schlesinger Jr. wrote of "the huge, complicated business of negotiating with Churchill" the book exposed in its lacerating prose.

The most personal, scabrous assessment of Churchill at that time came from an unlikely source: a Roosevelt, who had also spent a considerable amount of time with Eisenhower. In *As He Saw It*, Elliott Roosevelt, the second oldest son of Eleanor and Franklin, provided backstage accounts of some of the most important wartime conferences that involved FDR, Churchill, and (at Tehran and Yalta) Stalin. A dubious, memoirish narrative from start to finish—direct quotations provoke doubt about their authenticity—the "He" of the title referred to the president, who in this retelling of recent history seemed hell-bent on eliminating the British Empire and ending colonialism rather than defeating the Axis powers. The book, like Adamic's, didn't spare criticism of Churchill, and the younger Roosevelt acknowledged at the outset that the Fulton speech was a principal impetus for his best-selling book. That Eleanor Roosevelt wrote the foreword provided something of a familial imprimatur and an indirect slap of her own at the former (and future) prime minister.

Similar to Butcher's diary, with its multipart presentation in the *Saturday Evening Post*, Roosevelt's book was serialized in *Look* magazine. (At the time the *Saturday Evening Post* had a circulation approaching 4,000,000, with *Look* at nearly 2,500,000.) A full-page advertisement in the *New York Times* announcing the *Look* excerpts, complete with Eleanor Roosevelt's endorsement, accentuated the purported combative interplay between the prime minister and president. The first extract carried the title "FDR vs. Churchill—the Inside Story." The next one focused on "Quarrels at Casablanca," the third "How Churchill Fought with Stalin," and the final one "Did We Forge the Iron Curtain?"

The son might have thought he was channeling his father's perspective, but the theme of the individual articles forced the public to look at Churchill with more than a suspecting glance. The portrait, in fact, was deliberately nasty. On the first page of "FDR vs. Churchill," Elliott described his different roles at five foreign conferences: "a message-taker, errand-runner and drink-filler. (This last task was nearly full time in relation to one of the Big Three.) [Elliott is referring to Churchill—Ed.]" This five-word editorial note in *Look* twisted the knife, as did Elliott's remark in the book itself that on a visit to Chequers outside London he was summoned to the prime minister's chambers to find Churchill "stalking about the room, clad only in a cigar. Ho, I thought; here's something to tell my grandchildren about."[11] Elliott was the second Roosevelt to find Churchill in the state of nature and, like his father, unable to keep the experience to himself.

Even before the first article in *Look* appeared in the September 3, 1946, issue, Churchill was grumbling about the thirty-five-year-old Roosevelt, who served in the Army Air Force from 1940 until the end of the war. According to Lord Moran's account, dated August 8, Churchill told his doctor, "Elliott Roosevelt has been writing a foolish book; he attacks me."[12] The former prime minister was particularly annoyed at the accusation—by someone he dismissed as "not much of a fellow"—of delaying the cross-Channel invasion for two years before D-Day.

At the same point of his book, Moran related that Churchill told him about a "heated" argument between himself and his son, Randolph, two nights earlier: " 'I bellowed and he counter-bellowed, and I felt things weren't right here.' " Churchill motioned to his heart, saying that " 'it was like the ghost of what happened at Washington when I tried to open the window.' "[13] The painful incident in the White House during the night after his first speech to Congress on December 26, 1941, whether a minor heart attack or not, still worried him.

One of Churchill's most revealing statements about what he perceived as an avalanche of criticism concerning his wartime actions came in a May 5, 1948, letter to Truman. While asking presidential permission to quote from messages he sent to FDR in his memoirs, Churchill noted with prickly specificity what had been said about him by former U.S. government officials, including Cordell Hull, Henry Stimson, and Henry Morgenthau. The four-page letter even complains about what Elliott Roosevelt and Butcher had written in 1946.[14] The former prime minister was keeping score and remembering names. Truman granted the request, allowing Churchill to return the fire directed at him. He avoided making trips to America at this time until he could defend himself with his history of the war—as *he* saw it.

Combat memoirs kept publishers on their own war footing after the hostilities ended. In 1948, both Churchill and Eisenhower brought out books of their own intended to establish what they wanted on the public record about their decisions and actions. Neither would continue to be used as anyone's punching bag.

The Gathering Storm, the first volume of Churchill's six-book *The Second World War*, came out in June in America (and three months later in Britain), while Eisenhower's *Crusade in Europe* appeared in the States in November (and early in 1949 in the U.K.) Both works received massive exposure en route to commercial success. For example, six extended excerpts of *The Gathering Storm* were published by *Life* magazine, and the *New York Times* featured a nearly unbelievable thirty installments between April 16 and May 20. In early November, the *New York Herald Tribune* started to serialize *Crusade in Europe*. This series, too, involved thirty separate articles.[15] With a first printing of 150,000 copies as well as Book-of-the-Month Club sales (strategically timed for the Christmas season), Eisenhower, the president of Columbia University since the spring of 1948, could look ahead to a financial future far different from his decades of military service. Eisenhower's memoir came out in Britain less than a year after *The Gathering Storm* appeared, and shortly thereafter Churchill's second volume, *Their Fin-*

est Hour, was published—again with the promotion of several excerpts in *Life* and thirty installments in the *New York Times*. This time, as though to say "I'm back," Churchill spent ten days in the United States that coincided with release of the book. News coverage about it amplified reports about Churchill's meeting with Truman and a Boston speech on March 31, 1949, at the Massachusetts Institute of Technology's Mid-Century Convocation. Compared by commentators to his address at Fulton for its global importance, Churchill defended the West, especially "the fraternal association between the British Commonwealth of nations and the United States," in its struggle with the (in his word) "communized" world commanded by "thirteen men in the Kremlin."[16] Speaking at this convocation served as something of a prelude to Churchill being named *Time* magazine's "Man of the Half-Century" in the January 2, 1950, issue.

Eight weeks later, in the United Kingdom's general election, Conservatives picked up ninety seats and reduced Labour's majority in the House of Commons. In publishing precincts and political ones, Churchill was rebounding from his electoral setback five years earlier and the snide postwar criticism that rankled him. For Americans, his stature continued to rise later in 1950 when two more volumes of his war history were published—*The Grand Alliance* (in April) and *The Hinge of Fate* (in November)—with both documenting the U.S. role and involvement before and after Pearl Harbor. Curiously, the U.K. edition of *The Hinge of Fate* wasn't available until August of 1951, eight months after the American edition. To a certain extent, as Churchill looked to the United States for assistance to Britain in 1940 and 1941, a decade later he counted on lucrative publishing deals in America to help subsidize his own lifestyle that was anything but economical, as exposed and documented by David Lough in *No More Champagne: Churchill and His Money*.[17]

The widely circulated postwar accounts and the attention they received helped shape public opinion about the major figures involved and the decisions they made, particularly Churchill and Eisenhower.

Moreover, their books boosted their political fortunes: to win back 10 Downing Street for Churchill and to capture the White House for Eisenhower. Indeed, on October 26, 1951, Churchill steered the Conservative Party to its first majority in the House of Commons since he became head of the Tories in 1940. Six months earlier in 1951, Eisenhower took a leave of absence from Columbia to return to Europe as the first Supreme Allied Commander of the NATO military alliance, a post he occupied until June of 1952 when he returned to the United States to begin his first political campaign for the Republican Party's nomination for president.

Just seventy days after becoming a two-time prime minister, Churchill sought to bolster the U.K.-U.S. relationship and his own stature as a world figure by returning to Washington for a series of meetings with Truman and other government officials. When Churchill arrived on January 5, 1952, Truman's disapproval rating, according to a Gallup survey that week, was 67 percent, and in early February his approval mark dropped to 22 percent, the lowest in Gallup history. Not long afterward he announced he would forgo a reelection campaign. Bilateral discussions took place for a few days that January, and following a short trip to Canada, he returned to Washington to deliver his third address to a joint session of Congress on January 17. The main story on the front page of the next day's *New York Times* focused on Churchill's speech, with James Reston, who'd won a Pulitzer Prize in 1945 for his coverage of the Dumbarton Oaks conference, briskly summed up the address in his opening sentence: "Prime Minister Churchill gave Congress today a solemn but fairly hopeful report on the state of the universe."

Though Reston remarked that the seventy-seven-year-old's "voice was certainly not as clear or firm as it was the last time he addressed the Congress" in 1943, Churchill's method of composing until the moment of delivery hadn't changed. He still resembled a Fleet Street journalist with the deadline clock ticking. John Colville, the prime minister's longtime private secretary, described Churchill as still in bed fussing with his remarks when he was informed "the cars were at the door and we ought already to be leaving." According to his aide, the prime minister "got up, dressed and reached the Capitol with two minutes to spare."[18]

The last time Churchill visited Truman during his presidency was January 8, 1953, twelve days before Eisenhower's inauguration. During this trip to America—his ninth since 1941—Churchill spent more time in New York conferring with the president-elect than talking with the soon-to-retire incumbent. How the prime minister and the president-elect sized each other up in private at the beginning of their new relationship was revealingly documented in diaries. Eisenhower was candid in his assessment of "Winston," who, though "charming and interesting as ever," has become noticeably older with his thinking "unquestionably influenced by old prejudices or instinctive reaction." The "special place of partnership" between the United Kingdom and the United States continued to be Churchill's abiding pet subject.[19]

Eisenhower viewed the postwar world as vastly different and in need of new approaches. For him, Churchill was a prisoner of the past: "Winston is trying to relive the days of World War II." The incoming commander in chief looked back to bygone war days with the perspective from his experience: "In those days he had the enjoyable feeling that he and our president were sitting on some rather Olympian platform with respect to the rest of the world and directing world affairs from that point of vantage."[20]

Eisenhower's assessment of Churchill turned into a broader commentary on the desirability of older leaders going to the sidelines to allow younger people to serve in leadership posts. While considering Churchill's condition, he also extracted a lesson for himself or anyone yearning to cling to power. In a parenthetical note, he remarked: "(For myself I am determined that whatever the cause of my own retirement from public life, I will never stay around in active position so long that age itself will make me a deterrent to rather than an agent of reasonable action.)"[21] Several of the diary entries reflected the thinking of a shrewd surveyor of not just one person but of power in general.

Despite the wide smiles and saccharine statements of fellowship, the two men had serious reservations about each other in their elective offices. Right after Eisenhower's landslide victory in 1952 over Illinois governor Adlai Stevenson 55.2 percent to 44.3 percent (and thirty-nine of the forty-eight states), the prime minister told Colville: "For your private ear, I am greatly disturbed. I think this makes war much more probable."[22] On January 7, after Churchill met with Eisenhower, John Foster Dulles, and other Republicans, Colville recorded that his boss "was really worked up and, as he went to bed, said some very harsh things about the Republican party in general, and Dulles in particular."[23] Churchill's reservations about American leadership continued after Eisenhower's inauguration, and on July 24, 1953, Colville recorded that the prime minister, was: "Very disappointed in Eisenhower whom he thinks both weak and stupid. Bitterly regrets that the Democrats were not returned at the last Presidential Election."[24] Shortly after his remark to Colville, Churchill became more pointedly personal delivering his opinion of the six-month occupant of the White House to his niece Clarissa Eden, Anthony Eden's wife: "He is a nice man, but a fool."[25] Despite such snide remarks muttered to those close to him, Churchill's messages to Eisenhower carried the salutation "My dear Friend" or "My dear Ike."

Throughout 1953, deftly documented by Roger Hermiston in his study, *Two Minutes to Midnight*,[26] Churchill persisted in trying to organize a meeting of the U.K., U.S., and U.S.S.R. Each proposal was rejected by the Eisenhower administration, which viewed the Communist threat both at home and abroad at the top of its governing agenda. Why consort with an enemy in what the president and his State Department considered a futile exercise, even a waste of time?

Still, Churchill kept proposing high-level huddling to address major problems. Such personal diplomacy, with the world watching, animated him, nourished his ego, and kept the United Kingdom (as well as its leader) perceived as an international power. In a 1950 speech, he even coined a term for this approach when he advocated talks like those at Tehran and Yalta—"a parley at the summit." From then on, the word *summit,* which he had also used during his Christmas Eve remarks from the White House in 1941, signified heavyweight consultations between or among preeminent authorities with potentially consequential ramifications.

Churchill's animating ambition was "the building of a sure and lasting peace," the concluding (and often quoted) words of his speech on October 10, 1953, to the Conservative Party conference. In his first speech since his major stroke on June 23, he again pushed for a meeting, where he thought he could influence world affairs and reduce East-West tensions. That the so-called "Big Three" were ostensibly allies in wartime and that the postwar situation was in no way comparable didn't deter him from such bold overtures.

Clearly the relationship between the seventy-eight-year-old British leader and the sixty-two-year-old soldier-turned-politician would be on an entirely different plain from the way they worked together during the war years. The United States had become much less isolationist and more engaged in world affairs, while the British Empire was declining markedly in terms of its influence and wealth. In addition, Eisenhower was now head of state and in charge of the executive branch rather than a top military officer meeting with a principal ally to discuss—and often debate—strategy and tactics amid combat.

Aware of the new political dynamic of their leader-to-leader rapport, Churchill took pains to revise the sixth volume (*Triumph and Tragedy*) of *The Second World War.* Given the new situation, he was willing to delete his well-known criticism of Eisenhower's decisions during the final months of battle to avoid conflict between the two countries and to keep some semblance of the "special relationship" flourishing. On April 9, 1953, two weeks after Churchill was knighted by Queen Elizabeth II, he wrote Eisenhower that he had finished writing *Triumph and Tragedy* before returning as prime minister, and he wondered whether the president wanted to see relevant "extracts" prior to publication. "I know that nothing which I have written will damage our friendship," Churchill said. "But, now that you have assumed supreme political office in your country, I am most anxious that nothing should be published which might seem to others to threaten our current relations in our public duties or to impair the sympathy and understanding which exist between our countries."[27]

Despite Churchill's sniping in private—after the January 1953 meetings he referred to Eisenhower as "a real man of limited stature"[28]—he expunged his reservations about Eisenhower's war leadership, including this pointed passage that he struck from *Triumph and Tragedy*. It was intended to appear in the first paragraph of the chapter titled "The Final Advance": "Our troops could, and in my opinion should have liberated it [Prague], but in fact were restrained from doing so by the direct intervention of the highest American authorities. Berlin, Prague, and Vienna were needlessly yielded to the Soviets. Here may be discerned the Tragedy in our hour of Triumph."[29] Multiple emendations followed to make this version of history strategically tactful for the current political situation. To delete a key sentence explaining the book's title reflects the serious concern of the author-prime minister at offending a president just taking office. Air-brushing history might serve a political purpose, but what's lost is finding out those figures responsible for what Churchill views as a "Tragedy."[30]

Six weeks before *Triumph and Tragedy* was published in America on November 30, 1953, Churchill received word he'd won the Nobel Prize in Literature. That year's Nobel Peace Prize—an honor Churchill coveted—was awarded to George C. Marshall for his efforts through the European Recovery Program, popularly known as the Marshall Plan, to rebuild postwar Europe. A few days after Churchill's sixth war volume arrived at bookstores—like others in the series it was a Book-of-the-Month Club selection—he, Eisenhower, and French prime minister Joseph Laniel met in Bermuda for a conference to discuss the possibility of talks with the Soviets, the dangers of the atomic age, the future of Europe, the Far East, and other concerns.

At this conference, Eisenhower, in effect, unloaded on Churchill for wanting any association with the Soviet Union, which he compared to an unrepentant woman of easy virtue and lucrative lust incapable of changing. The prime minister might have been on a sunny island, but he was out in the cold. The president didn't want to hear any arguments running counter to a major thrust of his administration and, particularly, of the State Department led by John Foster Dulles, an avowed opponent of the Truman containment policy. He did, however, want to convey a positive impression in the wake of the high-level, widely covered gathering. Eisenhower flew directly from Bermuda to the United Nations in New York City to deliver what became known as his "Atoms for Peace" speech, which concluded that "the United States pledges before you—and therefore before the world—its determination to help solve the fearful atomic dilemma—to devote its entire heart and mind to find the way by which the miraculous inventiveness of man shall not be dedicated to his death, but consecrated to his life."[31]

In the December 19 issue of *The New Yorker* Richard H. Rovere called Churchill "the host and the moving spirit" of the three-power conclave, which was delayed from July because of the prime minister's June stroke. Similar to Roosevelt's attempt to conceal his handicap—detailed in Hugh Gregory Gallagher's study *FDR's Splendid Deception*—Churchill tried as best he could to keep information about the seriousness of his condition confidential.[32] Despite the many whispered and grumbled reservations of the prime minister about the president, he wasn't shy in attempting to schedule face-to-face reunions with Eisenhower. The two finally agreed to meet in Washington six months after the Bermuda conference. It would be their third parley since January of 1953, and this one would mark Churchill's return to the White House.

Close analysis of the only Republican president and administration between 1933 and 1969 prompted Princeton professor Fred I. Greenstein to christen the Eisenhower years as "the hidden-hand presidency."

The former military commander governed by using—in Greenstein's phrase—"an indirect leadership style," an approach that sought to distance the president from controversies over policy and grubby political infighting. In *The Hidden-Hand Presidency: Eisenhower as Leader*, Greenstein wrote: "A president who seeks influence and cultivates a reputation for not intervening in day-to-day policy-making will necessarily hide his hand more often than one who seeks recognition as an effective political operator."[33] Eisenhower's megawatt smile and easy-going manner conveyed the avuncular or grandfatherly image he wanted to project. Outside camera range, however, the realities of governing produced a different picture. The "hidden hand," with its stealth-like direction, was much closer to hands-on than hands-off, yet without discernible fingerprints. Richard Nixon suggested as much in his 1962 memoir, *Six Crises*, principally about his two terms as Eisenhower's vice president. Describing the chief executive he watched and served, Nixon candidly remarked: "He was a far more complex and devious man than most people realized, and in the best sense of those words." The last phrase of the sentence doesn't exactly blunt the sharp edges of the preceding words, and the observant understudy added about Eisenhower that "he usually preferred the indirect approach where it would serve him better than the direct attack on a problem."[34]

Churchill's visit to Washington in June of 1954 can be viewed as a variation of the hidden-hand method. More accurately it illustrated sleight-of-hand statecraft, the dexterous manipulation of events that led to consequences far different from the announced expectations. Intent to take another turn on the world stage, the prime minister followed the White House lead during the five days he was back in Washington, though he was becoming aware the years were taking their toll on him. In a poignant letter to Clementine, dated May 25, 1954, Churchill remarked that he had to draft a speech for delivery at Royal Albert Hall in London, admitting: "This is a toil which lies ahead of me, and I do not conceal from you that original composition is a greater burden than it used to be, while I dislike having my speeches made for me by others as much as I ever did."[35]

The prime minister proposed to make his third trip in three years to America for "some talks" in a letter to Eisenhower over two months before the visit. On June 11, the president, who sought to conduct the meetings during a weekend, wrote his soon-to-be guest: "It will be like old times to have a weekend with you. I know that it will be interesting and enjoyable and I am certainly hopeful that it will be profitable for both our countries."[36]

Yet, at his June 15 news conference, Secretary of State Dulles, who served as a U.S. senator from New York for four months in 1949 before losing a special election, downplayed the potential profitability of the upcoming visit by saying it would be "extremely informal" with "no agenda." The next day Eisenhower told reporters that Churchill was concerned about "the theory that there are such great rifts occurring among us." To tamp down such talk, the president said he decided to play host to "a friendly informal thing" over a weekend. He even said: "There are going to be no meetings as such. I expect him to stay at the White House with me and there will be people coming in and out."[37] Instead of suggesting anything resembling summitry, Eisenhower's phraseology sounded more apropos a social occasion: longtime friends spending a weekend of casual conviviality.

Scrupulous in sensing the climate being created, Churchill adopted Eisenhower's nonchalance. Although the prime minister concluded a June 10 letter to the president by noting, "I feel that we have reached a serious crisis in which the whole policy of peace through strength may be involved,"[38] Churchill's widely covered arrival statement gave no hint of "a serious crisis." After remarking that he'd traveled from "my fatherland to my mother's land," he said: "I've come with Anthony Eden [Britain's foreign secretary] to talk over a few family matters and try to make sure there are no misunderstandings."

The resonance of domesticity in the term "a few family matters"—

rather than "a serious crisis"—became a dominant theme in journalistic coverage of the visit, conforming to the scripted narrative of the White House. Interestingly, in a memoir about his first term, Eisenhower took a different approach from the administration's announced line, admitting that the talks began in "an atmosphere of furor brought about by exaggeration in the press of Anglo-American differences."[39] Blaming the press for "differences" or conflict followed, of course, in the long tradition of presidential friction with the fourth estate.

Unlike earlier White House sojourns, this one was different in several ways beyond the most obvious that it wasn't occurring during war when strategizing about future battles became the preoccupation. This time Eden was sharing the spotlight with Churchill and the entire British party numbered just twenty people rather than the scores that accompanied the prime minister in the 1940s. To a certain extent, this slimmed-down situation mirrored the postwar status of the United Kingdom and the British Empire: a much-reduced role in the world with less global reach. Moreover, in the eyes of some observers, the increasingly frail and faltering Churchill humanly symbolized the enfeebled imperium that he'd championed and defended since the era of Queen Victoria. All his talk of a "special relationship" helped to keep the United Kingdom standing right next to the nation that emerged from the war as an international superpower and economic heavyweight. The British Empire was in eclipse but still wanted to bask, if not in the sun, in the partially illuminated shadows of the world's newest colossus.

Government documents that appeared thirty-two years after the prime minister's visit related a much different story from Eisenhower's description of a no-agenda, no-formality weekend. Two days before Churchill's arrival, the president, secretary of state, and others in the administration devoted a lengthy meeting to discussing precise details of the visit and the matters to be discussed: the European Defense Community, the Near East (Egypt, Iran, Saudi Arabia, and Cyprus), withdrawal of U.K. forces from Korea, and East-West trade. The next day, Eisenhower, Dulles, and various aides met again to review planning, adding atomic matters and the dispute between America and Britain over the Guatemala government's pro-communist orientation. (A coup d'état, involving the U.S. Central Intelligence Agency, was staged during Churchill's visit, putting a military dictatorship in power.) Besides these high-level meetings to sketch out areas to examine, the State Department prepared "briefing papers for topics which the British were expected to raise." The subjects that were covered: the Soviet Union, atomic energy, China and Korea, Southeast and South Asia, Europe, the Middle East, Latin America, and economic matters.[40] Eisenhower might have forecast "no meetings as such," but all the advance work—in a way similar to how Churchill prepared prior to his first meetings with FDR after Pearl Harbor—belied the White House sessions on the schedule. The president also had formulated grand ideas about an appropriate way to conclude the "friendly informal thing" being arranged.

White House press secretary James Hagerty, who had been Thomas Dewey's publicist and spokesperson in the 1940s before joining the Eisenhower campaign in 1952, pointed out in his diary the extent to which Eisenhower personally sought to create a definite perception for projection and amplification by news sources. For instance, the president "was quite indignant that his orders had been changed" for Churchill's reception. Eisenhower intended that a modest ceremony take place at the South Portico right below the Truman balcony instead of the more ceremonial one facing north and traditionally used for foreign dignitaries. In Hagerty's account, the president wanted it at the South Portico "to make it a more informal welcome."[41]

After being greeted by the president and First Lady, Churchill went with the Eisenhowers to the White House living quarters on the second floor. Given an option of rooms for his stay, the prime minister immediately selected the one he wanted. "Churchill picked the Rose Room for himself and Eden was assigned the Lincoln Room," Hagerty noted, and did so "as a matter of sentiment."[42] Sentiment notwithstanding, Churchill's suite had been part of the White House renovation during the Truman presidency. The extensive changes prompted Eisenhower to give Churchill a tour of the new yet still familiar surroundings, which didn't impress Colville, his private secretary. "The White House is not attractive; it is too like a grand hotel inside," he jotted in his diary.[43] Before lunch, the two leaders had "a private conversation" in the Oval Office that lasted seventy-five minutes. As was the case for the discussions between Churchill and Roosevelt in the 1940s, the official government report offered no clue of the subjects covered, and there was no record kept.[44]

During the nearly two-hour luncheon meeting that involved Churchill, Eisenhower, Eden, Dulles, and a few others, it was as though participants engaged in what popular NBC television news anchor of the time, John Cameron Swayze, called "hopscotching the world." The U.S. memorandum about the first session was comprehensive: "Among the subjects discussed were Germany, France, Guatemala, the Hapsburg and Ottoman Empires, the Kerensky government in Russia, African colonies, the French position in North Africa, Indochina, the Oppenheimer case, the internal problem of Communism, the Boer War, World War II, the relationship of Communist China to Russia, the EDC [European Defense Community] and NATO and the Locarno Pact."[45]

This smorgasbord of subjects, with their range and breadth, didn't suggest the beginning of a leisurely "family" weekend. The memorandum also included this detail: "Before leaving the luncheon table the President suggested that whereas it seemed unnecessary to have any fixed agenda, it might be useful to have set down certain key words . . . as a checklist for discussion in order to make sure that no important topic was overlooked." He also proposed that written minutes, approved by the two governments, summarize "any decisions or agreements" coming out of their meetings. Churchill endorsed the president's far from casual recommendations.[46]

A second two-hour meeting followed lunch as well as a Rose Garden photo session of the four key figures talking among themselves. Given the sultry weather, the outdoor picture-taking, done at the urging of London newspapers, was brief. Early in the second discussion, Churchill raised the possibility of a summit involving the United States, United Kingdom, and Soviet Union, an *idée fixe* since returning to power. Eisenhower didn't completely close the door, but he countered that maybe Nixon and Dulles could initiate American involvement before the president participated in any significant proceedings. He also stipulated that representatives of the People's Republic of China would not be welcome, should that suggestion be proposed. Despite Churchill's desire to participate in another three-power summit, in part to dramatize himself as a peacemaker extraordinaire in reducing Cold War tensions, it was not to be. Eisenhower did not take part in any conference with Soviet leaders until July of 1955, almost four months after Churchill resigned as prime minister and as leader of the Conservative Party.

Several concerns first raised during their lunch received amplification in this substantive session. At one point, Churchill said "he was anxious to take some of the weight off the United States in its presentation of an anti-Communist front. He said, however, that England would never accept going to war in Indochina. He doubted that the United States would either."[47] At the time, the Viet Minh, supported by the Soviet Union and China, had the month before defeated the French in the Battle of Dien Bien Phu. The United States, clandestinely and largely through the CIA, had provided assistance to the French to try to help them defeat the Communist-backed forces. An American effort to draw the British into the colonial conflict, which had begun in 1946, failed, with the U.K. decision resulting in friction between the two governments.

As the situation unfolded in subsequent years, Churchill's prediction that the United States wouldn't go to war in Indochina proved calamitously inaccurate. As president, Eisenhower sent several hundred advisors to help the government of South Vietnam after the 1954 partition agreement of the Geneva Accords. Thousands of "advisors" followed later, and, ultimately, almost three million men and women with the U.S. military served in Vietnam until 1975, when the last Americans fled Saigon. Near the end of this White House meeting, the group took up another topic with deep roots and enduring claim to international significance: "the Arab-Israeli problem." The stated goal—"to relax tensions by our combined efforts"—was, in their estimation, "no definitive answer to the problem."[48]

One of the more significant discussions that Friday afternoon focused on what the government notetakers referred to, in a separate report, as "Atomic Energy Matters." Eisenhower brought up the decade-old concern of what information the two countries could exchange, while Churchill spoke in apocalyptic language about dangers arising from the weaponry being developed after the bombings of Hiroshima and Nagasaki in August nearly nine years earlier. Tests of a hydrogen bomb earlier in 1954—in the statement of the report—"transformed what had been to him [Churchill] a vague scientific nightmare into something which now dominates the whole world." Acknowledging Russian development of the bomb, the prime minister argued that "wars could have been fought with the A-bomb but that the H-bomb is something totally different." In this dawning, nuclear-obsessed world, Churchill saw the situation by invoking three words: "deterrent, alert and alarm."[49] The stakes—and growing fear—propelled the former warlord to concentrate on the cause of peace.

At the press briefing Hagerty conducted after the afternoon session, he focused on just two topics: the status of the European Defense Community, a never implemented six-country organization intended as a counterweight to the Soviet threat, and atomic matters. In both cases, they were Cold War matters of contention and unavoidable at the time for the two countries' policymakers and their publics. The long consultations following the morning arrival of the British contingent proved to be more than friendly chats, and subsequent activities that weekend followed a similar course. A devotee of afternoon siestas and a habitual night owl, Churchill kept to business throughout this Washington stay. With speculation making the rounds that he'd soon resign and be replaced by Eden, he knew he might not have another chance as prime minister to influence international affairs in direct concert with the United States.

As might be expected in the scripted theatrics of public diplomacy, the president's press secretary—described by one reporter as "quick-witted, quick-tempered and cool-nerved"—was more forthcoming in his diary than in front of journalists. Hagerty provided a behind-the-scenes look at how Churchill conducted himself during the conference. Probably because of the personal nature of his "observations," several of his statements do not appear in the government's record.

The press secretary and the president spoke early Saturday morning, and Eisenhower told Hagerty "that it was awfully difficult to talk with Churchill, that he refused to wear a hearing aid and consequently the President had to shout at him all the time in conversation." From this remark, Hagerty, a former *New York Times* political reporter, developed a picture of a somewhat unsteady lion in winter who still possessed an outsized personality that kept him going as a leader. Hagerty observed: "He is almost in the dotage period and gives the appearance at least of losing connection with the conversation that is going on in the room. However, when he speaks he still retains the forcefulness of delivery, the beautiful, ordered, and intelligent command of the English language although he doesn't seem to be able to stay on a point very long."[50] He added a poignant afterword to this portrayal by saying "I am sure the entire British delegation realizes that the Prime Minister is a very feeble old man and that he has not too long to live."[51] This prediction on life expectancy was off by a decade.

On Saturday morning, as the day before, Churchill and Eisenhower met together in the Oval Office without Eden or Dulles, who were conferring over at the State Department. This time a notetaker prepared a memorandum about what the two leaders discussed. A possible Big Three summit returned as the "primary subject of conversation," with Churchill again suggesting the dynamics of such a meeting. After Eisenhower mentioned the possibility of France participating, the prime minister commented: "Two is company; three is hard company; four is a deadlock." As the president seemed reluctant to agree, he volunteered that Churchill was advocating something foreign to him and outside his experience. Eisenhower remarked: "I am not afraid to meet anybody face to face to talk to him, but the world gets in a habit of expecting a lot."[52] Though Churchill persisted in dreaming about doing something bold, involving himself, to change the climate of the Cold War and reduce global tensions, he was never able to arrange such an event.

While his visitor seemed preoccupied with setting up a summit, Eisenhower had something entirely different on his mind. As the final result of the weekend's "friendly informal thing," Eisenhower wanted to see the two countries approve what he envisioned as "Atlantic Charter #2," an updated set of common principles similar to the eight-point statement issued after the first wartime meeting between Churchill and Roosevelt in August of 1941. Instead of a communiqué listing subjects addressed, he contemplated a document with lasting salience.[53] Churchill read the draft of the proposed charter, pronouncing it: "Damned good" and offered two small phrasing changes.[54] As it happened, revising the text continued for two more days—and a matter-of-fact summary of proceedings was also released to the White House press corps at the end of the long weekend.

Beginning with Churchill's first visit to Washington in late 1941, he always made a point of spending time with key members of Congress as well as other officials in the executive branch. In 1954, that meant a White House luncheon on June 26 for—the *New York Times* reported—twenty-eight members of Congress, ten members of the administration, and Earl Warren, the former California governor who had become chief justice of the Supreme Court nine months earlier. With no reporters in attendance, the only detailed account of the remarks made by Eisenhower and Churchill came from "notes"

Hagerty took, and they lack direct quotation. Introducing his guest, the president averred (in Hagerty's summary) "that no other citizen in the world could command so much admiration and respect as did the Prime Minister."[55] Churchill's talk combined ideological concerns—the danger to freedom from Communism—and more immediate matters. At one point, as Hagerty phrased it, Churchill said "that meeting jaw to jaw is better than war," another of his pitches for a summit that included the Soviets.[56]

One of Churchill's most often attributed bon mots—"to jaw-jaw is always better than to war-war"—can be traced to this luncheon. The *New York Times* on June 27 used that specific phrase in a page one headline and quoted the statement twice in its story. The same day the *Washington Post* quoted the prime minister on its front page as saying it's "better to talk jaw to jaw than have war." Others newspapers, including the *Chicago Tribune*, *Los Angeles Times* and *New York Herald Tribune*, published slight variations of the wording, with the *Herald Tribune* pointing out that the text of the fifteen-minute talk wasn't released to the press. The source it credited for the jaw-jaw quotation? Senate Minority Leader Lyndon B. Johnson.

Hagerty's briefing launched the colorful phrase on its way, as did his acknowledgment of the prime minister's fervent wish of meeting "at the summit," a Churchillian flourish that conveys both a policy and a performative approach. The British leader's self-confidence at being able to solve complicated problems facing the world animated him—in a similar way, though under very different circumstances, as it did during the 1940s. From his decades in politics, he also knew that well-timed praise and flattery would endear him to the public. Saying, in Hagerty's rendering, that "he had never had a visit to Washington so agreeable and pleasant as this one," Churchill went on to declare: "Thank God you have him [Eisenhower] at the head of your country and that your country is at the head of the world."[57] Whatever reservations Churchill might have had after Eisenhower's election seem to have faded, at least rhetorically, as they worked together. Moreover, the remarks, if remotely faithful to the prime minister's honest opinion, call into question what he really thought of previous White House stays during FDR's presidency and possibly of Roosevelt himself.

The only Saturday meeting among Churchill, Eisenhower, Eden, and Dulles focused on issues related to Egypt and the Suez Canal, including Britain's decision to reduce military forces there and America's intention to help the Egyptians economically and militarily. The "Memorandum of Conversation," prepared by the government, failed to note that the session, which began at 5 p.m., was briefly halted just after 5:30. A lightning storm with attendant winds clocked at sixty-six miles an hour roared through Washington. Churchill rushed from the president's study "like a little boy" (in Hagerty's phrase) to witness the destructive downpour that claimed two lives, according to local newspaper stories the next day. Colville described the madcap scene of the prime minister's eccentric enthusiasm of racing out of the meeting and urging everyone to go to the Solarium to witness the raging storm. The prime minister's secretary commented: "I can't imagine anybody else interrupting a meeting with the President of the United States, two Secretaries of State and two Ambassadors just for this purpose."[58] Churchill's excitement prompted amusement, but it also reflected his continuing sense of wonder, of being a firsthand observer of an adrenaline-rush phenomenon that old age hadn't extinguished.

On the next day, in contrast to his church-going during his first White House visit, the prime minister declined the chance to attend religious services with Eisenhower. Churchill had also begged off an earlier invitation for Sunday prayer with Eisenhower at the Bermuda conference six months earlier. At that time, he abstained by saying in a widely reported remark, "I will meet my Maker soon enough."

The remainder of Churchill's time in Washington more closely resembled the weekend among friends or family that the two governments had initially publicized. The prime minister and president conferred about the written documents that would be released, but there were no additional large meetings. Early Sunday afternoon, Churchill met privately with Dulles before the secretary of state and foreign minister sat down with their staffs to discuss the seating of the People's Republic of China at the United Nations—a move the United States strongly opposed and the U.K. thought deserved consideration. In their dialogue, the prime minister told Dulles of his eagerness to go to Moscow, and he also angled to have the top diplomat in the State Department convince Eisenhower of participating. (Letting go of a firm conviction wasn't in Churchill's constitution.) Dulles closed the door just as quickly and as firmly as he did the one on China, an action that didn't occur in the U.N. until 1971. Despite such substantive differences, the two countries were able to accommodate or camouflage differences of their viewpoints and, in the process, reduce the perception of friction and conflict. As the talks progressed, news coverage emphasized agreement among representatives of the two countries, and Churchill didn't miss any opportunity to herald the special relationship between the United Kingdom and the United States.

All the reporting, however, wasn't appreciated by the prime minister. That Sunday evening after the third White House dinner, he returned to the Rose Bedroom and, in the opinion of his doctor, Lord Moran, his preeminent patient was visibly perturbed. According to Moran, Churchill handed him Saturday's *Manchester Guardian* with a statement in a report by Alistair Cooke underlined in red ink: "Sir Winston has never yet managed to have a talk alone with President Eisenhower." Calling the assertion "absolute nonsense," Churchill fumed: "Why, I have spent about three hours every day talking to the President alone."[59]

The passage that offended its subject drew a sharp contrast between Churchill's wartime visits and the one in 1954, saying that the current conference would not feature "the intimate pow-wows between Roosevelt and Churchill in the war years." The offending article also noted "Sir Winston is ageing fast and that President Eisenhower is not, as Roosevelt always was, his own Secretary of State." This was the most prominent story on the newspaper's front page, and it appeared under the headline "Mr Eden Steals the Limelight," another dig at the prime minister, which brought into public view some of the concerns then being expressed about Churchill during his trip abroad.

Cooke, a respected journalist on both sides of the Atlantic who later became a popular, urbane broadcaster during the last decades of the twentieth century, wrote many admiring words about Churchill before the dispatch in question appeared. Cooke, for instance, had praised Churchill's book, *Maxims and Reflections*—noting at one point that "this brilliant anthology of Churchillisms . . . is more revealing of the best of him than any other single work by him or about him"—in a cover piece for the *New York Times Book Review* in March of 1949. His admiration far exceeded one example of perceived criticism. Indeed, after Churchill's death, Cooke sat down with Eisenhower for an extended television interview about one subject: Winston Churchill. The program was aired by the ABC network in 1967, and their colloquy subsequently appeared as a book, *General Eisenhower on the Military Churchill*, in 1970.[60]

Late on the morning of Monday, June 28, the four main figures and their staffs met briefly in Eisenhower's office to discuss the joint communiqué that would be released later that day. The so-called "Declaration," modeled on the Atlantic Charter, still required additional work as well as approval from the U.K. government in London. Eisenhower proposed a final talk on Tuesday morning before Churchill and his party left for meetings in Canada. Despite the deliberate downplaying beforehand, the bilateral conference turned out to be an extended weekend of serious business.

At that Monday meeting, the president and the prime minister handled the scheduling of the next day's session themselves. According to Hagerty, Eisenhower said: "Winston, I will be ready to meet you anytime you want. I get up at 6:30 and will be available from seven o'clock on." Churchill, an unashamed "tardy riser," balked at the early times suggested. When 11:30 was proposed, the prime minister responded: "That will be fine. That is more normal."[61]

Shortly after this exchange, Churchill left the White House to speak at a luncheon of the National Press Club. In his remarks, he focused on the need to reduce Cold War tensions. The warrior of the 1940s sought to be recognized as a conciliator in the 1950s, with several newspapers devoting page-one attention to what he said. In response to one question, he pushed for a new approach, implying, once again, the worth of a summit, and "that we ought to have a try for peaceful co-existence, a real good try for it." He recalled his "iron curtain" address, saying "I even remember making a speech at Fulton six years ago, which didn't get a very warm welcome in the United States, because it was so anti-Russian and anti-Communist; but I am not anti-Russian; I am violently anti-Communist."

Churchill might have been making a rather self-serving distinction; however, he was fighting to play a constructive role on the world stage at what he called a "doom-laden" time. Hagerty accompanied Churchill and his party to the Hotel Statler near the White House, which became the Capital Hilton in 1977. The press secretary described the prime minister's aides as being apprehensive that Churchill might stumble answering questions "he had not seen before and which were to be read to him on the spot." Despite the anxiety, "the old gentleman did a magnificent job" in Hagerty's estimation.[62]

Hagerty's judgment was reiterated in the journalistic coverage of the event, attended by more than 850 members of the fourth estate. Some newspapers, including the *New York Times*, Washington's *Evening Star*, and the *New York Herald Tribune*, published transcripts of the prime minister's opening remarks and his responses to the questions posed. The *Washington Post*, which devoted an editorial—"The Master's Voice"—to Churchill's appearance printed an entire page of pictures of the prime minister as well as a news article about the lunchtime session. The first question he was asked indirectly brought up the reported disputes between the United Kingdom and the United States: "At Quebec in 1943 (or 1944) you and Mr. Roosevelt spoke of the 'blazing friendship' between our two countries. What is the temperature of that friendship now?" Churchill thundered: "Normal." Later, he praised the president in words echoing what he had said at the Saturday lunch with Congressional leaders: "I rejoice that General Eisenhower is at the head of your country at the time when your country has been called upon to become the head of the world." Referred to in the *Post* as "the stooped old gentleman," the prime minister demonstrated he was spry enough politically to mend fences and to associate himself with a president then enjoying an approval rating (according to the Gallup Organization) of over 60 percent.

At the same time Churchill was emphasizing the value of the special relationship, the official communiqué explaining "these few days of friendly and fruitful conversations" circulated on the news wires to outlets around the world. The words "we," "our," and "agreed" recur throughout the sections about "Western Europe," "Southeast Asia," and "Atomic Matters." Any rifts or disagreements didn't receive an iota of attention.[63]

Following the luncheon, Churchill left the White House and moved to the British embassy for his last day in Washington. That evening during a dinner at the embassy, Vice President Nixon represented the president and sat next to the prime minister. Nixon, who had met Churchill on his airport arrival and would see him off the next afternoon, noted in his diary several direct quotations—almost as though he had made a recording of their conversation. Asked about accomplishments of the conference, Churchill purportedly responded, "I always seem to get inspiration and renewed vitality by contact with this great novel land of yours which sticks up out of the Atlantic." Later, he commented on the threat from Communism, remarking: "I think that I have done as much against the Communists as [Sen. Joseph] McCarthy has done for them." Nixon asked Churchill why the British didn't like McCarthy, the two-term senator from Wisconsin, who without evidence charged that Communists populated the federal government. The prime minister "said one thing they couldn't understand was why the Senate did not investigate all of the charges about his finances and other irregularities in getting elected and while he was Senator." Nixon jumped in to respond "that very possibly Senators did not want to set the precedent of investigating a colleague for fear that it might someday react in a case against themselves."[64] The remark was something of a verbal omen. Twenty years later Congressional investigations of Watergate-related misdeeds and illegalities resulted in Nixon's resignation from the presidency.

At the time Nixon spoke with Churchill, McCarthy was facing gale-force criticism from Democrats, independent-minded liberals, and segments of the press for his Red Scare campaign. Yet two nights before the embassy dinner, Nixon had been the headline speaker at a Republican Party dinner in McCarthy's home state of Wisconsin, and several of his statements echoed what the embattled senator was saying. One syndicated dispatch about the speech opened by focusing on alleged bungling by the Truman administration with Dean Acheson as secretary of state: "The 'Acheson' foreign policy was directly responsible for the loss of China, and if China had not been lost there would have been no Korean War and no crisis in Indo-China today, Vice President Richard M. Nixon declared here tonight." The "slam-bang political speech," as it was termed in the next sentence of the *New York Herald Tribune* report, kicked off the midterm Congressional campaign for Republicans, and a crowd of over three thousand cheered. The president, as usual, would hide his political hand and let his Number Two take charge of partisan brawling; however, as it turned out, Republicans lost control of both the House and the Senate in the November elections, Eisenhower's first midterm contest.

The final activity of the nearly five-day "weekend" conference was the release, in the phrase of a *New York Times* editorial, of "A New Atlantic Charter." The first item in the "Declaration" of the two leaders set the tone for the document's six points: "In intimate comradeship, we will continue our united efforts to secure world peace based upon the principles of the Atlantic Charter, which we reaffirm." High-minded, collaborative, forward-looking, the text avoided reference to the East-

West divide and Communism, though it advocated "self-government" and "independence," particularly on behalf of "formerly sovereign states now in bondage" and "nations now divided against their will." The statement later proposed slowing down the arms race and finding ways to transform "prodigious nuclear forces . . . to enrich and not to destroy mankind."[65]

What Eisenhower, Churchill, and others composed is not as historically significant as the original Atlantic Charter, but it is a serious joint approach to a world far different from the one that existed in the summer of 1941, and it also reflected the "intimate comradeship" the two countries were trying to convey at the conclusion of the conference. Taken together, all the sessions amounted to much more than what either side described would happen before the talks began, and the spirit of the sessions endured. Nineteen months later, this time with Eden as prime minister, the U.S. and U.K. governments released yet another "Declaration," titled "The Declaration of Washington," directly addressing the Cold War competition, Communism, and "the glorification and aggrandizement of the Soviet Communist State."[66] Eisenhower saw value in bold, charter-like statements promulgated by the two countries in what undoubtedly was an attempt to emulate Roosevelt. In his memoirs, Eden didn't devote much attention to the joint declaration, but he observed: "The President had taken considerable pains over this."[67]

Saying farewell to Churchill at the White House, Eisenhower told the prime minister's son-in-law and member of Parliament Christopher Soames, who married Mary Churchill in 1947: "Bring him back again, will you?" The wartime comrades, who now were (as one reporter described them) "the free world's two foremost leaders," continued to work for shared objectives, despite certain obstacles. In a short telegram to Clementine on June 29, Churchill ventured: "I think we have broken the backbone of our difficulties."[68]

While Churchill was visiting Canada, Eisenhower conducted a news conference that was dominated by reporters' queries about the just-completed conference—as well as Nixon's attack on Acheson for losing China and precipitating the Korean War. The president extolled the prime minister's abilities—saying his "admiration for him was as high as ever"—before defending his vice president for delivering a speech he said he hadn't read. In preparing to meet the press, Dulles told Hagerty that Eisenhower should try to interject that as a result of the visit "our two countries are closer than they had been for some time and that they had met as friends to talk over family difficulties."[69] Churchill had wanted and sought this trip to the White House to repair rifts and to defuse speculative stories about infighting in the relationship he prized above others. After all the sessions, it seemed as though the collaborative script written by the prime minister and president produced what both leaders pursued.

Churchill didn't return to America during his final nine months as prime minister. The two leaders, however, kept in close contact, largely through the exchange of letters or telegrams following the visit in 1954. Nearly fifty messages during that time addressed international issues and personal concerns. Indeed, a month after their White House meetings, Eisenhower sent a long, twenty-two-paragraph letter that focused on portions of their "Declaration" and Churchill's "confidential statement" of his intention "to shift the responsibility of the Premiership to other shoulders." The president proposed as part of Churchill's leave-taking "a thoughtful speech on the rights to self-government" and the "growing spirit of nationalism" as a reaction to colonialism.[70] Eisenhower's letter, dated July 22, was answered on August 8, and Churchill dodged the idea of a major speech to revert to his unending obsession of scheduling a Big Three conference: "Now, I believe, is the moment for parley at the summit. All the world desires it."[71] Neither leader followed the other's advice, taking up new concerns in their subsequent messages.

One of the most compelling letters Eisenhower composed after the June visit was not to Churchill but about him. Eight days after Churchill's eightieth birthday (on November 30, 1954), the president sent a longtime friend from Abilene, Edward (Swede) Hazlett, a detailed assessment of that day's political environment—including criticism of the twenty-second amendment limiting a president to two terms—and Eisenhower's opinion of human greatness as well as individuals he thought deserved that distinction. Saying essential qualities "would be vision, integrity, courage, understanding, the power of articulation either in the spoken or written form, and what we might call profundity of character," one person (in his view) stood out from the others he mentioned. That person was Churchill. "For my part," Eisenhower wrote, "I think I would say that he comes nearest to fulfilling the requirements of greatness in any individual that I have met in my lifetime. I have known finer and greater characters, wiser philosophers, more understanding personalities. But they did not achieve prominence either through carrying on duties of great responsibility or through giving to the world new thoughts and ideas."[72]

Eisenhower had the ability to look beyond past policy and strategic disagreements or personal frustrations to take the whole measure of someone he'd come to know and work with during the inferno of global war and, more recently, the wintry peace that followed. He didn't hide his esteem for Churchill and, in fact, it seemed to become more ardent following the 1954 visit. When—after months of foot-dragging—Churchill finally resigned as prime minister on April 5, 1955, Eisenhower went to the Rose Garden to deliver a public yet personal statement. It included a paragraph directly addressed to the British leader, who had counseled at his last cabinet meeting at 10 Downing Street: "Never be separated from the Americans."[73] The president said: "All of us in the free world can respect your decision, Sir Winston.... But we shall never accept the thought that we are to be denied your counsel, your advice. Out of your great experience, your great wisdom, and your great courage, the free world yet has much to gain."[74] The next day's *New York Times*, before quoting Eisenhower's entire statement about his "old and very dear friend," noted on page one: "It is not usual for the head of the United States Government to express himself so feelingly when the head of another government resigns from office."

Eisenhower's rhetorical ovation for Churchill didn't stop with his comrade's departure from 10 Downing Street. In the Eisenhower Presidential Library, a folder with Churchill's name on it contained the instruction to "Tuck this away in Sir Winston's file." Within the folder is a one-page, anticipatory tribute that Eisenhower prepared for release if Churchill had died before January 20, 1961, the date when the Eisenhower presidency would end. Saying "the world has lost one of the truly great men of our time," the president concentrated his remarks on Churchill's meaning in the United States: "For Sir Winston—in time of war and in time of peace—captured the imagination of all Americans. His indomitable courage and his indestructible belief in the society of free nations and in the dignity of free men became a symbol of our way of life. From him, America and all free lands gained added inspiration and determination to work for the maintenance of a just and enduring peace."[75]

What prompted Eisenhower to prepare his touching farewell? On February 2, 1958, the White House announced that Churchill and his wife would be the Eisenhowers' guests in April, when an exhibit of forty Churchill paintings was scheduled to be on display at the Smithsonian Institution in Washington. On February 18, however, the former prime minister became ill with what was diagnosed as a combination of pneumonia and pleurisy. The front page of the *New York Times* for February 20 reported that the lung problems still didn't prevent Churchill from smoking two cigars the previous day. Recurrence of the pneumonia in March resulted in postponement of the April visit to the White House. Churchill's frailty and bouts with illness probably prompted Eisenhower to have the statement at the ready, and the date on the file—"Jan. 1958 to November 1959"—is a strong clue.

Still a showman with talent for the dramatic, Churchill's planned return to America would have come at a time when his art and writing were receiving extensive attention. Besides the several-city exhibition of his canvases, the fourth volume of his *History of the English-Speaking Peoples* was published on March 17. Titled *The Great Democracies*, one "book" in this final volume of a project Churchill began in the 1930s was called "The Great Republic," and it concentrated on the American Civil War. Moreover, his long essay, "The Cold 'Peace' and Our Future," came out in the April 29 issue of *Look* magazine, featuring on its cover three photos along with short quotations of the author, including this first one: "Truman is worthy to be numbered among the greatest Presidents." At the beginning of the eleven-page article, Churchill reiterated his criticism of the American military for not being more aggressive in the final months of the European combat. Some sentences in just one paragraph pulled no punches:

> I had earnestly hoped that the Americans would not withdraw from the wide territories in Central Europe they had conquered before we met [at Yalta]. . . .
>
> The Americans seemed quite unconscious of the situation, and the satellite states, as they came to be called, were occupied by Russian troops. Berlin was already in their hands, though Field Marshal [Bernard L.] Montgomery could have taken it had he been permitted. . . .
>
> The Russians had occupied Prague with, as it seemed, the approval of the Americans.

The name of "Eisenhower" didn't appear in Churchill's bill of particulars, but anyone acquainted with the details about the war's end in Europe would surely know who the Supreme Allied Commander was during this period. What's curious about the essay—the headnote in *Look* says, "These may well be the last words Sir Winston will ever write for publication"—is that it served as the epilogue for the single volume abridgment of Churchill's 1,250,000-word history of the war. Titled simply *Memoirs of the Second World War*, the nearly 500,000 words of the condensation wasn't published until February 1959. Was *Look* hoping to capitalize on the planned visit in 1958, with its varied activities, rather than wait for the appearance of the abridgment and its added epilogue?

Churchill's lingering reservations about how the final months of the war played out—prompting Alan Brooke to quote Churchill in his diary for April 1, 1945, "There is only one thing worse than fighting with allies, and that is fighting without them!"[76]—didn't mar planning for his twelfth trip to America that involved meetings with a president during the previous eighteen years. This one—from May 4 to May 8 of 1959—would be almost entirely different from his earlier one in 1954. Eisenhower, rather than Churchill, encouraged the visit, and from the start both figures saw it as a friendly, social reunion: something of a sentimental journey and sojourn for the eighty-four-year-old former prime minister. Looking ahead to their time together, the president jested in one letter dated January 20, 1959, that they would have fun deciding which particular military figure was really responsible for winning World War II. Eisenhower was well aware that jousting over appropriate or deserved credit continued to be waged in memoirs and reminiscences coming out on both sides of the Atlantic. The postwar prose battle that began with the books published in 1946 continued.

Churchill arrived in New York on May 4 after his first flight in a jet, the Comet, of the British Overseas Airways Corporation. The president's personal plane then brought him and his party of four to Washington, where Eisenhower himself greeted his guest at the airport. Since the first term, when the administration's protocol dictated that the president would designate others to welcome high-level or notable visitors, the policy had changed. Eisenhower now decided whether he'd personally take part in an arrival ceremony, which he had also done two years earlier on the first U.S. state visit of Queen Elizabeth II and Prince Philip.

Even before Churchill stepped foot on American soil again, a *New York Times* editorial offered "a hearty welcome" to "the Olympian Man of the Century." Eisenhower was more restrained in his remarks about his "dear friend of wartime days." In reply, Churchill noted he expected "a quiet visit" before dropping a small incendiary device on the otherwise jolly proceedings: "I always love coming to America. But I shall not say—as most people who are traveling nowadays about the world seem to do—everything I think." Without being specific, Churchill's sly words took aim at his fellow countryman, Field Marshal Montgomery, who in an hour-long television interview with Edward R. Murrow and Charles Collingwood of CBS News that aired on April 28 criticized Eisenhower's leadership both during the war and as president. At one point for the American audience, he opined: "Your leaders are not awfully well. Mr. Dulles is in the hospital with cancer; your president has had three very serious illnesses; the head of your State Department [Christian A. Herter] today walks about on two crutches [from arthritis]." All in all, Montgomery, who was in Moscow at the time, judged U.S. leadership as "rather suspect," statements the press circulated prominently. Though frail and unable to move around without difficulty, Churchill could still land a jab in defense of his White House host.

While the previous visit was billed—despite what it turned out to be—as a "weekend" get-together, suggesting leisurely conversation rather than serious policy-oriented sessions, Churchill arrived in 1959 on a Monday and most of that work-week in the executive mansion revolved around him. This time there wasn't any debate over which portico to use. The more formal north one was chosen for the arrival of the president and his guest. What didn't change—and never varied during his six sojourns of residence at 1600 Pennsylvania Avenue—was the suite where he stayed: the Rose Bedroom.

Churchill remained asleep the next morning, May 5, when Eisenhower was conducting a press conference. One questioner inquired whether Montgomery's carping had come up in the previous evening's discussion with Churchill. Like the former prime minister, the president seemed ready with a stinging retort: "Well, I think that we tried to talk about important things." Once laughter subsided, Eisenhower spoke more generally about his visitor: "We had a nice talk at a family dinner about numerous questions around the world, both personalities and issues."

Montgomery's broadside wasn't the only controversial subject related to Churchill's visit that arose with journalists that Tuesday morning. Former president Harry Truman's decision to decline Eisenhower's invitation to return to the White House for a dinner with the former prime minister prompted a reporter to wonder whether Truman was "avoiding or evading" a meeting with his successor.[77] Truman and Eisenhower had been friendly governmental colleagues before the 1952 campaign, but antipathy subsequently developed about, among other things, Eisenhower's handling, or mishandling, of McCarthy. Concerning the dinner, Truman blamed Eisenhower—"the invitation came too late—as intended"—and had taken to referring to the president in private by a nickname appropriated from a character created by the early twentieth-century author and humorist Ring Lardner: "Alibi Ike."[78] The sentimental reuniting for two former allies wouldn't take place without personal pique or political quarreling intervening.

While reporters filed their stories about the news conference, Churchill and Eisenhower made a melancholy journey to what was then called Walter Reed Army Medical Center outside Washington to visit John Foster Dulles and George Marshall. Neither Dulles nor Marshall had long to live, with Dulles passing away nineteen days later and Marshall, a stroke victim, dying on October 16. Over the fireplace in the sitting room of the Dulles suite hung Eisenhower's oil portrait of Churchill, which the subject judged as "very good." On the same trip away from the White House, the two also stopped at the government's arboretum to admire the azaleas in bloom, a favorite flower of Churchill. The president had arranged his schedule to accommodate his visitor, a kindness even more evident the next day.

Repeating a practice Roosevelt had initiated, Eisenhower took Churchill to his home outside Washington—his farm at Gettysburg, Pennsylvania. After a brief helicopter ride, the president showed off his nearly two hundred acres and his home, which was completed in 1955. Besides a tour by golf cart with Eisenhower as chauffeur, the two inspected the Civil War battlefields around Gettysburg from the air, seeing the location of Pickett's Charge and other pivotal places. Many historians think the fate of the Confederate cause was determined between July 1 and 3, 1863, on the terrain they were viewing, and Churchill, who had written at length about "the Gettysburg campaign" in *The Great Democracies*, now could see from the air where the war's most costly engagement—an estimated fifty thousand were killed or wounded there—was fought. Decades earlier, he had toured the battlefields by car and on foot, but this was his first panoramic perspective by air.

That evening at a "stag" dinner in the White House, both Eisenhower and Churchill delivered their only formal remarks of the visit. The president traced their friendship to first meeting Churchill "in this house . . . in the same room that he is now occupying." While Eisenhower mostly evoked the past, Churchill reverted to a theme he'd repeatedly championed in America since the early 1940s: the necessity for "comradeship" of English-speaking peoples: "I feel most strongly that our whole effort should be to work together. . . . I think that it is in close and increasing fellowship, the brotherhood of English-speaking peoples, that we must work."[79] Churchill's last prepared remarks he delivered in the White House might have sounded anachronistic amid the emergence of so many new countries and the global decline of colonization, but they expressed a concept at the center of his thinking.

As he'd done in 1954, Churchill moved to the British embassy early the next afternoon, on May 7, following a send-off at the White House that numbered approximately three hundred cheering people. His three nights in the Rose Bedroom meant that he'd occupied those quarters for some fifty days since December 22, 1941. On this trip—unlike the previous one—Eisenhower accepted an invitation for dinner at the embassy that night. One name on Churchill's proposed list of attendees was removed by the U.S. administration. Former secretary of state Dean Acheson would not be welcome in the company of the president, the vice president, or others. The Associated Press dispatch about the dinner began with this lead: "President Eisenhower and Sir Winston Churchill reminisced again last night with World War II comrades at the last of three stag dinners." The phrase "reminisced again" could serve as a principal reason and thrust of the trip, and they reunited three months later in London at the U.S. ambassador's home for yet another dinner involving prominent war figures during Eisenhower's two-week trip to Germany, Britain, and France.

In a memoir, Anthony Montague Browne, Churchill's secretary during his final years and the recipient of a Distinguished Flying Cross during the war, provided a behind-the-scenes account of Churchill's last Washington visit that described the determination of the former prime minister to return to America and touched on Montgomery's televised criticism. The First Viscount Montgomery of Alamein had been the president's White House guest twice—in 1953 and 1958—making his armchair judgments more personally wounding to Eisenhower. Montague Browne even reported a health scare that prompted him to call Lord Moran back in London.

Churchill showed the aide a black mark on the tip of one of his fingers, and a Washington doctor, who was summoned, diagnosed the condition as gangrene. The prospect of a quick return to Britain arose, but Churchill rejected the idea: "I don't care what's wrong with my bloody finger," and he refused to change any of his schedule.[80] Moran urged secrecy when he discussed the malady with the American physician. During both his first and his last White House visits, Churchill felt the need to seek medical care while he was staying in the same quarters. Both times his circulatory system was the suspected cause of the problems.

Churchill departed from Washington as he arrived—on the president's own plane. At the end of a weekend in New York at Bernard

Baruch's home, Churchill offered a brief farewell at Idlewild Airport before the return flight to London. Thanking his "great friend," the president, for making his stay "a memorable one," Churchill concluded: "I would like to bid you farewell on this note: As long as the United States and Great Britain are united, the future is one of high hope, both for ourselves and for the free world." The cause that had brought him across the Atlantic after Pearl Harbor and so many times since then still dominated his thinking and public remarks.

Churchill's last visit was front page news across the United States, with lasting impact on those with whom he had contact. Ann C. Whitman, Eisenhower's longtime personal secretary who served throughout both terms, offered her assessment that "it was the most historic and memorable event of all the years at the White House." Commenting that Eisenhower treated Churchill "like a son would treat an aging father and was just darling with him," Whitman explained why the president acted so solicitously: "Sir Winston is feeble and has difficulty talking, so much so that communication is at times practically impossible. But little things show that, as his secretary [Montague Browne] said, he takes everything in.... For instance, he noticed a picture of Field Marshall [*sic*] Montgomery in the President's trophy room. He simply looked at it and shrugged his shoulders with a gesture that implied more than a thousand words." The secretary, who became Nelson A. Rockefeller's chief of staff during his two-plus years as vice president from late 1974 to early 1977, summed up the visit by noting its effect on Eisenhower and the pleasure it gave him that Churchill "would come all this way to renew his friendship. To see Sir Winston is to look upon history—a history that is heroic and great."[81]

When Montague Browne returned to London, he prepared a "Private and Confidential" memorandum for the British ambassador in Washington, Sir Harold Caccia, about the White House visit that was more revealing than the version in his memoir. At one point in this account, the president referred to Murrow as "a snake," and Churchill received credit for "smoothing the ruffled feathers" of Montgomery's invective.

Montague Browne viewed the interaction between Churchill and Eisenhower much the same way Whitman did. "During the three days we were in the White House the President showed an affectionate care and consideration for Sir Winston and spent a great deal of time with him," Churchill's aide remarked. The report then focused on Eisenhower, saying the president's "working day seems to be from about half past eight in the morning until luncheon. In the afternoon, when he was not with Sir Winston, he seemed either to be resting or taking light exercise."[82] Montague Browne had worked with Churchill since September of 1952 and observed a more energetic schedule for the figure he assisted. Whether his appraisal is fair to Eisenhower is debatable. Yet, by 1959, the president had recovered from a serious heart attack in 1955, surgery for a bowel obstruction in 1956, and a stroke in 1957. A less strenuous—more hands-off—agenda in the last phase of his second term was not unreasonable, though each of the nights Churchill was in Washington the president served as host or as featured invitee at dinners. The president was on duty each evening, and these occasions qualify as work-related responsibilities to most people.

Right after Churchill arrived back home, Lord Moran stopped to check on his most illustrious patient. The trip had extracted its toll—"He was so tired that he could hardly keep awake," Moran observed—but Clementine told the doctor that her husband " 'loved the visit. I think he wanted to go to America before he died, because of his mother.' "[83]

Churchill's motivation to cross the Atlantic came from more than a son's love for the birthplace of a parent. Even at the age of eighty-five, he still wanted to perform in the public arena and on the world stage, whether through political action or by the power of his prose. Shortly before this jaunt to the United States, Churchill—to the disapproval of Clementine—decided to be a candidate once again for his seat in Parliament from the Woodford constituency in Essex. The October 1959 contest to remain in the Commons—the twenty-first he'd waged since 1899—would be his last and the sixteenth time he won. He served until September 25, 1964, four months before his death. Throughout those years, Churchill and Eisenhower corresponded with regularity—and they continued to do what they could to defend the free world they helped shape through war and peace for almost a quarter-century.

EPILOGUE

John F. Kennedy considered Winston Churchill his hero, and also, as historian Arthur M. Schlesinger Jr. wrote, "his greatest admiration."[1] Churchill's almost unprecedented combination of political, literary, and oratorical prowess provided Kennedy with a figure in the public arena to emulate. Eighty-two days after his inauguration in 1961, the forty-three-year-old president learned that the British statesman, exactly twice his age, happened to be a passenger aboard a yacht that had docked in the Hudson River following a month's long Caribbean cruise. With the voyage—courtesy of Aristotle Onassis, the Greek shipping tycoon and future husband of Jacqueline Bouvier Kennedy—at an end, Churchill was scheduled to return to London the next day from Idlewild Airport, just as he'd done in 1959 on his last visit to the White House.

Kennedy proposed a different itinerary. In a phone call, he offered to fly the former prime minister from New York to Washington so the two could talk and spend time together at the White House. Mindful of Churchill's frailty and difficulties in concentrating, his secretary, Anthony Montague Browne, who took the call, declined the invitation. He wrote afterward: "The thought of America, and indeed the world, seeing him at his worst was not endurable." Kennedy, according to Montague Browne, understood the decision, saying, "Please give him my warmest and most admiring good wishes."[2]

But Kennedy's esteem never waned. Two Aprils later, the president presided over a first of its kind White House ceremony. On April 9, 1963, Kennedy formally conferred honorary U.S. citizenship on a foreign national. Both chambers of Congress—the Senate unanimously—had approved a resolution making Churchill an American, a recognition of his "exceptional merit." With the extended Churchill family watching the Rose Garden proceedings from their London home on the BBC's live (and ostentatiously promoted) satellite broadcast, Kennedy signed the legislation, Public Law 88–6, and delivered a brief address. In her syndicated column that appeared the next day, Mary McGrory tartly observed, "The President read his remarks with the air of a man who knows only honorable defeat awaits any man entering a prose tourney with the great word-marshal of the 20th century who, as he said, 'mobilized the English language and sent it into battle.' "

Trepidatious or not, Kennedy soldiered on, emphasizing the word "freedom" in his speech and praising the honoree's linguistic mobilization.[3] Neither Kennedy nor McGrory gave proper credit to the author of the striking image describing words as weapons. Edward R. Murrow, a pioneer radio and television journalist for CBS News, coined the remark nearly a decade earlier, on November 30, 1954, during a broadcast marking the eightieth birthday "of perhaps the most considerable man to walk the stage of history in our time." Murrow had reported, bravely and memorably, from London during the war, and in championing Churchill's four-score years, Murrow recognized how the former prime minister had "mobilized the English language and sent it into battle to steady his fellow countrymen and hearten those Europeans upon whom the long dark night of tyranny had descended."[4] Truth be told, though, Murrow probably didn't mind the purloining of his remark. As it happened, Murrow attended the citizenship ceremony as an invited government official. In 1961,

Kennedy appointed him director of the United States Information Agency, which was created in 1953.

The president concluded his remarks with a flourish: "By adding his name to our rolls, we mean to honor him—but his acceptance honors us much more. For no statement or proclamation can enrich his name now—the name Sir Winston Churchill is already legend."[5] Unlike Franklin Roosevelt, Harry Truman, or Dwight Eisenhower, Kennedy never had the chance to spend time with Churchill as president, but the history-making ceremony just outside the executive mansion served as something of a star-spangled substitute.

Randolph Churchill then read a six-paragraph statement that his father had composed for the occasion. Besides being a message of gratitude for the recognition "without parallel," the text included fighting words directed at anyone belittling the United Kingdom in the international community: "I reject the view that Britain and the Commonwealth should now be relegated to a tame and minor role in the world. . . . Let no man underrate our energies, our potentialities, and our abiding power for good."[6] Churchill made yet another plea for "unity of the English-speaking peoples," particularly through an enduring, special relationship between the United Kingdom and the United States. "In this century of storm and tragedy I contemplate with high satisfaction the constant factor of the interwoven and upward progress of our peoples," Randolph read. "Our comradeship and our brotherhood in war were unexampled. We stood together, and because of that fact the free world now stands."[7] A signature phrase—"this century of storm and tragedy"—made clear the source of the words spoken on his behalf that overcast Tuesday afternoon. One *Washington Post* account of the proceedings noted, "Heavy clouds floated overhead, but the scene was brightened by some of the most luminous prose ever heard in Washington."

The text of Churchill's entire statement appears as the final address in the massive eight-volume, 8,917-page compilation of his complete speeches spanning sixty-six years. Fittingly or not, these final words were delivered not in the House of Commons but at the White House. Churchill had made the Rose Bedroom his home in Washington. Now in the Rose Garden he was reaching the peak of a personal summit.

Shortly before the citizenship ceremony, Schlesinger, the natty, bowtie-preferring professor on leave from Harvard to serve as a special assistant to Kennedy, wrote a newspaper column for the *Sunday Telegraph* in Britain, explaining why Churchill would become "the first Atlantic citizen, the imperishable symbol of the Atlantic Communion." The cartoon illustrating the essay depicted a smiling Statue of Liberty with an illumined cigar—rather than a torch—held proudly aloft to light the way.

Like Kennedy, Schlesinger revered Churchill and praised his devotion to freedom and democracy in *The Vital Center*. In a memoir he wrote a half century later, Schlesinger included an anecdote about Churchill's defense of Britain's place in the world. The prolific historian and devout Democrat reported that Dean Acheson, Truman's secretary of state throughout his second term, from 1949 to 1953, was the source of the comment on Britain's imperial decline and its search for a new role. Schlesinger happened to be standing next to Acheson at the ceremony and heard him mutter: "Well, it hasn't taken Winston long to get used to American ways. He was not an American citizen for three minutes before he began attacking an ex-Secretary of State."[8]

Acheson's jocular criticism notwithstanding, editorial writers and commentators applauded Churchill's newest distinction, which the recipient, it was reported, prized above others he'd been awarded, including his Nobel Prize in Literature. One of the first congratulatory letters to Churchill arrived from Dwight Eisenhower. After remarking that he was "more than delighted," the former president became nostalgic. Extinguished, as was the case during the 1959 White House visit, were any smoldering embers from what Eisenhower often referred to as their "quite warm arguments" during the war or their later disagreements in the early 1950s when they were both in office. Now "friendship" and "admiration" prompted the fellowship of comrades. "Frequently these days I cannot help wish that you and I might be able to meet occasionally, as in former days, to converse on matters of interest to our two nations. I miss those contacts and those discussions—sorely." Eisenhower's letter is now displayed with Churchill's passport-resembling "Honorary Citizen Document" in an exhibition case at the Churchill War Rooms in London.

Eisenhower's valediction to his note is one word: "Affectionately." For earlier letters during his presidency, the more common closing sentiment was "As ever," "With warm regard," or "Your Devoted Friend." As years passed and their actions as well as words became public, the human bond between the two men seemed to grow stronger and warmer. During his last White House visit, Churchill wrote Clementine on May 5, 1959: "Here I am. All goes well & the President is a real friend."[9] That avowal of friendship was also reflected in Eisenhower's autobiographical report about his first term in office, *The White House Years: Mandate for Change, 1953–1956*. The former president described the personal dynamics of their amicability, and twice in the space of four paragraphs at the end of one chapter expressed his "admiration and affection" for his comrade of the past two decades.[10]

Eisenhower's emotional sentiments for Churchill were shared by millions of Americans. Beginning in 1948 and continuing for the next seventeen years, Churchill appeared near the top of the "most admired" rankings conducted by the Gallup Poll. In 1964, the last time he qualified for consideration, he finished second to Lyndon B. Johnson, the landslide winner of that year's presidential election, and ahead of both Eisenhower and Martin Luther King Jr., the recipient of the Nobel Peace Prize in 1964.[11]

Churchill died on January 24, 1965, at the age of ninety. President Johnson had been hospitalized for three-and-a-half days just before the funeral, and, after being advised not to travel, he named a three-person delegation to represent the United States: Supreme Court Chief Justice Earl Warren, Secretary of State Dean Rusk, and Ambassador to the United Kingdom David K. E. Bruce. The exclusion of newly inaugurated Vice President Hubert H. Humphrey garnered criticism on both sides of the Atlantic, and at a press conference shortly after the memorial rites Johnson admitted that he "may have made a mistake." In his memoir, *The Education of a Public Man*, Humphrey acknowledged that not being selected "succeeded in driving a small wedge between Johnson and me,"[12] a wedge that would widen later in their term.

The most prominent American to participate in the four-day state funeral was Eisenhower, who was invited by the Churchill family. The five-star general, who had his army commission reactivated by Kennedy after leaving the White House and preferred to be called "General Eisenhower" instead of "Mr. President," delivered a tribute broadcast internationally by the BBC as the coffin was transported by barge down the River Thames to Waterloo Station. Burial took place at St. Martin's Church in Bladon, just outside the grounds of Blenheim Palace in Oxfordshire, where Churchill was born in 1874. Eisenhower described his unique association with Churchill and the pride of two countries to recognize him as a "soldier, statesman and citizen." Besides looking back, the former president peered into the future: "Among all the things so written or spoken [about Churchill], there will ring out through all the centuries one incontestable refrain: He was a champion of freedom."[13]

Churchill's death prompted an outpouring of biographical and historical chronicles as well as first-person tributes and remembrances. Newspapers, magazines, television networks, book publishing, and the recording industry flooded the marketplace with Churchilliana. Eisenhower contributed the introduction to *Churchill: The Life Triumphant*, a hardcover volume produced by American Heritage Magazine and United Press International that appeared in March of 1965.

That same month *The Atlantic* devoted its cover and ten articles to remembering, in its phrase, "The Greatest Englishman." Eleanor Roosevelt's contribution carried the title "Churchill at the White House," and the former First Lady didn't romanticize her opinions about her husband's frequent houseguest. "I have to confess that I was frightened of Mr. Churchill," she declared. "I was solicitous for his comfort, but I was always glad when he departed, for I knew that my husband would need a rest, since he had carried his usual hours of work in addition to the unusual ones Mr. Churchill preferred."[14] The "unusual" hours were just the tip of her iceberg of reservations.

Mrs. Roosevelt recorded the serious disagreement she had with Churchill over the rendering of a statue honoring FDR, which was unveiled in London's Grosvenor Square on April 12, 1948. The widow steadfastly wanted to show him standing, while Churchill advocated on behalf of the more familiar, from photographs and newsreels, seated position that Roosevelt's handicap so often imposed on him. Ultimately, Mrs. Roosevelt won the argument, but her statuarial antagonist was never, in her judgment, "reconciled."

The former First Lady's most stunning remembrance came in the second-to-last paragraph of her essay-reminiscence. It described an episode few people would want revealed, given the occasion of her writing shortly after the death of the person being celebrated with fifty pages of words and pictures. Mrs. Roosevelt, however, could be as fearless as her husband, and she used self-deprecating tact to make her point. At lunch one time, she noted, Churchill turned to her and assertively inquired, " 'You never have really approved of me, have you?' " Taken aback, Mrs. Roosevelt, who referred to herself as "an unimportant person," said she "hesitated a moment and finally said, 'I don't think I ever disapproved, sir,' but I think he remained convinced that there were things he and I did not agree upon, and perhaps there were a number!"[15] The coy final words, along with the exclamation point for emphasis, provided more than a suggestion of the multitude of viewpoints where the two didn't see eye to eye.

Whether Churchill ever learned that Mrs. Roosevelt went to FDR in the hope of acquiring Blair House is not known. However, the history on the Blair House website revealed: "Winston Churchill's frequent trips to Washington helped convince President Franklin Roosevelt of the need for official diplomatic housing." The background statement explained why: "Franklin Roosevelt, Jr., recalls the morning his mother found the prime minister wandering towards the family's private quarters at 3 a.m., trademark cigar in hand, to rouse the sleeping president for more conversation. He met Eleanor first, however, who firmly persuaded him to wait until breakfast."[16] As noted earlier, the individual who provoked Mrs. Roosevelt never stayed across the street.

Though illness prevented Johnson from attending Churchill's funeral, he served as the principal speaker in October 1965, when a bronze bust of Churchill was donated to the art collection of the White House. In his prepared remarks, Johnson called the former British prime minister "one of America's greatest citizens," adding wryly that the White House "most certainly would have been Winston Churchill's home for several four-year terms if he had been *born* an American citizen."[17] The bust, a gift of several World War II colleagues, including Eisenhower and W. Averell Harriman, was originally placed on display outside the Diplomatic Reception Room on the ground floor of the White House. Now its location changes at the discretion of the president in office.

Since 2013, another bust of Churchill has been exhibited in Washington at the U.S. Capitol, and it has a direct connection to his first wartime visit to meet with Roosevelt as well as the delivery of his first address to a joint meeting of Congress. Authorized by a resolution of the House of Representatives in 2011, the timing observed the seventieth anniversary of Churchill's speech on December 26, 1941. On the pedestal of the bust below Churchill's name are three identifying designations:

STATESMAN
DEFENDER OF FREEDOM
HONORARY U.S. CITIZEN

Under those terms and carved into the limestone base are words from the concluding sentence of his 1941 speech: "In days to come, the

British and American peoples will, for their own safety and for the good of all, walk together in majesty, in justice and in peace." Those words and thousands more were composed just down the street in the Rose Bedroom.

In *Farewell the Trumpets*, the concluding volume of *The Pax Britannica Trilogy*, Jan Morris used Churchill's funeral as the grand, ceremonial finale of the British Empire. Metaphorically inspired, the orchestrated obsequies might have been somewhat imprecise, according to Morris, who wrote that Churchill, "intellectually" at least, "was more an internationalist than an imperialist. . . . Churchill was much more at home with Americans than with Australians or Canadians."[18]

Often when he came to America after Pearl Harbor, Churchill did, indeed, make himself at home in the White House. He knew as well as anyone that global leadership was dramatically shifting, giving U.S. presidents a dominant role in decision-making and action-taking. Throughout his two premierships, he sought to establish his place at the new summit of power, and he continued traveling to Washington, first amid the storm of war and later in the quest for peace. For this internationalist and imperialist, the main stage of history now existed at 1600 Pennsylvania Avenue—so that was where he wanted to parley and perform, as only he could.

ACKNOWLEDGMENTS

Research for this book began in 2016 with the first of two grants from the University of Notre Dame's Institute for Scholarship in the Liberal Arts. The following year a Visiting Research Fellowship at the Rothermere American Institute (University of Oxford) provided immersion in primary sources as well as a perfect headquarters for trips to the National Archives at Kew, the British Library, the Imperial War Museum, and the Churchill Archives Centre at Churchill College (University of Cambridge). Hal Jones and Huw David were commendable hosts during the time at Rothermere, and Allen Packwood, the director of the Churchill Archives, made each of several forays to Cambridge rewarding and beneficial. He and Jessica Collins at the Centre answered questions and located documents with alacrity and professionalism.

Trips to the presidential libraries of Franklin D. Roosevelt, Harry S. Truman, and Dwight D. Eisenhower furnished necessary background about Churchill's trips to Washington in the 1940s and 1950s. Kirsten Carter and Virginia Lewick at the Roosevelt Presidential Library in Hyde Park, New York, and Linda K. Smith at the Eisenhower Presidential Library in Abilene, Kansas, responded to specific inquiries with astute advice. Staffs at the Borthwick Institute for Archives at the University of York, the Library of Congress, the

New York Public Library, and the Theodore M. Hesburgh Library at Notre Dame were most cooperative in finding sources—with Tracey Morton of the Hesburgh Library Interlibrary Loan Office deserving a special salute of appreciation. In addition, the Department of Manuscripts and Archives at Yale University's Sterling Memorial Library kindly digitized the diaries of Henry L. Stimson for consultation and quotation.

Matthew Costello, the Chief Education Officer at the White House Historical Association (WHHA), replied to many inquiries as the project developed and also oversaw publication of an early précis of the book that appeared on the WHHA website.

At Notre Dame, where I taught from 1980 until 2018, my two academic homes—the Department of American Studies and the John W. Gallivan Program in Journalism, Ethics & Democracy—continued to offer gracious assistance in the shuffle to emeritus status. Both Jason Ruiz, the chair of American Studies, and Jason Kelly, the director of the Gallivan Program, kindly helped to underwrite reproduction fees. Katie Schlotfeldt in American Studies and Mary Jo Young in the Gallivan Program also assisted enormously along the way. Two American Studies graduates—Tessa Bangs and Madeline Doctor—carefully assembled and organized newspaper articles and research documents. The word godsend comes to mind for their work. Dave Klawiter, the senior systems engineer in the university's Creative Computing Group, genially—and repeatedly—helped a thumby operator of technology prepare the manuscript for the publisher.

Robert Weil, executive editor and vice president of Liveright, a division of W. W. Norton, warmly encouraged this project and offered wise counsel from our first meeting in the summer of 2018 to the completion of the manuscript in 2023. He deserves all the recognition and respect he has earned internationally in the republic of letters. Haley Bracken, a junior editor at Liveright, deftly and cheerfully responded to many authorial questions as the book took shape and moved through the publishing process. Editorial assistants Kadiatou Keita and Luke Swann kindly helped carry the manuscript over the finish line.

This book is dedicated to Gail Bancroft and Kenneth Socha. From the first fugitive thoughts of a possible book about Churchill's White House days, Gail and Ken have shown a keen interest and thoughtfully acted on that interest. One day a nifty little camera arrived in the mail to make it easier to work in archives and libraries. Another time they providentially helped make possible a necessary research trip to Britain. When the costs of photographs selected for reprinting exceeded original budgetary expectations, they promptly provided assistance. A few words on the dedication page are certainly not adequate to express an author's sincere gratitude—and neither is this paragraph.

Once again, Judy Schmuhl endured a writer's wayward ways and helped immeasurably, even lovingly, in bringing another book to THE END. From now on, the author will be more dutiful on the home front and elsewhere. Promise.

APPENDIX

THREE ADDRESSES WRITTEN IN THE WHITE HOUSE

ADDRESS TO U.S. CONGRESS, DECEMBER 26, 1941

Members of the Senate and of the House of Representatives of the United States, I feel greatly honoured that you should have invited me to enter the United States Senate Chamber and address the representatives of both branches of Congress. The fact that my American forebears have for so many generations played their part in the life of the United States, and that here I am, an Englishman, welcomed in your midst, makes this experience one of the most moving and thrilling in my life, which is already long and has not been entirely uneventful. I wish indeed that my mother, whose memory I cherish across the vale of years, could have been here to see. By the way, I cannot help reflecting that if my father had been American and my mother British, instead of the other way around, I might have got here on my own. In that case, this would not have been the first time you would have heard my voice. In that case, I should not have needed any invitation, but, if I had, it is hardly likely that it would have been unanimous. So perhaps things are better as they are. I may confess, however, that I do not feel quite like a fish out of water in a legislative assembly where English is spoken.

I am a child of the House of Commons. I was brought up in my father's house to believe in democracy. "Trust the people"—that was his message. I used to see him cheered at meetings and in the streets by crowds of workingmen way back in those aristocratic Victorian days when, as Disraeli said, the world was for the few, and for the very few. Therefore I have been in full harmony all my life with the tides which have flowed on both sides of the Atlantic against privilege and monopoly, and I have steered confidently towards the Gettysburg ideal of "government of the people, by the people, for the people." I owe my advancement entirely to the House of Commons, whose servant I am. In my country, as in yours, public men are proud to be the servants of the State and would be ashamed to be its masters. On any day, if they thought the people wanted it, the House of Commons could by a simple vote remove me from my office. But I am not worrying about it at all. As a matter of fact, I am sure they will approve very highly of my journey here, for which I obtained the King's permission in order to meet the President of the United States and to arrange with him for all that mapping-out of our military plans, and for all those intimate meetings of the high officers of the armed services of both countries, which are indispensable for the successful prosecution of the war.

I should like to say, first of all, how much I have been impressed and encouraged by the breadth of view and sense of proportion which I have found in all quarters over here to which I have had access. Anyone who did not understand the size and solidarity of the foundations of the United States might easily have expected to find an excited, disturbed, self-centred atmosphere, with all minds fixed upon the novel, startling, and painful episodes of sudden war, as they hit America. After all, the United States have been attacked and set upon by three most powerfully armed dictator states. The greatest military power in Europe, the greatest military power in Asia. Japan, Germany, and Italy have all declared, and are making, war upon you, and the quarrel is opened which can only end in their overthrow or yours. But here in Washington, in these memorable days, I have found an

Olympian fortitude which, far from being based upon complacency, is only the mask of an inflexible purpose and the proof of a sure and well-grounded confidence in the final outcome. We in Britain had the same feeling in our darkest days. We, too, were sure that in the end all would be well. You do not, I am certain, underrate the severity of the ordeal to which you and we have still to be subjected. The forces ranged against us are enormous. They are bitter, they are ruthless. The wicked men and their factions who have launched their peoples on the path of war and conquest know that they will be called to terrible account if they cannot beat down by force of arms the peoples they have assailed. They will stop at nothing. They have a vast accumulation of war weapons of all kinds. They have highly trained and disciplined armies, navies, and air services. They have plans and designs which have long been contrived and matured. They will stop at nothing that violence or treachery can suggest.

It is quite true that, on our side, our resources in man-power and materials are far greater than theirs. But only a portion of your resources is as yet mobilized and developed, and we both of us have much to learn in the cruel art of war. We have, therefore, without doubt, a time of tribulation before us. In this time some ground will be lost which it will be hard and costly to regain. Many disappointments and unpleasant surprises await us. Many of them will afflict us before the full marshalling of our latent and total power can be accomplished. For the best part of twenty years the youth of Britain and America have been taught that war was evil, which is true, and that it would never come again, which has been proved false. For the best part of twenty years the youth of Germany, Japan, and Italy, have been taught that aggressive war is the noblest duty of the citizen, and that it should be begun as soon as the necessary weapons and organisation have been made. We have performed the duties and tasks of peace. They have plotted and planned for war. This, naturally, has placed us, in Britain, and now places you in the United States at a disadvantage which only time, courage, and strenuous, untiring exertions can correct.

We have indeed to be thankful that so much time has been granted to us. If Germany had tried to invade the British Isles after the French collapse in June, 1940, and if Japan had declared war on the British Empire and the United States at about the same date, no one can say what disasters and agonies might not have been our lot. But now, at the end of December, 1941, our transformation from easy-going peace to total war efficiency has made very great progress. The broad flow of munitions in Great Britain has already begun. Immense strides have been made in the conversion of American industry to military purposes, and now that the United States are at war it is possible for orders to be given every day which in a year or eighteen months hence will produce results in war power beyond anything which has yet been seen or foreseen in the dictator states. Provided that every effort is made, that nothing is kept back, that the whole man-power, brain-power, virility, valour, and civic virtue of the English-speaking world, with all its galaxy of loyal, friendly, or associated communities and states—provided all that is bent unremittingly to the simple and supreme task, I think it would be reasonable to hope that the end of 1942 will see us quite definitely in a better position than we are now, and that the year 1943 will enable us to assume the initiative upon an ample scale.

Some people may be startled or momentarily depressed when, like your President, I speak of a long and hard war. But our peoples would rather know the truth, sombre though it be. And after all, when we are doing the noblest work in the world, not only defending our hearths and homes but the cause of freedom in other lands, the question of whether deliverance comes in 1942, 1943, or 1944, falls into its proper place in the grand proportions of human history. Sure I am that this day—now—we are the masters of our fate; that the task which has been set us is not above our strength; that its pangs and toils are not beyond our endurance. As long as we have faith in our cause and an unconquerable will-power, salvation will not be denied us. In the words of the Psalmist: "He shall not be afraid of evil tidings; his heart is fixed, trusting in the Lord." Not all the tidings will be evil.

On the contrary, mighty strokes of war have already been dealt against the enemy; the glorious defence of their native soil by the Russian armies and people have inflicted wounds upon the Nazi tyranny and system which have bitten deep, and will fester and inflame not only in the Nazi body but in the Nazi mind. The boastful Mussolini has crumpled already. He is now but a lackey and a serf, the merest utensil of his master's will. He has inflicted great suffering and wrong upon his own industrious people. He has been stripped of his African empire. Abyssinia has been liberated. Our armies in the East, which were so weak and ill-equipped at the moment of French desertion, now control all the regions from Teheran to Benghazi, and from Aleppo and Cyprus to the sources of the Nile.

For many months we devoted ourselves to preparing to take the offensive in Libya. The very considerable battle, which has been proceeding there the last six weeks in the desert, has been most fiercely fought on both sides. Owing to the difficulties of supply on the desert flanks, we were never able to bring numerically equal forces to bear upon the enemy. Therefore we had to rely upon superiority in the numbers and qualities of tanks and aircraft, British and American. Aided by these, for the first time, we have fought the enemy with equal weapons. For the first time we have made the Hun feel the sharp edge of those tools with which he has enslaved Europe. The armed forces of the enemy in Cyrenaica amounted to about 150,000, of whom about one-third were Germans. General [Claude] Auchinleck set out to destroy totally that armed force. I have every reason to believe that his aim will be fully accomplished. I am so glad to be able to place before you, members of the Senate and of the House of Representatives, at this moment when you are entering the war, proof that with proper weapons and proper organization we are able to beat the life out of the savage Nazi. What Hitler is suffering in Libya is only a sample and foretaste of what we must give him and his accomplices, wherever this war shall lead us, in every quarter of the globe.

There are good tidings also from blue water. The life-line of supplies which joins our two nations across the ocean, without which all might fail, is flowing steadily and freely in spite of all the enemy can do. It is a fact that the British Empire, which many thought eighteen months ago was broken and ruined, is now incomparably stronger and is growing stronger with every month. Lastly, if you will forgive me for saying it, to me the best tidings of all is that the United States, united as never before, have drawn the sword for freedom and cast away the scabbard.

All these tremendous facts have led the subjugated peoples of Europe to lift up their heads again in hope. They have put aside for ever the shameful temptation of resigning themselves to the conqueror's will. Hope has returned to the hearts of scores of millions of men and women, and with that hope there burns the flame of anger against the brutal, corrupt invader, and still more fiercely burn the fires of hatred and contempt for the filthy quislings whom he has suborned. In a dozen famous ancient states, now prostrate under the Nazi yoke, the masses of the people, of all classes and creeds, await the hour of liberation, when they too will be able once again to play their part and strike their blows like men. That hour will strike, and its solemn peal will proclaim that night is past and that the dawn has come.

The onslaught upon us, so long and so secretly planned by Japan, has presented both our countries with grievous problems for which we could not be fully prepared. If people ask me, as they have a right to ask me in England, "Why is it that you have not got an ample equipment of modern aircraft and army weapons of all kinds in Malaya and in the East Indies?" I can only point to the victories General Auchinleck has gained in the Libyan campaign. Had we diverted and dispersed our gradually growing resources between Libya and Malaya, we should have been found wanting in both theatres. If the United States have been found at a disadvantage at various points in the Pacific Ocean, we know well that it is to no small extent because of the aid which you have been giving to us in munitions for the defence of the British Isles and for the Libyan campaign, and, above all, because of your help in the battle of the Atlantic, upon which all depends, and which has in consequence been successfully and prosperously maintained. Of course it would have been much better, I freely admit, if we had had enough resources of all kinds to be at full strength at all threatened points; but considering how slowly and reluctantly we brought ourselves to large-scale preparations, and how long these preparations take, we had no right to expect to be in such a fortunate position.

The choice of how to dispose of our hitherto limited resources had to be made by Britain in time of war, and by the United States in time of peace; and I believe that history will pronounce that upon the whole—and it is upon the whole that these matters must be judged—the choice made was right. Now that we are together, now that we are linked in a righteous comradeship of arms, now that our two considerable nations, each in perfect unity, have joined all their life energies in a common resolve, a new scene opens upon which a steady light will glow and brighten.

Many people have been astonished that Japan should in a single day have plunged into war against the United States and the British Empire. We all wonder why, if this dark design, with all its laborious and intricate preparations, had been so long filling their secret minds, they did not choose our moment of weakness eighteen months ago. Viewed quite dispassionately, in spite of the losses we have suffered and the further punishment we shall have to take, it certainly appears to be an irrational act. It is, of course, only prudent to assume that they have made very careful calculations and think they see their way through. Nevertheless, there may be another explanation. We know that for many years past the policy of Japan has been dominated by secret societies of subalterns and junior officers of the Army and Navy, who have enforced their will upon successive Japanese cabinets and parliaments by the assassination of any Japanese statesmen who opposed, or who did not sufficiently further, their aggressive policy. It may be that these societies, dazzled and dizzy with their own schemes of aggression and the prospect of early victories, have forced their country against its better judgment into war. They have certainly embarked upon a very considerable undertaking. For after the outrages they have committed upon us at Pearl Harbour, in the Pacific Islands, in the Philippines, in Malaya, and in the Dutch East Indies, they must now know that the stakes for which they have decided to play are mortal.

When we consider the resources of the United States and the British Empire compared to those of Japan, when we remember those of China, which has so long valiantly withstood invasion and when also we observe the Russian menace which hangs over Japan, it becomes still more difficult to reconcile Japanese action with prudence or even with sanity. What kind of a people do they think we are? Is it possible they do not realize that we shall never cease to persevere against them until they have been taught a lesson which they and the world will never forget?

Members of the Senate, and Members of the House of Representatives, I turn for one moment more from the turmoil and convulsions of the present to the broader basis of the future. Here we are together facing a group of mighty foes who seek our ruin; here we are together defending all that to free men is dear. Twice in a single generation the catastrophe of world war has fallen upon us; twice in our lifetime has the long arm of fate reached across the ocean to bring the United States into the forefront of the battle. If we had kept together after the last war, if we had taken common measures for our safety, this renewal of the curse need never have fallen upon us.

Do we not owe it to ourselves, to our children, to mankind tormented, to make sure that these catastrophes shall not engulf us for the third time? It has been proved that pestilences may break out in the Old World, which carry their destructive ravages into the New World, from which, once they are afoot, the New World cannot by any means escape. Duty and prudence alike command first that the germ-centres of hatred and revenge should be constantly and vigilantly surveyed and treated in good time, and, secondly, that an adequate organization should be set up to make sure that the pestilence can be controlled at its earliest beginnings before it spreads and rages throughout the entire earth.

Five or six years ago it would have been easy, without shedding a drop of blood, for the United States and Great Britain to have insisted on fulfilment of the disarmament clauses of the treaties which Germany signed after the Great War; that also would have been the opportunity for assuring to Germany those materials which we declared in the Atlantic Charter should not be denied to any nation, victor or vanquished. That chance has passed. It is gone. Prodigious hammer-strokes have been needed to bring us together again, or, if you allow me to use other language, I will say that he must indeed have a blind soul who cannot see that some great purpose and design is being worked out here below, of which we have the honour to be the faithful servants. It is not given to us to peer into the mysteries of the future. Still, I avow my hope and faith, sure and inviolate, that in the days to come the British and American peoples will for their own safety and for the good of all walk together side by side in majesty, in justice, and in peace.

ADDRESS TO U.S. CONGRESS, MAY 19, 1943

Mr. President, Mr. Speaker, and Members of the Senate and the House of Representatives. Seventeen months have passed since I last had the honour to address the Congress of the United States. For more than 500 days, every day a day, we have toiled and suffered and dared shoulder to shoulder against the cruel and mighty enemy. We have acted in close combination or concert in many parts of the world, on land, on sea, and in the air. The fact that you have invited me to come to Congress again a second time, now that we have settled down to the job, and that you should welcome me in so generous a fashion, is certainly a high mark in my life, and it also shows that our partnership has not done so badly.

I am proud that you should have found us good allies, striving forward in comradeship to the accomplishment of our task without grudging or stinting either life or treasure, or, indeed, anything that we have to give. Last time I came at a moment when the United States was aflame with wrath at the treacherous attack upon Pearl Harbour by Japan, and at the subsequent declarations of war upon the United States made by Germany and Italy. For my part I say quite frankly that in those days, after our long—and for a whole year lonely—struggle, I could not repress in my heart a sense of relief and comfort that we were all bound together by common peril, by solemn faith and high purpose, to see this fearful quarrel through, at all costs, to the end.

That was the hour of passionate emotion, an hour most memorable in human records, an hour, I believe, full of hope and glory for the future. The experiences of a long life and the promptings of my blood have wrought in me the conviction that there is nothing more important for the future of the world than the fraternal association of our two peoples in righteous work both in war and peace.

So in January, 1942, I had that feeling of comfort, and I therefore prepared myself in a confident and steadfast spirit to bear the terrible blows which were evidently about to fall on British interests in the Far East, which were bound to fall upon us, from the military strength of Japan during a period when the American and British fleets had lost, for the time being, the naval command of the Pacific and Indian Oceans.

One after another, in swift succession, very heavy misfortunes fell upon us, and upon our Allies, the Dutch, in the Pacific theatre. The Japanese have seized the lands and islands they so greedily coveted. The Philippines are enslaved, the lustrous, luxuriant regions of the Dutch East Indies have been overrun. In the Malay Peninsula and at Singapore we ourselves suffered the greatest military disaster, or at any rate the largest military disaster, in British history.

Mr. President, Mr. Speaker, all this has to be retrieved, and all this and much else has to be repaid. And here let me say this: let no one suggest that we British have not at least as great an interest as the United States in the unflinching and relentless waging of war against Japan. And I am here to tell you that we will wage that war, side by side with you, in accordance with the best strategic employment of our forces, while there is breath in our bodies and while blood flows in our veins.

A notable part in the war against Japan must, of course, be played by the large armies and by the air and naval forces now marshalled by Great Britain on the eastern frontiers of India. In this quarter there lies one of the means of bringing aid to hard-pressed and long-tormented China. I regard the bringing of effective and immediate aid to China as one of the most urgent of our common tasks.

It may not have escaped your attention that I have brought with me to this country and to this conference Field Marshal [Archibald] Wavell and the other two Commanders-in-Chief from India. Now, they have not travelled all this way simply to concern themselves about improving the health and happiness of the Mikado of Japan. I thought it would be good that all concerned in this theatre should meet together and thrash out in friendly candour, heart to heart, all the points that arise; and there are many.

You may be sure that if all that was necessary was for an order to be given to the great armies standing ready in India to march towards the Rising Sun and open the Burma Road, that order would be given this afternoon. The matter is, however, more complicated, and all movement or infiltration of troops into the mountains and jungles to the North-East of India is very strictly governed by what your American military men call the science of logistics.

But, Mr. President, I repudiate, and I am sure with your sympathy, the slightest suspicion that we should hold anything back that could be usefully employed, or that I and the Government I represent are not as resolute to employ every man, gun, and airplane that can be used in this business, as we have proved ourselves ready to do in other theatres of the war.

In our conferences in January, 1942, between the President and myself, and between our high expert advisers, it was evident that, while the defeat of Japan would not mean the defeat of Germany, the defeat of Germany would infallibly mean the ruin of Japan. The realisation of this simple truth does not mean that both sides should not proceed together, and indeed the major part of the United States forces is now deployed on the Pacific fronts. In the broad division which we then made of our labours, in January, 1942, the United States undertook the main responsibility for prosecuting the war against Japan, and for helping Australia and New Zealand to defend themselves against a Japanese invasion, which then seemed far more threatening than it does now.

On the other hand, we took the main burden on the Atlantic. This was only natural. Unless the ocean life-line which joins our two peoples could be kept unbroken, the British Isles and all the very considerable forces which radiate therefrom would be paralysed and doomed. We have willingly done our full share of the sea work in the dangerous waters of the Mediterranean and in the Arctic convoys to Russia, and we have sustained, since our alliance began, more than double the losses in merchant tonnage that have fallen upon the United States.

On the other hand, again, the prodigious output of new ships from the United States building-yards has, for six months past, overtaken, and now far surpasses, the losses of both Allies, and if no effort is relaxed there is every reason to count upon the ceaseless progressive expansion of Allied shipping available for the prosecution of the war.

Our killings of the U-boat, as the Secretary of the Navy will readily confirm, have this year greatly exceeded all previous experience, and the last three months, and particularly the last three weeks, have yielded record results. This of course is to some extent due to the larger number of U-boats operating, but it is also due to the marked improvement in the severity and power of our measures against them, and of the new devices continually employed.

While I rate the U-boat danger as still the greatest we have to face, I have a good and sober confidence that it will not only be met and contained but overcome. The increase of shipping tonnage over sinkings provides, after the movement of vital supplies of food and munitions has been arranged, that margin which is the main measure of our joint war effort.

We are also conducting from the British Isles the principal air offensive against Germany, and in this we are powerfully aided by the United States Air Force in the United Kingdom, whose action is chiefly by day as ours is chiefly by night. In this war numbers count more and more, both in night and day attacks. The saturation of the enemy's flak, through the multiplicity of attacking planes and the division and diversion of his fighter protection by the launching of several simultaneous attacks, are rewards which will immediately be paid from the substantial increases in British and American numbers which are now taking place.

There is no doubt that the Allies already vastly outnumber the hostile air forces of Germany, Italy, and Japan, and still more does the output of new aeroplanes surpass the output of the enemy. In this air war, in which both Germany and Japan fondly imagined that they would strike decisive and final blows, and terrorise nations great and small into submission to their will—in this air war it is that these guilty nations have already begun to show their first real mortal weakness. The more continuous and severe the air fighting becomes, the better for us, because we can already replace casualties and machines far more rapidly than the enemy, and we can replace them on a scale which increases month by month.

Progress in this sphere is swift and sure, but it must be remembered that the preparation and development of airfields, and the movement of the great masses of ground personnel on whom the efficiency of modern air squadrons depends, however earnestly pressed forward, are bound to take time.

Opinion, Mr. President, is divided as to whether the use of air power could by itself bring about a collapse in Germany or Italy. The experiment is well worth trying, so long as other measures are not excluded. Well, there is certainly no harm in finding out. But however that may be, we are all agreed that the damage done to the enemy's war potential is enormous.

The condition to which the great centres of German war industry, and particularly the Ruhr, are being reduced, is one of unparalleled devastation. You have just read of the destruction of the great dams which feed the canals, and provide the power to the enemy's munition works. That was a gallant operation, costing eight out of the nineteen Lancaster bombers employed, but it will play a very far-reaching part in reducing the German munitions output.

It is the settled policy of our two staffs and war-making authorities to make it impossible for Germany to carry on any form of war industry on a large or concentrated scale, either in Germany, in Italy, or in the enemy-occupied countries. Wherever these centres exist or are developed, they will be destroyed, and the munitions populations will be dispersed. If they do not like what is coming to them, let them disperse beforehand on their own. This process will continue ceaselessly with ever-increasing weight and intensity until the German and Italian peoples abandon or destroy the monstrous tyrannies which they have incubated and reared in their midst.

Meanwhile, our air offensive is forcing Germany to withdraw an ever larger proportion of its war-making capacity from the fighting fronts in order to provide protection against air attack. Hundreds of fighter aircraft, thousands of anti-aircraft cannon, and many hundreds of thousands of men, together with a vast share of the output of the war factories, have already been assigned to this purely defensive function. All this is at the expense of the enemy's power of new aggression, and of his power to resume the initiative.

Surveying the whole aspect of the air war, we cannot doubt that it is a major factor in the process of victory. That, I think, is established as a solid fact. It is agreed between us all that we should, at the earliest moment, similarly bring our joint air power to bear upon the military targets in the home lands of Japan. The cold-blooded execution of the United States airmen by the Japanese government is a proof, not only of their barbarism, but of the dread with which they regard this possibility.

It is the duty of those who are charged with the direction of the war to overcome at the earliest moment the military, geographical, and political difficulties, and begin the process, so necessary and desirable, of laying the cities and other munitions centres of Japan in ashes, for in ashes they must surely lie before peace comes back to the world.

That this objective holds a high place in the present conference is obvious to thinking men, but no public discussion would be useful upon the method or sequence of events which should be pursued in order to achieve it. Let me make it plain, however, that the British will participate in this air attack on Japan in harmonious accord with the major strategy of the war. That is our desire. And the cruelties of the Japanese enemy make our airmen all the more ready to share the perils and sufferings of their American comrades.

At the present time, speaking more generally, the prime problem which is before the United States, and to a lesser extent before Great Britain, is not so much the creation of armies or the vast output of munitions and aircraft. These are already in full swing, and immense progress, and prodigious results, have been achieved. The problem is rather the application of those forces to the enemy in the teeth of U-boat resistance across the great ocean spaces, across the narrow seas, or on land through swamps, mountains, and jungles in various quarters of the globe.

That is our problem. All our war plans must, therefore, be inspired, pervaded, and even dominated by the supreme object of coming to grips with the enemy under favourable conditions, or at any rate tolerable conditions—we cannot pick and choose too much—on the largest scale, at the earliest possible moment, and of engaging that enemy wherever it is profitable, and indeed I might say wherever it is possible, to do so. Thus, in this way, shall we make our enemies in Europe and in Asia burn and consume their strength on land, on sea, and in the air with the maximum rapidity.

Now you will readily understand that the complex task of finding the maximum openings for the employment of our vast forces, the selection of the points at which to strike with the greatest advantage to those forces, and the emphasis and priority to be assigned to all the various enterprises which are desirable, is a task requiring constant supervision and adjustment by our combined staffs and heads of governments.

This is a vast, complicated process, especially when two countries are directly in council together, and when the interests of so many other countries have to be considered, and the utmost good will and readiness to think for the common cause, the cause of all the United Nations, are required from everyone participating in our discussions. The intricate adjustments and arrangements can only be made by discussion between men who know all the facts, and who are and can alone be held accountable for success or failure. Lots of people can make good plans for winning the war if they have not got to carry them out. I dare say if I had not been in a responsible position I should have made a lot of excellent plans, and very likely should have brought them in one way or another to the notice of the executive authorities.

But it is not possible to have full and open argument about these matters. It is an additional hardship to those in charge that such questions cannot be argued out and debated in public except with enormous reticence, and even then with very great danger that the watching and listening enemy may derive some profit from what he overhears. In these circumstances, in my opinion, the American and British press and public have treated their executive authorities with a wise and indulgent consideration, and recent events have vindicated their self-restraint. Mr. President, it is thus that we are able to meet here today in all faithfulness, sincerity, and friendship.

Geography imposes insuperable obstacles to the continuous session of the combined staff and executive chiefs, but as the scene is constantly changing, and lately I think I may say constantly changing for the better, repeated conferences are indispensable if the sacrifices of the fighting troops are to be rendered fruitful, and if the curse of war which lies so heavily upon almost the whole world is to be broken and swept away within the shortest possible time.

I therefore thought it my duty, with the full authority of His Majesty's Government, to come here again with our highest officers in order that the combined staffs may work in the closest contact with the chief executive power which the President derives from his office, and in respect of which I am the accredited representative of Cabinet and Parliament.

The wisdom of the founders of the American Constitution led them to associate the office of Commander-in-Chief with that of the Presidency of the United States. In this they were following the precedents which were successful in the days of George Washington. It is remarkable that after more than 150 years this combination of political and military authority has been found necessary, not only in the United States, but in the case of Marshal Stalin in Russia and of Generalissimo Chiang Kai-shek in China. Even I, as Majority Leader in the House of Commons—one branch of the Legislature—have been drawn from time to time, not perhaps wholly against my will, into some participation in military affairs.

Modern war is total, and it is necessary for its conduct that the technical and professional authorities should be sustained and if necessary directed by the heads of government, who have the knowledge which enables them to comprehend not only the military but the political and economic forces at work, and who have the power to focus them all upon the goal.

These are the reasons which compelled the President to make his long journey to Casablanca, and these are the reasons which bring me here. We both earnestly hope that at no distant date we may be able to achieve what we have so long sought—namely, a meeting with Marshal Stalin and if possible with Generalissimo Chiang Kai-shek. But how and when and where this is to be accomplished is not a matter upon which I am able to shed any clear ray of light at the present time, and if I were I should certainly not shed it.

In the meanwhile we do our best to keep the closest association at every level between all the authorities of all the Allied countries engaged in the active direction of the war. It is my special duty to promote and preserve this intimacy and concert between all parts of the

British Commonwealth and Empire, and especially with the great self-governing Dominions, like Canada, whose Prime Minister is with us at this moment, whose contribution is so massive and invaluable. There could be no better or more encouraging example of the fruits of our consultations than the campaign in Northwest Africa, which has just ended so well.

One morning in June last, when I was here, the President handed me a slip of paper which bore the utterly unexpected news of the fall of Tobruk, and the surrender, in unexplained circumstances, of its garrison of 25,000 men. That indeed was a dark and bitter hour for me, and I shall never forget the kindness and the wealth of comradeship which our American friends showed me and those with me in such adversity. Their only thought was to find the means of helping to restore the situation, and never for a moment did they question the resolution or fighting quality of our troops. Hundreds of Sherman tanks were taken from the hands of American divisions and sent at the utmost speed round the Cape of Good Hope to Egypt. When one ship carrying fifty tanks was sunk by torpedo, the United States government replaced it and its precious vehicles before we could even think of asking them to do so. The Sherman was the best tank in the desert in the year 1942, and the presence of these weapons played an appreciable part in the ruin of Rommel's army at the battle of Alamein and in the long pursuit which chased him back to Tunisia.

And at this time, June of last year, when I was here last, there lighted up those trains of thought and study which produced the memorable American and British descent upon French Northwest Africa, the results of which are a cause of general rejoicing. We have certainly a most encouraging example here of what can be achieved by British and Americans working together heart and hand. In fact, one might almost feel that if they could keep it up there is hardly anything that they could not do, either in the field of war or in the not less tangled problems of peace.

History will acclaim this great enterprise as a classic example of the way to make war. We used the weapon of sea power, the weapon in which we were strongest, to attack the enemy at our chosen moment and at our chosen point. In spite of the immense elaboration of the plan, and of the many hundreds, thousands even, who had to be informed of its main outlines, we maintained secrecy and effected surprise.

We confronted the enemy with a situation in which he had either to lose invaluable strategical territories, or to fight under conditions most costly and wasteful to him. We recovered the initiative, which we still retain. We rallied to our side French forces which are already a brave—and will presently become a powerful—army under the gallant General [Henri] Giraud. We secured bases from which violent attacks can and will be delivered by our air power on the whole of Italy, with results no one can measure, but which must certainly be highly beneficial to our affairs.

We have made an economy in our strained and straitened shipping position worth several hundreds of great ships, and one which will give us the advantage of far swifter passage through the Mediterranean to the East, to the Middle East, and to the Far East. We have struck the enemy a blow which is the equal of Stalingrad, and most stimulating to our heroic and heavily engaged Russian allies. All this gives the lie to the Nazi and Fascist taunt that parliamentary democracies are incapable of waging effective war. Presently we shall furnish them with further examples.

Still, I am free to admit that in North Africa we builded better than we knew. The unexpected came to the aid of the design and multiplied the results. For this we have to thank the military intuition of Corporal Hitler. We may notice, as I predicted in the House of Commons three months ago, the touch of the master hand. The same insensate obstinacy which condemned Field Marshal [Friedrich] von Paulus and his army to destruction at Stalingrad has brought this new catastrophe upon our enemies in Tunisia.

We have destroyed or captured considerably more than a quarter of a million of the enemy's best troops, together with vast masses of material, all of which had been ferried across to Africa after paying a heavy toll to British submarines and British and United States aircraft. No one could count on such follies. They gave us, if I may use the language of finance, a handsome bonus after the full dividend had been earned and paid.

At the time when we planned this great joint African operation, we hoped to be masters of Tunisia even before the end of last year; but the injury we have now inflicted upon the enemy, physical and psychological, and the training our troops have obtained in the hard school of war, and the welding together of the Anglo-American staff machine—these are advantages which far exceed anything which it was in our power to plan. The German lie factory is volubly explaining how valuable is the time which they bought by the loss of their great armies. Let them not delude themselves.

Other operations which will unfold in due course, depending as they do upon the special instruction of large numbers of troops and upon the provision of a vast mass of technical apparatus, these other operations have not been in any way delayed by the obstinate fighting in Northern Tunisia.

Mr. President, the African war is over. Mussolini's African Empire and Corporal Hitler's strategy are alike exploded. It is interesting to compute what these performances have cost these two wicked men and those who have been their tools or their dupes. The Emperor of Abyssinia sits again upon the throne from which he was driven by Mussolini's poison gas. All the vast territories from Madagascar to Morocco, from Cairo to Casablanca, from Aden to Dakar, are under British, American, or French control. One continent at least has been cleansed and purged for ever from Fascist or Nazi tyranny.

The African excursions of the two dictators have cost their countries in killed and captured 950,000 soldiers. In addition, nearly 2,400,000 gross tons of shipping have been sunk and nearly 8,000 aircraft destroyed, both of these figures being exclusive of large numbers of ships and aircraft damaged. There have also been lost to the enemy 6,200 guns, 2,550 tanks and 70,000 trucks—which is the American name for lorries, and which, I understand, has been adopted by the combined staffs in Northwest Africa in exchange for the use of the word petrol in place of gasolene.

These are the losses of the enemy in the three years of war, and at the end of it all what is it that they have to show? The proud German Army has by its sudden collapse, sudden crumpling and breaking up, unexpected to all of us, the proud German Army has once again proved the truth of the saying, "The Hun is always either at your throat or at your feet"; and that is a point which may have its bearing upon the future. But for our part at this milestone in the war we can say: "One continent redeemed."

The Northwest African campaign, and particularly its Tunisian climax, is the finest example of the co-operation of the troops of three different countries and of the combination under one supreme commander of the sea, land, and air forces which has yet been seen. In particular, the British and American staff work, as I have said, has matched the comradeship of the soldiers of our two countries striding forward side by side under the fire of the enemy.

It was a marvel of efficient organisation which enabled the Second American Corps, or rather Army, for that was its size, to be moved 300 miles from the Southern sector, which had become obsolete through the retreat of the enemy, to the Northern coast, from which, beating down all opposition, they advanced and took the fortress and harbour of Bizerte. In order to accomplish this march of 300 miles, which was covered in twelve days, it was necessary for this very considerable army, with its immense modern equipment, to traverse at right angles all the communications of the British First Army, which was already engaged or about to be engaged in heavy battle; and this was achieved without in any way disturbing the hour-to-hour supply upon which that Army depended. I am told that these British and American officers worked together without the slightest question of what country they belonged to, each doing his part in the military organisation which must henceforward be regarded as a most powerful and efficient instrument of war.

There is honour, Mr. President, for all; and I shall at the proper time and place pay my tribute to the British and American commanders by land and sea who conducted or who were engaged in the battle. This only will I say now: I do not think you could have chosen any man more capable than General Eisenhower of keeping his very large, heterogeneous force together, through bad times as well as good, and of creating the conditions of harmony and energy which were the indispensable elements of victory.

I have dwelt in some detail, but I trust not at undue length, upon these famous events; and I shall now return for a few minutes to the general war, in which they have their setting and proportion. It is a poor heart that never rejoices; but our thanksgiving, however fervent, must be brief.

Heavier work lies ahead, not only in the European, but, as I have indicated, in the Pacific and Indian spheres; and the President and I, and the combined staffs, are gathered here in order that this work may be, so far as lies within us, well conceived, and thrust forward without losing a day.

Not for one moment must we forget that the main burden of the war on land is still being borne by the Russian armies. They are holding at the present time no fewer than 190 German divisions and twenty-eight satellite divisions on their front. It is always wise, while doing justice to one's own achievements, to preserve a proper sense of proportion; and I therefore mention that these figures of the German forces opposite Russia compare with the equivalent of about fifteen divisions which we have destroyed in Tunisia, after a campaign which has cost us about 50,000 casualties. That gives some measure of the Russian effort, and of the debt which we owe to her.

It may well be that a further trial of strength between the German and Russian armies is impending. Russia has already inflicted injuries upon the German military organism which will, I believe, prove ultimately mortal; but there is little doubt that Hitler is reserving his supreme gambler's throw for a third attempt to break the heart and spirit and destroy the armed forces of the mighty nation which he has already twice assaulted in vain.

He will not succeed. But we must do everything in our power that is sensible and practicable to take more of the weight off Russia in 1943. I do not intend to be responsible for any suggestion that the war is won, or that it will soon be over. That it will be won by us I am sure. But how and when cannot be foreseen, still less foretold.

I was driving the other day not far from the field of Gettysburg, which I know well, like most of your battlefields. It was the decisive battle of the Civil War. No one after Gettysburg doubted which way the dread balance of war would incline, yet far more blood was shed after the Union victory at Gettysburg than in all the fighting which went before. It behooves us, therefore, to search our hearts and brace our sinews and take the most earnest counsel, one with another, in order that the favourable position which has already been reached both against Japan and against Hitler and Mussolini in Europe shall not be let slip.

If we wish to abridge the slaughter and ruin which this war is spreading to so many lands and to which we must ourselves contribute so grievous a measure of suffering and sacrifice, we cannot afford to relax a single fibre of our being or to tolerate the slightest abatement of our efforts. The enemy is still proud and powerful. He is hard to get at. He still possesses enormous armies, vast resources, and invaluable strategic territories. War is full of mysteries and surprises. A false step, a wrong direction, an error in strategy, discord or lassitude among the Allies, might soon give the common enemy power to confront us with new and hideous facts. We have surmounted many serious dangers, but there is one grave danger which will go along with us till the end. That danger is the undue prolongation of the war. No one can tell what new complications and perils might arise in four or five more years of war. And it is in the dragging-out of the war at enormous expense, until the democracies are tired or bored or split, that the main hopes of Germany and Japan must now reside. We must destroy this hope, as we have destroyed so many others, and for that purpose we must beware of every topic, however attractive, and every tendency, however natural, which turns our minds and energies from this supreme objective of the general victory of the United Nations. By singleness of purpose, by steadfastness of conduct, by tenacity and endurance, such as we have so far displayed—by these, and only by these, can we discharge our duty to the future of the world and to the destiny of man.

ADDRESS AT HARVARD UNIVERSITY, SEPTEMBER 6, 1943

President Conant, Mr. Governor of the Commonwealth of Massachusetts, gentlemen of the university, ladies and gentlemen here assembled.

The last time I attended a ceremony of this character was in the spring of 1941, when, as Chancellor of Bristol University, I conferred a degree upon the United States Ambassador, Mr. [John] Winant, and *in absentia* upon President [James] Conant, our [Harvard's] President, who is here today and presiding over this ceremony. The blitz was running hard at that time, and the night before, the raid on Bristol had been heavy. Several hundreds had been killed and wounded. Many houses were destroyed. Buildings next to the University were still burning, and many of the University authorities who conducted the ceremony had pulled on their robes over uniforms begrimed and drenched; but all was presented with faultless ritual and appropriate decorum, and I sustained a very strong and invigorating impression of the superiority of man over the forces that can destroy him.

Here now, today, I am once again in academic groves—groves is, I believe, the right word—where knowledge is garnered, where learning is stimulated, where virtues are inculcated and thought encouraged. Here, in the broad United States, with a respectable ocean on either side of us, we can look out upon the world in all its wonder and in all its woe. But what is this that I discern as I pass through your streets, as I look round this great company?

I see uniforms on every side. I understand that nearly the whole energies of the University have been drawn into the preparation of American youth for the battlefield. For this purpose all classes and courses have been transformed, and even the most sacred vacations have been swept away in a round-the-year and almost round-the-clock drive to make warriors and technicians for the fighting fronts.

Twice in my lifetime the long arm of destiny has reached across the oceans and involved the entire life and manhood of the United States in a deadly struggle. There was no use in saying "We don't want it; we won't have it; our forebears left Europe to avoid these quarrels; we have founded a new world which has no contact with the old." There was no use in that. The long arm reaches out remorselessly, and everyone's existence, environment, and outlook undergo a swift and irresistible change. What is the explanation, Mr. President, of these strange facts, and what are the deep laws to which they respond? I will offer you one explanation—there are others, but one will suffice.

The price of greatness is responsibility. If the people of the United States had continued in a mediocre station, struggling with the wilderness, absorbed in their own affairs, and a factor of no consequence in the movement of the world, they might have remained forgotten and undisturbed beyond their protecting oceans: but one cannot rise to be in many ways the leading community in the civilised world without being involved in its problems, without being convulsed by its agonies and inspired by its causes.

If this has been proved in the past, as it has been, it will become indisputable in the future. The people of the United States cannot escape world responsibility. Although we live in a period so tumultuous that little can be predicted, we may be quite sure that this process will be intensified with every forward step the United States make in wealth and in power. Not only are the responsibilities of this great republic growing, but the world over which they range is itself contracting in relation to our powers of locomotion at a positively alarming rate.

We have learned to fly. What prodigious changes are involved in that new accomplishment. Man has parted company with his trusty friend the horse and has sailed into the azure with the eagles, eagles being represented by the infernal—I mean internal—combustion engine. Where, then, are those broad oceans, those vast staring deserts? They are shrinking beneath our very eyes. Even elderly Parliamentarians like myself are forced to acquire a high degree of mobility.

But to the youth of America, as to the youth of Britain, I say "You cannot stop." There is no halting-place at this point. We have now reached a stage in the journey where there can be no pause. We must go on. It must be world anarchy or world order.

Throughout all this ordeal and struggle which is characteristic of our age, you will find in the British Commonwealth and Empire good comrades to whom you are united by other ties besides those of state policy and public need. To a large extent, they are the ties of blood and history. Naturally, I, a child of both worlds, am conscious of these.

Law, language, literature—these are considerable factors. Common conceptions of what is right and decent, a marked regard for fair play, especially to the weak and poor, a stern sentiment of impartial justice, and above all the love of personal freedom, or as Kipling put it: "Leave to live by no man's leave underneath the law"—these are common conceptions on both sides of the ocean among the English-speaking peoples. We hold to these conceptions as strongly as you do.

We do not war primarily with races as such. Tyranny is our foe. Whatever trappings or disguise it wears, whatever language it speaks, be it external or internal, we must for ever be on our guard, ever mobilised, ever vigilant, always ready to spring at its throat. In all this, we march together. Not only do we march and strive shoulder to shoulder at this moment under the fire of the enemy on the fields of war or in the air, but also in those realms of thought which are consecrated to the rights and the dignity of man.

At the present time we have in continual vigorous action the British and United States Combined Chiefs of Staff Committee, which works immediately under the President and myself as representative of the British War Cabinet. This committee, with its elaborate organisation of staff officers of every grade, disposes of all our resources and, in practice, uses British and American troops, ships, aircraft, and munitions just as if they were the resources of a single state or nation.

I would not say there are never divergences of view among these high professional authorities. It would be unnatural if there were not. That is why it is necessary to have a plenary meeting of principals every two or three months. All these men now know each other. They trust each other. They like each other, and most of them have been at work together for a long time. When they meet they thrash things out with great candour and plain, blunt speech, but after a few days the President and I find ourselves furnished with sincere and united advice.

This is a wonderful system. There was nothing like it in the last war. There never has been anything like it between two allies. It is reproduced in an even more tightly-knit form at General Eisenhower's headquarters in the Mediterranean, where everything is completely intermingled and soldiers are ordered into battle by the Supreme Commander or his deputy, General [Harold] Alexander, without the slightest regard to whether they are British, American, or Canadian, but simply in accordance with the fighting need.

Now in my opinion it would be a most foolish and improvident act on the part of our two governments, or either of them, to break up this smooth-running and immensely powerful machinery the moment the war is over. For our own safety, as well as for the security of the rest of the world, we are bound to keep it working and in running order after the war—probably for a good many years, not only until we have set up some world arrangement to keep the peace, but until we know that it is an arrangement which will really give us that protection we must have from danger and aggression, a protection we have already had to seek across two vast world wars.

I am not qualified, of course, to judge whether or not this would become a party question in the United States, and I would not presume to discuss that point. I am sure, however, that it will not be a party question in Great Britain. We must not let go of the securities we have found necessary to preserve our lives and liberties until we are quite sure we have something else to put in their place which will give us an equally solid guarantee.

The great Bismarck—for there were once great men in Germany—is said to have observed towards the close of his life that the most potent factor in human society at the end of the nineteenth century was the fact that the British and American peoples spoke the same language. That was a pregnant saying. Certainly it has enabled us to wage war together with an intimacy and harmony never before achieved among allies.

This gift of a common tongue is a priceless inheritance, and it may well some day become the foundation of a common citizenship. I like to think of British and Americans moving about freely over each other's wide estates with hardly a sense of being foreigners to one another. But I do not see why we should not try to spread our common language even more widely throughout the globe and, without seeking selfish advantage over any, possess ourselves of this invaluable amenity and birthright.

Some months ago I persuaded the British Cabinet to set up a committee of ministers to study and report upon Basic English. Here you have a plan. There are others, but here you have a very carefully wrought plan for an international language capable of a very wide transaction of practical business and interchange of ideas. The whole of it is comprised in about 650 nouns and 200 verbs or other parts of speech—no more indeed than can be written on one side of a single sheet of paper.

What was my delight when, the other evening, quite unexpectedly, I heard the President of the United States suddenly speak of the merits of Basic English, and is it not a coincidence that, with all this in mind, I should arrive at Harvard, in fulfilment of the long-dated invitations to receive this degree, with which President Conant has honoured me? For Harvard has done more than any other American university to promote the extension of Basic English. The first work on Basic English was written by two Englishmen, Ivor Richards, now of Harvard, and C.K. Ogden, of Cambridge University, England, working in association.

The Harvard Commission on English Language Studies is distinguished both for its research and its practical work, particularly in introducing the use of Basic English in Latin America; and this Commission, your Commission, is now, I am told, working with secondary schools in Boston on the use of Basic English in teaching the main language to American children and in teaching it to foreigners preparing for citizenship.

Gentlemen, I make you my compliments. I do not wish to exaggerate, but you are the head-stream of what might well be a mighty fertilising and health-giving river. It would certainly be a grand convenience for us all to be able to move freely about the world—as we shall be able to do more freely than ever before as the science of the world develops—be able to move freely about the world, and be able to find everywhere a medium, albeit primitive, of intercourse and understanding. Might it not also be an advantage to many races, and an aid to the building-up of our new structure for preserving peace? All these are great possibilities, and I say: "Let us go into this together. Let us have another Boston Tea Party about it."

Let us go forward as with other matters and other measures similar in aim and effect—let us go forward in malice to none and good will to all. Such plans offer far better prizes than taking away other people's provinces or lands or grinding them down in exploitation. The empires of the future are the empires of the mind.

It would, of course, Mr. President, be lamentable if those who are charged with the duty of leading great nations forward in this grievous and obstinate war were to allow their minds and energies to be diverted from making the plans to achieve our righteous purposes without needless prolongation of slaughter and destruction.

Nevertheless, we are also bound, so far as life and strength allow, and without prejudice to our dominating military tasks, to look ahead to those days which will surely come when we shall have finally beaten down Satan under our feet and find ourselves with other great allies at once the masters and the servants of the future. Various schemes of achieving world security while yet preserving national rights, traditions and customs are being studied and probed.

We have all the fine work that was done a quarter of a century ago by those who devised and tried to make effective the League of Nations after the last war. It is said that the League of Nations failed. If so, that is largely because it was abandoned, and later on betrayed: because those who were its best friends were till a very late period infected with a futile pacifism: because the United States, the originating impulse, fell out of the line: because, while France had been bled white and England was supine and bewildered, a monstrous growth of aggression sprang up in Germany, in Italy, and Japan.

We have learned from hard experience that stronger, more efficient, more rigorous world institutions must be created to preserve peace and to forestall the causes of future wars. In this task the strongest victorious nations must be combined, and also those who have borne the burden and heat of the day and suffered under the flail of adversity; and, in this task, this creative task, there are some who say: "Let us have a world council and under it regional or continental councils," and there are others who prefer a somewhat different organisation.

All these matters weigh with us now in spite of the war, which none can say has reached its climax, which is perhaps entering for us, British and Americans, upon its most severe and costly phase. But I am here to tell you that, whatever form your system of world security may take, however the nations are grouped and ranged, whatever derogations are made from national sovereignty for the sake of the larger synthesis, nothing will work soundly or for long without the united effort of the British and American peoples.

If we are together nothing is impossible. If we are divided all will fail.

I therefore preach continually the doctrine of the fraternal association of our two peoples, not for any purpose of gaining invidious material advantages for either of them, not for territorial aggrandisement or the vain pomp of earthly domination, but for the sake of service to mankind and for the honour that comes to those who faithfully serve great causes.

Here let me say how proud we ought to be, young and old alike, to live in this tremendous, thrilling, formative epoch in the human story, and how fortunate it was for the world that when these great trials came upon it there was a generation that terror could not conquer and brutal violence could not enslave. Let all who are here remember, as the words of the hymn we have just sung suggest, let all of us who are here remember that we are on the stage of history, and that whatever our station may be, and whatever part we have to play, great or small, our conduct is liable to be scrutinised not only by history but by our own descendants.

Let us rise to the full level of our duty and of our opportunity, and let us thank God for the spiritual rewards He has granted for all forms of valiant and faithful service.

NOTES

PROLOGUE

1. Winston S. Churchill, *The Grand Alliance* (Boston: Houghton Mifflin, 1950), 606.
2. Kay Halle, ed., *Winston Churchill on America and Britain: A Selection of His Thoughts on Anglo-American Relations* (New York: Walker, 1970), 48.
3. Winston S. Churchill, *Great Contemporaries* (New York: W. W. Norton, 1991), 237. The original essay, "While the World Watches," was published in *Collier's* on December 29, 1934, and later collected as "Roosevelt from Afar" in the revised, second edition of *Great Contemporaries* (London: Thornton Butterworth, 1938).
4. Warren F. Kimball, ed., *Churchill & Roosevelt: The Complete Correspondence* (Princeton, NJ: Princeton University Press, 1984), 1:24.
5. Martin Gilbert, *Churchill: A Life* (London: Pimlico, 2000), 522.
6. J. B. West with Mary Lynn Kotz, *Upstairs at the White House: My Life with the First Ladies* (New York: Coward, McCann & Geoghegan, 1973), 39.
7. Robert Klara, *The Hidden White House: Harry Truman and the Reconstruction of America's Most Famous Residence* (New York: Thomas Dunne Books, 2013), 87.
8. Winston S. Churchill, *Closing the Ring* (Boston: Houghton Mifflin, 1951), 282.

CHAPTER 1: ALONE NO MORE

1. Lord Moran, *Churchill: The Struggle for Survival, 1940–1965, Taken from the Diaries of Lord Moran* (Boston: Houghton Mifflin, 1966), 11.
2. Warren F. Kimball, ed., *Churchill & Roosevelt: The Complete Correspondence* (Princeton, NJ: Princeton University Press, 1984), 1:292.

3. John Barnes and David Nicholson, eds., *The Empire at Bay: The Leo Amery Diaries, 1929–1945* (London: Hutchinson, 1988), 756.
4. Frank Wilson and Beth Day, *Special Agent: A Quarter Century with the Treasury Department and the Secret Service* (New York: Holt, Rinehart and Winston, 1965), 145.
5. Wilson and Day, *Special Agent*, 156.
6. William Seale, *The President's House: A History* (Washington, DC: White House Historical Association, 1986), 2: 992–93.
7. A. Merriman Smith, *Thank You, Mr. President* (New York: Harper & Brothers, 1946), 130.
8. Kimball, *Churchill & Roosevelt: Complete Correspondence*, 1: 284.
9. Kimball, *Churchill & Roosevelt: Complete Correspondence*, 1: 286.
10. Geoffrey Green, *The Conference Diaries of Flight Sergeant Geoffrey Green*, December 13 and December 16, 1941, Churchill Archives Centre, Churchill College, Cambridge.
11. Mary Soames, ed., *Winston and Clementine: The Personal Letters of the Churchills* (Boston: Houghton Mifflin, 1999), 461.
12. W. Averell Harriman, "Trip to U.S. with 'P.M.', December 1941," W. Averell Harriman Papers, Library of Congress, box 161, file December 20–31, 1941. Some entries from these journals can be found in *Special Envoy: To Churchill and Stalin, 1941–1946* by W. Averell Harriman and Elie Abel (New York: Random House, 1975).
13. Soames, *Winston and Clementine*, 459–61.
14. Eleanor Roosevelt, "My Day," December 24, 1941, https://erpapers.columbian.gwu.edu/browse-my-day-columns.
15. Henrietta Nesbitt, *White House Diary* (Garden City, NY: Doubleday, 1948), 269–70.
16. Eleanor Roosevelt, *My Day*, December 24, 1941, https://erpapers.columbian.gwu.edu/browse-my-day-columns.
17. Eleanor Roosevelt, *This I Remember* (New York: Harper & Brothers, 1949), 224.
18. Winston S. Churchill, *The Grand Alliance* (Boston: Houghton Mifflin, 1950), 648.
19. Churchill, *Grand Alliance*, 663.
20. Churchill, *Grand Alliance*, 654.
21. Churchill, *Grand Alliance*, 657.
22. Churchill, *Grand Alliance*, 658.
23. Churchill, *Grand Alliance*, 660.
24. "Research Starters: US Military by the Numbers," National WWII Museum, New Orleans, LA, https://www.nationalww2museum.org/students-teachers/student-resources/research-starters/research-starters-us-military-numbers.
25. Green, *Conference Diaries of Geoffrey Green*, December 23, 1941.
26. Alonzo Fields, *My 24 Years in the White House* (New York: Coward-McCann, 1961), 81–82.
27. John Colville, *The Fringes of Power: 10 Downing Street Diaries, 1939–1955* (New York: W. W. Norton, 1985), 136.

28. Colville, *Fringes of Power*, 624.
29. *Foreign Relations of the United States: The Conferences at Washington, 1941–1942 and Casablanca, 1943* (Washington, DC: Department of State Publication 8414/Government Printing Office, 1968), 77.
30. Andrew Roberts, *Churchill: Walking with Destiny* (New York: Viking, 2018), 2.
31. Robert Dallek, *Franklin D. Roosevelt: A Political Life* (New York: Viking, 2017), 25.
32. *Press Conferences of President Franklin D. Roosevelt*, Franklin D. Roosevelt Presidential Library, Press Conference #794, December 23, 1941, 386.
33. Press Conference #794, 388.
34. Churchill, *Grand Alliance*, 663.
35. Press Conference #794, 383.
36. Churchill, *Grand Alliance*, 663.
37. Martin Gilbert, *Continue to Pester, Nag and Bite: Churchill's War Leadership* (Toronto: Vintage Canada, 2004), 11.
38. *Foreign Relations of the United States: The Conferences at Washington, 1941–1942 and Casablanca, 1943*, 81–82.
39. David Brinkley, *Washington Goes to War* (New York: Alfred A. Knopf, 1988), 102.
40. Robert Rhodes James, ed., *Winston S. Churchill: His Complete Speeches, 1897–1963* (New York: Chelsea House Publishers, 1974), 6:6535.
41. *Foreign Relations of the United States: The Conferences at Washington, 1941–1942 and Casablanca, 1943*, 268.
42. *Foreign Relations of the United States: The Conferences at Washington, 1941–1942 and Casablanca, 1943*, 95.
43. *Foreign Relations of the United States: The Conferences at Washington, 1941–1942 and Casablanca, 1943*, 95.
44. Ian Jacob, Diary (typewritten) about "Operation Arcadia," in The Papers of Sir Ian Jacob, Churchill Archives Centre, Churchill College, Cambridge, 25–26.
45. Jacob, Diary, 45.
46. Jacob, Diary, 60.
47. Andrew Roberts, *The Holy Fox: A Biography of Lord Halifax* (London: Weidenfeld and Nicolson, 1991), 274.
48. Lord Halifax, *Lord Halifax Diaries* (University of York: York Digital Library), December 27, 1941, 556.
49. Lord Halifax, *Secret Diary*, Borthwick Institute for Archives, University of York, March 25, 1942, 41.
50. Halifax, *Lord Halifax Diaries*, December 25, 1941, 555.
51. Michael F. Reilly as told to William J. Slocum, *Reilly of the White House* (New York: Simon & Schuster, 1947), 125.
52. Elliott Roosevelt and James Brough, *A Rendezvous with Destiny: The Roosevelts of the White House* (New York: G. P. Putnam's Sons, 1975), 307.
53. James, *Churchill: His Complete Speeches*, 6:6536.
54. James, *Churchill: His Complete Speeches*, 6:6537.
55. James, *Churchill: His Complete Speeches*, 6:6538.

56. James, *Churchill: His Complete Speeches*, 6:6537.
57. James, *Churchill: His Complete Speeches*, 6:6540.
58. James, *Churchill: His Complete Speeches*, 6:6541.
59. Martin Gilbert, ed. *The Churchill War Papers*, vol. 3, *The Ever-Widening War* (New York: W. W. Norton, 2001), 1696.
60. Vivian A. Cox, *Seven Christmases: Second World War Memoirs of Lieutenant Commander Vivian A. Cox, R.N.V.R.*, ed. Nick Thorne (Sevenoaks, Kent, U.K.: Nikkay Associates, 2010), 121.
61. Cox, *Seven Christmases*, 122.
62. William M. Rigdon with James Derieux, *White House Sailor* (Garden City, NY: Doubleday, 1962), 12.
63. Martin Gilbert, ed., *The Churchill Documents*, vol. 17, *Testing Times, 1942* (Hillsdale, MI: Hillsdale College Press, 2014), 11.
64. Gilbert, ed., *Churchill Documents*, 17:14.
65. Halifax, *Lord Halifax Diaries*, January 3, 1942, 560.
66. Churchill, *Grand Alliance*, 683.
67. Grace Tully, *F.D.R., My Boss* (New York: Charles Scribner's Sons, 1949), 305.
68. Geoffrey C. Ward, ed., *Closest Companion: The Unknown Story of the Intimate Friendship between Franklin Roosevelt and Margaret Suckley* (Boston: Houghton Mifflin, 1995), 385.
69. Cordell Hull, *The Memoirs of Cordell Hull*, vol. 2 (New York: Macmillan, 1948), 1124.
70. Halifax, *Lord Halifax Diaries*, January 4, 1942, 560.
71. Mackenzie King, *Diaries of William Lyon Mackenzie King*, Library and Archives, Government of Canada, December 5, 1942, 4.
72. Walter Henry Thompson, *Assignment: Churchill* (New York: Farrar, Straus and Young, 1955), 248–49.
73. Gerald Pawle, *The War and Colonel Warden* (New York: Alfred A. Knopf, 1963), 142.
74. Gilbert, *Churchill War Papers*, 3:1676.
75. Gilbert, *Churchill War Papers*, 3:1699.
76. Cox, *Seven Christmases*, 125.
77. Martin Gilbert and Larry Arnn, eds., *The Churchill Documents*, vol. 18, *One Continent Redeemed, January–August 1943* (Hillsdale, MI: Hillsdale College Press, 2015), 1270.
78. J. B. West with Mary Lynn Kotz, *Upstairs at the White House: My Life with the First Ladies* (New York: Coward, McCann & Geoghegan, 1973), 39.
79. Robert E. Sherwood, *Roosevelt and Hopkins: An Intimate History* (New York: Harper & Brothers, 1948), 442–43.
80. Margaret Truman, *The President's House: A First Daughter Shares the History and Secrets of the World's Most Famous Home* (New York: Ballantine Books, 2003), 217–18.
81. Cox, *Seven Christmases*, 125.
82. Giles Milton, *The Ministry of Ungentlemanly Warfare: Churchill's Mavericks: Plotting Hitler's Defeat* (London: John Murray, 2016), 192.
83. Kimball, *Churchill & Roosevelt: Complete Correspondence*, 1:131.

84. Churchill, *Grand Alliance*, 697.
85. John Colville, "Memoir," in *Action This Day: Working with Churchill*, ed. John Wheeler-Bennett (London: Macmillan, 1968), 112.
86. Moran, *Churchill*, 17.
87. Moran, *Churchill*, 17–18.
88. Moran, *Churchill*, 21.
89. Martin Gilbert, *Churchill: A Life* (London: Pimlico, 2000), 714.
90. Mary Soames, *Clementine Churchill: The Biography of a Marriage* (Boston: Houghton Mifflin, 1979), 350.
91. Roberts, *Churchill*, 703.
92. Churchill, *Grand Alliance*, 691.
93. King, *Diaries of Mackenzie King*, December 27, 1941, 6.
94. Moran, *Churchill*, 22.
95. Thompson, *Assignment: Churchill*, 259.
96. Walter Thompson, *Beside the Bulldog: The Intimate Memoirs of Churchill's Bodyguard* (London: Apollo, 2003), 105.
97. Franklin D. Roosevelt, State of the Union Address to Congress, January 6, 1942, Franklin D. Roosevelt Presidential Library, file number 1409–A, 20.
98. *Foreign Relations of the United States: The Conferences at Washington, 1941–1942 and Casablanca, 1943*, 171.
99. King, *Diaries of Mackenzie King*, January 8, 1942.
100. *Foreign Relations of the United States: The Conferences at Washington, 1941–1942 and Casablanca, 1943*, 209.
101. Churchill, *Grand Alliance*, 683.
102. Basil Woon, *Roosevelt, World Statesman* (London: Peter Davies, 1942), 182.
103. Gilbert, *Churchill Documents*, 17:53.
104. Gilbert, *Churchill Documents*, 17:21.
105. Oliver Harvey, *The War Diaries of Oliver Harvey*, ed. John Harvey (London: Collins, 1978), 86.
106. See several letters in W. Averell Harriman Papers, Library of Congress, box 161, folder 6, January 1942.
107. Gilbert, *Churchill Documents*, 17:92–94.
108. Henry L. Stimson, Diary, Manuscripts and Archives, Yale University Library, January 8–11, 1942, 2.
109. Henry L. Stimson and McGeorge Bundy, *On Active Service in Peace and War* (New York: Harper & Brothers, 1948), vol. 2, 413.
110. Stimson and Bundy, *On Active Service in Peace and War*, 2:414.
111. James, *Churchill: His Complete Speeches*, 6:6569.
112. Halifax, *Lord Halifax Diaries*, February 18, 1942, 582.
113. Eleanor Roosevelt, *This I Remember*, 242–43.
114. Curtis Roosevelt, *Upstairs at the Roosevelts': Growing Up with Franklin and Eleanor* (Lincoln, Nebraska: Potomac Books, 2017), 180.
115. Joseph P. Lash, Joseph P. Lash Papers, Franklin D. Roosevelt Presidential Library, Diary, January 1, 1942.

116. Fulton Oursler, *Behold This Dreamer: An Autobiography by Fulton Oursler*, ed. Fulton Oursler Jr. (Boston: Little, Brown, 1964), 424.

CHAPTER 2: DEFEAT AND DISGRACE

1. Alex Danchev and Daniel Todman, eds., *War Diaries, 1939–1945: Field Marshal Lord Alanbrooke* (Berkeley: University of California Press, 2001), 265.
2. Lord Halifax, *Lord Halifax Diaries* (University of York: York Digital Library), June 18, 1942, 647.
3. Halifax, *Lord Halifax Diaries*, June 18, 1942, 647.
4. Winston S. Churchill, *The Hinge of Fate* (Boston: Houghton Mifflin, 1950), 377.
5. Churchill, *Hinge of Fate*, 377.
6. Gerald Pawle, *The War and Colonel Warden* (New York: Alfred A. Knopf, 1963), 167–68.
7. Geoffrey C. Ward, ed., *Closest Companion: The Unknown Story of the Intimate Friendship between Franklin Roosevelt and Margaret Suckley* (Boston: Houghton Mifflin, 1995), 162.
8. Warren F. Kimball, ed., *Churchill & Roosevelt: The Complete Correspondence* (Princeton, NJ: Princeton University Press, 1984), 1:491.
9. James Roosevelt with Bill Libby, *My Parents: A Differing View* (Chicago: Playboy Press, 1976), 206.
10. Kimball, *Churchill & Roosevelt: Complete Correspondence*, 1:421.
11. Kimball, *Churchill & Roosevelt: Complete Correspondence*, 1:422.
12. Winston S. Churchill, *The Grand Alliance* (Boston: Houghton Mifflin, 1950), 698.
13. William D. Hassett, *Off the Record with F.D.R., 1942–1945* (New Brunswick, NJ: Rutgers University Press, 1958), 67.
14. W. Averell Harriman, "W.A. Harriman Personal Notes: Trip to Hyde Park Saturday, June 20, 1942," W. Averell Harriman Papers, Library of Congress, box 162, folder 2.
15. Kimball, *Churchill & Roosevelt: Complete Correspondence*, 1:441.
16. "Memorandum of Conference Held at the White House, by Mr. Samuel H. Cross, Interpreter," *Foreign Relations of the United States: Diplomatic Papers, 1942, Europe, Vol. 3* (Washington, DC: Department of State Publication 7165 /Government Printing Office, 1961), 577.
17. Henry L. Stimson and McGeorge Bundy, *On Active Service in Peace and War* (New York: Harper & Brothers, 1948), 2:421.
18. Churchill, *Hinge of Fate*, 381.
19. Churchill, *Hinge of Fate*, 382.
20. Henry L. Stimson, Diary, Manuscripts and Archives, Yale University Library, June 20, 1942, 3.
21. Grace Tully, *F.D.R., My Boss* (New York: Charles Scribner's Sons, 1949), 302–3.
22. Tully, *F.D.R., My Boss*, 303–4.
23. John Martin, *Downing Street: The War Years* (London: Bloomsbury, 1991), 81.

24. Churchill, *Hinge of Fate*, 382.
25. Churchill, *Hinge of Fate*, 383.
26. Daniel Allen Butler, *Field Marshal: The Life and Death of Erwin Rommel* (Philadelphia: Casemate, 2015), 222.
27. Churchill, *Hinge of Fate*, 383.
28. Doris Kearns Goodwin titled one chapter in *No Ordinary Time*, her Pulitzer Prize-winning history of the Roosevelts during World War II, "What Can We Do to Help?" Without providing a source, Roger Daniels in *Franklin D. Roosevelt: The War Years, 1939–1945* dramatized the moment: "The Briton was stunned. After a few moments, Roosevelt turned to him and asked, 'Is there anything we can do to help?'" The repetition of the story, with the quotation in whatever formulation, derived most probably from Churchill's own recollection of the meeting. It appears in several books by Martin Gilbert and Andrew Roberts as well as in Churchill biographies by Roy Jenkins, John Keegan, and Max Hastings, to name a few. In *The Mantle of Command: FDR at War, 1941–1942* and *War and Peace: FDR's Final Odyssey D-Day to Yalta, 1943–1945*, Nigel Hamilton repeated Roosevelt's reputed question, citing *The Memoirs of General Lord Ismay* each time. However, in *War and Peace*, Hamilton quoted what Ismay wrote the second time in his memoirs about the same incident. This time Churchill's principal military assistant made the moment more personal: "Winston, what can we do to help?" Was the putative question with or without direct address? It might seem a minor matter, but it raises some suspicion about the precision of the quotation itself. Ismay rather than Churchill was the source in Hamilton's two volumes. Ismay's memoirs were published in 1960, a decade after Churchill's *The Hinge of Fate* appeared. Lord Moran reprised the question in *Churchill: The Struggle for Survival, 1940–1965*, which was published in 1966. By the time the books by Ismay and Moran appeared, the Churchillian version of the six-word query had become the widely accepted portrayal of a key, human moment in World War II.
29. Eleanor Roosevelt, *This I Remember* (New York: Harper & Brothers, 1949), 252.
30. The official U.S. government document about the conference—*Foreign Relations of the United States: The Conferences at Washington, 1941–1942 and Casablanca*—does not include Roosevelt's question (though it came out eighteen years after Churchill's *The Hinge of Fate*), but it does note "the news of the British reversal was quickly met by the American decision to ship immediately to the British forces in Africa the 300 tanks and 100 cannon previously assigned to the United States First Armored Division." Stimson discussed Tobruk and Churchill's visit in his diary and in *On Active Service in Peace and War*, as did Robert Sherwood in *Roosevelt and Hopkins: An Intimate History*. FDR's poignant question did not appear in any of these accounts, and Sherwood, a lauded dramatist, would no doubt have been predisposed to cite such a moving line, if he were aware of it.
31. See Oliver Harvey, *The War Diaries of Oliver Harvey*, ed. John Harvey (London: Collins, 1978), 227.

32. Robert Rhodes James, ed., *Winston S. Churchill: His Complete Speeches, 1897–1963* (New York: Chelsea House Publishers, 1974), 7:6780.
33. *Press Conferences of President Franklin D. Roosevelt*, Franklin D. Roosevelt Presidential Library, Press Conference #899, May 25, 1943, 341.
34. Churchill, *Hinge of Fate*, 383.
35. Stimson and Bundy, *On Active Service in Peace and War*, 2:423–24.
36. *Foreign Relations of the United States: The Conferences at Washington, 1941–1942 and Casablanca, 1943*, 437.
37. *Foreign Relations of the United States: The Conferences at Washington, 1941–1942 and Casablanca, 1943*, 438.
38. Stimson, Diary, June 22, 1942, 4.
39. Churchill, *Hinge of Fate*, 384.
40. Peter G. Boyle, ed., *The Churchill-Eisenhower Correspondence, 1953–1955* (Chapel Hill: The University of North Carolina Press, 1990), 201.
41. Harvey, *War Diaries of Oliver Harvey*, 133–34.
42. Churchill, *Hinge of Fate*, 386–87.
43. Lord Moran, *Churchill: The Struggle for Survival, 1940–1965* (Boston: Houghton Mifflin, 1966), 42–43.
44. Stimson, Diary, June 23–25, 1942, 4.
45. Moran, *Churchill: The Struggle for Survival, 1940–1965*, 43.
46. Mackenzie King, *Diaries of William Lyon Mackenzie King*, Library and Archives, Government of Canada, June 25, 1942, 6.
47. King, *Diaries of Mackenzie King*, June 25, 1942, 5.
48. King, *Diaries of Mackenzie King*, June 25, 1942, 7.
49. *Foreign Relations of the United States: The Conferences at Washington, 1941–1942 and Casablanca, 1943*, 483.
50. Michael F. Reilly as told to William J. Slocum, *Reilly of the White House* (New York: Simon and Schuster, 1947), 127.
51. The letter is among the papers of John Martin, Churchill Archives Centre, Churchill College, Cambridge.
52. Reilly, *Reilly of the White House*, 128.
53. Danchev and Todman, *War Diaries, 1939–1945*, 272.
54. Danchev and Todman, *War Diaries, 1939–1945*, 273.
55. James, *Churchill: His Complete Speeches*, 6:6648.
56. James, *Churchill: His Complete Speeches*, 6:6649.
57. Forrest C. Pogue, *George C. Marshall: Ordeal and Hope, 1939–1942* (New York: Viking Press, 1966), 330.
58. Jean Edward Smith, *FDR* (New York: Random House, 2007), 561.
59. Kimball, *Churchill & Roosevelt: The Complete Correspondence*, 1:670.

CHAPTER 3: "WINSTON'S TRAVELLING CIRCUS"

1. Lord Halifax, "Secret Diary, 1941–1945," Borthwick Institute for Archives, University of York, May 6, 1943, 72.
2. Winston S. Churchill, *The Hinge of Fate* (Boston: Houghton Mifflin, 1950), 603.

3. Robert Rhodes James, ed., *Winston S. Churchill: His Complete Speeches, 1897–1963* (New York: Chelsea House Publishers, 1974), 6: 6693.
4. James, *Churchill: His Complete Speeches*, 6:6706.
5. James, *Churchill: His Complete Speeches*, 6:6694.
6. *Foreign Relations of the United States: The Conferences at Washington and Quebec, 1943* (Washington, DC: Department of State Publication 8552/Government Printing Office, 1970), 17.
7. *Foreign Relations of the United States: Conferences at Washington and Quebec, 1943*, 17.
8. W. Averell Harriman, "W.A. Harriman—Memorandum of Dinner with the Prime Minister on board SS QUEEN MARY Thursday, May 6, 1943," W. Averell Harriman Papers, Library of Congress, box 164, folder 3.
9. Churchill, *Hinge of Fate*, 788.
10. Churchill, *Hinge of Fate*, 791.
11. William D. Leahy, *I Was There: The Personal Story of the Chief of Staff to Presidents Roosevelt and Truman Based on His Notes and Diaries Made at the Time* (New York: Whittlesey House, 1950), 158–59.
12. Henry L. Stimson, Diary, Manuscripts and Archives, Yale University Library, May 10, 1943, 1.
13. Kenneth Pendar, *Adventure in Diplomacy: Our French Dilemma* (New York: Dodd, Mead, 1945), 154.
14. Dwight D. Eisenhower, *Crusade in Europe* (Garden City, NY: Doubleday, 1948), 195–96.
15. Robert E. Sherwood, *Roosevelt and Hopkins: An Intimate History* (New York: Harper & Brothers, 1948), 9. "Being a writer by trade, I tried continually to study him, to try to look beyond his charming and amusing and warmly affectionate surface into his heavily forested interior. But I could never really understand what was going on in there."
16. *Foreign Relations of the United States: The Conferences at Washington and Quebec, 1943*, 51.
17. Elizabeth Nel, *Mr. Churchill's Secretary* (London: Hodder and Stoughton, 1958), 104.
18. *Press Conferences of President Franklin D. Roosevelt*, Franklin D. Roosevelt Presidential Library, press conference #896, May 14, 1943, 313–14.
19. James, *Churchill: His Complete Speeches*, 7: 6774.
20. Denis Smyth, *Deathly Deception: The Real Story of Operation Mincemeat* (Oxford: Oxford University Press, 2010), 229.
21. Two popular books, later made into eponymous movies, told the story of this intricate operation: *The Man Who Never Was* (1953) by Ewen Montagu and *Operation Mincemeat: The True Spy Story That Changed the Course of World War II* (2010) by Ben Macintyre.
22. *Foreign Relations of the United States: The Conferences at Washington and Quebec, 1943*, 76.
23. *Foreign Relations of the United States: The Conferences at Washington and Quebec, 1943*, 76.
24. Alex Danchev and Daniel Todman, eds., *War Diaries, 1939–1945: Field*

Marshal Lord Alanbrooke (Berkeley: University of California Press, 2001), 403.

25. Danchev and Todman, *War Diaries, 1939–1945*, 404.
26. Churchill, *Hinge of Fate*, 795.
27. Churchill, *Hinge of Fate*, 795–96.
28. Gerald Pawle, *The War and Colonel Warden* (New York: Alfred A. Knopf, 1963), 231–32.
29. Churchill, *Hinge of Fate*, 796.
30. Winston S. Churchill, "If Lee Had Not Won the Battle of Gettysburg," *Scribner's*, December 1930, 588.
31. See Winston S. Churchill, *The Great Democracies* (New York: Dodd, Mead, 1958), "The Great Republic," 131–263.
32. See David S. Wyman, *The Abandonment of the Jews: America and the Holocaust, 1941–1945* (New York: Pantheon Books, 1984).
33. Bernard M. Baruch, *Baruch: The Public Years* (New York: Holt, Rinehart and Winston, 1960), 300.
34. Nel, *Mr. Churchill's Secretary*, 105.
35. Lord Halifax, *Lord Halifax Diaries* (University of York: York Digital Library), May 18, 1943, 846.
36. James, *Churchill: His Complete Speeches*, 7:6776.
37. James, *Churchill: His Complete Speeches*, 7:6776.
38. James, *Churchill: His Complete Speeches*, 7:6780.
39. James, *Churchill: His Complete Speeches*, 7:6783.
40. *Foreign Relations of the United States: The Conferences at Washington and Quebec, 1943*, 134.
41. Alben W. Barkley, *That Reminds Me—* (Garden City, NY: Doubleday, 1954), 211.
42. Grace Tully, *F.D.R., My Boss* (New York: Charles Scribner's Sons, 1949), 329–30.
43. Mackenzie King, *Diaries of William Lyon Mackenzie King*, Library and Archives, Government of Canada, May 19, 1943, 1.
44. Danchev and Todman, *War Diaries, 1939–1945*, 407.
45. *Foreign Relations of the United States: The Conferences at Washington and Quebec, 1943*, 122–23.
46. King, *Diaries of Mackenzie King*, May 18, 1942, 2.
47. King, *Diaries of Mackenzie King*, May 19, 1942, 4.
48. Winston S. Churchill, *The Grand Alliance* (Boston: Houghton Mifflin, 1950), 655.
49. *Foreign Relations of the United States: The Conferences at Washington and Quebec, 1943*, 138.
50. Halifax, *Lord Halifax Diaries*, May 20, 1943, 848.
51. Halifax, *Lord Halifax Diaries*, May 20, 1943, 848.
52. *Foreign Relations of the United States: The Conferences at Washington and Quebec, 1943*, 155.
53. Danchev and Todman, *War Diaries, 1939–1945*, 408.
54. Halifax, *Lord Halifax Diaries*, May 21, 1943, 848.

55. See Oliver Harvey, *The War Diaries of Oliver Harvey*, ed. John Harvey (London: Collins, 1978), 227.
56. Halifax, *Lord Halifax Diaries*, May 22, 1943, 849.
57. *Foreign Relations of the United States: The Conferences at Washington and Quebec, 1943*, 171.
58. *Foreign Relations of the United States: The Conferences at Washington and Quebec, 1943*, 171.
59. Halifax, *Lord Halifax Diaries*, May 23, 1943, 851.
60. Churchill, *Hinge of Fate*, 810.
61. Stimson, Diary, May 25, 1943, 1.
62. Churchill, *Hinge of Fate*, 800.
63. Danchev and Todman, *War Diaries, 1939–1945*, 410–11.
64. Harvey, *War Diaries of Oliver Harvey*, 261.
65. Halifax, *Lord Halifax Diaries*, May 23, 1943, 851.
66. *Foreign Relations of the United States: The Conferences at Washington and Quebec, 1943*, 220.
67. *Foreign Relations of the United States: The Conferences at Washington and Quebec, 1943*, 220.
68. *Foreign Relations of the United States: The Conferences at Washington and Quebec, 1943*, 377.
69. *Foreign Relations of the United States: The Conferences at Washington and Quebec, 1943*, 377.
70. Stimson, Diary, May 27, 1943, 2–3.
71. William D. Hassett, *Off the Record with F.D.R., 1942–1945* (New Brunswick, NJ: Rutgers University Press, 1958), 169.
72. Mary Soames, ed., *Winston and Clementine: The Personal Letters of the Churchills* (Boston: Houghton Mifflin, 1999), 482–83.
73. Lord Moran, *Churchill: The Struggle for Survival, 1940–1965* (Boston: Houghton Mifflin, 1966), 103.
74. "War Cabinet 81 (43)," conclusions, June 5, 1943, National Archives, Kew, 1.
75. "War Cabinet 81 (43)," conclusions, June 5, 1943, 3.

CHAPTER 4: FORWARD TOWARD VICTORY

1. W. Averell Harriman and Elie Abel, *Special Envoy to Churchill and Stalin, 1941–1946* (New York: Random House, 1975), 221.
2. W. Averell Harriman, "W. A. Harriman—Conversations with the Prime Minister en route to the United States on board SS *QUEEN MARY*—August 5–6, 1943," W. Averell Harriman Papers, Library of Congress, box 164, folder 8.
3. W. A. Harriman, "Memorandum of dinner at the Citadel, Quebec, with the President and Prime Minister, Tuesday, August 24, 1943," W. Averell Harriman Papers, box 164, folder 8.
4. Warren F. Kimball, ed., *Churchill & Roosevelt: The Complete Correspondence* (Princeton, NJ: Princeton University Press, 1984), 2:382.
5. Winston S. Churchill, *Closing the Ring* (Boston: Houghton Mifflin, 1951), 82.

6. Gerald Pawle, *The War and Colonel Warden* (New York: Alfred A. Knopf, 1963), 242.
7. Walter Henry Thompson, *Assignment: Churchill* (New York: Farrar, Straus and Young, 1955), 280.
8. Geoffrey C. Ward, ed., *Closest Companion: The Unknown Story of the Intimate Friendship between Franklin Roosevelt and Margaret Suckley* (Boston: Houghton Mifflin, 1995), 229.
9. Ward, *Closest Companion*, 230.
10. Blanche Wiesen Cook, *Eleanor Roosevelt: The War Years and After* (New York: Viking, 2016), 3:477. "ER anticipated serious illuminating discussions during Churchill's visit. As she prepared days of entertainment for the prime minister and his daughter, she looked forward to an exploration of the controversies Churchill had traveled so far to settle with her husband." Unfortunately, other subjects intruded on the complexities of contemporary affairs. "She was disappointed," Cook wrote. "Everybody made small talk. Nothing of substance was discussed in her presence."
11. Joseph P. Lash, *A World of Love: Eleanor Roosevelt and Her Friends, 1943–1962* (Garden City, NY: Doubleday, 1984), 54–55.
12. W. A. Harriman, "Memorandum of dinner at Hyde Park, New York—Saturday, August 14, 1943," W. Averell Harriman Papers, box 164, folder 8.
13. Eleanor Roosevelt, "My Day," August 17, 1943, https://erpapers.columbian.gwu.edu/browse-my-day-columns.
14. Samuel L. Rosenman, *Working with Roosevelt* (New York: Harper & Brothers, 1952), 387.
15. See *Foreign Relations of the United States: The Conferences at Washington and Quebec, 1943* (Washington, DC: Department of State Publication 8552/Government Printing Office, 1970), 830–31.
16. Churchill, *Closing the Ring*, 82.
17. Lash, *World of Love*, 54.
18. David L. Roll, *The Hopkins Touch: Harry Hopkins and the Forging of the Alliance to Defeat Hitler* (Oxford and New York: Oxford University Press, 2013), 284.
19. Doris Kearns Goodwin, *No Ordinary Time: Franklin & Eleanor Roosevelt: The Home Front in World War II* (New York: Simon & Schuster, 1994), 459.
20. Kimball, *Churchill & Roosevelt: Complete Correspondence*, 2:388.
21. *Foreign Relations of the United States: The Conferences at Washington and Quebec, 1943*, 472.
22. Larry Collins, *The Secrets of D-Day* (Beverly Hills, CA: Phoenix Books, 2006), 4.
23. Martin Gilbert and Larry P. Arnn, eds., *The Churchill Documents: One Continent Redeemed, January–August 1943* (Hillsdale, MI: Hillsdale College Press, 2015), 18:2218.
24. Alex Danchev and Daniel Todman, eds., *War Diaries, 1939–1945: Field Marshal Lord Alanbrooke* (Berkeley: University of California Press, 2001), 441.
25. Danchev and Todman, *War Diaries, 1939–1945*, 442.
26. Churchill, *Closing the Ring*, 85.

27. Danchev and Todman, *War Diaries, 1939–1945*, 444.
28. Churchill, *Closing the Ring*, 85.
29. *Foreign Relations of the United States: The Conferences at Washington and Quebec, 1943*, 880.
30. *Foreign Relations of the United States: The Conferences at Washington and Quebec, 1943*, 896.
31. See pages 84–85 of Churchill's *Closing the Ring.*
32. Anthony Eden, *The Eden Memoirs: The Reckoning* (London: Cassell, 1965), 402.
33. Elizabeth Nel, *Mr. Churchill's Secretary* (London: Hodder and Stoughton, 1958), 114.
34. John Martin, *Downing Street: The War Years* (London: Bloomsbury, 1991), 115.
35. Nel, *Mr. Churchill's Secretary*, 114–15.
36. Alexander Cadogan, *The Diaries of Sir Alexander Cadogan, 1938–1945,* ed. David Dilks (New York: G. P. Putnam's Sons, 1972), 558–59.
37. Ward, *Closest Companion*, 235.
38. Russell D. Buhite and David W. Levy, eds., *FDR's Fireside Chats* (Norman: University of Oklahoma Press, 1992), 269.
39. David Brinkley, *Washington Goes to War* (New York: Alfred A. Knopf, 1988), 102.
40. Pawle, *War and Colonel Warden*, 247.
41. Robert H. Pilpel, *Churchill in America, 1895–1961: An Affectionate Portrait* (New York: Harcourt Brace Jovanovich, 1976), 199.
42. Martin Gilbert and Larry P. Arnn, eds., *The Churchill Documents: Fateful Questions, September 1943 to April 1944* (Hillsdale, MI: Hillsdale College Press, 2017), 19:43.
43. Lord Moran, *Churchill: The Struggle for Survival, 1940–1965* (Boston: Houghton Mifflin, 1966), 124.
44. Nel, *Mr. Churchill's Secretary*, 116.
45. Moran, *Churchill*, 124.
46. Churchill, *Closing the Ring*, 124.
47. Robert Rhodes James, ed., *Winston S. Churchill His Complete Speeches, 1897–1963* (New York: Chelsea House Publishers, 1974), 7:6825.
48. Robert E. Sherwood, *Roosevelt and Hopkins: An Intimate History* (New York: Harper & Brothers, 1948), 750.
49. John Colville, "Memoir," in *Action This Day: Working with Churchill*, ed. John Wheeler-Bennett (London: Macmillan, 1968), 97.
50. James, *Churchill His Complete Speeches*, 7:6825–26.
51. James, *Churchill His Complete Speeches*, 7:6826.
52. James, *Churchill His Complete Speeches*, 7:6827.
53. Gilbert and Arnn, *Churchill Documents: Fateful Questions*, 19:113.
54. Gilbert and Arnn, *Churchill Documents: Fateful Questions*, 19:195.
55. H. G. Nicholas, ed., *Washington Despatches, 1941–1945: Weekly Political Reports from the British Embassy* (Chicago: University of Chicago Press, 1981), 193.

56. Nicholas, *Washington Despatches, 1941–1945*, 245.
57. Isaiah Berlin, *Letters, 1928–1946,* ed. Henry Hardy (Cambridge: Cambridge University Press, 2004), 467. Berlin's lofty opinion of Churchill continued beyond his wartime service, and he made it dramatically public after he returned to Oxford. In 1949, he wrote a sweeping review of the first volume of Churchill's war memoirs, *The Gathering Storm*, for *The Atlantic Monthly*. Titled simply "Mr. Churchill" in *The Atlantic* and republished a few months later in the U.K. as "Mr Churchill and FDR" in *Cornhill Magazine*, the article made clear Berlin's unadulterated admiration for its subject. Within a year, the text even appeared as a short book, *Mr Churchill in 1940*, and the slim volume was reissued on both sides of the Atlantic the year before Churchill's death in 1965.
58. Berlin, *Letters, 1928–1946*, 456.
59. For the tenth anniversary of FDR's death, the BBC asked Berlin, by then a well-known public intellectual with a global reputation, to prepare a twenty-five-minute broadcast to recognize the date. Roosevelt died on April 12, 1945, and the tribute aired April 12, 1955. Berlin published his remarks, "Roosevelt through European Eyes," in the July 1955 issue of *The Atlantic*. Noting that Roosevelt "was one of the few statesmen in the twentieth or any other century who seemed to have no fear at all of the future," Berlin never mentioned the disapproval he relayed to his parents in 1943. Near the end, in fact, he stated that FDR "showed that it is possible to be politically effective and yet benevolent and civilized," and, more broadly, "Mr. Roosevelt's example strengthened democracy everywhere." Had Berlin changed his mind, as he never did vis-à-vis Churchill? Did the media assignment-tribute demand a monologue of commendation, requiring suppression of criticism to the point of hypocrisy? Berlin subsequently positioned his *Atlantic* essays about Churchill and Roosevelt as the first and second ones in his collection, *Personal Impressions*, first published in 1980.
60. Cadogan, *Diaries of Sir Alexander Cadogan,* 559–60.
61. Harriman Papers, box 164, folder 9, September 1–14, 1943.
62. Oliver Harvey, *The War Diaries of Oliver Harvey*, ed. John Harvey (London: Collins, 1978), 291.
63. Eden, *Eden Memoirs: The Reckoning*, 405.
64. Geoffrey Green, *The Conference Diaries of Flight Sergeant Geoffrey Green*, September 7, 1943, Churchill Archives Centre, Churchill College, Cambridge.
65. *Foreign Relations of the United States: The Conferences at Washington and Quebec, 1943*, 1215.
66. Churchill, *Closing the Ring*, 137.
67. Churchill, *Closing the Ring*, 138.
68. Hastings Ismay, *The Memoirs of General Lord Ismay* (New York: Viking Press, 1960), 320.
69. William D. Leahy, William D. Leahy Papers, Library of Congress, Diaries, box 5, microfilm reel no. 3, September 11, 1943, 27.
70. William D. Hassett, *Off the Record with F.D.R., 1942–1945* (New Brunswick, NJ: Rutgers University Press, 1958), 201.
71. Churchill, *Closing the Ring*, 142.

72. W. Averell Harriman Papers, Library of Congress, box 164, folder 9, September 1–14, 1943.
73. Emma Soames, ed., *Mary Churchill's War: The Wartime Diaries of Churchill's Youngest Daughter* (New York: Pegasus Books, 2022), 223–24.
74. Soames, *Mary Churchill's War*, 234.
75. Soames, *Mary Churchill's War*, 238.
76. Soames, *Mary Churchill's War*, 239.
77. Mary Soames, *Clementine Churchill: The Biography of a Marriage* (Boston: Houghton Mifflin, 1979), 448.
78. Lord Halifax, *Lord Halifax Diaries* (University of York: York Digital Library), December 6, 1941, 544.
79. Moran, *Churchill*, 127–28.
80. Ward, *Closest Companion*, 238–39.
81. Kimball, *Churchill & Roosevelt: Complete Correspondence*, 3:139.
82. Kimball, *Churchill & Roosevelt: Complete Correspondence*, 2:447.
83. Gilbert and Arnn, *Churchill Documents: Fateful Questions*, 19:158–59.
84. James, *Churchill: His Complete Speeches*, 7:7289.
85. Halifax, *Lord Halifax Diaries*, August 18, 1943, 891.
86. James, *Churchill: His Complete Speeches*, 7:6849.
87. James, *Churchill: His Complete Speeches*, 7:6845.
88. Henry L. Stimson, Diary, Manuscripts and Archives, Yale University Library, October 28, 1943, 1–2.

CHAPTER 5: A SECRET RENDEZVOUS

1. Warren F. Kimball, ed., *Churchill & Roosevelt: The Complete Correspondence* (Princeton, NJ: Princeton University Press, 1984), 3:54.
2. Kimball, *Churchill & Roosevelt: Complete Correspondence*, 3:59.
3. Kimball, *Churchill & Roosevelt: Complete Correspondence*, 3:64.
4. Kimball, *Churchill & Roosevelt: Complete Correspondence*, 3:143–44.
5. Kimball, *Churchill & Roosevelt: Complete Correspondence*, 3:157.
6. Kimball, *Churchill & Roosevelt: Complete Correspondence*, 3:249.
7. Kimball, *Churchill & Roosevelt: Complete Correspondence*, 3:250.
8. Kimball, *Churchill & Roosevelt: Complete Correspondence*, 3:272.
9. Susan Butler, ed., *My Dear Mr. Stalin: The Complete Correspondence between Franklin D. Roosevelt and Joseph V. Stalin* (New Haven, CT: Yale University Press, 2005), 129.
10. Kimball, *Churchill & Roosevelt: Complete Correspondence*, 2:278–79.
11. Kimball, *Churchill & Roosevelt: Complete Correspondence*, 2:283.
12. Frances Perkins, *The Roosevelt I Knew* (New York: Viking Press, 1946), 84.
13. Perkins, *The Roosevelt I Knew*, 85.
14. Winston S. Churchill, *Closing the Ring* (Boston: Houghton Mifflin, 1951), 373.
15. Churchill, *Closing the Ring*, 374.
16. *Foreign Relations of the United States, Diplomatic Papers: The Conferences at Cairo and Tehran, 1943* (Washington, DC: Department of State Publication 7187/Government Printing Office, 1970), 585.

17. John Gunther, *Roosevelt in Retrospect: A Profile in History* (New York: Harper & Brothers, 1950), 17.
18. Jon Meacham, *Franklin and Winston: An Intimate Portrait of an Epic Friendship* (New York: Random House, 2003), 265–66.
19. John Wheeler-Bennett, ed., *Action This Day: Working with Churchill* (London: Macmillan, 1968), 96. See footnote 1 in John Colville, "Memoir," in *Action This Day.*
20. Mackenzie King, *Diaries of William Lyon Mackenzie King,* Library and Archives, Government of Canada, September 11, 1944, 1.
21. King, *Diaries of Mackenzie King,* September 11, 1944, 1.
22. King, *Diaries of Mackenzie King,* September 11, 1944, 1.
23. Winston S. Churchill, *Triumph and Tragedy* (Boston: Houghton Mifflin, 1953), 155.
24. *Foreign Relations of the United States: The Conference at Quebec* (Washington, DC: Department of State Publication 8627/Government Printing Office, 1972), 326.
25. *Foreign Relations of the United States: The Conference at Quebec,* 327.
26. *Foreign Relations of the United States: The Conference at Quebec,* 348.
27. *Foreign Relations of the United States: The Conference at Quebec,* 477.
28. *Press Conferences of President Franklin D. Roosevelt,* Franklin D. Roosevelt Presidential Library, Press Conference #968, September 16, 1944, 117–18.
29. Lord Moran, *Churchill: The Struggle for Survival, 1940–1965* (Boston: Houghton Mifflin, 1966), 197.
30. John Colville, *The Churchillians* (London: Weidenfeld and Nicolson, 1981), 93.
31. Robert J. Cruikshank, "SECRET" memorandum to John Martin, September 15, 1944. In Martin's book *Downing Street: The War Years* (London: Bloomsbury, 1991), he writes: "At past conferences some of my worst troubles have been about the press; but this time Brendan [Bracken, Minister of Information] has given us Cruikshank, head of the American division of the Ministry of Information and formerly editor of the *Star*, and there could not be a better man for the job." (p. 161)
32. Churchill, *Triumph and Tragedy, 160.*
33. See page 82 of Churchill, *Closing the Ring.* The U.S. government's official record, *Foreign Relations of the United States: The Conferences at Washington and Quebec 1943,* included this sentence: "It was not Roosevelt's custom to record his conversations with Churchill, and although Harry Hopkins was present at Hyde Park, nothing has been found in the Hopkins Papers concerning the substance of the discussions there." See *Foreign Relations of the United States: The Conferences at Washington and Quebec, 1943* (Washington DC: Department of State Publication 8552/Government Printing Office, 1970), 832.
34. In David Reynolds' investigation of the composition of the six volumes of *The Second World War,* titled *In Command of History* (New York: Random House, 2005), he cited Churchill's paragraph about Hopkins' diminished status and then tried to untangle the knots of the past: "This paragraph was published

in *Life* magazine's serialization of *Closing the Ring* on 8 October 1951 and in the American book version the following month. But on 1 November Robert Sherwood told Houghton Mifflin that, when researching his biography of Hopkins, he was told by Churchill that this episode occurred when Churchill visited Hyde Park after the *second* Quebec conference, in 1944. This message was hastily relayed to Churchill, and Deakin unearthed documentary evidence confirming that Hopkins had been present at Hyde Park in September 1944 but not in August 1943. There was still time to delete the passage from the British edition of *Closing the Ring*, but it was printed in almost exactly the same words in both editions of volume 6. Americans therefore read the same story twice—about events more than a year apart!" See 365–66.

35. Gerald Pawle, *The War and Colonel Warden* (New York: Alfred A. Knopf, 1963), 324.
36. Mary Soames, *Clementine Churchill: The Biography of a Marriage* (Boston: Houghton Mifflin, 1979), 474.
37. Soames, *Clementine Churchill*, 474.
38. Soames, *Clementine Churchill*, 474.
39. See Anna Roosevelt Halsted Papers, Franklin D. Roosevelt Presidential Library, box 66.
40. Geoffrey C. Ward, ed., *Closest Companion: The Unknown Story of the Intimate Friendship between Franklin Roosevelt and Margaret Suckley* (Boston: Houghton Mifflin, 1995), 327.
41. Eleanor Roosevelt, "My Day," September 25, 1944, https://erpapers.columbian.gwu.edu/browse-my-day-columns.
42. Roosevelt, "My Day," September 19, 1944, https://erpapers.columbian.gwu.edu/browse-my-day-columns.
43. Joseph P. Lash, *A World of Love: Eleanor Roosevelt and Her Friends, 1943–1962* (Garden City, NY: Doubleday, 1984), 139–40.
44. Soames, *Clementine Churchill*, 475.
45. Clementine Churchill, The Papers of Clementine Ogilvy Spencer-Churchill, Baroness Spencer-Churchill of Chartwell, Churchill Archives Centre, Churchill College, Cambridge, September 1944 diary, 22.
46. William D. Leahy, *I Was There: The Personal Story of the Chief of Staff to Presidents Roosevelt and Truman Based on His Notes and Diaries Made at the Time* (New York: Whittlesey House, 1950), 263.
47. *Foreign Relations of the United States: The Conference at Quebec*, 498.
48. Leahy, *I Was There*, 264.
49. John Barnes and David Nicholson, eds., *The Empire at Bay: The Leo Amery Diaries, 1929–1945* (London: Hutchinson, 1988), 432.
50. Leahy, *I Was There*, 265.
51. Leahy, *I Was There*, 265.
52. *Foreign Relations of the United States: The Conference at Quebec*, 492.
53. Alexander Cadogan, *The Diaries of Sir Alexander Cadogan, 1938–1945*, ed. David Dilks (New York: G. P. Putnam's Sons, 1972), 667.
54. Alex Danchev and Daniel Todman, eds., *War Diaries, 1939–1945: Field Marshal Lord Alanbrooke* (Berkeley: University of California Press, 2001), 590.

55. See Danchev and Todman, *War Diaries, 1939–1945*, 592–93. Brooke added this postscript to the September 14 entry: "The fact that dear old patient Pug [Ismay] had at last reached the end of his tether and could stand Winston's moods no longer is some indication of what we had been through."
56. Robert E. Sherwood, *Roosevelt and Hopkins: An Intimate History* (New York: Harper & Brothers, 1948), 847.
57. Churchill, *Triumph and Tragedy*, 344.
58. Churchill, *Triumph and Tragedy*, 397.
59. Walter Henry Thompson, *Assignment: Churchill* (New York: Farrar, Straus and Young, 1955), 303.
60. Lord Halifax, *Lord Halifax Diaries* (University of York: York Digital Library), April 12, 1945, 1333.
61. Halifax, *Lord Halifax Diaries*, April 13, 1945, 1333.
62. Cadogan, *Diaries of Sir Alexander Cadogan, 1938–1945*, 727.
63. Churchill, *Triumph and Tragedy*, 479.
64. Churchill, *Triumph and Tragedy*, 473.
65. Robert Rhodes James, ed., *Winston S. Churchill: His Complete Speeches, 1897–1963* (New York: Chelsea House Publishers, 1974), 7:7139.
66. James, *Churchill: His Complete Speeches*, 7:7141.
67. Harold Nicolson, *The War Years, 1939–1945: Volume II of Diaries and Letters*, ed. Nigel Nicolson (New York: Atheneum, 1967), 449.
68. John Colville, *The Fringes of Power: 10 Downing Street Diaries, 1939–1955* (New York: W. W. Norton, 1985), 589.
69. Moran, *Churchill: Struggle for Survival, 1940–1965*, 370.
70. Churchill, *Triumph and Tragedy*, 479.
71. Moran, *Churchill: Struggle for Survival, 1940–1965*, 371.
72. Kimball, *Churchill & Roosevelt: Complete Correspondence*, 3:574.
73. See file marked "Churchill, Winston: 1943" in Franklin D. Roosevelt Presidential Library.
74. Elliott Roosevelt, ed., *F.D.R.: His Personal Letters, 1928–1945* (New York: Duell, Sloan and Pearce, 1950), 2:1456.
75. Perkins, *The Roosevelt I Knew*, 383.
76. Elliott Roosevelt, *As He Saw It* (New York: Duell, Sloan and Pearce, 1946), 38.
77. Colville, *Fringes of Power*, 461.
78. Colville, *Fringes of Power*, 624.
79. Sherwood, *Roosevelt and Hopkins*, 363.
80. Sherwood, *Roosevelt and Hopkins*, 364.
81. Anthony Eden, *The Eden Memoirs: The Reckoning* (London: Cassell, 1965), 478.
82. Ian Jacob, "Memoir," in *Action This Day: Working with Churchill*, ed. John Wheeler-Bennett (London: Macmillan, 1968), 206.
83. Jacob, *Action This Day*, 207.
84. Jacob, *Action This Day*, 207–8.
85. Jacob, *Action This Day*, 208.

86. Arthur M. Schlesinger Jr., *Journals, 1952–2000*, eds. Andrew Schlesinger and Stephen Schlesinger (New York: Penguin Press, 2007), 575.
87. Walter Graebner, *My Dear Mr. Churchill* (Boston: Houghton Mifflin, 1965), 98.
88. Roy Jenkins, *Churchill* (London: Macmillan, 2001), 912.
89. Jenkins, *Churchill*, 784.
90. Jenkins, *Churchill*, 785.
91. Edith Benham Helm, *The Captains and the Kings* (New York: G. P. Putnam's Sons, 1954), 210. *The New York Times* review, on May 23, 1954, referred to the reported secret, month-long stay of the Churchills as the book's "newsiest tidbit" without making any effort to verify whether it happened.
92. J. B. West with Mary Lynn Kotz, *Upstairs at the White House: My Life with the First Ladies* (New York: Coward, McCann & Geoghegan, 1973), 40.
93. See Ward, ed., *Closest Companion*, 322–25 for Daisy Suckley's detailed report of the visit.

CHAPTER 6: THE COLD PEACE

1. Robert H. Ferrell, ed., *Off the Record: The Private Papers of Harry S. Truman* (New York: Harper & Row, 1980), 51.
2. Dwight D. Eisenhower, *Crusade in Europe* (Garden City, NY: Doubleday, 1948), 446.
3. Robert Rhodes James, ed., *Winston S. Churchill: His Complete Speeches, 1897–1963* (New York: Chelsea House Publishers, 1974), 7:7294.
4. James, *Churchill: His Complete Speeches*, 7:7296.
5. Eleanor Roosevelt, "My Day," March 14, 1946, https://erpapers.columbian.gwu.edu/browse-my-day-columns.
6. Harry C. Butcher, *My Three Years with Eisenhower: The Personal Diary of Captain Harry C. Butcher, USNR* (New York: Simon & Schuster, 1946), 75.
7. Merle Miller, *Ike the Soldier: As They Knew Him* (New York: G. P. Putnam's Sons, 1987), 381. In *The New York Times*, Charles Poore called *My Three Years with Eisenhower* "easily the most interesting book about the war that has come this way." That review appeared on the day of publication in April. Two days later Poore devoted a second review to the diary, noting at one point: "Mr. Churchill, in particular, was forever trying to get him [Eisenhower] to change his plans," even threatening to resign as prime minister over one military decision. On April 28, the cover and most of an inside page of *The New York Times* Sunday book section were devoted to Butcher's book, with Churchill's role also prominent in it.
8. Louis Adamic, *Dinner at the White House* (New York: Harper & Brothers, 1946), 26.
9. Adamic, *Dinner at the White House*, 96.
10. Eleanor Roosevelt, "My Day," August 24, 1946, https://erpapers.columbian.gwu.edu/browse-my-day-columns.
11. Elliott Roosevelt, *As He Saw It* (New York: Duell, Sloan and Pearce, 1946), 57.
12. Lord Moran, *Churchill: The Struggle for Survival, 1940–1965* (Boston: Houghton Mifflin, 1966), 336.

13. Moran, *Churchill: Struggle for Survival*, 337.
14. Churchill letter to Truman, Churchill Archives Centre, Churchill College, May 5, 1948 (CHUR 4/23A-B).
15. Announcing *Crusade in Europe* and the newspaper's involvement, *The New York Herald Tribune* reported Eisenhower's book "will be the largest nonfiction publishing venture in history." The syndicated excerpts to "thousands of newspapers" in the United States and internationally meant: "More newspapers will print the series than any other similar newspaper serialization in history." Churchill and Eisenhower—along with their publishers—seemed in something of a skirmish, if not war, for readership and sales.
16. See "The Twentieth Century—Its Promise and Its Realization" in James, *Churchill: His Complete Speeches*, 7:7801–10.
17. See David Lough, *No More Champagne: Churchill and His Money* (New York: Picador, 2015).
18. John Colville, *The Fringes of Power: 10 Downing Street Diaries, 1939–1955* (New York: W. W. Norton, 1985), 639–40.
19. Robert H. Ferrell, ed., *The Eisenhower Diaries* (New York: W. W. Norton, 1981), 222.
20. Ferrell, *Eisenhower Diaries*, 223.
21. Ferrell, *Eisenhower Diaries*, 224.
22. Colville, *Fringes of Power*, 654.
23. Colville, *Fringes of Power*, 662.
24. Colville, *Fringes of Power*, 672.
25. Clarissa Eden, *Clarissa Eden: A Memoir: From Churchill to Eden*, ed. Cate Haste (London: Weidenfeld & Nicolson, 2007), 142.
26. See Roger Hermiston, *Two Minutes to Midnight: 1953—The Year of Living Dangerously* (London: Biteback, 2021).
27. Peter G. Boyle, ed., *The Churchill-Eisenhower Correspondence, 1953–1955* (Chapel Hill: The University of North Carolina Press, 1990), 40. See David Reynolds, *In Command of History: Churchill Fighting and Writing the Second World War* (New York: Random House, 2005) for his meticulous study of the composition, editing, and publication of Churchill's six volumes. Chapter Twenty-Eight, "A Very Diplomatic History," details the extent to which Churchill doctored the manuscript to avoid transatlantic friction.
28. Colville, *Fringes of Power*, 665.
29. Allen Packwood, ed., *Cosmos Out of Chaos: Introducing the Churchill Archives Centre* (Cambridge: Churchill College, 2009), 53.
30. In Anthony Montague Browne, *Long Sunset: Memoirs of Winston Churchill's Last Private Secretary* (London: Cassell, 1995), Montague Browne noted that Churchill "made considerable changes in Volume VI of his war memoirs, then nearing publication, to remove any criticism of Eisenhower." He went on to observe: "The published version was mild. A pity, I thought. History is history, and you don't do much good by failing to illuminate the grosser errors. To which the reply is, of course, that you don't do much good by offending the new US President either." See page 154.

31. "Atoms for Peace" speech, Dwight David Eisenhower's Papers as President, Dwight D. Eisenhower Presidential Library, Speech Series, box 5, United Nations Speech, 12/8/53, page 9.
32. See Hugh Gregory Gallagher, *FDR's Splendid Deception* (New York: Dodd, Mead 1985).
33. Fred I. Greenstein, *The Hidden-Hand Presidency: Eisenhower as Leader* (New York: Basic Books, 1982), 59.
34. Richard M. Nixon, *Six Crises* (Garden City, NY: Doubleday, 1962), 161.
35. Mary Soames, ed., *Winston and Clementine: The Personal Letters of the Churchills* (Boston: Houghton Mifflin, 1999), 579.
36. Boyle, *Churchill-Eisenhower Correspondence*, 145.
37. "The President's Press Conference, June 16, 1954," The American Presidency Project, University of California at Santa Barbara, https://www.presidency.ucsb.edu/Documents/the-presidents-news-conference-470.
38. Boyle, *Churchill-Eisenhower Correspondence*, 144.
39. Dwight D. Eisenhower, *The White House Years: Mandate for Change, 1953–1956* (Garden City, NY: Doubleday, 1963), 368.
40. See page 1074, *Foreign Relations of the United States, 1952–1954*, vol. 6, *Western Europe and Canada, Part 1* (Washington, DC: Department of State Publication 9489/Government Printing Office, 1986).
41. Papers of James C. Hagerty, 1953–1961, Diary entries, box number 1, Eisenhower Presidential Library, June 25, 1954, 1. Hagerty diary entries that have been published appear in *The Diary of James C. Hagerty: Eisenhower in Mid-Course, 1954–1955*, edited by Robert H. Ferrell (Bloomington: Indiana University Press, 1983) and also in *Foreign Relations of the United States, 1952–1954*, vol. 6, *Western Europe and Canada, Part 1.*
42. Hagerty, Diary, June 25, 1954, 1.
43. Colville, *Fringes of Power*, 692.
44. *Foreign Relations of the United States, 1952–1954*, vol. 6, *Western Europe and Canada, Part 1*, 1076.
45. *Foreign Relations of the United States, 1952–1954*, vol. 6, *Western Europe and Canada, Part 1*, 1077.
46. *Foreign Relations of the United States, 1952–1954*, vol. 6, *Western Europe and Canada, Part 1*, 1078.
47. *Foreign Relations of the United States, 1952–1954*, vol. 6, *Western Europe and Canada, Part 1*, 1083.
48. *Foreign Relations of the United States, 1952–1954*, vol. 6, *Western Europe and Canada, Part 1*, 1084.
49. *Foreign Relations of the United States, 1952–1954*, vol. 6, *Western Europe and Canada, Part 1*, 1085–86.
50. Ferrell, *Diary of James C. Hagerty*, 77.
51. Ferrell, *Diary of James C. Hagerty*, 78.
52. *Foreign Relations of the United States, 1952–1954*, vol. 6, *Western Europe and Canada, Part 1*, 1098–99.
53. *Foreign Relations of the United States, 1952–1954*, vol. 6, *Western Europe and Canada, Part 1*, 1097.

54. *Foreign Relations of the United States, 1952–1954*, vol. 6, *Western Europe and Canada, Part 1*, 1099.
55. *Foreign Relations of the United States, 1952–1954*, vol. 6, *Western Europe and Canada, Part 1*, 1101.
56. *Foreign Relations of the United States, 1952–1954*, vol. 6, *Western Europe and Canada, Part 1*, 1102–3.
57. *Foreign Relations of the United States, 1952–1954*, vol. 6, *Western Europe and Canada, Part 1*, 1104.
58. Colville, *Fringes of Power*, 693.
59. Moran, *Churchill: Struggle for Survival*, 602.
60. See James Nelson, ed., *General Eisenhower on the Military Churchill: A Conversation with Alistair Cooke* (New York: W. W. Norton, 1970).
61. *Foreign Relations of the United States, 1952–1954*, vol. 6, *Western Europe and Canada, Part 1*, 1114–15.
62. *Foreign Relations of the United States, 1952–1954*, vol. 6, *Western Europe and Canada, Part 1*, 1115.
63. See "Statement by President Eisenhower and Prime Minister Churchill," *Foreign Relations of the United States, 1952–1954*, vol. 6, *Western Europe and Canada, Part 1*, 1132.
64. Richard Nixon, *RN: The Memoirs of Richard Nixon* (New York: Grosset & Dunlap, 1978), 158–59.
65. *Foreign Relations of the United States, 1952–1954*, vol. 6, *Western Europe and Canada, Part 1*, 1130.
66. "Declaration of Washington," February 1, 1956, in *American Foreign Policy: Current Documents, 1956* (Washington, DC: Department of State Publication 6811/Government Printing Office, 1959), 445.
67. Anthony Eden, *The Eden Memoirs: Full Circle* (London: Cassell, 1960), 336.
68. Martin Gilbert, *Winston S. Churchill: Never Despair* (Boston: Houghton Mifflin, 1988), 8:1010.
69. Hagerty, Diary, June 30, 1954, 2.
70. Boyle, *Churchill-Eisenhower Correspondence*, 162–63.
71. Boyle, *Churchill-Eisenhower Correspondence*, 167.
72. Robert Griffith, ed., *Ike's Letters to a Friend, 1941–1958* (Lawrence: University Press of Kansas, 1984), 140.
73. Martin Gilbert, *Churchill and America* (New York: Free Press, 2005), 436.
74. "Sir Winston Churchill Retirement," Dwight David Eisenhower's Papers as President, Dwight D. Eisenhower Presidential Library, Speech Series, box 12, 4/5/55.
75. "Churchill, Winston, Jan. 1958 to November 1959 (5)," Dwight David Eisenhower's Papers as President 1953–1961," Dwight D. Eisenhower Presidential Library, box 20.
76. Alex Danchev and Daniel Todman, eds., *War Diaries, 1939–1945: Field Marshal Lord Alanbrooke* (Berkeley: University of California Press, 2001), 680.
77. "The President's News Conference, May 5, 1959," The American Presidency Project, University of California at Santa Barbara, https://www.presidency.ucsb.edu/documents/the-presidents-news-conference-229.

78. Ferrell, *Off the Record*, 381–82.
79. Robert Rhodes James, ed., *Winston S. Churchill His Complete Speeches, 1897–1963* (New York: Chelsea House Publishers, 1974), 8:8694.
80. Montague Browne, *Long Sunset,* 262.
81. Ann C. Whitman Papers, diary, Eisenhower Presidential Library, box 41, May 4–5, 1959.
82. Anthony Montague Browne memorandum, Churchill Archives Centre, Churchill College, May 21, 1959 (CHUR 2/298).
83. Moran, *Churchill: Struggle for Survival*, 800.

EPILOGUE

1. Arthur M. Schlesinger Jr., *A Thousand Days: John F. Kennedy in the White House* (Boston: Houghton Mifflin, 1965), 84.
2. Anthony Montague Browne, *Long Sunset: Memoirs of Winston Churchill's Last Private Secretary* (London: Cassell, 1995), 290.
3. "Remarks on Signing Honorary Citizenship for Sir Winston Churchill, 9 April, 1963," Papers of John F. Kennedy, Presidential Papers, President's Office Files, DOI:JFKPOF-043–032–p0006 and JFKPOF-043–032–p0007, John F. Kennedy Presidential Library, 6–7.
4. Edward R. Murrow, *In Search of Light: The Broadcasts of Edward R. Murrow, 1938–1961,* ed. Edward Bliss Jr. (New York: Alfred A. Knopf, 1967), 275–76.
5. "Remarks on Signing Honorary Citizenship for Sir Winston Churchill, 9 April, 1963," DOI: JFKPOF-043–032–p0009 and JFKPOF-043–032–p0010, John F. Kennedy Presidential Library, 9–10.
6. Robert Rhodes James, ed., *Winston S. Churchill: His Complete Speeches, 1897–1963* (New York: Chelsea House Publishers, 1974), 8:8709.
7. James, *Churchill: His Complete Speeches*, 8:8709.
8. Arthur M. Schlesinger Jr., *A Life in the 20th Century: Innocent Beginnings, 1917–1950* (Boston: Houghton Mifflin, 2000), 386.
9. Mary Soames, ed., *Winston and Clementine: The Personal Letters of the Churchills* (Boston: Houghton Mifflin, 1999), 633.
10. Dwight D. Eisenhower, *The White House Years: Mandate for Change, 1953–1956* (Garden City, NY: Doubleday, 1963), 530–31.
11. See Frank Newport, David W. Moore, and Lydia Saad, "Most Admired Men and Women: 1948–1998," Gallup News Service, https://news.gallup.com/poll/3415/most admired-men-women-19481998.aspx.
12. Hubert H. Humphrey, *The Education of a Public Man: My Life and Politics,* ed. Norman Sherman (Garden City, NY: Doubleday, 1976), 419.
13. Dwight D. Eisenhower Papers, Post Presidential, 1961–1969, Speech Series (A70–32), Dwight D. Eisenhower Presidential Library, box 8, SP-1, "Tribute to Sir Winston Churchill," 1/30/65.
14. Eleanor Roosevelt, "Churchill at the White House," *The Atlantic Monthly,* March 1965, 78–79.
15. Roosevelt, "Churchill at the White House," 80.

16. See "History of the Home," Blair House Foundation, https://blairhouse.org/history.
17. Lyndon B. Johnson, "Reading cards, '10/6/65, Remarks of the President upon Accepting Bust of Winston Churchill,'" statements files, box 164, LBJ Presidential Library.
18. Jan Morris, *Farewell the Trumpets: An Imperial Retreat* (London: Folio Society, 1992), 461.

BIBLIOGRAPHY

Abramson, Rudy. *Spanning the Century: The Life of W. Averell Harriman, 1891–1986*. New York: William Morrow, 1992.

Adamic, Louis. *Dinner at the White House*. New York: Harper & Brothers, 1946.

Alanbrooke, Alan Brooke. *War Diaries, 1939–1945, Field Marshal Lord Alanbrooke*. Edited by Alex Danchev and Daniel Todman. Berkeley: University of California Press, 2001.

Ashley, Maurice. *Churchill as Historian*. London: Secker & Warburg, 1968.

Barkley, Alben W. *That Reminds Me—*. Garden City, NY: Doubleday, 1954.

Barnes, John, and David Nicholson, eds. *The Empire at Bay: The Leo Amery Diaries 1929–1945*. London: Hutchinson, 1988.

Baruch, Bernard M. *Baruch: The Public Years*. New York: Holt, Rinehart and Winston, 1960.

Bercuson, David, and Holger Herwig. *One Christmas in Washington: Roosevelt and Churchill Forge the Grand Alliance*. Woodstock, NY: Overlook Press, 2005.

Berlin, Isaiah. *Letters, 1928–1946*. Edited by Henry Hardy. Cambridge: Cambridge University Press, 2004.

———. *Personal Impressions*, expanded edition. Edited by Henry Hardy. Princeton, NJ: Princeton University Press, 2001.

Beschloss, Michael. *Presidents of War*. New York: Crown, 2018.

Blake, Robert, and Wm. Roger Louis, eds. *Churchill*. New York: W. W. Norton, 1993.

Bland, Larry I., ed. *George C. Marshall Interviews and Reminiscences for Forrest C. Pogue*. Lexington, VA: George C. Marshall Research Foundation, 1991.

Blum, John Morton. *From the Morgenthau Diaries: Years of War, 1941–1945*. Boston: Houghton Mifflin, 1967.

———, ed. *The Price of Vision: The Diary of Henry A. Wallace, 1942–1946*. Boston: Houghton Mifflin, 1973.

Boyle, Peter G., ed. *The Churchill-Eisenhower Correspondence, 1953–1955*. Chapel Hill: University of North Carolina Press, 1990.

Brinkley, David. *Washington Goes to War*. New York: Alfred A. Knopf, 1988.

Browne, Anthony Montague. *Long Sunset: Memoirs of Winston Churchill's Last Private Secretary*. London: Cassell, 1995.

Buhite, Russell D., and David W. Levy, eds. *FDR's Fireside Chats*. Norman: University of Oklahoma Press, 1992.

Burns, James MacGregor. *Roosevelt: The Lion and the Fox*. New York: Harcourt, Brace & World, 1956.

———. *Roosevelt: The Soldier of Freedom*. New York: Harcourt Brace Jovanovich, 1970.

Butcher, Harry C. *My Three Years with Eisenhower: The Personal Diary of Captain Harry Butcher, USNR*. New York: Simon & Schuster, 1946.

Butler, Daniel Allen. *Field Marshal: The Life and Death of Erwin Rommel*. Philadelphia: Casemate, 2015.

Butler, Susan, ed. *My Dear Mr. Stalin: The Complete Correspondence between Franklin D. Roosevelt and Joseph V. Stalin*. New Haven, CT: Yale University Press, 2005.

Cadogan, Alexander. *The Diaries of Sir Alexander Cadogan*. Edited by David Dilks. New York: G. P. Putnam's Sons, 1972.

Chadakoff, Rochelle, ed. *Eleanor Roosevelt's My Day: Her Acclaimed Columns, 1936–1945*. New York: Pharos Books, 1989.

Churchill, Winston S. *Great Contemporaries*. New York: W. W. Norton, 1991.

——— *A History of the English-Speaking Peoples*, 4 vols. New York: Dodd, Mead, 1956–1958/London: Cassell, 1956–1958.

———. *The Second World War*, 6 vols. Boston: Houghton Mifflin, 1948–1953/London: Cassell, 1948–1954.

Clarke, Peter. *Mr Churchill's Profession: Statesman, Orator, Writer*. London: Bloomsbury, 2012.

Collins, Larry. *The Secrets of D-Day*. Beverly Hills, CA: Phoenix Books, 2006.

Colville, John. *The Churchillians*. London: Weidenfeld and Nicolson, 1981.

———. *Footprints in Time*. London: Collins, 1976.

———. *The Fringes of Power: 10 Downing Street Diaries, 1939–1955*. New York: W. W. Norton, 1985.

Cook, Blanche Wiesen. *Eleanor Roosevelt: The War Years and After*, vol. 3, *1939–1962*. New York: Viking, 2016.

Cooke, Alistair. *Memories of the Great and the Good*. New York: Arcade, 1999.

Dallek, Robert. *Franklin D. Roosevelt: A Political Life*. New York: Viking, 2017.

Daniels, Roger. *Franklin D. Roosevelt: The War Years, 1939–1945*. Urbana: University of Illinois Press, 2016.

D'Este, Carlo. *Warlord: A Life of Winston Churchill at War, 1874–1945*. New York: Harper, 2008.

Donovan, Robert J. *Confidential Secretary: Ann Whitman's 20 Years with Eisenhower and Rockefeller*. New York: E. P. Dutton, 1988.

Eade, Charles, ed. *Churchill: By His Contemporaries*. London: Hutchinson, 1953.

Eden, Anthony. *The Eden Memoirs: Full Circle*. London: Cassell, 1960.

———. *The Eden Memoirs: The Reckoning*. London: Cassell, 1965.

Eden, Clarissa. *Clarissa Eden: A Memoir: From Churchill to Eden*. Edited by Cate Haste. London: Weidenfeld & Nicolson, 2007.

Eisenhower, Dwight D. *Crusade in Europe*. Garden City, NY: Doubleday, 1948.

———. *The White House Years: Mandate for Change, 1953–1956.* Garden City, NY: Doubleday, 1963.

Ferrell, Robert H., ed. *The Diary of James C. Hagerty: Eisenhower in Mid-Course, 1954–1955.* Bloomington: Indiana University Press, 1983.

———, ed. *The Eisenhower Diaries.* New York: W. W. Norton, 1981.

Fields. Alonzo. *My 24 Years in the White House.* New York: Coward-McCann, 1961.

Gallagher, Hugh Gregory. *FDR's Splendid Deception.* New York: Dodd, Mead, 1985.

Gardner, Brian. *Churchill in Power: As Seen by His Contemporaries.* Boston: Houghton Mifflin, 1970.

Gilbert, Martin. *Churchill: A Life.* New York: Holt, 1991.

———. *Churchill and America.* New York: Free Press, 2005.

———. *Continue to Pester, Nag and Bite: Churchill's War Leadership.* Toronto: Vintage Canada, 2004.

———. *Road to Victory: Winston S. Churchill 1941–1945.* London: Heinemann, 1986.

———, ed. *The Churchill War Papers.* 3 vols. New York: W. W. Norton, 2001.

Goodwin, Doris Kearns. *Leadership in Turbulent Times.* New York: Simon & Schuster, 2018.

———. *No Ordinary Time: Franklin and Eleanor Roosevelt: The Home Front in World War II.* New York: Simon & Schuster, 1994.

Graebner, Walter. *My Dear Mr. Churchill.* Boston: Houghton Mifflin, 1965.

Greenstein, Fred I. *The Hidden-Hand Presidency: Eisenhower as Leader.* New York: Basic Books, 1982.

Griffith, Robert, ed. *Ike's Letters to a Friend, 1941–1958.* Lawrence, Kansas: University Press of Kansas, 1984.

Grove, Noel. *Inside the White House: Stories from the World's Most Famous Residence.* Washington, DC: National Geographic, 2013.

Gunther, John. *Roosevelt in Retrospect: A Profile in History.* New York: Harper & Brothers, 1950.

Halle, Kay, ed. *Winston Churchill on America and Britain.* New York: Walker, 1970.

Hamilton, Nigel. *Commander in Chief: FDR's Battle with Churchill, 1943.* Boston: Houghton Mifflin Harcourt, 2016.

———. *The Mantle of Command: FDR at War, 1941–1942.* Boston: Houghton Mifflin Harcourt, 2014.

———. *War and Peace: FDR's Final Odyssey D-Day to Yalta, 1943–1945.* Boston: Houghton Mifflin Harcourt, 2019.

Harriman, W. Averell, and Elie Abel. *Special Envoy to Churchill and Stalin, 1941–1946.* New York: Random House, 1975.

Harvey, Oliver. *The War Diaries of Oliver Harvey.* Edited by John Harvey. London: Collins, 1978.

Hassett, William D. *Off the Record with F.D.R. 1942–1945.* New Brunswick, NJ: Rutgers University Press, 1958.

Hastings, Max. *Operation Chastise: The RAF's Most Brilliant Attack of World War II.* New York: HarperCollins, 2020.

———. *Winston's War: Churchill, 1940–1945.* New York: Alfred A. Knopf, 2010.

Helm, Edith Benham. *The Captains and the Kings.* New York: G. P. Putnam's Sons, 1954.

Hermiston, Roger. *Two Minutes to Midnight: 1953—The Year of Living Dangerously.* London: Biteback, 2021.

Hickman, Tom. *Churchill's Bodyguard.* London: Headline Book, 2005.

Hopkins, Michael F., Saul Kelly, and John W. Young, eds. *British Ambassadors to the United States, 1939–77.* London: Palgrave Macmillan, 2009.

Humes, James C. *Eisenhower and Churchill: The Partnership That Saved the World.* Roseville, CA: Prima, 2001.

Humphrey, Hubert H. *The Education of a Public Man: My Life and Politics.* Edited by Norman Sherman. Garden City, NY: Doubleday, 1976.

Ignatieff, Michael. *Isaiah Berlin: A Life.* New York: Metropolitan Books, 1998.

Ismay, Hastings. *The Memoirs of General Lord Ismay.* New York: Viking Press, 1960.

Jenkins, Roy. *Churchill.* London: Macmillan, 2001.

———. *Franklin Delano Roosevelt.* New York: Times Books, 2003.

Johnson, Paul. *Churchill.* New York: Viking Penguin, 2009.

Keegan, John. *The Second World War.* New York: Viking, 1990.

———. *Winston Churchill.* New York: Penguin, 2002.

Kershaw, Ian. *Personality and Power: Builders and Destroyers of Modern Europe.* New York: Penguin Press, 2022.

Kimball, Warren F., ed. *Churchill & Roosevelt: The Complete Correspondence*, 3 vols. Princeton, NJ: Princeton University Press, 1984.

Klara, Robert. *The Hidden White House: Harry Truman and the Reconstruction of America's Most Famous Residence.* New York: Thomas Dunne Books, 2013.

Larson, Arthur. *Eisenhower: The President Nobody Knew.* New York: Charles Scribner's Sons, 1968.

Larson, Erik. *The Splendid and the Vile: A Saga of Churchill, Family and Defiance during the Blitz.* New York: Crown, 2020.

Lash, Joseph P. *Eleanor and Franklin: The Story of Their Relationship Based on Eleanor Roosevelt's Private Papers.* New York: W. W. Norton, 1971.

———. *A World of Love: Eleanor Roosevelt and Her Friends, 1943–1962.* Garden City, NY: Doubleday, 1984.

Lavery, Brian. *Churchill Goes to War: Winston's Wartime Journeys.* Annapolis, MD: Naval Institute Press, 2007.

Leahy, William D. *I Was There: The Personal Story of the Chief of Staff to Presidents Roosevelt and Truman Based on His Notes and Diaries Made at the Time.* New York: Whittlesey House, 1950.

Lehrman, Lewis E. *Churchill, Roosevelt & Company.* Guilford, CT: Stackpole Books, 2017.

Lough, David. *No More Champagne: Churchill and His Money.* New York: Picador, 2015.

Lovell, Richard. *Churchill's Doctor: A Biography of Lord Moran.* New York: Parthenon, 1993.

Maier, Thomas. *When Lions Roar: The Churchills and the Kennedys.* New York: Crown, 2014.

Martin, John. *Downing Street: The War Years.* London: Bloomsbury, 1991.

Meacham, Jon. *Franklin and Winston: An Intimate Portrait of an Epic Friendship.* New York: Random House, 2003.

Miller, Merle. *Ike The Soldier: As They Knew Him*. New York: G. P. Putnam's Sons, 1987.

Milton, Giles. *The Ministry of Ungentlemanly Warfare: Churchill's Mavericks: Plotting Hitler's Defeat*. London: John Murray, 2016.

Moran, Lord. *Churchill: The Struggle for Survival 1940–1965, Taken from the Diaries of Lord Moran*. Boston: Houghton Mifflin, 1966.

Morgan, Frederick. *Overture to Overlord*. Garden City, NY: Doubleday, 1950.

Morris, Jan. *Farewell the Trumpets: An Imperial Retreat*. London: Folio Society, 1992.

Murrow, Edward R. *In Search of Light: The Broadcasts of Edward R. Murrow, 1938–1961*. Edited by Edward Bliss Jr. New York: Alfred A. Knopf, 1967.

Nel, Elizabeth. *Mr. Churchill's Secretary*. London: Hodder and Stoughton, 1958.

Nelson, James, ed. *General Eisenhower on the Military Churchill: A Conversation with Alistair Cooke*. New York: W. W. Norton, 1970.

Nesbitt, Henrietta. *White House Diary*. Garden City, NY: Doubleday, 1948.

Nicholas, H. G., ed. *Washington Despatches 1941–1945: Weekly Political Reports from the British Embassy*. Chicago: University of Chicago Press, 1981.

Nixon, Richard M. *RN: The Memoirs of Richard Nixon*. New York: Grosset & Dunlap, 1978.

Oursler, Fulton. *Behold This Dreamer!* Edited by Fulton Oursler Jr. Boston: Little, Brown, 1964.

Packwood, Allen. *How Churchill Waged War: The Most Challenging Decisions of the Second World War*. Yorkshire: Frontline Books, 2018.

———, ed. *Cosmos Out of Chaos: Introducing the Churchill Archives Centre*. Cambridge: Churchill College, 2009.

Parks, Lillian Rogers, with Frances Spatz Leighton. *My Thirty Years Backstairs at the White House*. Bronx, NY: Ishi Press International, 2008.

Pawle, Gerald. *The War and Colonel Warden*. New York: Alfred A. Knopf, 1963.

Pendar, Kenneth. *Adventure in Diplomacy: Our French Dilemma*. New York: Dodd, Mead, 1945.

Perkins, Frances. *The Roosevelt I Knew*. New York: Viking Press, 1946.

Pickersgill, J. W. *The Mackenzie King Record*, vol. 1, 1939–1944. Toronto: University of Toronto Press, 1960.

Pilpel, Robert H. *Churchill in America: 1895–1961: An Affectionate Portrait*. New York: Harcourt Brace Jovanovich, 1976.

Pogue, Forrest C. *George C. Marshall: Ordeal and Hope*. New York: Viking Press, 1966.

Purnell, Sonia. *Clementine: The Life of Mrs. Winston Churchill*. New York: Viking, 2015.

Reardon, Terry. *Winston Churchill and Mackenzie King: So Similar, So Different*. Toronto: Dundurn, 2012.

Reilly, Michael F., as told to William J. Slocum. *Reilly of the White House*. New York: Simon & Schuster, 1947.

Reynolds, David. *In Command of History: Churchill Fighting and Writing the Second World War*. New York: Random House, 2005.

Rigdon, William M., with James Derieux. *White House Sailor*. Garden City, NY: Doubleday, 1962.

Roberts, Andrew. *Churchill: Walking with Destiny*. New York: Viking, 2018.

———. *The Holy Fox: A Biography of Lord Halifax*. London: Weidenfeld & Nicolson, 1991.

———. *Masters and Commanders: The Military Geniuses Who Led the West to Victory in WWII*. London: Allen Lane, 2008.

Roll, David L. *The Hopkins Touch: Harry Hopkins and the Forging of the Alliance to Defeat Hitler*. Oxford and New York: Oxford University Press, 2013.

Roosevelt, Curtis. *Upstairs at the Roosevelts': Growing up with Franklin and Eleanor*. Lincoln, NE: Potomac Books, 2017.

Roosevelt, Eleanor. *Autobiography*. New York: Harper, 1961.

———. *This I Remember*. New York: Harper & Brothers, 1949.

Roosevelt, Elliott. *As He Saw It*. New York: Duell, Sloan and Pearce, 1946.

———, ed. *F.D.R.: His Personal Letters, 1928–1945*, vol. 2. New York: Duell, Sloan and Pearce, 1950.

Roosevelt, Elliott, and James Brough. *A Rendezvous with Destiny: The Roosevelts of the White House*. New York: G. P. Putnam's, 1975.

Roosevelt, James, with Bill Libby. *My Parents: A Differing View*. Chicago: Playboy Press, 1976.

Rosenman, Samuel I. *Working with Roosevelt*. New York: Harper & Brothers, 1952.

Rovere, Richard H. *The Eisenhower Years*. New York: Farrar, Straus and Cudahy, 1956.

Rowley, Hazel. *Franklin and Eleanor: An Extraordinary Marriage*. New York: Farrar, Straus and Giroux, 2010.

Sandys, Celia. *Chasing Churchill: The Travels of Winston Churchill*. London: HarperCollins, 2003.

Schlesinger, Arthur M., Jr. *Journals: 1952–2000*. Edited by Andrew Schlesinger and Stephen Schlesinger. New York: Penguin Press, 2007.

———, *A Life in the 20th Century: Innocent Beginnings, 1917–1950*. Boston: Houghton Mifflin, 2000.

———, *A Thousand Days: John F. Kennedy in the White House*. Boston: Houghton Mifflin, 1965.

Seale, William. *Blair House: The President's Guest House*. Washington, DC: The White House Historical Association, 2016.

———. *The President's House: A History*, 2 vols. Washington, DC: White House Historical Association, 1986.

Sherwood, Robert E. *Roosevelt and Hopkins: An Intimate History*. New York: Harper & Brothers, 1948.

Shinkle, Peter. *Uniting America: How FDR and Henry Stimson Brought Democrats and Republicans Together to Win World War II*. New York: St. Martin's Press, 2022.

Smith, A. Merriman. *Thank You, Mr. President*. New York: Harper & Brothers, 1946.

Smith, Jean Edward. *Eisenhower in War and Peace*. New York: Random House, 2012.

———. *FDR*. New York: Random House, 2007.

Smith, Kathryn. *The Gatekeeper: Missy LeHand, FDR, and the Untold Story of the Partnership That Defined a Presidency*. New York: Simon & Schuster, 2016.

Smyth, Denis. *Deathly Deception: The Real Story of Operation Mincemeat*. Oxford: Oxford University Press, 2010.

Soames, Emma, ed. *Mary Churchill's War: The Wartime Diaries of Churchill's Youngest Daughter.* New York: Pegasus Books, 2022.
Soames, Mary. *Clementine Churchill: The Biography of a Marriage.* Boston: Houghton Mifflin, 1979.
———. *A Daughter's Tale: The Memoir of Winston Churchill's Youngest Child.* New York: Random House, 2011.
———, ed. *Winston and Clementine: The Personal Letters of the Churchills.* Boston: Houghton Mifflin, 1999.
Stafford, David. *Roosevelt and Churchill: Men of Secrets.* Woodstock: Overlook Press, 1999.
Stimson, Henry L., and McGeorge Bundy. *On Active Service in Peace and War,* 2 vols. New York: Harper & Brothers, 1948.
Thompson, Neville. *The Third Man: Churchill, Roosevelt, Mackenzie King, and the Untold Friendships That Won WWII.* Toronto: Sutherland House, 2021.
Thompson, Walter Henry. *Assignment: Churchill.* New York: Farrar, Straus and Young, 1955.
Thompson, Walter. *Beside the Bulldog: The Intimate Memoirs of Churchill's Bodyguard.* London: Apollo, 2005.
Thompson, W. H. *I Was Churchill's Shadow.* London: Christopher Johnson, 1951.
Trethewey, Rachel. *The Churchill Sisters: The Extraordinary Lives of Winston and Clementine's Daughters.* New York: St. Martin's Press, 2021.
Truman, Margaret. *The President's House: A First Daughter Shares the History and Secrets of the World's Most Famous Home.* New York: Ballantine Books, 2003.
Tully, Grace. *F.D.R., My Boss.* New York: Charles Scribner's Sons, 1949.
Vale, Allister, and John Scadding. *Winston Churchill's Illnesses, 1886–1965.* Barnsley, England: Frontline Books, 2020.
Ward, Geoffrey C., ed. *Closest Companion: The Unknown Story of the Intimate Friendship between Franklin Roosevelt and Margaret Suckley.* Boston: Houghton Mifflin, 1995.
West, J. B., with Mary Lynn Kotz. *Upstairs at the White House: My Life with the First Ladies.* New York: Coward, McCann & Geoghegan, 1973.
Wheeler-Bennett, John, ed. *Action This Day: Working with Churchill.* London: Macmillan, 1968.
Whitcomb, John, and Claire Whitcomb. *Real Life at the White House: Two Hundred Years of Daily Life at America's Most Famous Residence.* New York: Routledge, 2000.
Wilroy, Mary Edith, and Lucie Prinz. *Inside Blair House.* Garden City, NY: Doubleday, 1982.
Wilson, Frank, and Beth Day. *Special Agent: A Quarter Century with the Treasury Department and the Secret Service.* New York: Holt, Rinehart and Winston, 1965.
Winfield, Betty Houchin. *FDR and the News Media.* Urbana: University of Illinois Press, 1990.
Woon, Basil. *Roosevelt, World Statesman.* London: Peter Davies, 1942.

INDEX

ABOUT THE AUTHOR

Robert Schmuhl is the Walter H. Annenberg-Edmund P. Joyce Chair Emeritus in American Studies and Journalism at the University of Notre Dame. He joined the Notre Dame faculty in 1980 and since 2016 has been an adjunct professor in the School of Law and Government at Dublin City University. He is the author or editor of more than a dozen books, including *Statecraft and Stagecraft: American Political Life in the Age of Personality* (1990), *Wounded Titans: American Presidents and the Perils of Power* (1996), *In So Many Words: Arguments and Adventures* (2006), *Ireland's Exiled Children: America and the Easter Rising* (2016), and *The Glory and the Burden: The American Presidency from the New Deal to the Present* (2022). He lives in South Bend, Indiana.